Treasury of Religious Plays

Selected and Edited by

THELMA SHARMAN BROWN
Associate Secretary of Promotion and Sales
Missionary Education Movement

Introduction by

HAROLD EHRENSPERGER

ASSOCIATION PRESS
347 Madison Avenue
New York 17, N. Y.

137

To Mother

Introduction

A FACT, too obvious to need saying, is that the church has been without good dramatic material in the form of plays. Ironically enough this is true of the one institution that has a source book which is filled with more dramatic material than has ever been found in any other single book. Pages of this book devoted to the life of Jesus of Nazareth and the activities of his followers are packed with drama.

Still more ironic is the fact that the people called Christian are not themselves creating dramatic material; they are not *living* their religion in contemporary society. If they were, they would know that to live a way of life according to the example of Jesus is to live every day dramatically. This means a kind of living patterned after a tangible ideal, directed by an inner sanction, in accordance with standards which are high and noble. It means living in terms of others and in terms of the social patterns that create community; it means the happiness in living which arises from the give-and-take of co-operative living; it means living courageously, flouting smallness and selfishness. It means the life of Jesus, even though relatively, truly manifesting itself in each of our lives today.

Living which is in keeping with such purposes, standards, and judgments is religious living. It creates the kind of incidents and stuations which we call dramatic. When these are sifted and condensed into the space and time of scenes, and when they come alive before a congregation, we have a religious play. When this play purges, teaches, inspires, and exalts the congregation, as well as the group creating the play, the experience has been a religious one.

Christianity in its inception, in the glorious parts of its history, and in its contemporary expression, is the storehouse of content for religious plays. It is difficult to understand why so few truly religious plays have been derived from the Bible, why the lives of the saints and the great, heroic figures of the past have not yielded more good drama, and why the conflict and struggle of contemporary man attempting to live deeply and truly according to his conscience has not given us the greatest plays of our day. Unfortunately what we often call "religious drama" frightens both the sincere writer and the skillful technician. We shall need to reject much that has been paraded under the name of religion, and still more we shall need to discover the sincerely effective drama that arises when true religion, giving meaning to existence, comes into life.

True religious drama can deal with any subject matter. The religious character of the play results from the treatment given to its content and the audience-response it evokes. True religious drama must always be done sincerely, with the least possible amount of show and trappings. It must never be a show. It must never be an occasion for the participants to show off. It should be an experience which comprises the intelligence and logic of a sermon, a demonstration of decision and consequence, a spur to and a foretaste of perfection, and an incitement to action. It makes its appeal through the senses, all of them, giving the experience completeness and a capacity for mental and emotional stimulation.

This *Treasury of Religious Plays* is an attempt to give groups working in the church a ready book of materials arranged in a convenient form. Those who know religious literature will be familiar with the name of the compiler of this volume as a person who has dedicated her life to the cultivation of taste and judgment in the use of literature for the church. Those familiar with drama in the church will recognize many of the plays selected by Miss Brown as the old and tested ones. Miss Brown has called her collection a *treasury,* which means that what is here will have to be dug out, unlocked, and put into use. This is the process to be followed by anyone who makes a play come to life before a congregation: First, there will be the search for the treasure—a good play that will stimulate and activate a group when it is produced. Then the treasure must be unlocked from the printed page. For even the simplest and most unpretentious play can be set free from its pages by people who are sincerely trying to make it breathe and live. Religious drama is born when the play, no longer merely words, in action moves from an effective beginning to a still more effective ending. A play may not be great, it may not even be good by the highest standards. Yet if a director is wise in the use of drama, and is at the same time a person conscious of the religious growth possible in the producing of a play, if he is willing to make every effort to get everything out of a play which can possibly be gotten, and if he is willing to work with the group toward the high end for which all plays in the church ought to be produced, then the production even of a mediocre play can be a worth-while experience. The test will be the value of the experience to the congregation and the producing group. This is not to say we do not want good plays, or that they are not our greatest need today; it is to suggest that we must work with our available material and make it have as much value as possible. Only as we are able to do this will we be able to convince competent playwrights that there is a readiness worthy of their efforts. Let us hope, too, that in time we shall be able to convince a few great writers that in the religious interpretation of life alone will they achieve the peak of satisfaction in their work.

Here are twenty plays locked in a treasury. How valuable they are will depend upon how effectively they are set free, how convincingly they are brought to life, and how well they serve the educational and worship functions of the church. May their treasure be found as we translate their meaning into our lives.

HAROLD EHRENSPERGER

Editorial Secretary of the Student Department of the Board of Education of the Methodist Church. Editor, motive, official magazine of the Methodist Student Movement.

Table of Contents

ix

Preface

"Sir," confided the Greeks to Philip, "we would see Jesus."

"Where is he?" the wise men had inquired. "We have seen his star in the East and want to worship him."

"Behold him!" said the preacher to the throngs beside the River Jordan, and an attentive fisherman eagerly called his brother to share the good news.

"Come and see a man who told me all I ever did," confessed a woman of Samaria to her townsmen.

Mary Magdelene ran to the disciples. "Come and see the place where the Lord lay!"

From then until today a never-ending procession has sought Jesus. Now as then he is the wise teacher, the sympathetic friend, the miraculous healer, the emancipator, the peacemaker, the evangelist, and the saviour of the world. His friends, now as then, have used his message as well as the dramatic incidents of his life to show him to others, and the drama is an increasingly popular method of interpretation.

This *Treasury of Religious Plays* grew out of repeated requests for additional dramatic material. Calls came from leaders in churches, schools, and other organizations, from librarians and booksellers in many parts of the country.

"Where can I find a Christmas play with a missionary emphasis?" asked the president of a missionary society.

"We want an Easter play that has meaning for today," wrote the director of religious life on a college campus.

"Our young people's forum is studying various versions of Scripture." The program chairman needed something to make the discussions more vital.

A high school teacher was worried because her students seemed to regard truth lightly, and juvenile delinquency had led to tragedy in their community. "Perhaps a play would help, if it isn't 'preachy,'" she suggested.

The counselor of an older boys' camp wanted a play on peace, "With an all-male cast, of course."

"We have been offered time on our local radio station for a Christmas play and we want something different from the regular nativity scene," explained the director of a Y.W.C.A. in a growing western town.

The pastor of a large city church needed an appropriate

drama for his Sunday evening worship hour, "Something that
will help our congregation to appreciate our Christian heritage."

And the superintendent of a small rural Sunday school
couldn't put on a big Christmas play "because we haven't
good players, and there isn't any curtain. But we want our
pupils to see Jesus as the reason for Christmas."

The plays in this anthology were selected in answer to such
inquiries; for in different words, but just as earnestly as did
the New Testament Greeks and the wise men, our generation
is saying, "We would see Jesus."

Since most churches and many other organization produce
dramatic services at Christmas and Easter, here are a variety
of plays for these seasons.

Other plays were included because of the times in which
we live. We should remember our heritages—religious freedom, democracy, literacy, good homes, and God's Word.

But our freedoms have been only partly won. Until they
are, let plays on peace, on race relations, on evangelism, and
missions speak and stir to action.

This is a time of unusual responsibility for young people.
Stewardship of all life, love, and integrity need to be vividly
interpreted. Young people like not only to attend religious
dramas but to participate in them; thus many of the plays in
this book are especially suited to youth and several include
parts for children.

Although most of these selections have present-day settings,
three are based upon historic events. Two are adapted from
classical fiction and several drawn from biblical episodes. One
is a dramatic poem, another is satire, and four may be used
on radio.

Through characters in this treasury we become better acquainted with people of Austria, China, Old England, Ancient Palestine, Russia, Mexico, India, and Syria, as well as
colonial and present-day America.

A chief factor in selecting a play is the number of characters. One play in this volume may use as many as eighteen
players though the average is between six and eight, and a few
need five persons or less.

Another important question is the length of the performance. The majority of these plays run about twenty, thirty, or forty minutes. One requires one and one-half hours, while two may be played within fifteen minutes.

Some of the selections in this book are very simple to stage and to act. Others require more experience and more elaborate settings. A few have been favorites through the years, though many are comparatively new. Most of them have not been available before in book form.

Although this compilation is not exhaustive, an examination of the table of contents and the indices will suggest further subjects and a variety of uses. We hope there will be something for everyone within its pages.

Please read carefully the word of warning with reference to the use of all material in *Treasury of Religious Plays*. See page iv. Note that the plays presented here are for reading purposes only. If you wish to produce a play, nearly all of them are available at booksellers in single copies. Specific information is stated at the beginning of each play. Whether or not royalties are to be paid for production is also indicated. Be sure to follow all instructions for presentation and make adequate arrangements with the author or publisher, all of whom have been very generous in allowing us to reprint their work.

May I thank each one: Mr. Theodore Johnson and Mr. Carl Johnson, Baker's Plays; Mr. Pat Beaird, Abingdon-Cokesbury Press; Mr. Christopher O'Leary, Samuel H. French Company; Mr. Robert Willett, Willett-Clark and Company, Dr. Alfred D. Moore, Committee on World Literacy and Christian Literature; Dr. Franklin D. Cogswell, Friendship Press; Mrs. Rockwell Smith, Evanston, Illinois, and Mrs. Marion Wefer of Philadelphia, Pennsylvania.

I also should like to express my sincere appreciation for helpful suggestions by Miss Juanita Baker and Miss Betty Poff of the Baptist Sunday School Board, and Robert Scott Steele, associate editor of *motive*, Methodist Publishing House, and my gratitude to all who had part in the preparation of the manuscript.

THELMA SHERMAN BROWN

The Birth of the Song, "Silent Night"
An Original Historical Radio Drama
by
FLORENCE FELTEN FRENCH

Characters:

NARRATOR	ELIZABETH GRUBER
FATHER GRUBER	BERTA
MOTHER GRUBER	PASTOR MOHR
FRANZ GRUBER	FIRST PASTOR

TIME: Early 19th Century.

PLACE: Austria.

LENGTH: Thirty minutes.

ANNOUNCER. *(Your usual opening)*

(*Music: Fade in organ playing "Silent Night"; cross-fade to man humming same tune: sustain briefly, then fade and sneak out under following:*)

NARRATOR. Let me tell you about the man who is humming that tune. His name is Franz Xavier Gruber. Just one hundred twenty-eight years ago tonight (*Christmas Eve, 1946*), he hummed that tune for the first time . . . it was his tune . . . and his choir would sing it in the little church in Oberndorf, Austria. Otherwise you would never have heard of him. He was once an ordinary boy . . . but a boy with nimble fingers . . . for weaving with his father and two older brothers . . . and for something else which was a secret between his mother and himself. They lived in Hochburg, near the Danube . . . (*Fading*) This ordinary peasant family of weavers. . . .

FATHER GRUBER. I'm proud of you Franz. And to be perfectly frank with you, for a boy of twelve, your weaving is far finer than that of your two older brothers. One of these days, you'll be a great weaver, my son.

1

FRANZ. (*Tensely*) Please don't say that, Father. I can't stand the thought of weaving much longer.

FATHER GRUBER. (*Authoritatively*) That's enough, Franz. Do you realize you're speaking to your father?

FRANZ. (*Apologetically*) I'm sorry, Father.

FATHER GRUBER. I'm partly to blame. I should know better than to praise you. It never pays. . . . What have you there, Mamma?

MOTHER GRUBER. (*Fading in*) They're Franzl's wooden pegs, Joseph. He had them in the wall behind his bed. I'm sorry, Franzl. They broke off when I made your bed.

FATHER GRUBER. (*Angrily*) In the wall, Anna? Franz, did you cut a hole in the wall for these pegs?

FRANZ. Yes, I did, but . . .

FATHER GRUBER. (*Interrupting*) That's enough. You ought to be ashamed of yourself, Franz! I have too much to do already keeping up the house! And now you add to my trouble by deliberately spoiling the wall.

FRANZ. (*Insistently*) Please let me explain! I didn't mean to spoil the wall. I just put these pieces of wood there to practice finger exercises.

FATHER GRUBER. (*Explosively*) Finger exercises! So! You don't get enough finger exercises in your weaving. I'll see to it that you get more!

FRANZ. (*Excitedly*) Oh no, no, Father! Don't give me any more weaving. I couldn't stand it! It's a different kind of finger exercise I need. Using these wooden pegs keeps me in practice for spinet and organ playing.

FATHER GRUBER. (*Impatiently puzzled*) What do you mean . . . we've no spinet . . . we've no organ!

FRANZ. (*Struggling*) I know. But I go to Herr Peterlechner's. He lets me use his. He even teaches me how to play.

FATHER GRUBER. (*Explosively*) Teaches you! And who pays for these lessons?

FRANZ. (*Quietly*) He doesn't charge me anything.

FATHER GRUBER. (*With exasperation*) Franz, you should know better than to accept lessons from Andreas Peterlechner. He's a teacher and should be paid!

MOTHER GRUBER. Come, come, Joseph. Don't be so hard on Franzl. You should be pleased that he wants to learn. Don't scold him for it.

FATHER GRUBER. *(Impatiently)* Anna, you stay out of this! In this family we pay for what we get!

MOTHER GRUBER. All right, Joseph. Then I'll make it up to Herr Peterlechner. Franzl, you can take over some fresh coffee kuchen when you go for your lesson tonight.

FATHER GRUBER. You'll do nothing of the kind, Anna. Franz, you're not going for your lesson tonight or any other night!

MOTHER GRUBER. Oh, Papa, be reasonable. Franzl *must* go tonight. He's promised Herr Peterlechner to take his place at the church organ tomorrow morning. Poor Herr Peterlechner has been sick all week.

FATHER GRUBER. *(Unbelievingly)* Anna, what are you saying? Franz—play the organ for the service? I won't have it, I tell you. It's bad enough to have him disgrace us at home . . . but in public . . . that's too much!

MOTHER GRUBER. *(Firmly)* Who said he was going to disgrace us? Just wait and see . . . you'll be proud of him. But now let's stop arguing. It's time for supper. . . . Franzl will have to hurry to get to his lesson on time. While you wash up, I'll put the soup on the table.

(Music: Organ playing church music of period suggestive of Franz playing in church: swelling to climax then fading out.)

FATHER GRUBER. *(Reproachfully)* Ach, Anna. You shouldn't have strutted so! Now the whole congregation knows you're as proud as a peacock!

MOTHER GRUBER. *(Defensively)* Why shouldn't they? I want them to know that I'm proud of our Franzl. How many children twelve years old could play the organ the way he did? Answer me that!

FATHER GRUBER. Not any around here!

MOTHER GRUBER. *(Reprovingly)* Joseph, I told you not to scold him for trying to learn.

FATHER GRUBER. *(Repentantly)* All right, I admit I was wrong. I'll make up for it, Anna.

MOTHER GRUBER. But how can you, after the way you talked to him last night?

FATHER GRUBER. *(Confidently)* Never you fear, Anna, I can do it. I've made plans on my way back from church. Did you see the spinet in Bruger's window?

MOTHER GRUBER. *(Uninterestedly)* No, I never even looked in the window. *(Proudly)* All I could think of was how well Franzl played and how surprised people were.

FATHER GRUBER. *(Pointedly)* That's the very thing that made me look at the spinet. I mean to buy it for him.

MOTHER GRUBER. *(Incredulously)* *Buy* it! Don't talk foolishly. Poor folks like us buying a spinet. People would think we'd gone crazy!!

FATHER GRUBER. *(Reassuringly)* No, they wouldn't. And it doesn't cost so much—only five gulden.

MOTHER GRUBER. *(Mockingly)* *Only* five gulden! Why we don't have that much to our name!

FATHER GRUBER. *(Confidently)* No . . . but I know how we can get it. Now is the time . . . . during the holiday season . . . when folks buy more linens. I'll do extra weaving nights.

MOTHER GRUBER *(Tearfully pleased)* Oh, Joseph, I could cry. You *are* a good man. *(Quickly)* Look here . . . why couldn't I earn something too . . . my cookies aren't too bad . . . I could bake Christmas cookies and sell them.

FATHER GRUBER *(Encouragingly)* *"Too bad!"* They're the best in the neighborhood, Anna! We'll make so much. . . . I'll tell you what we'll do. . . .

MOTHER GRUBER. What more?

FATHER GRUBER. *(With growing excitement)* We'll save anything we make more than five gulden . . . we'll start a fund to send Franz to Burghausen.

MOTHER GRUBER. *(Puzzled)* Why in the world do you want to send him *away*?

FATHER GRUBER. That's where the great teacher, George Hartdobler, lives. Franz must be apprenticed to him.

MOTHER GRUBER. *(Unbelievably)* How you've changed since last night! I can hardly believe my ears. . . .

FATHER GRUBER. *(Annoyed)* Don't fuss, Anna. . . .

MOTHER GRUBER. *(Hastily interrupting)* Ach no, Joseph. I only mean I'm so happy you've these wonderful plans for Franzl . . . *(worried)* still . . . the other children . . . we have them to think of too. It's hardly fair to them to give Franzl so much and them so little. . . .

FATHER GRUBER. *(Impatiently interrupting)* You can always find something to worry about, can't you, Anna? Doesn't it occur to you that they too will be proud of a famous brother?

MOTHER GRUBER. *(Warningly)* Famous! Now you're building castles too high in the air. Watch out, Joseph. They'll topple over.

(Music: Sneak in organ playing a few Bach exercises: Segue to more difficult composition of period suggesting real musical accomplishment, fading off with music with a love motif.)

ELIZABETH. *(Enthusiastically)* What a big day this has been for you, Franzl!

FRANZ. I'm glad you could come, Elizabeth. If only my father and mother could have been here too! You know it was Father's idea that I come to study under Herr Hartdobler. Now that I have my diploma, Father's dreams are realized.

ELIZABETH. And in only one year, Franzl! It *is* too bad they couldn't come. How proud they would have been. What honors heaped upon you. I've never heard you play better!

FRANZ. *(Really pleased)* I'm glad if you thought so!

ELIZABETH. *(Earnestly)* I surely did. But, Franzl . . . what are you hiding behind your back?

FRANZ. *(Hesitatingly)* It's a surprise I got today. I brought it along because I thought it might interest you, too.

ELIZABETH. *(Delightedly)* Oh, has it something to do with me?

FRANZ. *(Hesitatingly)* I'd like to think it does. But I guess you'll have to decide that.

ELIZABETH. My, you are mysterious today. *(Sound: Unwrapping of paper with following line)* Come . . . let's see it. . . . How disappointing! Just a piece of paper!

FRANZ. But read it, Elizabeth. It's my appointment to teach at Arnsdorf.

ELIZABETH. An appointment so soon! How splendid! Tell me about it!

FRANZ. There isn't much to tell. I'll be the typical country schoolteacher.

ELIZABETH. And you'll have a choirmaster post I hope?

FRANZ. Unfortunately, no. But Herr Hartdobler says there's a church only two miles away . . . in Oberdorf . . . something may turn up there.

ELIZABETH. He ought to know. Oh I'm sure there'll be an opening. Then why do you look so glum, Franzl? You don't seem a bit happy over it.

FRANZ. *(Struggling)* Well . . . you see, there's a large apartment in the schoolhouse. . . . I can't help feeling I'd be lonesome in such a big place. I've been wondering . . . of course I haven't much to offer . . . a small salary . . . a house for you and your children . . . a regular job . . . that's all . . . but . . . well, Elizabeth, would you marry me and live there with me?

ELIZABETH. *(Starting to cry)* Oh, Franzl. . . .

FRANZ. *(Interrupting hastily).* Please don't cry. . . .

ELIZABETH. Franzl dear, you don't understand.

FRANZ. *(Dejectedly)* I was afraid it would be this way. That's why I've waited so long.

ELIZABETH. *(Triumphantly through her tears)* Franzl, dear, I'm the one who has waited so long. I'd given up hope. I told myself . . . why should Franzl, just reaching manhood, marry a widow with two children. . . .

FRANZ. Oh, Elizabeth . . . how could you harbor such thoughts . . . when I'm so fond of Kitty and Berta? But will they want me for a father?

ELIZABETH. Franzl, darling, they'll adore you for a father! And I . . . I'm the happiest woman alive! I'd love to live in that house with you!

(Music: Punctuate Elizabeth's final line with full swelling organ chords expressive of the thrill Franz has when Elizabeth assents: segue to peaceful family type of music in period: sneak out. Sound: off mike, gradually fading in—simultaneously beat of horses' hoofs, sleigh bells, crunch of snow: then man's voice calling [off mike] "Whoa": Cut sound.)

FRANZ. *(Calling off mike)* Mamma, have Kitty wear her warm scarf. Hurry, everybody—the sleigh's here. Berta, you can't carry such a big basket even if you are the oldest child. Mamma, put on your warm coat.

ELIZABETH. *(Answering off mike then gradually fading in)* Franz, how silly. I should know how to dress for Christmas in Arnsdorf. *(On mike)* After all, this is the eleventh Christmas we've taken baskets to the poor.

FRANZ. *(Reminiscently)* Yes, Mamma. Eleven years we've

been here. Now Berta is old enough for a midnight service. This big house . . . so full of children's laughter these eleven years. How would I have lived in it alone?

ELIZABETH. *(Appreciatively)* Franzl, we've so much to be thankful for. Why, the children's own father couldn't have done more for them than you have. *(Directly and quickly)* There now. All the baskets are packed in the sleigh. Here we go, children. . . . Come on, Papa . . . don't be so slow.

(Sound: [Simultaneously with "Don't be so slow" sneak in] crunch of snow and approaching footsteps: continue through Elizabeth's line "Oh, yes, do come with us, Joseph.")

FRANZ. Don't be in such a hurry, Mamma. . . . Here comes Pastor Mohr.

ELIZABETH. What brings him from Oberdorf on the day before Christmas?

CHILDREN'S VOICES. *(Simultaneously)* You came just in time. Do get into the sleigh with us, Pastor Mohr. We're just ready to start. Here's a basket for you to give.

ELIZABETH. Oh yes, do come with us, Joseph.

MOHR. Thank you, Elizabeth. I am tempted . . . but I've come on pressing business to see your husband.

ELIZABETH. *(Disappointedly)* Oh dear me, then Franz can't come either?

FRANZ. *(Reprovingly)* Elizabeth, you surprise me. Where are your manners?

ELIZABETH. *(Apologetically)* Please excuse me, Joseph. . . . Oh I do hope no one has died this time of year!

MOHR. Oh no, nothing like that. *(Lightly)* I come on a pleasant mission. I've brought a present . . . and I want Franz to do it up in a holiday wrapping. It's for everyone who comes to the midnight service tonight.

CHILDREN'S VOICES. *(Simultaneously)* Think of that! I'm glad I'm old enough to stay up late now. I wish I could go too, Papa. I wonder what the present is. Maybe I can go next year.

BERTA. Oh, Pastor Mohr. I can't believe it . . . you're only joking.

MOHR. *(Laughing)* What a doubting child you have, Franz.

FRANZ. *(Jokingly)* Berta takes after her mother.

ELIZABETH. *(Banteringly)* How mean you are, Franz.

BERTA. *(Seriously)* But, Pastor Mohr . . . it'd have to be a *big* present for the whole congregation . . . and I don't see you carrying any.

MOHR. *(Reassuringly)* I have one, Berta. It's right here in my pocket.

BERTA. *(With wonder)* Mama, to have *so much* from something *so small* . . . why, it sounds like a miracle to me. . . .

ELIZABETH. Perhaps it *is* a miracle, Berta. Miracles have happened before at Christmas time. *(Quickly)* But now let's get back into the sleigh again, children. It's starting to snow. We'll have to hurry. Good-bye.

(Sound: [*Begin simultaneously on mike and fade out at end of chorus of Children's Voices:*] *Horses' hoofs, crunch of snow, sleigh bells.)*

CHILDREN'S VOICES. *(Simultaneously on mike: fade gradually 'til completely off)* Isn't it exciting! Oh, I can hardly wait! How I wish I could go. Let's see if we can guess. Wish you were coming along! Good-bye. Good-bye.

(Sound: Cut.)

FRANZ. *(Curiously)* Joseph, what in the world is this mysterious present you have for all of us?

MOHR. Before I tell you, Franz, I want a promise.

FRANZ. But, Joseph, how can I promise when I don't know what I'm promising?

MOHR. I wouldn't ask it, Franz, if I didn't know that you could carry it out.

FRANZ. Well, all right, Joseph, I promise. Now, what is it?

MOHR. Do you remember at our last choir rehearsal . . . I said we needed a new Christmas song?

FRANZ. *(Vaguely remembering)* Y-e-s.

MOHR. I wasn't joking. Hear are the words. That's my present. Yours will be the music.

FRANZ. *(Unbelievingly)* You want *me* to write the music?

MOHR. Yes. Why not? You've composed songs before.

FRANZ. *(Modestly)* Yes, but never in such a short time. Tell me . . . who wrote the words?

MOHR. *(Quietly)* I did.

FRANZ. *(Matter-of-factly)* Let's go into the study. . . . *(Suddenly awakening to Mohr's words)* What? *You* wrote them, Joseph? I didn't know you wrote poetry.

MOHR. *(Modestly)* Oh, occasionally. *(Hesitatingly)* May I read you the first verse?

FRANZ. Do read it!

MOHR. *(Reading)*

> Silent Night! Holy Night!
> All is calm, all is bright
> Round yon Virgin Mother and Child.
> Holy Infant so tender and mild,
> Sleep in heavenly peace,
> Sleep in heavenly peace.

FRANZ. *(Genuinely impressed)* Beautiful! To think you can write poetry like that!

MOHR. *(Modestly)* Oh it's nothing wonderful.

FRANZ. Indeed it is! It's remarkable!

MOHR. *(Appreciatively)* I'm pleased you like it. *(Persistently)* And now, Franz . . . your promise . . . the music.

FRANZ. Good heavens, man. It's five now. Only six more hours before the midnight service. I'm not a magician, Joseph. I'm a mere musician.

MOHR. *(Laughingly)* I know. I wouldn't have brought it to you, were you a magician. *(Pleading earnestly)* I just want a simple melody. You can do it easily.

FRANZ. *(Dubiously)* No, Joseph, I'm afraid I can't.

JOSEPH. Of *course* you can. I'll sit next to the spinet. Then I can help you with the words while you pick out the notes.

FRANZ. You're bound to have your own way, aren't you? *(Suddenly relieved at a new thought)* But, Joseph . . . you know the mice gorged themselves on the organ . . . it's out of commission . . . we can't use it tonight.

MOHR. I know it's not working. But the organ builder is there now trying to fix it.

FRANZ. *(Still doubtful)* It's in bad shape. Can he have it ready for tonight?

MOHR. No, frankly, he can't. It'd take another week at least.

FRANZ. *(Greatly relieved)* Well, then, Joseph. It's out of the question . . . we can't possibly do this thing for tonight . . . next Christmas . . . I'd be glad to plan on that.

MOHR. But I've my heart set on it for tonight! *(Suddenly inspired)* I know what we can do!

FRANZ. What?

Mohr. We can do without the organ!

Franz. *(Firmly)* I'm sorry to disappoint you, Joseph, but I wouldn't think of trying a new song without accompaniment.

Mohr. Oh, of course not. I didn't mean that . . . but that guitar on the wall . . . you play that, don't you?

Franz. *(Feeling trapped)* Yes . . . but . . . now, Joseph, I can't play that guitar at the service . . . if that's what you're thinking!

Mohr. But why not? It'll be novel! The people will never forget it. . . . Come now, say you'll do it. Remember . . . you promised.

Franz. I know I promised, Joseph. But it's too short a time. . . . I can't do it. . . . *(Suddenly touched by his friend's disappointment)* Oh well, don't look so glum. . . . I'll try, Joseph.

Mohr. Oh, thank you, Franz! You'll never know what this means to me. Just write the guitar accompaniment and several parts so that we can lead the boys' choir in singing it. If you come just a few minutes earlier than usual, we'll have time for practice.

Franz. *(Laughingly)* Joseph, what an optimist you are!

Mohr. *(Enthusiastically)* What a musician you are! I've known so for a long time. *(Fading)* Now the whole congregation will know it tonight. Auf Wiedersehen, Franz.

Franz. *(Fading)* Auf Wiedersehen.

(Sound: Fade in ringing of church bells calling people to service: Sustain briefly. Fading under with:)

Berta. *(Hushed voice of wonder)* Oh, Mama, isn't the church beautiful tonight?

Elizabeth. Lovelier than I've ever seen it before, Berta.

Berta. Mama—what a big tree! Look at those little wooden men under it.

Elizabeth. They're the carved figures of the three wise men.

Berta. See . . . they have something in their hands, Mama.

Elizabeth. Gifts, Berta, for the Christ Child.

Berta. Mama, do you know what gift Pastor Mohr has for us? The one he asked Papa to wrap?

Elizabeth. No, dear, it's a secret between the two of them. You'll soon know. Here comes the Pastor now.

BERTA. But, Mama, where's Pastor Mohr? I thought he'd conduct the service.

ELIZABETH. *(In hushed voice)* Oh no, you see, he's the *assistant* pastor, and for the Christmas Eve service, he's needed to help your father with the choir boys. *(Fading)* Sh-h-h, Berta . . . the Pastor. . . .

FIRST PASTOR. *(In even rhythm: full rich tones)* How happy we all are tonight as we gather to celebrate the birth of the Christ Child. Of all nights in the year, this is the most holy. But tonight is not only the most holy of *this* whole year . . . but of all our years together, for it brings to us the birth of a beautiful new Christmas song . . . a song written and composed in our very midst by our beloved assistant pastor and our cherished choir director. It is a melody which should make the words, "Silent Night! Holy Night!" forever a part of Christmas.

(Music: Chorus at first with guitar accompaniment then organ: Eight voices singing with guitar accompaniment.)
> Silent Night! Holy Night!
> All is calm, all is bright

(Sneak in organ accompaniment, with more voices.)
> Round yon Virgin Mother and Child.
> Holy Infant so tender and mild,

(Up full chorus and swell organ to climax.)
> Sleep in heavenly peace,
> Sleep in heavenly peace.

(Sustain organ softly with tune under:)

NARRATOR. *(Fading in)* Yes, Franzl was just an ordinary boy . . . but with nimble fingers . . . for weaving . . . and something else which *was* a secret between his mother and himself. But now he became a man . . . it was no longer a secret. His tune was carried home by the organ builder, who then sang it for the Strassers, a well-known Tyrolean quartet. These Strassers sold gloves and sang songs in the market squares of Europe. Now they had a new song to sing—Franz's song. But as they sang *Silent Night* over all the countryside, they forgot to mention that it belonged to him. That is how it came to be known as a folksong. Only the director of the Royal Court Orchestra in Berlin grew curious about its origin. . . . He wrote about it to Austria . . . and found out what you already know . . . that a modest man, an organist with nimble fingers, was the composer . . . Franz Xavier Gruber.

(Music: Organ continue tune, swelling into majestic finale.)

ANNOUNCER. You have been listening to the ————'s presentation of "The Birth of the Song, 'Silent Night,'" an original historical radio drama by Florence Felten French. This production was made possible by special arrangement with Walter H. Baker Company, Boston. Those appearing in the cast were—

A Christmas Carol

by

CHARLES DICKENS

Adapted as a half-hour radio broadcast

by

FREDERICK GARRIGUS

Characters:

EBENEZER SCROOGE	MRS. CRATCHIT
FRED, *his nephew*	MARTHA CRATCHIT
BOB CRATCHIT	PETER CRATCHIT
GHOST OF CHRISTMAS PAST	TINY TIM
GHOST OF CHRISTMAS PRESENT	FIRST MAN
GHOST OF CHRISTMAS FUTURE	SECOND MAN
A SOLICITOR	WOMAN
MARLEY'S GHOST	JOE
A GIRL	BOY

PLACE: England.

TIME: 19th century.

LENGTH: Thirty minutes.

FRED. *(Fades in)* A merry Christmas, Uncle! God save you!

SCROOGE. Bah! Humbug!

FRED. Christmas a humbug, Uncle? You don't mean *that*, I'm sure!

SCROOGE. I do! Out upon merry Christmas! What's Christmastime to you but a time for paying bills without money; a time for finding yourself a year older, and not an hour richer; a time for balancing your books and having every item in 'em through a round dozen of months presented dead against you? If I had my will, every idiot who goes about with "Merry Christmas" on his lips should be boiled with his own pudding, and buried with a stake of holly through his heart! He should!

13

Fred. Uncle!

Scrooge. Nephew, keep Christmas your own way, and let me keep it in mine.

Fred. Keep it! But you *don't* keep it!

Scrooge. Let me leave it alone, then! Much good may it do you! Much good it has ever done you!

Fred. There are many things from which I might have derived good, by which I might have profited, I dare say, Christmas among the rest. But I am sure I have always thought of Christmastime, when it has come round, as a good time; a kind, forgiving, charitable, pleasant time; and I say, God bless it!

Bob. Amen!

Scrooge. Let me hear another sound from you, Bob Cratchit, and you'll keep your Christmas by losing your situation! As for you, nephew, you're quite a powerful speaker, sir; I wonder you don't go into Parliament.

Fred. Don't be angry, Uncle. Come! Dine with us tomorrow.

Scrooge. I—I'll see you in—

Fred. But why? Why, Uncle?

Scrooge. Why did you get married, nephew?

Fred. Because I fell in love!

Scrooge. Because you fell in love! Good afternoon!

Fred. Nay, Uncle, but you never came to see me before that happened. Why give it as a reason for not coming now?

Scrooge. Good afternoon!

Fred. I am sorry, with all my heart, to find you so resolute. But I have made the trial in homage to Christmas ,and I'll keep my Christmas humor to the last. So, a merry Christmas, Uncle!

Scrooge. Good afternoon!

Fred. And a happy New Year, Uncle!

Scrooge. Good afternoon!

Fred. And a merry Christmas to you, Bob Cratchit!

Bob. A merry Christmas, sir! God bless it!

Scrooge. Bah! Humbug!

[*Pause.*

Solicitor. (*Voice fades in*) Beg pardon, sir, but is this Scrooge and Marley's?

SCROOGE. It is!

SOLICITOR. Have I the pleasure of addressing Mr. Scrooge or Mr. Marley?

SCROOGE. Jacob Marley has been dead these seven years. He died seven years ago this very night.

SOLICITOR. At this festive season of the year, Mr. Scrooge, it is more than usually desirable that we should make some slight provision for the poor and destitute, who suffer greatly at the present time.

SCROOGE. Are there no prisons?

SOLICITOR. Plenty of prisons, Mr. Scrooge. But a few of us are trying to raise a fund to buy the poor some meat and drink, and means of warmth. What shall I put you down for?

SCROOGE. Nothing!

SOLICITOR. You wish to be anonymous, Mr. Scrooge?

SCROOGE. I wish to be left alone! Since you ask me what I wish, sir, that is my answer. I don't make merry myself at Christmas, and I can't afford to make idle people merry. I help to support the prisons and the workhouses—those who are badly off must go there!

SOLICITOR. Many can't go there, sir, and many would rather die.

SCROOGE. If they would *rather* die, they had better do it, and decrease the surplus population. Good afternoon!

SOLICITOR. *(Fade out on the last of this speech)* Good afternoon, Mr. Scrooge, and a merry Christmas to you!

SCROOGE. Bah! Humbug! *(Pause)* Here you, Bob Cratchit!

BOB. Yes, sir.

SCROOGE. You'll want all day tomorrow, I suppose?

BOB. *(Timidly)* If it's quite convenient, sir.

SCROOGE. It's *not* convenient, and it's not fair! If I was to stop half a crown for it, you'd think yourself mightily ill-used, I'll be bound!

BOB. Yes, sir.

SCROOGE. And yet you don't think *me* ill-used, when I pay a day's wages for no work.

BOB. It's only once a year, sir.

SCROOGE. A poor excuse for picking a man's pocket every twenty-fifth of December! But I suppose you must have the whole day. Be here all the earlier *next* morning!

Bob. I shall indeed, sir. Good night, Mr. Scrooge, and a merry Christmas to you!

> [*Voice fades out on this speech.*

Scrooge. Bah! Humbug!

(*Music cue. A few measures of Christmas music fades in and, after ten seconds, fades down and out. Pause.*)

(*Sound effect. First, a single bell rings; this peal is taken up by several bells, and continues for a few seconds. Stop. The sound of a chain being dragged over the floor fades in, becomes very near, and stops. Pause.*)

Scrooge. (*Terrified*) A ghost! I know him! Marley's ghost! (*Coldly*) How now! What do you want with me?

Marley's Ghost. Much!

Scrooge. Who are you?

Marley's Ghost. Ask me who I *was.*

Scrooge. Who *were* you then?

Marley's Ghost. In life I was your partner, Jacob Marley.

Scrooge. Mercy! Dreadful apparition, why do you trouble me? Why do spirits walk the earth, and why do they come to me?

Marley's Ghost. It is required of every man that the spirit within him should walk abroad among his fellowmen; and if that spirit goes not forth in life, it is condemned to do so after death. In life my spirit never roved beyond the narrow limits of our money-changing hold; and weary journeys lie before me!

Scrooge. Seven years dead. And traveling all the time? You travel fast?

Marley's Ghost. On the wings of the wind.

Scrooge. You might have got over a quantity of ground in seven years.

Marley's Ghost. O blind man, blind man! Not to know that no space of regret can make amends for one life's opportunities misused! Yet I was like this man; I once was like this man!

Scrooge. (*Falteringly*) But you were always a good man of business, Jacob.

Marley's Ghost. Business! Mankind was my business; but hear me! My time is nearly gone! I cannot tell you all I would. A very little time is permitted me. I cannot rest, I cannot stay, I cannot linger anywhere! Hear me!

Scrooge. I will. But don't be hard upon me? Don't be flowery, Jacob, pray!

Marley's Ghost. I am here tonight to warn you that you have yet a chance and hope of escaping my fate. A chance and hope of *my* procuring, Ebenezer!

Scrooge. You were always a good friend to me, Jacob. Thank'ee.

Marley's Ghost. You will be haunted by three Spirits.

Scrooge. Is that the chance and hope you mentioned, Jacob? I—I think I'd rather not!

Marley's Ghost. Without their visits, you cannot hope to shun the path I tread. Expect the first tomorrow night, when the bell tolls one. Expect the second on the next night at the same hour. The third, upon the next night, when the last stroke of twelve has ceased to vibrate. Look to see me no more. And look that, for your own sake, you remember what has passed between us!

[*Fade out on last line.*

(*Music cue. Christmas fades in and, after five seconds, fades down and out. Pause.*)

(*Sound effect. Clock strikes a deep, dull, hollow one. Pause. Whirring sound fades in and stops.*)

Scrooge. Are you the spirit, sir, whose coming was foretold to me?

Ghost of the Past. I am!

Scrooge. Who and what are you?

Ghost of the Past. I am the Ghost of Christmas Past.

Scrooge. *Long* past?

Ghost of the Past. No. *Your* past. The things that you will see with me are shadows of the things that have been; they will have no consciousness of us.

Scrooge. What business brings you here?

Ghost of the Past. Your welfare. Rise, and walk with me!

[*Pause.*

Scrooge. (*In supplication*) Not out of the window, Spirit! I am mortal, and liable to fall!

Ghost of the Past. Bear but a touch of my hand upon

your heart, and you shall be upheld in more than this! Come!
(Pause)

> *(Music cue. Violin and piano fade in softly playing "Sir
> Roger de Coverley"—the music continues to play softly
> underneath the dialogue until the music cue.)*

GHOST OF THE PAST. Do you know this office, Ebenezer
Scrooge?

SCROOGE. Know it! I was apprenticed here! And there's
old Fezziwig! Bless his heart, it's Fezziwig, alive again! *(Pause)*
And there's Dick Wilkins, to be sure! My old fellow-ap-
prentice, bless me, yes. There he is. He was very much at-
tached to me was Dick. Dear, dear! *(Pause. Reminiscently)*
What parties we had in this office on Christmas Eve! And
old Fezziwig and Mrs. Fezziwig—they always danced top couple
in the Sir Roger de Coverley, just as they're doing it there
now. Those were happy times, Spirit! And how very grateful
we all were to old Fezziwig for those Christmas Eves!

GHOST OF THE PAST. A small matter to make these silly folks
so full of gratitude.

SCROOGE. A *small* matter, Spirit?

GHOST OF THE PAST. Old Fezziwig spent but a few pounds of
your mortal money—three or four, perhaps. Is *that* so much,
that he deserves this praise?

SCROOGE. It isn't that, Spirit. He had the power to render
us happy or unhappy; to make our service light or burden-
some; a pleasure or a toil. Say that his power lies in words
and looks; in things so slight and insignificant that it is impossible to add and count 'em up; what then? The happiness
he gives is quite as great as if it cost a fortune. *(Pause)*

GHOST OF THE PAST. What's the matter, Scrooge?

SCROOGE. Oh—nothing particular.

GHOST OF THE PAST. Something, I think.

SCROOGE. No, no! I should like to be able to say a word
or two to my clerk just now. That's all.

GHOST OF THE PAST. My time grows short! Come with me!
Quick!

> *(Music cue. Dance music fades down quickly, and cuts out.
> Pause.)*

GHOST OF THE PAST. Do you know this scene, Scrooge?

SCROOGE. Yes; again it is myself, with one I loved. I was a young man on that fatal day, Spirit!

(Music cue. Music plays softly "Drink to Me Only With Thine Eyes" underneath the following dialogue to Music Cue.)

GHOST OF THE PAST. Listen to what they say!

GIRL. It matters little to you, Ebenezer, very little. Another idol has displaced me; and if it can comfort you in time to come, as I would have tried to do, I have no just cause to grieve.

YOUTHFUL SCROOGE. What idol has displaced you?

GIRL. A golden one. You fear the world too much. I have seen your nobler aspirations fall off one by one, until the master-passion, gain, engrosses you. Have I not?

YOUTHFUL SCROOGE. What then? Even if I have grown so much wiser, what then? I am not changed toward you. Have I ever sought release from our engagement?

GIRL. In words, no. Never.

YOUTHFUL SCROOGE. In what, then?

GIRL. In a changed nature; in an altered spirit; in another atmosphere of life; another hope as its great end. If you were free today, tomorrow, can even I believe that you would choose a dowerless girl; or, choosing her, do I not know that your repentance and regret would surely follow? I do; and I release you. With a full heart, for the love of him you once were.

SCROOGE. Spirit! Remove me from this place!

(Music cue. Music fades down and cuts out in next speech.)

GHOST OF THE PAST. I told you these were the shadows of the things that *have* been. That they are *what* they are, do not blame me!

SCROOGE. Remove me! I cannot bear it! Leave me! Take me back! Haunt me no longer! *(Fade out this last speech and fade in music)*

(Music cue. Lively music fades in on this last speech. Stop music after five seconds.)

(Sound effect. Whirring sound fades up and in; continue for three seconds and cut out.)

GHOST OF THE PRESENT. Look up! Look up, and know me

better, man! I am the Ghost of Christmas Present. Look upon me! YOU have never seen the like of me before!

SCROOGE. Never!

GHOST OF THE PRESENT. Have never walked forth with the younger members of my family; meaning (for I am very young) my elder brothers, born in these later years?

SCROOGE. I don't think that I have. I'm afraid I have not. Have you many brothers, Spirit?

GHOST OF THE PRESENT. More than eighteen hundred!

SCROOGE. A tremendous family to provide for!

GHOST OF THE PRESENT. Will you come forth with me, Ebenezer Scrooge?

SCROOGE. Spirit, conduct me where you will. I went forth last night on compulsion, and I learnt a lesson which is working now. Tonight, if you have aught to teach me, let me profit by it.

GHOST OF THE PRESENT. Touch my robe!

(*Music cue. Lively Christmas music fades in and, after four seconds, fades down and then continues diminuendo underneath the following dialogue until the music cue.*)

GHOST OF THE PRESENT. Do you know this home, Ebenezer Scrooge?

SCROOGE. Why it's my clerk's home! It's Bob Cratchit's home!

GHOST OF THE PRESENT. Ay, Bob Cratchit's house! Your clerk, Bob, who pockets on Saturdays but fifteen copies of his Christian name! Yet the Ghost of Christmas Present blesses his four-roomed house with the sprinklings of his torch! Listen! (*Pause*)

MRS. CRATCHIT. What has ever got your precious father, then? And your brother Tiny Tim! And Martha warn't as late last Christmas day, by half an hour!

PETER. Here's Martha, Mother! Hurrah! That's *such* a goose, Martha!

MR. CRATCHIT. Why bless your heart alive, my dear, how late you are!

MARTHA. We'd a deal of work to finish up last night, and had to clear away this morning, Mother!

MRS. CRATCHIT. Well! Never mind, so long as you are come.

Sit ye down before the fire, my dear, and have a warm. Lord bless ye!

PETER. No, No! There's Father and Tiny Tim coming! Hide, Martha, hide!

BOB. *(Fades in)* Why, where's our Martha?

MRS. CRATCHIT. Not coming, Bob!

BOB. Not coming!—Not coming upon Christmas day!

MARTHA. *(Laughingly)* I'm here, Father!

BOB. Martha!

MRS. CRATCHIT. And how did Tiny Tim behave, Bob?

BOB. As good as gold, and better! You know, he told me, coming home, that he hoped the people saw him in the church, because he was a cripple, and it might be pleasant to them to remember, upon Christmas day, who made the lame beggars walk and blind men see. *(Pause)*

MRS. CRATCHIT. Is the punch ready, Bob?

BOB. It is, and for the first toast I'll give you Mr. Scrooge, the Founder of the Feast!

MRS. CRATCHIT. The Founder of the Feast indeed! I wish I had *him here!* I'd give him a piece of *my mind* to feast upon, and I hope he'd have a *good* appetite for it!

BOB. My dear, the children! Christmas day!

MRS. CRATCHIT. It *should* be Christmas day, I'm sure, on which one drinks the health of such an odious, stingy, hard, unfeeling man as Mr. Scrooge. You *know* he is, Robert! Nobody knows it better than *you* do, poor fellow!

BOB. My dear, Christmas day.

MRS. CRATCHIT. I'll drink his health for your sake, Robert, and the day's not for his! Long life to him! A merry Christmas and a happy New Year! He'll be very merry and very happy, I have no doubt!

BOB. Come, a merry Christmas to us all, my dears. God bless us!

TINY TIM. God bless us, every one!

(Music cue. Stop music. Pause.)

(Sound effect. Clock tolls twelve. Pause.)

(Sound effect. Whirring sound fades up and in. Stop. Pause.)

SCROOGE. I am in the presence of the Ghost of Christmas Yet to Come?

GHOST OF THE FUTURE. You are!

SCROOGE. Ghost of the Future! I fear you more than any spectre I have seen! But, as I know your purpose is to do me good, and as I hope to live to be a better man from what I was, I am prepared to bear you company, and do it with a thankful heart.

GHOST OF THE FUTURE. Follow me!

SCROOGE. Lead on! Lead on! The night is waning fast, and it is precious time to me, I know. Lead on, Spirit! *(Pause)*

GHOST OF THE FUTURE. Stop here on this corner, and listen. *(Pause)*

FIRST MAN. *(Voice fades in)* No, I don't know much about it either way. I only know he's dead.

SECOND MAN. When did he die?

FIRST MAN. Last night, I believe.

SECOND MAN. What has he done with his money?

FIRST MAN. I haven't heard. He hasn't left it to me, that's all I know! Bye-bye! *(Pause)*

GHOST OF THE FUTURE. Follow me, Ebenezer Scrooge, to yet another scene! *(Pause)*

WOMAN. *(Voice fades in)* Look *here,* old Joe, *here's* a chance!

JOE. *(Eagerly)* What have you got to sell? What have you got to sell?

WOMAN. Half a minute's patience, Joe, and *you* shall *see!* Every person has a right to take care of *themselves!* *He* always did! Who's the *worse* for the loss of a few old things like these? Not a *dead* man, I suppose?

JOE. No, I suppose not!

WOMAN. If he had been *natural* in his lifetime, he'd have had somebody to look *after* him when he was struck with Death, instead of lying gasping out his *last there, alone,* by *himself!*

JOE. It's the truest word that was ever spoke, it's a judgment on him!

WOMAN. I wish it was a little *heavier* judgment, and it *should* have been, you may *depend* on it, if I could have laid my hands on anything else. Open that bundle, old Joe, and let me know the value of it. Speak out plain! *(Short pause)*

JOE. What do you call this? Bed curtains?

WOMAN. Ah! Bed curtains! Don't drop that oil upon the blankets, now!

JOE. *His* blankets?

WOMAN. Whose *else* do you think? *He* isn't likely to take cold without 'em, I dare say!

SCROOGE. I see, I see! The case of this unhappy man might be my own. My life tends that way now. Spirit, let me see some tenderness connected with a death, or this dark chamber, Spirit, will be forever present to me!

GHOST OF THE FUTURE. Follow me! *(Pause)*

SCROOGE. Bob Cratchit's home again! But why are they all so quiet? What's that the boy is reading?

(Music cue. The quiet music of a Christmas hymn plays softly underneath the following dialogue to the music cue.)

PETER. *(Slowly, as if reading)* "And he took a little child, and set him in the midst of them." *(Pause)* What's the matter, Mother, why have you stopped your needlework?

MRS. CRATCHIT. The color hurts my eyes. There, now they're better again. It makes them weak to work by candle-light; and I wouldn't show weak eyes to your father when he comes home for the world. It must be near his time.

PETER. Past it, rather. But I think he has walked a little slower than he used, since Tiny Tim is gone, Mother.

MRS. CRATCHIT. I have known him walk, with Tiny Tim upon his shoulder, very fast indeed!

PETER. And so have I, often!

MRS. CRATCHIT. But Tiny Tim was very light to carry, and his father loved him so, that it was no trouble—no trouble. Ah, there's your father at the door! *(Pause)*

BOB. *(Fade in)* Hello, Mother. Hello, Peter!

MRS. CRATCHIT. You're late, dear. You went to the grave today, then, Robert?

BOB. Yes, my dear. I wish you could have gone. It would have done you good to see how green a place it is. But you'll see it often. I promised Tiny Tim that I would walk there on a Sunday. My little, little child! My little child!

(Fade out on this speech and broken sobs. Pause.)

(Music cue. Fade out music.)

SCROOGE. Specter, something informs me that our parting

moment is at hand. I know it, but I know not how. Before
you leave me, answer me one question. Are these the shadows
of things that will be, or are they shadows of the things that
may be only?

GHOST OF THE FUTURE. Men's courses will foreshadow certain ends, to which, if persevered in, they must lead. But if
the courses be departed from the ends will change.

SCROOGE. Say that it is thus with what you show me! Spirit!
Hear me! I am not the man I was. I will not be the man I
must have been but for this intercourse. Why show me this,
if I am past all hope? Assure me that I yet may change these
shadows you have shown me by an altered life! *(Pause)* I will
honor Christmas in my heart, and try to keep it all the year!
I will live in the Past, the Present, and the Future! I will not
shut out the lessons that they teach!

(*Sound effect. Into the last part of the above speech fade up
the sound of church bells pealing. Continue loudly for
a few seconds, and then fade down and peal intermit-
tently underneath following dialogue to the Sound Cue.*)

SCROOGE. Why it's morning! It's a clear, bright day, and I
am in my own room!

(*Sound effect. Window opens.*)

SCROOGE. *(Calls out)* Hallo! Hallo, there! What's today?

BOY. *(From a distance)* Eh?

SCROOGE. What's today, my fine fellow?

BOY. *(Nearer)* Today! Why it's CHRISTMAS DAY!

SCROOGE. It's Christmas day! I haven't missed it! Hallo,
there my fine fellow!

BOY. Hallo!

SCROOGE. Do you know the Poulterer's, in the next street
but one, at the corner?

BOY. I should hope I did!

SCROOGE. An intelligent boy! A remarkable boy! Do you
know whether they've sold the prize turkey that was hanging
up there? Not the *little* prize turkey—the *big* one?

BOY. What! The one as big as me?

SCROOGE. What a delightful boy. It's a pleasure to talk to
him! Yes, my buck!

BOY. It's hanging there now!

SCROOGE. Is it? Go and buy it!

Boy. Walk-ER!

SCROOGE. No, no, I am in earnest. Go and buy it and tell 'em to bring it here, that I may give the man the direction where to take it. Come back with the man, and I'll give you a shilling. Come back with him in less than five minutes, and I'll give you half a crown! *(To himself)* I'll send it to Bob Cratchit's! He shan't know who sends it. It's twice the size of Tiny Tim! Joe Miller never made such a joke as sending it to Bob's will be!

(Music cue. Old English Christmas air fades in, plays for ten seconds, and then fades down and out. Pause.)

(Sound effect. Clock strikes nine. Pause.)

SCROOGE. *(Gleefully)* He's late! The day after Christmas, and Bob Cratchit's late for work! Ah, there he comes. *(Pause. Gruffly)* Hallo! What do you mean by coming here at this time of day, Bob Cratchit?

BOB. I am very sorry, sir! I *am* behind my time!

SCROOGE. You are? Yes! I think you are! Step this way, if you please, sir!

BOB. It's only once a year, sir. It shall not be repeated. I was making rather merry yesterday, sir.

SCROOGE. Now, I'll tell what, my friend. I am not going to stand this sort of thing any longer! And therefore I am about to raise your salary! A merry Christmas, Bob! *(Earnestly)* A merrier Christmas, Bob, my good fellow, than I have given you for many a year! I'll raise your salary, and endeavor to assist your struggling family, and we shall discuss your affairs this very afternoon, over a Christmas bowl of smoking bishop, Bob! Make up the fires, and buy a second coal scuttle before you dot another "i," Bob Cratchit!

(Musical closing. Christmas music fades in on this last speech, and play forte for a few seconds then quickly changes to diminuendo, and so continues underneath the dialogue of the closing announcement.)

CURTAIN

White Christmas

A Missionary Play in One Act

by

DOROTHY CLARKE WILSON

Characters:

WILLIAM MARSHALL CHARLIE
KATE MARSHALL JOHN LIANG
BOB MARSHALL THE SMALL ONE
CAROLYN MARSHALL MRS. MILTON CRAIG
JUNIE MARSHALL

TIME: Modern Christmas.

PLACE: United States.

LENGTH: About 40 minutes.

SCENE.—*A living room in the house of William Marshall. The furnishings show evidences of luxury. Entrances left and right into other parts of the house. Center, rear, French doors or a large window, outside of which there is snow falling. It is a soft, sticky snow, and, although it is too dark outside to see from within the actual falling of the snow, there are shining particles clinging to the panes and small drifts are visible piled against the sashes. At left, rear, is a Christmas tree, hung with bright-colored ornaments and white packages. On the tree, in a conspicuous place facing front is a large, flaxen-haired doll. Just beneath, on a table, is a miniature representation of the manger scene.*

(As the curtain rises Junie enters right, on tiptoe, as if afraid of disturbing the beauty of the tree. She gazes at it delightedly, fingering some of the ornaments, but very carefully so as not to break them. She goes to the manger scene and bends over it, rearranging the small objects several times until she is perfectly satisfied. She hums softly "Away in a Manger" as she does so. Carolyn enters right, followed by Charlie, who carries a stepladder. In her hand is a resplendent Christmas tree angel, made of tinsel and paper.)

JUNIE. *(Clasping her hands)* Oh, oh! A real angel! Are you going to hang it on the tree, Carrie?

CAROLYN. *(Pointing to a spot beneath the tree)* Put it here, Charlie. *(Sharply)* Look out! Be careful! Those ornaments break easily. *(As one falls to the floor)* There! You should have been more careful.

CHARLIE. *(Bowing, his face expressionless)* I sweep it up, miss.

CAROLYN. Very well. But that doesn't put it together again. Sometimes you're very clumsy, Charlie.

(Charlie *backs toward the door right.* Carolyn *mounts the ladder, knocking down one of the colored balls as she does so.)*

JUNIE. Oh! Look, Carrie, you broke one yourself—a great big one, and Charlie only broke a little, teeny-weeny one.

CAROLYN. Be quiet, Junie! *(Turning to* Charlie) Well! What are you standing there staring for? Why don't you go?

CHARLIE. *(Still expressionless)* Yes, miss.

He goes out.

JUNIE. *(Coming close to the ladder and looking up at* Carolyn) I think you're mean to Charlie. You're always hurtin' his feelings. I can tell by the way his eyes look.

CAROLYN. *(Hanging the angel as high as possible on the tree)* Nonsense! Charlie isn't like us, Junie. He belongs to a different race and has a different set of emotions entirely. He'd walk all over us if we treated him like a white person—even like a white servant. Look, Junie! How's that?

JUNIE. *(A little wistfully)* It's nice for a goldy-crinkly one. But I'd like to see just one really truly one. Don't they have really truly angels, Carrie? There are really truly babies—and really truly stars.

CAROLYN. You're a funny little mite, aren't you? But I do wish you wouldn't call me Carrie. Call me Lyn if you want to, but I hate Carrie.

(Bob *enters right. Like* Carolyn, *he is dressed for the party which is to take place that evening.)*

BOB. Oh, is that so, Carrie! I'm so glad to know that, Carrie. Merry Christmas, Carrie. And happy New Year, too, Carrie, my dear.

CAROLYN. *(Making a wild pass for his hair and nearly falling off the stepladder)* Bob! You nuisance! College hasn't

improved you a particle. Here! Take this stepladder out in
the kitchen again, will you?

BOB. Not on your life. What do you think we hire a Chink
for, anyway? Just to brighten up the house with a little color?
(Charlie *enters right, with brush and dustpan, in time to
hear the last speech. He sweeps up the remains of the broken
decorations, then with an impassive face removes the stepladder.* Bob, *perching on the arm of a chair, hands in pockets*)
That fellow gives me the creeps. I watched him then, and I'll
swear all the time he was in the room his face never moved a
muscle. Do you suppose he's human?

JUNIE. (*Precisely*) Charlie has a little girl. I've seen her.
She's just as big as I am, and her name is the Small One—
only it's something different in Chinese. And he lives on the
top floor of a big house over on Water Street. And there are
red geraniums in the windows.

CAROLYN. (*Moving toward the window and looking out*)
For goodness' sake, how did you find out all that?

JUNIE. I asked him. And once I played a perfectly lovely
game with his little girl, and it was lots of fun.

CAROLYN. (*Absently*) Well, you'd better not tell Mother
about it. (*Looking out of window*) Oh, dear! It's snowing
terribly. I don't see why it had to go and snow on the night
of my party. As if enough hadn't gone wrong already with
Uncle David's letter coming.

BOB. (*Walking around the tree*) Old tree looks pretty well
loaded down, but I'm not interested in the small stuff. Say,
Sis, what's chances for that new roadster I wrote Dad about?
Chick Meader, my roommate, has a honey. All the boys at
"U" have something to ride around in. I say it's a disgrace—

CAROLYN. Well, I don't see it hanging anywhere on the
tree, do you? I'm more interested in that long package over
there in the corner. It might be—well, lots of things. I'd like
to look and see if my name's on it.

BOB. Well, gee, I've got a good mind not to go back to "U"
if Dad doesn't come across with that roadster. I'll be the
laughing stock of the whole crowd.

(Kate Marshall *enters right. She is a handsome, fashionably
dressed woman in the early forties, with a perpetually
nervous air and lines of worry on her forehead. She carries a paper and pencil.*)

KATE. *(Reprovingly)* Bob Marshall, I'm ashamed of you. Here you haven't been in the house a half an hour and haven't even seen your father—and yet all you can talk about is a new car.

BOB. Well, gee, Mom, all the fellows have them. You ought to know how the wind blows. Tell me, is he or isn't he going to be a good sport and give me one?

KATE. *(Sitting down and going over her list)* I don't know. And I can't think about anything, just now. I've got too many things on my mind. I've been all the afternoon straightening out the charity baskets that the church is sending—the chairman of the committee having a nervous breakdown at the last minute threw everything on my shoulders, and such a tangle! And here I've just found out that we forgot to send any present to Aunt Catherine—I don't know how I ever missed her, and she sent us that lovely tea set last year from Tiffany's. It must have cost at least fifty dollars. And now at the last minute the orchestra for Carolyn's party has backed out—

CAROLYN. *(In dismay)* The orchestra's backed out! And the party not an hour away! Oh, whatever are we going to do!

KATE. I called up Jake's trio, and they agreed to come.

CAROLYN. Oh, dear! Jake's isn't nearly so good. I just knew something else would go wrong—and just when I'd set my heart on everything being just right!

KATE. *(Pondering over her lists)* And I can't remember whether I sent any invitations to the Dudley Staples family. If I didn't, it would be a terrible *faux pas.*

BOB. *(Flippantly)* Why don't you call them up and ask them? *(He has been crawling about under the tree examining labels)* It's all right, Sis. The long package has your name on it.

CAROLYN. *(Immediately diverted)* Oh, dear, I'd like to know what it is. I'm sure that's the one Dad had delivered from Mercier's.

JUNIE. *(From her seat on a low stool near the tree)* I know what's in it. Daddy told me. It's a fur—Oh! *(Clapping her hand over her mouth)* He made me promise not to tell.

CAROLYN. *(Eyes shining)* It's a fur coat, isn't it, Junie? Oh, I knew it, I knew it. We're going to have a real Christmas this year. Dad's been awfully good-natured lately, ever since he put across that deal with Mr. Milton Craig.

BOB. *(Hopefully)* Then maybe I'll get the car. I'm going to ask him. Where is Dad, anyway? Getting ready for the party?

KATE. *(Suddenly becoming conscious of the children)* No, I only wish he were.

CAROLYN. My goodness, Bob doesn't know, does he? He wasn't here when Uncle David's letter came.

BOB. What letter?

CAROLYN. Oh, the letter that told all about it. You see, brother mine, *(pausing for effect)* we have a guest coming for Christmas. And Dad's gone down to the docks to meet him.

(Junie, *wearied with grown-up conversation, strolls out of the room.)*

BOB. Down to the docks! You don't mean Uncle David!

CAROLYN. No, darling, not Uncle David. One of Uncle David's dear converted heathens, one of our Chinese brothers.

KATE. *(Protesting)* Now, Carolyn, you know that isn't the right attitude. We're all interested in the work your Uncle David is trying to do as a missionary—

BOB. *(Chortling and throwing himself into a chair)* Ha, that's a good one! Just in time, too, for your swell party. You can have him in the receiving line.

CAROLYN. *(Maliciously)* Yes, laugh, why don't you? You won't feel like it after you've read Uncle David's letter. Uncle David asked as a special favor that you introduce him to all of your friends at the "U." He's going to be a student there next semester.

BOB. *(Starting indignantly out of his chair)* Well, I'd just like to see myself!

CAROLYN. Get the letter, Mother. You might as well read it out loud. They'll be coming any time now, and Bob might as well be prepared.

KATE. I wish you wouldn't speak that way, Carolyn. You know we are all interested in your Uncle David's work. Your father—

BOB. Has practically supported it financially. Oh, yes, we know all about it. Go ahead and read the letter, Mother.

(Kate *goes to a small center table, finds the letter, and, sit-*

ting down again, adjusts her glasses. Carolyn *glances
maliciously at* Bob.)

KATE. *(Reading)* "My dear brother, I received your note
with its most welcome enclosure, and, as I told you in my last
letter, thanks to the very wonderful co-operation you and your
church have shown, our work here is forging ahead. I can't
help wishing you would tell me more about yourself—it has
been so many years since we have met and shared experiences
that sometimes we seem almost like strangers. Yet I know this
is not so. By the continued support you have given my work
through the years. I know that we must be working together
for the building of the kingdom of God—"

CAROLYN. Skip all that, Mother. It's just what Uncle David
always writes. Read the last part.

KATE. *(Turning several pages)* "And now, Bill, I'm going
to ask a favor of you and give you a chance to share personally
in one of the most satisfying pieces of work God has ever permitted me—and you, also—to do. For it is the extra money
you sent in your last check which has made this thing possible. I am sending a young Chinese to America for a year in
your own state university—one of the finest specimens of
young Christian manhood I have ever been privileged to
know. He is a graduate of our own mission college, speaks
English almost as well as you do yourself, and would do credit
to any group. He comes from a very fine, old, Chinese family,
and his parents have been Christians for a number of years.
His father, in fact, is an instructor of Chinese literature in
our mission college. I have great hopes for John. John Liang,
the boy's name is. If I had nothing else to show for all the
years' work I have put in over here in China than what I
have been able to do for this boy, it would still have been more
than worth while. Now here, Bill, is where your part comes
in, yours and your family's. John will be landing at your own
city docks just about the time you get this letter—December
24 his boat is scheduled to get in. You can look it up in the
lists—the *Eastern Empress* sailing from Hong Kong. He will
be a perfect stranger to America and American ways—in fact,
he has never known any Americans except myself and a few
of the missionaries here in the school—and naturally I want
him to get the best possible introduction to them both. I

want you to take him to your own home, Bill, until the university opens, and treat him as one of the family. Let him see what a good Christian American home is like. And Bob is in the university now, isn't he—your fine boy that I have never seen! Ask Bob for me if he will not take John under his wing for the first few days, help him to get acquainted with the professors, introduce him to his own friends. John is like an own son to me, and as such I entrust him to you. Affectionately, David."

(There is a silence after Kate *finishes reading. At some time during the reading* Charlie *appears in the entrance left. He stands unobserved, waiting patiently, stolidly, for he has come to make a request of Mrs. Marshall.)*

BOB. Well, I'll be————! I say, what an awful mess to put a fellow in! And just when I've got into a decent frat, too. The fellows will think I'm crazy, lugging around a dirty Chink. Gosh, Mom, I haven't got to do it, have I? I'd never be able to live it down.

KATE. *(Folding the letter and putting it away)* You'll have to ask your father. He thinks a great deal of your Uncle David, and of course he's head of the church missionary committee. But personally I shouldn't think a foreigner with limited means would feel at home with the group you go with in college.

BOB. *(Eagerly)* No, you're right he wouldn't. A swell frat's the last place he'd want to be. The Y.M.C.A.'s the place for him.

CAROLYN. You should worry. You've got a whole week to do it in. Think of my party. The guests will be coming inside of an hour, and Dad may be coming back any time—with *him* —right in the middle of it! And it was going to be such a perfect party!

KATE. Carolyn, my dear, I've told you we'll manage somehow to keep this—this young man from spoiling your party— *(Suddenly spying* Charlie, *who has been standing immovable.)* Charlie! What are you doing there? How long have you been there?

CHARLIE. *(Stolidly)* I come. I ask missy. I wait.

KATE. *(Assuming her usual role with* Charlie *which is that of using his own dialect, or what she imagines is his dialect)*

All light. This time all light. But next time—no stand like that. No wait. You understand, Charlie?

CHARLIE. Yes, missy.

CAROLYN. For goodness sake talk English to him, Mother. He can understand English as well as you.

KATE. *(Patiently)* Carolyn, my dear, I had Chinese servants before you were born. *(To* Charlie) All light. Now can ask. Only be quick about it.

(Junie *returns to the room and regards the proceedings with interest.)*

CHARLIE. Tomollow—he Chlismas. I no work tomollow? I have Chlismas at home? What?

KATE. *(Aghast)* Have Christmas at home! Not work! You mean you're asking me for a holiday—on Christmas! *(Assuming role again)* No, Charlie. Sorry. No can. No can possible. Big party tonight. Lots clear up in morning. Big dinner tomollow. Lot company. Understand?

CHARLIE. *(Gravely)* I understand.

KATE. *(Trying to be kind and understanding)* Some time —you have Chinese day—like Chlismas Amelican day. Then you have holiday. All light? Understand?

CHARLIE. *(Bowing, his face still expressionless)* I understand.

[He goes out left.

BOB. Of all the nerve! Asking for Christmas day off! He'll be asking for the Fourth of July next, telling us he has to go and put a wreath on the grave of his grandfather who fought in the Revolution!

CAROLYN. *(Glancing out the window)* Gracious, here's Father! And he has—has *him* with him.

(William Marshall *enters right, followed by* John Liang. *The former is a typical middle-aged American business man, a bit heavy in spots, excellently dressed, obviously keen-minded. The latter is a young Chinese with a fine, pleasant face, perpetually smiling. Except for the slight slant to his eyes and the yellowish tinge to his skin, he might be any fine, athletic type of young American manhood, for his clothes are fairly well cut, and he speaks English only with a slight accent. There are flakes of snow on the overcoats of both men.)*

WILLIAM. *(Cheerfully)* Well, we're going to have a white

Christmas, all right. It's still snowing for all it's worth. *(There is a sudden awkward silence)* Folks—this is—Mr. Liang, only he seems to think it will be easier if we call him John. *(John steps forward, smiling)* And—er—John, this is my wife, Mrs. Marshall—my son, Bob—my daughter, Carolyn—and little Junie over there by the tree—

> *(The Marshall family seems suddenly to have run out of speech, and there is another awkward silence or would be, if the enthusiastic personality of John Liang did not immediately dominate the situation. Junie alone is undisturbed. She crosses the room and offers her hand.)*

JUNIE. I'm pleased to meet you.

JOHN. And I'm certainly pleased to meet you all—you don't know how pleased. *(He looks around the circle and smiles even more broadly)* Mr. David has told me all about you—every one of you—and showed me all your pictures. What is it you call them—short snaps?

JUNIE. *(Delighted)* Oh! How funny! You mean snapshots.

KATE. *(Extending her hand)* We are glad to meet any friend of David's.

> (Charlie *appears, as if by magic, to take the men's overcoats. There is a sudden apprehension among the* Marshalls *as to how he will receive the guest, but* Charlie's *face is as expressionless as usual.* Kate *relaxes in relief.)*

WILLIAM. Sit down—er—John, sit down. Make yourself at home—as we Americans say. Things are just a little—er—unusual around here. We're observing Christmas tomorrow, as you probably know.

JOHN. *(His face lighting a little more, if possible)* Yes, and to think that I should arrive in time to see the real Christmas in the real America! I saw it all as I came by in the car—all the trees in the houses, the bright candles in the windows, the glad faces on everybody, and I thought to myself, "Now have I come at last to the good country of my Mr. David, where so many people are like him, Christian," and my heart is like a warm glow, I am so happy.

> *(The Marshalls are a little embarrassed.* William *sits down and gestures* John *to do the same.* Kate *sits on the edge of her chair.* Carolyn, *obviously anxious to get the guest out of the way as soon as possible, stands impatiently behind him, signaling her mother.)*

CAROLYN. *(Mumbling)* If you'll excuse me—*(She starts for the door.)*

WILLIAM. Where are you going, daughter? Our guest has only just come.

CAROLYN. *(Sulkily)* I have a few things to do before the party.

KATE. That's all right, run along, dear, Mr.—Mr. Liang will excuse you, I'm sure. *(Trying to play the gracious hostess)* Mr. Marshall writes that you are planning to attend school here at the university. I'm sure I hope you'll like it.

JOHN. *(Leaning forward, his face again alight)* Like it! All my life I have dreamed of it. And now it is you, Mr. Marshall, who have made it possible. *(He takes a leather wallet from his pocket and holds it almost caressingly)* When Mr. David laid this in my hand—this five hundred dollars that you had sent—and told me it was at last my dream come true, I could not at first believe it. My father gets not much money. He has many children. I thought I must work a long time before I could get money to pay for my dream of your American college. And then Mr. David told me—that your heart too is in China! It will be you and me working together—to make my dream of Christian China come true.

BOB. *(In genuine amazement)* Five hundred dollars! Why, you can't go to the "U" a month on five hundred dollars.

WILLIAM. *(Somewhat sarcastically)* You mean you couldn't.

JOHN. *(Smiling)* No? Ah, then I work, I find something to do. These hands are not—what you call it?—lazy. *(In putting the wallet back into his pocket,* John *has been reminded of something. From another pocket he pulls a little Chinese doll and holds it out smilingly to* Junie.*)*

JUNIE. Oh! What a cunning little doll! May I look at it?

JOHN. *(Smiling, as he gives it to her)* You may have it. I brought it for you.

JUNIE. *(Delighted)* For me? Oh—thank you. I like it. All my dolls are just the same. But this one has a yellow face.

JOHN. This is a Chinese doll. At Christmas in my home we make the little Jesus in the cradle and the sheep tenders, as you have over there on the table, and this is the doll we had for the little child one.

JUNIE. Oh! You mean you have it just the same, only all the little dolls are yellow?

JOHN. Yes. That's right.

JUNIE. (*Running to the table*) I'm going to take my little white doll out of the manger and put the little yellow one in. (*She does, in spite of* Kate's *frown*) There! The little yellow doll fits lots better. The white one was too big.

KATE. (*Restlessly, looking at her watch*) We'd better show Mr.—Mr. Liang to his room, William. He must be tired after his long journey. Perhaps he will feel like resting this evening.

WILLIAM. Oh, there's no hurry—(*Catching* Kate's *warning glance*) Er—which room did you want him to have, Kate? The north one might be pleasanter.

KATE. (*Hurriedly, not looking at* William) I've arranged for Mr.—Mr. Liang on the third floor, William, next to Charlie's room. There are to be several guests staying over from the party, and I thought he might find it pleasanter—

WILLIAM. (*A little blankly*) Oh! Very well. (*To* Charlie, *who has appeared as if by magic at the moment wanted*) Take our guest to his room, Charlie. Mrs. Marshall says it has been made ready.

JOHN. How can I make known to you the gratitude I feel? You make me a most honored guest—I who am but a stranger deserving nothing. You know not what it means to be like this, in such a great country where so many homes are lighted with the Christmas candle, so many peoples, everywhere, keeping the Great One's birthday.

KATE. The attic room, Charlie.

(Charlie *nods, his face impassive, and leads the way out.* John *follows, bowing to his host and hostess. At the door* Charlie *stops, with a formal bow, and lets the guest precede him.* Carolyn *enters left.*)

WILLIAM. Say, what's the idea stuffing him way off up in that attic room? We've got plenty of rooms on the second story. I'd never be able to explain to David—

KATE. (*Patiently*) Now, William, I've thought of all that. But you'll never have to explain to David, and you most certainly would have to explain to the Milton Craigs if they found you'd put a Chinaman in the room next to theirs. You know how people like the Milton Craigs feel about such things, and I thought you wouldn't want to offend them just now.

WILLIAM. Yes. You're right, Kate. I'm depending on

Craig's support to put across a big deal—and a lot of people have prejudices—I'm sure you're right. It would be pleasanter for him on the third floor.

BOB. *(Skeptically)* For him! Ha, that's a good one!

CAROLYN. And Dad, you've just got to keep him away from the party somehow. I'd never hear the last of it. All the crowd would think I had invited him.

KATE. Yes, William, you must arrange that. As you say, so many people have prejudices. If any of the guests should happen to get a glimpse of him, which I hope they won't, they must think he's a servant. He really isn't bad looking at all for an Oriental. He'd make a splendid looking butler.

BOB. Wonder what Charlie thinks, seeing us entertain another Chink right in the parlor.

KATE. *(Worriedly)* Yes, and that's another reason why we must be careful. I've taken such pains all these years to keep Charlie on his proper level.

CAROLYN. *(Wheedlingly, slipping her arm about her father's neck)* I'll tell you what, Dad. You can keep John Chinaman right here in this room and show him your collection. That's a full evening's job once you get started, and we can keep all the crowd out of this room easily enough.

WILLIAM. But I'd counted on getting a chat with Craig about that Western Steamship stock. It looks like a big thing.

CAROLYN. Oh, you can afford to forget business for one evening. After that big deal you put over, you're entitled to take it easy for a while.

WILLIAM. *(Settling himself comfortably in an easy chair)* I'll say that was a good deal. For the first time since the beginning of the depression I'm able to face Christmas with some degree of cheerfulness.

BOB. *(Jumping to his feet, immediately seizing his opportunity)* Gee, that's great, Dad. It's good to have a dad that knows how to do things. Some of the fellows' old men are way down and out—can't afford to buy them even the cheapest kind of a car to run around in—

CAROLYN. *(Despairingly)* Oh, Bob, don't start that now.

BOB. Well, I was only just making a statement—It seems to me if you've got a lot of money to throw around on Chinamen—

WILLIAM. *(Who is in a magnanimous mood)* Don't worry, son. I got your letter. We're going to have a real Christmas this year. If you don't believe it, look what I've got for your mother. *(He draws a slim box from his pocket, opens it, and shows it to Bob.)*

BOB. Oh, gee!

WILLIAM. *(With satisfaction)* Genuine, too, my boy. I told you we were going to have a real Christmas.

CAROLYN. And you will show him your collection, won't you, Daddy?

JUNIE. *(Who has been bending over the manger scene, apparently oblivious of all else)* Why don't you want the nice man to go to your party, Carrie?

CAROLYN. *(Impatiently)* Oh—you wouldn't understand.

BOB. *(Solemnly)* Ask your Uncle Dudley, Pet. I believe in telling people the truth. It's because the gentleman is yellow. In other words, unbleached, unlike the great and only Anglo-Saxons.

JUNIE. *(Puzzled)* But that Jimmy Atkinson's yellow, too. You said he was yourself. And he's coming to the party.

BOB. *(With a howl of mirth)* Ha, that's a good one! Hear that, folks? *(Seriously)* You see it makes a difference, Pet, whether the yellow's on the inside or out.

CAROLYN. I don't think you're a bit funny.

KATE. *(Absently checking over a list)* Orchestra—ices—palms —lights—I think I've remembered everything. Oh, yes—I must tell Charlie to bring some sandwiches and coffee for Mr.—Mr. Liang.

BOB. Call him John, Mother. You'll never get used to the other name.

KATE. *(With a little shiver)* I couldn't. It doesn't seem right calling a—heathen John. I'd never get used to it.

(A bell rings distantly in another part of the house.)

CAROLYN. *(Eagerly)* There's the bell. They're beginning to come. Do I look all right, Mother? *(She pirouettes on her toes.)*

BOB. Like a million dollars. I wish you were.

CAROLYN. Come on, let's go. *(She and Bob go out left.)*

WILLIAM. *(Following)* Let me know when the Milton Craigs arrive.

KATE. *(To* Junie, *who is still bending over the manger scene)* It's your bedtime, Junie.

JUNIE. Oh, Mother—Christmas Eve! Please let me sit up just a little longer?

KATE. Well—just a few minutes. But—do take that awful little doll out of the manger, Junie. I couldn't say anything when that man was here, but—well I just don't like the looks of it.

JUNIE. Why, Mother?

KATE. Well—it just doesn't look right. The Chinese can observe Christmas any way they want to, I suppose, but we're living in America, not in China.

JUNIE. *(Thoughtfully)* Mother.

KATE. *(On her way out, turning a little impatiently)* What is it, darling?

JUNIE. Was Jesus an American?

KATE. *(Amused)* Why, no, of course not. There weren't any Americans when he was on earth. Jesus was an—an Oriental. *(A sudden startled look comes over her face, and she pauses an instant)* Just a few minutes, dear, don't forget.

(She goes out, and Junie stands over the manger scene. She rearranges the objects carefully, humming the tune of "Away in a Manger." John *enter right.)*

JOHN. Ah, they have all gone—all but the little one? *(He sits down and looks kindly at* Junie.) I have a little sister at home, just about as big as you.

JUNIE. *(Coming to his side)* You have? Is she white like me or yellow like Charlie's little girl?

JOHN. Her face is yellow, like Charlie's little girl. And she has very bright, dark eyes that light up like little candles when she smiles, and she has straight black hair, not curly like yours. And if you were to say her name in English, you would have to call her Peach Blossom.

JUNIE. *(Clapping her hands)* Oh, I like that. It's lots prettier than my name. Charlie's little girl is called Small One. Isn't that a funny name?

JOHN. Do you like to play with Charlie's little girl?

JUNIE. Yes, only Mother doesn't let me. Charlie's a servant, and you mustn't play with servants' little girls, you know, even the white ones.

JOHN. *(Slowly)* Oh, mustn't you? No. I didn't know that.

JUNIE. But I did play with her once, when Mother didn't know, and we had lots of fun. I like the little yellow doll. Did it belong to the little Peach Blossom?

JOHN. Yes. It belonged to Peach Blossom. You see, your Uncle David had told her about you, and she wanted you to have it. She has one just like it to put in her cradle.

JUNIE. *(Regretfully)* I had to take mine out again. Mother told me to. She said the little Jesus doll ought to be white. Maybe your little Peach Blossom didn't know the little Jesus doll ought to be white. P'raps nobody ever told her.

JOHN. *(Slowly)* No. You're right. I guess—nobody ever told her.

JUNIE. Here's Charlie with your supper. *(As* Charlie *enters left with tray)* Oh, Charlie, I've got something for you for Christmas. You wait right here, won't you, while I go and get it, and don't tell Mother.

CHARLIE. *(His face lighting with a great affection)* Yes, little missy. I wait. (Charlie *takes the tray to a small table at the extreme right of the stage, or he may take it offstage right, supposedly into an adjoining alcove. While he is gone,* John *sits thoughtfully. Presently the old enthusiasm comes back into his face, he rises, and approaches the tree, standing and looking up at it with awe and reverence on his face.* Charlie *returns and stands stolidly watching him. Impassively, after a pause, bowing low)* Your supper, sir. I get him ready, sir.

JOHN. *(Turning quickly)* Oh! Thank you. But you shouldn't have bothered. Mrs. Marshall is too kind. I did not need refreshment. Tell me, is your name really Charlie?

CHARLIE. Mis' Marshall's servant allays name Charlie. He have white face, he Henly, he have yellow face, he Charlie. I have yellow face, so I Charlie. *(Bowing again)* Your supper, sir. He wait. *(He starts for exit left.)*

JOHN. Wait a minute, Charlie. I want to talk to you. Don't you see, I've just come to America. I came in today on a ship from Hong Kong. It's all new to me. It must have been new to you once, too. There are so many things we ought to talk about. (Charlie *remains stolidly passive)* How long have you been in this country, Charlie?

CHARLIE. Ten years, sir.

JOHN. Think of it! Ten years! Ten Christmases—like this. Ten times to spend the Great One's birthday in company with so many millions who love and serve him. I envy you, Charlie.

CHARLIE. *(Bowing)* Your supper, sir. He wait. *(Again* Charlie *starts to go out left and again* John *stops him.)*

JOHN. Charlie—(Charlie *turns)* tell me this one thing more. Charlie—surely—you are a Christian?

(There is a long silence. Then Charlie *bows.)*

CHARLIE. I *was*—a Christian.

JOHN. You mean—you aren't any longer?

CHARLIE. I was Chlistian—in China. I come to Amelica. Now I no longer Chlistian.

JOHN. But—Charlie—

CHARLIE. *(Bowing himself out, this time with finality)* Your supper, sir. He wait.

(John stands looking after him, a puzzled, thoughtful expression on his face. He turns toward the small table and sits down, almost out of view of the rest of the stage. Presently the Small One *enters left. She tiptoes to the tree and stands looking up at it, an ecstatic expression on her face. She utters a long, delighted "Oh!" and lifts her arms high toward the flaxen-haired doll hanging above her head.* Junie *enters right, a large, clumsily wrapped package in her hand.)*

JUNIE. *(Going toward the* Small One) Hello, Charlie's Small One. Did you come to look at my tree?

SMALL ONE. *(Drawing back in fright)* Oh!

JUNIE. *(Kindly)* Don't be afraid. Nobody's going to hurt you. *(She takes the* Small One's *hand)* Come on with me. We'll go up and look at it closer.

(The Small One *again approaches the tree, this time clinging tightly to* Junie's *hand. She looks up again at the doll.)*

SMALL ONE. Pretty! So Pretty!

JUNIE. You like the doll? She is pretty, isn't she? My mother bought her for me, I think. Wait a minute. I'll let you hold her. She's going to be mine just as soon as Santa Claus comes to take the presents off the tree, so I guess I can take her down if I want to. *(She climbs up on a chair, removes the doll, and places it in the* Small One's *arms. The big dark eyes widen ecstatically. The* Small One *utters little crooning sounds and presses the doll closer in her arms. She sits down under the tree and rocks the doll back and forth, while* Junie *watches her with satisfaction)* You like her, don't you? Did you ever have a doll like that? *(The* Small One *shakes her head)* Well, *(slowly)* you could have that one if—you want her. I've got lots more.

SMALL ONE. *(Breathlessly)* Take home? Keep?

JUNIE. *(More enthusiastically)* Yes, I'd like to have you have her. I guess I won't miss her—not much. Besides, I have my little yellow doll.

CHARLIE. *(Entering left and spying the* Small One) You! You foolish Small One! You know what you do? You take rice from our mouths. Come quick! Don't let missy see!

JUNIE. *(Giving him the parcel)* Oh—Charlie! Here's the present. *(He hides it quickly behind him as* Kate *enters.)*

KATE. *(Sternly)* What's this? What are you doing, Junie? Who is that child, and what is she doing with your doll?

*(*Charlies *slips the parcel behind the tree.)*

JUNIE. *(Taking the* Small One's *hand)* This is Charlie's little girl, Mother, and her name is the Small One, and *(hesitating)* I've given her my new doll for a Christmas present.

KATE. *(Turning to* Charlie, *so angry that she forgets her usual method of address)* What does this mean, Charlie? Really, I must say I am surprised. And you've been such an ideal servant, too, all these years, until now. I never even knew you had a child. *(Very quietly* Charlie *takes the doll from the* Small One's *arms and hangs it back on the tree. Then he stands stolidly waiting.* Kate, *annoyed)* Well—haven't you got anything to say for yourself? *(*Charlie *is still silent)* All light. Can go now. But no let happen again. Understand? *(*Charlie *bows, takes the* Small One's *hand, and goes out left.* Kate, *still vexed)* The very idea! I've always known you couldn't trust an Oriental, and that proves it. You have to watch them every minute.

JUNIE. *(Distressed)* But, Mother, I gave her the doll. I've got lots more, and I didn't really need it. And she hasn't any doll at all.

KATE. *(Patiently)* Junie, my dear, do you realize that that is an imported doll, with clothes made by a real Parisian dressmaker, and that it cost me a great deal of money? It certainly isn't an appropriate gift for an unkempt little foreigner who probably doesn't have the slightest idea even of the meaning of Christmas. I'll tell you what we'll do. I'll have one of the church charity baskets sent around in the morning to Charlie's family, and we'll put some cheap little toys in it. You can pick them out yourself. That will be a nice, kind thing to do, I'm sure. Now go to bed, child. It's getting late, and I must go back to the party. (Junie *goes out reluctantly. Suddenly* Kate *spies* John, *who has been standing quietly by the small table at the right of the stage. She is taken aback at the moment, wondering how much he has heard*) Oh, Mr.—Mr. Liang. I didn't know you had come down. I hope you haven't been waiting long?

JOHN. *(The smile gone from his face)* Not long, Mrs. Marshall. My Chinese friend was good enough to bring me a lunch, but I had already eaten at the docks.

KATE. *(Bewildered)* Your—Oh, I see. You mean Charlie. By the way, Mr.—Mr. Liang, I'm sorry it happened so, but my daughter is having a few friends in tonight—just a few intimate friends, you understand, for a little party, and we all thought it might be better—that is, that you might not enjoy meeting strangers the first night you came.

JOHN. Please, Mrs. Marshall, make not even the smallest difference in your plans for me. I should be glad to meet any friends of you and my Mr. David. I count them not strangers who join in a common remembrance of the Great One's birthday. I pray you, do not trouble—

KATE. *(Confused)* Oh, it's no trouble at all. I'm sure you must be tired after your long trip, and Mr. Marshall is so anxious to show you his collection. He's very proud of it and always has to show it to everybody that comes. He's in the library now, but he'll be right in.

JOHN. Perhaps he would like me to join him there?

KATE. *(Stopping him with a gesture)* No, no. You see, there are people in the library, and I am sure you would find it pleasanter here. You won't be so likely to be disturbed. And now if you'll excuse me. There are so many things to attend to. You—you will wait, won't you, Mr.—Mr. Liang?

JOHN. *(Somewhat bewildered by her obvious confusion)* Why—certainly, if you wish. But I dislike to cause Mr.

Marshall any trouble. *(Left alone,* John *looks thoughtfully after his hostess. He stands still for a long time thinking, then walks rather aimlessly across the room toward the tree. Pausing to look at it, he walks around it, and stops to look at it from the left side, where he stands unobserved by* Bob *and* Carolyn, *who enter right.)*

CAROLYN. Bob, come in here a minute, won't you, where no one will hear us. You can spare a minute from the dancing.

(There is a brief echo of noise and merriment from outside while the door opens and closes.)

BOB. Well, what is it now? Got another wall-flower you want me to play up to? If you have, nothing doing—

CAROLYN. *(Much disturbed)* Listen, Bob, Dad is still in the library with the Milton Craigs, and he hasn't even started to get out his collection. And that Chinaman's likely to come downstairs almost any time. Couldn't you just stay around for a while and watch—

BOB. While you make eyes at that rich Randall fellow! Nothing doing! I see now why you wanted everything to go just so. No wonder you didn't want a Chink popping up to spoil everything. He'd be about as popular with the blue-blooded Randalls as a cat in a cage of pet canaries.

CAROLYN. I know it. If Phil Randall ever found out we had friends like that, everything would be all up. And he does like me, Bob, I know he does. Won't you please do something. Go and tell Dad—

BOB. Nix. Do it yourself. I'm sick of acting one way to a fellow's face and another way behind his back. If you ask me, this Liang guy isn't such a bad sort. If he could just get bleached out a bit!

CAROLYN. But, Bob, he's impossible. He acts as if he thought he was every bit as good as—as good as we are. I've got to do something. He'd just ruin my party. Won't you please—

BOB. Oh, all right, all right. I'll tell Dad. I'll stick my head in the library door and yell, "Look out for the Yellow Peril!" That'll fetch him. *(He goes out right.)*

(Gay young voices offstage call "Carolyn!" "Lyn, darling! where are you?")

CAROLYN. Coming! *(She goes out right.)*

(John *comes from behind the tree. He walks slowly to the center of the stage. He looks tired, stunned. Without realizing what he is doing, he sits down in a chair and passes his hand wearily across his forehead. Presently he gets up again and walks aimlessly to the table containing the miniature manger scene, stands looking down at it. After a long moment he reaches out his hand and seems about to sweep the whole thing onto the floor, but at this moment* William *enters. He carries a large box under his arm.*)

William. *(Cordially)* Oh, here you are! Hope the folks haven't been neglecting you. Fact is, we had a few friends in this evening. Just a few young folks. You're tired probably and wouldn't care to meet any outsiders tonight. It gets on a fellow's nerves when he's tired, to meet a lot of strangers. I thought it might be pleasanter if you and I could have a little chat right here by ourselves. We're far enough away so the music won't bother us, and we can have a cozy little evening together—that is, if you're not too tired. *(Hopefully)* Perhaps you would feel more like going to bed.

(During William's *somewhat rambling speech* Charlie *has entered and picked up the tray. He catches* John's *eye over* William's *head and gives him a slow, sardonic smile, into which is cast all the bitter wisdom that ten years of disillusionment have given him.* John *is no longer the smiling, hopeful enthusiast of a few minutes before. He looks older and grayer, and the youthful, buoyant spirit seems to have gone out of him.*)

John. *(Quietly)* Whatever you say, Mr. Marshall. I am not tired. But I dislike to cause you any trouble to entertain me.

William. Oh, it's no trouble, no trouble at all. Fact is, I would enjoy having a little chat with you. And later on I'd like to show you my collection. A little hobby of mine that I find quite interesting—old American coins. *(He gestures;* John *to a chair, and they sit down.* Charlie *still hovers in the background with the tray. He appears to be looking out of the window)* Well, Charlie, what are you waiting for? They'll be needing you to help serve the ices.

Charlie. Yes, sir. Velly big storm, sir. Going to have velly white Chlismas—velly white, I say. *(With another significant glance at* John, *he goes out left, surreptitiously picking up* Junie's *present to him from behind the tree as he does so.)*

WILLIAM. *(Getting up and looking out of the window)* That's an expression we have here in the north. We say we have a white Christmas when the ground is covered with snow. I guess we're going to have one this year, all right.

JOHN. *(Half to himself)* White Christmas. White Christmas, you call it, do you? Yes, I should say it was going to be—very white.

WILLIAM. Must be a good two feet of it by this time.

JOHN. Two feet? Oh, I see. You mean the snow. Yes, of course.

WILLIAM. *(Sitting down and groping for a subject of conversation)* Well, suppose you tell me about my brother. He's well, I suppose.

JOHN. Mr. David? Oh—yes. Mr. David is quite well.

WILLIAM. Looked kind of thin in the last snapshots he sent us. David always did take things hard. Probably he thinks he has the whole future of China on his shoulders.

JOHN. *(Quietly)* Yes. I believe he does think exactly that.

WILLIAM. *(Settling back comfortably)* Well, we're behind him in everything he's trying to do, although of course in recent years most of us haven't been able to help financially as much as we would like to. I've always been a great believer in missions, and I've tried to keep my church interested. I've told them more than once, we ought to keep our missionary contributions on a level with all our other charities. Christian America has always stood for helping the weaker brother, no matter what his race or color may be.

JOHN. *(In a peculiar voice)* Yes. Exactly. Christian America—helping the weaker—brother. I think I am beginning—to see.

WILLIAM. That's one thing we've always insisted on in our local church and city charities. I suppose our church is sending out about one hundred baskets this Christmas season—to all sorts and conditions of people. In fact, I know they are. My wife happens to have charge of it. But we never ask what color a man's face is or even if his religion is the same as ours. He needs something we have to give him, and we're glad to give it. It's our duty as Christians, you understand.

JOHN. *(Slowly)* Yes. I understand. I think I understand

—perfectly. One of my own people expressed the idea exactly when he wrote—let's see, how would one express it in your language?—"The lion that has eaten his fill lets even the cat lick his whiskers." Or, as it was once said to One greater than he, "Even the dogs eat of the crumbs which fall from the master's table."

WILLIAM *(Hardly knowing how to take this)* Er—yes—yes. I've heard the Chinese poets were very clever.

BOB. *(Suddenly entering left)* Mr. Craig's trying to find you, Dad. He says if you're going to show your collection to a friend, he'd like to see it too.

WILLIAM. *(Starting up out of his chair)* Craig! He isn't coming in here, I hope!

(Mrs. Milton Craig *appears in the entrance right. She is a rather large, fashionably dressed woman with a slightly imposing manner.)*

MRS. CRAIG. Oh, here you are, Mr. Marshall! I wondered where you had disappeared to with that friend of yours. Mr. Craig is looking everywhere for you.

WILLIAM. Oh—Mrs. Craig! Er—tell Mr. Craig I'll be right with him. I—er—just a little matter of business—

MRS. CRAIG. *(Coming farther into the room)* Don't move, Mr. Marshall—please. Milton says you are going to show your collection to a friend, and if you are, do let us see it, too. We've heard so much about it. *(She has now come far enough into the room to get a good view of* John, *who has risen, and stands, straight and impassive, beside his chair. The expression of* Mrs. Craig's *face changes very noticeably, from curiosity to amazement, and from amazement to a sudden disdainful coldness. She is like a gushing stream become suddenly frozen. At this moment* Kate *appears in the entrance right, and stands regarding the tableau with something akin to horror.)* Oh! I beg your pardon. I see I have interrupted—

WILLIAM. *(Confused and embarrassed)* Not at all, not at all, Mrs. Craig. Er—won't you sit down? I—er—I was just going to open my collection.

MRS. CRAIG. *(Turning away with a frigid little smile)* No, no. Don't let me keep you from your—friend. Some other time—perhaps—

WILLIAM. (*Keenly distressed at the thought of offending the* Craigs) Er—wait a minute, Mrs. Craig. As I said—a little matter of business—I'll be right with you—

JOHN. (*Suddenly pulling the leather wallet from his pocket and taking out the bills it contains. As he speaks there is something in his voice that arrests the attention of all in the room*) I not keep you any longer, Mr. Marshall. Our business, it is now all done, is it not? See—I return to you the money you so kindly give to poor unfortunate. Now I no longer need, so I give it back to you—(*He places the bills in* William's *hands.*)

(*Hardly knowing what he is doing,* William *closes his fingers about them.*)

WILLIAM. You—you—what? I don't understand.

JOHN. You give money to poor Chinese in need. You have so good kind heart. You want to help poor weak yellow brother. But Chinese cannot take. He return to you—so. Always will he remember. Always will he be grateful. (*John bows, his face grave and impassive, while* William *stands holding the money, speechless. He knows now what* John *is trying to do for him, and while he feels an intense embarrassment and not a little shame, both emotions are tempered by a strong relief.* John, *his voice grave but with a flicker of irony in his eyes*) Perhaps sometime the kind Mr. Marshall find job for poor unfortunate yellow man. The Chinese, he make velly good Amelican servant.

MRS. CRAIG. (*Turning to* Kate *with a smile*) I've heard your husband was one of the most charitable men in the city, Mrs. Marshall, and this proves it. Generous with charities, Milton says, means hard-headed in business. When you get through dispensing your charities, Mr. Marshall, you'll find us in the library. We do want to see your collection. (*Smiling pleasantly, she goes out right, her arm tucked in* Kate's.)

(*There is a long silence after their departure.* John *continues to stand straight and impassive, his head slightly bowed as in thought.* William *is much embarrassed.* Bob *watches the two intently, in his eyes a combination of amusement and irony.*)

BOB. (*Breaking the silence at last*) Well, Dad—I should say it was up to you to thank the gentleman—for getting you out of an embarrassing situation with the utmost skill. If you ask me, the honors for that engagement went all to China.

WILLIAM. (*Trying to pass off the matter lightly*) Well—I suppose I do owe him an apology. But I think John understands the situation as well as we do, and he certainly rendered me a great favor that time. It would have been a big blow to me just now to lose Craig's business friendship, and Craig is one of those men who have peculiar prejudices. I'm sure you understand that none of us feel that way, John. Kate and I are both keenly interested in the whole missionary enterprise. (John *remains silent. Finally, conscious that he is still holding the money in his hand,* William *with a little embarrassed laugh holds it out to* John) Well—now that these have served their purpose, I'll return them. (*As* John *stands motionless, making no gesture to take them*) Why, what's the matter? They're yours. Why don't you take them?

(John *slowly shakes his head.*)

JOHN. (*Quietly*) No, Mr. Marshall. They are not mine. They were yours in the beginning, and now they are yours again. I have given them back to you.

WILLIAM. (*Aghast*) What—what do you mean? Are you crazy? That—that was just a little joke.

JOHN. It was not a joke. On the contrary, it was most deadly serious. I meant everything I said. I cannot take your charity.

WILLIAM. (*Sputtering, almost angrily*) But you're not taking my charity. I gave this money to be used in mission work. Don't you understand? It's been my money that's made you what you are. If it weren't for me, you'd likely still be a poor, ignorant heathen.

BOB. Tone down, Dad. I don't blame him for not taking your money. I'd do the same myself. And it's Uncle David who's made him what he is, not just your money.

JOHN. Now do I understand why the light your great people has striven to shed abroad has not long since swept the whole earth into flame. You have sent it out as one hands out a crust to the beggar at his gate and not as one who invites his neighbor in to sup with him and to share the bounties with which God has blessed him. You have tried to give other men your God done up in white paper and tied with a white string, and bundled in a Christmas basket. *(After a pause, more gently)* Do you suppose the Chinese has not also, like you, a pride in his race, in his color? Does the sun envy the moon because her face is paler than his own? Would you believe me if I told you that to me your pale faces were ugly and unsightly did I not see them even as Mr. David has all these years seen mine?

BOB. I—I never thought of that. I suppose we do look kind of funny to you.

JOHN. *(Very quietly, speaking to* Bob *now instead of to* William) I came here tonight believing that your great America was Christian, that her people were even as my Mr. David, who taught me to love all men and to treat them as my brothers, but I am mistaken. I came with my hand stretched out in friendship, and you made me think that you, too, were my friends, while all the time you were ashamed of my presence and despised me because of my color. Now have I seen the truth, and I have passed through a great darkness. I thought at first that you had taken away from me my Christ, as you have taken Him away from Charlie, as you must have taken Him away from so many others—because you have put upon Him a white face and stripped Him of His simple oriental dress and placed strange words upon His lips. But I can see now it is only my dream you have taken away. For the Christ I know cannot be changed or even touched by human littleness. His face is neither white nor black nor brown nor yellow, but only a vast and shining radiance. And I am going back to take Him to my people.

WILLIAM. *(Uncertainly)* But—what is to become of your dream? You said it was the dream of your life, this year in our American college. We can't let you go back without getting what you came for—

BOB. *(Jumping up, suddenly eager)* Good heavens, Dad, are you blind? Don't you see, he's just been telling us what it might be—if we'd only all work together. Why—it isn't just that we've got something over here to give him—it's that he's got something to give us. Talk about missions! Why, if we could all go into it the way John says, we'd change the whole world all over. We'd solve all our problems—war, economic strife, and all the rest. We've been doling out charity to other nations long enough. Why not try sharing a while—sharing ourselves as well as our pocketbooks—making the Chinese laundryman around the corner as much our brother as the fellow over in Peking—*(He stops, a bit shamefaced, then goes toward* John) I say—I'm sorry for the way we've acted tonight. We've all treated you like dirt, and I know it. But I'd like to be real friends with you, honest I would. What do you say? Will you stay and go to the "U" this winter if I go without my car and use that money to help pay our way?

JOHN. *(A sudden light breaking over his face)* You really mean that? You'd give up the car you wanted—

BOB. Sure. And—there's nothing charity about it this time. I—I can't just express it, but—well, you've got something I want, and I know it. We've both got pretty big jobs to do—and maybe we can help each other.

JOHN. *(His face glowing with emotion)* Yes—I believe we can—help each other.

(Bob puts out his hand and John clasps it in a long friendly grip.)

BOB. *(Putting his arm across the other's shoulders)* Say—I'd like to take you into the other room and have you meet some of the fellows—

(Together they move toward exit right. William stands looking after them for a moment, then he looks down at the bills in his hand.)

CURTAIN

The Shepherd's Story

A Nativity Play in One Act

by

HARRY GREENWOOD GROVER

Characters:

> RACHEL   JESSE   NARRATOR

SCENE: Jesse's home.

TIME: The First Christmas.

LENGTH: About ten minutes.

(This is written in such a way as to make it available as a reading or radio or stage presentation.)

NARRATOR. A long time ago and far, far away, if a man were to try to walk to the place, there dwelt on the edge of a little town a shepherd and his wife. His name was JESSE and his wife's name was RACHEL. They had lived happily together for many years but had no children in their home. Perhaps because he had no wealth to tempt robbers, he felt that he did not need to live within the walls of the near-by town. But probably JESSE had never thought of that reason, but dwelt here because his father and his grandfather and his father's fathers had dwelt here before him. It was, besides, a comfortable little house with ground about it where RACHEL might have flowers to make her house gay and a little garden of herbs and vegetables to go with the meat from the flock, and most important, here JESSE might be near his flock. For beyond their dwelling, on the side away from the town, stretched green pastures fed by still waters. Here, long before the days of JESSE's fathers, shepherds had led their flocks by day and watched with the stars over them by night. There is a window down right; a door center; a fireplace left with stools; table center with stools right and left.

It is a winter morning. The sun has not yet risen, but

RACHEL is up, kneeling before the hearth fire, preparing her husband's morning meal. For he will be in soon, tired after his night's work afield and cold and hungry as work-folk always are. RACHEL is a lovely picture as she works in the light of the hearth fire. She has lovely dark eyes, much color from being out in wind and sun where her tasks call her. You see, her house is small and has few windows, so that it is a natural thing for her to go out of doors to do her work in the light. The linen and wool in her dress were made with her own hands and embroidered at her threshold in the sunshine or at the door of some neighbor woman. There are dishes on the floor by the fire, rugs and sheepskins aplenty to sit upon, and near the hearth a flat shallow basket filled with grain.

At the door is JESSE: tall and bronzed and bearded, wearing a rough brown robe thrown round his shoulders and carrying something wrapped up in a sheepskin which he puts down very carefully by the door. RACHEL, who is very busy at the hearth with her back to the door, does not turn around as he enters and so does not see the bundle. As the only light is from the hearth and she stays there at her tasks, her shadow keeps the secret of JESSE's bundle till the end. They greet each other with the usual greeting of their country and time.

JESSE. Peace, Rachel.

RACHEL. Peace to thee, Jesse.

JESSE. And to this house.

RACHEL. *(Turns to fire)* Cold?

JESSE. What?

RACHEL. Art thou cold?

JESSE. *(As if not hearing or dazed)* Cold?

RACHEL. Art thou cold, I say? Shut the door.

JESSE. *(Puts down bundle near door)* Nay, I am not cold.

RACHEL. It turned cold in the night. With all thy work, I suppose thou wouldst not mind.

JESSE. Yea.

RACHEL. Is all well with thy flock?

JESSE. What?

RACHEL. What ails thee, Jesse? Art gone deaf?

JESSE. Nay, I think not. Mine ears perhaps—What didst thou say?

RACHEL. Thy flock? Was all well with thy flock during the night watches?

JESSE. Yea.

RACHEL. Any more lambs?

JESSE. Yea.

RACHEL. And all well?

JESSE. All save one.

RACHEL. What chanced?

JESSE. The mother died.

RACHEL. And didst thou not fetch it to me to tend? *(He does not answer but looks up as if listening to something beyond the room.)* Jesse, art thou numb with cold? Come warm thyself. Sit here by the hearth while I get something to break thy fast. Art stricken dumb? Canst not hear?

JESSE. *(Sits at hearth)* Aye, I hear all. 'Tis thou that dost not hear.

RACHEL. Hear what? I hear everything. 'Tis thou.

JESSE. Nay. I hear the song.

RACHEL. The song? What dost thou mean? What hath happened to thee? Thou art as strange as when thou toldest thy dream of the Shining One. Thou needst meat. Here, come break thy fast. I have baked bread for thee. Come eat. And let be thy dreams of Shining Ones.

JESSE. Nay, Rachel, this was no dream. I have not slept all through the night.

RACHEL. *(Sits beside him, her arm about his shoulders)* 'Tis sleep thou needst, then! But first break thy fast. Then thou mayst sleep the day through. I will tend thy flock.

JESSE. Nay, I do not need sleep. This was better than sleep, far better. This time there were many Shining Ones and singing. Oh, such songs I never heard! 'Tis all within mine head now. Mine ears are full of it. And a great light rose in the east, a star bigger than many stars together. Methought the sun! And we were sore afraid, till the Shining One spake.

RACHEL. What is this, Jesse, more dreams grown out of the one thou toldest me of last year? Come, thou art tired or sick. Come eat.

JESSE. But this was not a dream. The shepherds all round saw it. All were wakened and talked about it. We were frightened. Ask any of them.

RACHEL. And one spake?

JESSE. Yea.

RACHEL. What did he say?

JESSE. "Follow the star!"

RACHEL. But surely, thou didst not leave thy flock to follow a dream-star?

JESSE. Nay, I did not.

RACHEL. I should think not! At eanling time the flock hath need of thy tendance.

JESSE. Yea, I stayed. But the twain who were with me went, James and Mark.

RACHEL. *(Rising)* What canst thou mean? Oh, thou art sick.

JESSE. Nay

RACHEL. What canst thou mean? Went where?

JESSE. After the star, Rachel.

RACHEL. Oh, Jesse, thou wert ever a simple man! Where would a man ever get to following a star?

JESSE. But the Shining One said. 'Twas not the star they sought. The star was leading them to—

RACHEL. To what? Treasure?

JESSE. Yea, treasure, Rachel, a babe! Is not a babe treasure? It would be to us.

RACHEL. Yea, in truth. But the Lord has not blessed his handmaiden. I know how thou longst for a babe, thou are so tender to all little things. But babes be not found 'neath stars any more than pots of gold at rainbows' ends, thou simple man.

JESSE. But the Shining One had given a sign that when they should see the star straight above them, there should be found a babe, in swaddling clothes and lying in a manger.

RACHEL. In a barn, eh? Stars do not tell when poor folk are born in barns.

JESSE. There was no room in the inn. 'Twas but a carpenter on his way to taxing, they found.

RACHEL. Oh, then art o'erwrought. What canst thou mean by all this to-do over babes and angels and barns?

JESSE. Nay, but they found the babe, just as he said. And heard the same song.

RACHEL. The same song thou saidst was aringing in thine ears?

Jesse. Yea, and hear it still: "Peace on earth." O, Rachel, that's what my soul longeth for, peace on earth. Dost thou not remember how the prophets spake to our fathers saying the time would come when men should beat their swords into ploughshares and their spears into pruning hooks?

Rachel. Yea, yea, but what has this to do with the star and the babe? Was the babe aught save any that may have been born this night?

Jesse. The Shining One said, "It is the Savior. The Prince of Peace." I cannot tell. I did not see.

Rachel. But the others followed the star and came back and told thee?

Jesse. Yea.

Rachel. And didst thou not long to go?

Jesse. Thou knowest! And I went.

Rachel. But thou saidst thou didst not see? 'Twas not so easy following a star? 'Twas all a dream?

Jesse. Nay, nay, I did go after the others returned. I found the inn they told me of and went to the barn as they had said. But at the door, ere I could enter, I met a man in sore distress. In his arms, he bore a new born babe, his first born. With haste he seized me and with grievous moans and sobbing told me how his wife had but then gone down the shadowy vale of death. He begged me to take the babe she left and keep it warm till he could fetch a nurse for it. But going thence along the road, dazed or crazed with grief he plunged or fell—I shall never know—

Rachel. Not the father, too?

Jesse. Yea, the two were gone. And no one there knew aught of either, their kindred or their country. And so I fetched the babe.

Rachel. Thou hast fetched a babe? Where hast thou bestowed him? Jesse, tell me!

Jesse. Dost thou in truth want the babe?

Rachel. Want it? Dost thou mean he will be ours?

Jesse. In truth, if thou wilt.

Rachel. Thou knowest. Where is he? Hasten, go. Thou saidst thou hadst a lamb. *(She quickly prepares a cradle using the basket near the hearth that was filled with grain while* Jesse *goes to the door)* Hasten. Art not gone?

Jesse. Nay, 'tis here. *(He brings very carefully the precious bundle and hands it to his wife)* 'Tis like a lamb. So young and soft a thing! But we have no cradle.

RACHEL. What need of a real cradle? The fowls of the air have no cradles. This basket—

JESSE. A basket?

RACHEL. Yea, what could be better? This winnowing basket, round and like a bird's nest. *(Emptying contents of basket into a bowl on the table)* I'll turn the wheat out into this bowl and have a cradle in a twinkling. Give me the lambskin there! Now what could be better! And, oh, the babe! 'Tis like a rose! *(She lays it in the cradle and bends over it as all mothers have since the world began)* The Rose of Sharon! Is he not beautiful? A bundle of myrrh! A cluster of camphire! Was the other babe as lovely?

JESSE. Yea, I think. I did not see.

RACHEL. And thou didst so long to see?

JESSE. Yea, but this one had need of me.

RACHEL. Yea, thou art good to all little things that have need. Fetch some milk. *(She places basket on floor near window. Suddenly looking up as if listening)* What is that noise?

JESSE. What?

RACHEL. Dost thou not hear, the song?

JESSE. Oh, aye, the song I heard. Now thou canst hear!

RACHEL. Yea, Peace on Earth. *(The LIGHT through window brightens gradually around the basket.)*

JESSE. The angel's song I spake of: "Peace on Earth." I always dream of peace on earth, 'mongst men. *(He stands by the side of his wife and they look down in love at the babe lying peacefully there before them)* Peace, peace, to thee, little one!

RACHEL. *Our* little one, Jesse.

JESSE. Yea, wife.

RACHEL. The gift of God to us.

JESSE. The messenger of peace I have so longed to see.

RACHEL. Yea, peace!

CURTAIN

A Child Is Born

by

STEPHEN VINCENT BENÉT

NOTE

Mr. Archibald MacLeish, poet and Librarian of Congress, asked Mr. Benét to write THE UNITED NATIONS PRAYER to be used in connection with the celebration of Flag Day, 1942. It was incorporated in President Franklin D. Roosevelt's Flag Day speech over an international network on the evening of June 14.

This modern drama of the Nativity was written for the program, "Cavalcade of America," and broadcast over the National Broadcasting Company's network on the night of December 21, 1942. The play was so successful that it was repeated by popular request on the same program on the evening of December 20, 1943.

Characters:

NARRATOR	DISMAS, a thief
THE INNKEEPER	VOICE OF A PREFECT
THE INNKEEPER'S WIFE	VOICES OF SOLDIERS
LEAH }	AND OFFICERS
SARAH } Servants at the inn	VOICES OF KINGS
A SOLDIER	VOICES OF SHEPHERDS
JOSEPH OF NAZARETH	

SCENE: The kitchen of an inn. There is a flight of stairs leading to the rooms above. The door of the kitchen opens on the street.

(Music, as broadcast opens. It fades. Narrator speaks.)

NARRATOR. I'm your narrator. It's my task to say
Just where and how things happen in our play,
Set the bare stage with words instead of props
And keep on talking till the curtain drops.
So you shall know, as well as our poor skill
Can show you, whether it is warm or chill,
Indoors or out, a battle or a fair,
In this, our viewless theater of the air.
It's an old task—old as the human heart,
Old as those bygone players and their art
Who, in old days when faith was nearer earth,
Played out the mystery of Jesus' birth
In hall or village green or market square
For all who chose to come and see them there,
And, if they knew that Herod, in his crown,
Was really Wat, the cobbler of the town,
And Tom, the fool, played Abraham the Wise,
They did not care. They saw with other eyes.
The story was their own—not far away,
As real as if it happened yesterday,
Full of all awe and wonder yet so near,
A marvelous thing that could have happened here
In their own town—a star that could have blazed
On their own shepherds, leaving them amazed,
Frightened and questioning and following still
To the bare stable—and the miracle.

So we, tonight, who are your players too,
Ask but to tell that selfsame tale to you
In our own words, the plain and simple speech
Of human beings, talking each to each,
Troubled with their own cares, not always wise,
And yet, at moments, looking toward the skies.

The time is—time. The place is anywhere.
The voices speak to you across the air
To say that once again a child is born.
A child is born.
"I pray you all, give us your audience

And hear this matter with reverence."
  (Music)
There is a town where men and women live
Their lives as people do in troubled times,
Times when the world is shaken. There is an inn.
A woman sings there in the early morning.
  (Music, fading into the voice of a woman—the innkeeper's
    wife—singing as she goes about her household tasks.)
  INNKEEPER'S WIFE. In Bethlehem of Judea
There shall be born a child,
A child born of woman
And yet undefiled.
He shall not come to riches,
To riches and might,
But in the bare stable
He shall be Man's light.
He shall not come to conquest,
The conquest of kings,
But in the bare stable
He shall judge all things.
King Herod, King Herod,
Now what will you say
Of the child in the stable
This cold winter day?
I hear the wind blowing
Across the bare thorn,
I fear not King Herod
If this child may be born,
  (Sound of steps coming down a flight of stone stairs. A
    man's voice, rough and suspicious—the voice of the inn-
    keeper. The innkeeper is middle-aged—his wife some-
    what younger)
  INNKEEPER. Singing again! I told you not to sing!
  WIFE. I'm sorry. I forgot.
  INNKEEPER. Forgot? That's fine!
That's wonderful! That answers everything!
The times are hard enough and bad enough
For anyone who tries to keep an inn,
Get enough bread to stick in his own mouth

And keep things going, somehow, in his town.
The country's occupied. We have no country.
You've heard of that, perhaps?
You've seen their soldiers, haven't you? You know
Just what can happen to our sort of people
Once there's a little trouble? Answer me!
    WIFE. *(Wearily)* I've seen. I know.
    INNKEEPER. You've seen. You know. And you keep singing
       songs!
Not ordinary songs—the kind of songs
That might bring in a little bit of trade,
Songs with a kind of pleasant wink in them
That make full men forget the price of the wine,
The kind of songs a handsome girl can sing
After their dinner to good customers
—And, thanks to me, the inn still has a few!—
Oh no! You have to sing rebellious songs
About King Herod!
    WIFE. I'm sorry. I forgot.
    INNKEEPER. Sorry? Forgot? You're always saying that!
Is it your business what King Herod does?
Is it your place to sing against King Herod?
    WIFE. I think that he must be a wicked man,
A very wicked man.
    INNKEEPER. Oh, la, la, la!
Sometimes *I* think your ways will drive me mad.
Are you a statesman or a general?
Do you pretend to know the ins and outs
Of politics and why the great folk do
The things they do—and why we have to bear them?
Because it's we—we—we
Who have to bear them, first and last and always,
In every country and in every time.
They grind us like dry wheat between the stones.
Don't you know that?
    WIFE. I know that, somehow, kings
Should not be wicked and grind down the people.
I know that kings like Herod should not be.
    INNKEEPER. All right—all right. I'm not denying that.
I'm reasonable enough. I know the world.

I'm willing to admit to anyone
At least behind closed doors
   (He drops his voice)
That Herod isn't quite my sort of king
And that I don't approve of all he does.
Still, there he is. He's king. How will it help
If I go out and write on someone's wall
   (In a whisper)
"Down with King Herod!"
   (His voice comes up again)
What's it worth?
The cross for me, the whipping post for you,
The inn burned down, the village fined for treason,
Just because one man didn't like King Herod.
For that's the way things are.
   WIFE. Yet there are men—
   INNKEEPER. Oh yes, I know—fanatics, rabble, fools,
Outcasts of war, misfits, rebellious souls,
Seekers of some vague kingdom in the stars—
They hide out in the hills and stir up trouble,
Call themselves prophets, too, and prophesy
That something new is coming to the world,
The Lord knows what!
     Well, it's a long time coming,
And, meanwhile, we're the wheat between the stones.
   WIFE. Something must come.
   INNKEEPER. Believe it if you choose,
But, meantime, if we're clever, we can live
And even thrive a little—clever wheat
That slips between the grinding stones and grows
In little green blade-sprinkles on the ground.
At least, if you'll not sing subversive songs
To other people but your poor old husband.
   (Changing tone)
Come, wife, I've got some news.
I didn't mean to be so angry with you.
You've some queer fancies in that head of yours
—Lord, don't I know!—but you're still the tall girl
With the grave eyes and the brook-running voice
I took without a dower or a price

Out of your father's house because—oh, well—
Because you came. And they've not been so bad,
The years since then. Now have they?
   WIFE. No.
   INNKEEPER. That's right.
Give us a kiss.
   (Pause)
     I couldn't help the child.
I know you think of that, this time of year.
He was my son, too, and I think of him.
I couldn't help his dying.
   WIFE. No, my husband.
   INNKEEPER. He stretched his little arms to me and died.
And yet I had the priest—the high priest, too.
I didn't spare the money.
   WIFE. No, my husband.
I am a barren bough. I think and sing
And am a barren bough.
   INNKEEPER. Oh, come, come, come!
   WIFE. The fault is mine. I had my joyous season,
My season of full ripening and fruit
And then the silence and the aching breast.
I thought I would have children. I was wrong,
But my flesh aches to think I do not have them.
I did not mean to speak of this at all.
I do not speak of it. I will be good.
There is much left—so much.
The kindness and the bond that lasts the years
And all the small and treasurable things
That make up life and living. Do not care
So much. I have forgotten. I'll sing softly,
Not sing at all. It was long past and gone.
Tell me your news. Is it good news?
   INNKEEPER *(Eagerly)* The best!
The prefect comes to dinner here tonight
With all his officers—oh yes, I know,
The enemy—of course, the enemy—
But someone has to feed them.
   WIFE. And they'll pay?

INNKEEPER. Cash.
WIFE. On the nail?
INNKEEPER. Yes.
WIFE. Good.
INNKEEPER. I thought you'd say so.
Oh, we'll make no great profit—not tonight—
I've seen the bill of fare they asked of me,
Quails, in midwinter! Well, we'll give them—quails!
And charge them for them, too! You know the trick?
WIFE. Yes.
INNKEEPER. They must be well served. I'll care for that,
The honest innkeeper, the thoughtful man,
Asking, "Your worship, pray another glass
Of our poor wine! Your worship, is the roast
Done to your worship's taste? Oh, nay, nay, nay,
Your worship, all was settled in the bill,
So do not spoil my servants with largesse,
Your worship!"—And he won't. He pinches pennies.
But, once he's come here, he will come again,
And we shall live, not die, and put some coin,
Some solid, enemy and lovely coin
Under the hearthstone, eh?
Spoil the Egyptians, eh?
  (He laughs)
That's my war and my battle and my faith.
The war of every sane and solid man
And, even if we have no child to follow us,
It shall be won, I tell you!
  (There is a knock at the outer door)
Hark! What's that?
I'll go—the maids aren't up yet—lazybones!
  (The knock is repeated, imperatively)
INNKEEPER. *(Grumbling)* A minute—just a minute!
It's early yet—you needn't beat the door down.
This is an honest inn.
  (He shoots the bolts and opens the door, while speaking)
Good morning.
SOLDIER'S VOICE. Hail Caesar! Are you keeper of this inn?
INNKEEPER. Yes, sir.

SOLDIER. Orders from the prefect. No other guests shall
be entertained at your inn tonight after sundown. The prefect
wishes all the rooms to be at the disposal of his guests.

INNKEEPER. All the rooms?

SOLDIER. You understand plain Latin, don't you?

INNKEEPER. Yes, sir, but—

SOLDIER. Well?

INNKEEPER. Sir, when the prefect first commanded me,
There was a party of my countrymen
Engaged for a small room—he'd hear no noise—
No noise at all—

SOLDIER. This is the prefect's feast—the Saturnalia—
You've heard your orders.

INNKEEPER. Yes, sir. Yes, indeed sir.

SOLDIER. See they are carried out! No other guests!
Hail Caesar!

INNKEEPER. *(Feebly)* Hail Caesar!
(He slams the door)
Well, that's pleasant.
All rooms at the disposal of the prefect!
No other guests! I'll have to warn Ben-Ezra.
But he's a sound man—he will understand.
We'll cook his mutton here and send it to him
And the wine, too—a bottle of good wine—
The second best and let the prefect pay for it!
That will make up. No other guests. Remember
No other guests!

WIFE. I will remember.

INNKEEPER. Do so.
It is an order. Now, about the quail.
You'll make the sauce. That's the important thing
A crow can taste like quail, with a good sauce.
You have your herbs?

WIFE. Yes.

INNKEEPER. Well then, begin, begin!
It's morning and we haven't too much time
And the day's bitter cold. Well, all the better.
They'll drink the more but—all this work to do
And the fire barely started! Sarah! Leah!
Where are those lazy servants? Where's the fish?
Where's the new bread? Why haven't we begun?

Leah and Sarah, come and help your mistress!
I'll rouse the fools! There's work to do today!
(He stamps up the stairs. She moves about her business)
  WIFE. *(Singing)* In Bethlehem of Judea
There was an inn also.
There was no room within it
For any but the foe.
No child might be born there.
No bud come to bloom.
For there was no chamber
And there was no room.
  (Her voice fades off into music which swells up and down)
  NARRATOR. And the day passed and night fell on the town,
Silent and still and cold. The houses lay
Huddled and dark beneath the watching stars
And only the inn windows streamed with light—
  (Fade into offstage noise of a big party going on upstairs)
  1ST VOICE. *(Offstage)* Ha, ha, ha! And then the Cilician
    said to the Ethiopian. He said—
  2ND VOICE. *(Offstage)* Well, I remember when we first took
    over Macedonia. There was a girl there—
  3D VOICE. *(Offstage)* Quiet, gentlemen, quiet—the prefect
    wishes to say a few words—
  PREFECT'S VOICE. *(Off)* Gentlemen—men of Rome—mind-
    ful of Rome's historic destiny—and of our good friend
    King Herod—who has chosen alliance with Rome rather
    than a useless struggle—keep them under with a firm
    hand—
  SARAH. What is he saying up there?
  LEAH. I don't know.
I don't know the big words. The soldier said—
  SARAH. You and your soldier!
  LEAH. Oh, he's not so bad.
He brought me a trinket—see!
  SARAH. You and your Roman trinkets! I hate serving them.
I'd like to spit in their cups each time I serve them.
  LEAH. You wouldn't dare!
  SARAH. Wouldn't I, though?
  (There are steps on the stairs as the innkeeper comes down)
  INNKEEPER. Here, here,
What's this, what's this, why are you standing idle?

They're calling for more wine!

   SARAH. Let Leah serve them.

She likes their looks!

   WIFE. Sarah!

   SARAH. *(Sighs)* Yes, mistress.

   WIFE. Please, Sarah—we've talked like this so many times.

   SARAH. Very well, mistress. But let her go first.

   (To Leah)

Get up the stairs, you little soldier's comfort!

I hope he pinches you!

   LEAH. Mistress, it's not my fault. Does Sarah have to—

   WIFE. Oh go, go—both of you!

   (They mutter and go upstairs)

   INNKEEPER. Well, that's a pretty little tempest for you.

You ought to beat the girl. She's insolent

And shows it.

   WIFE. We can't be too hard on her.

Her father's dead, her brother's in the hills,

And yet she used to be a merry child.

I can remember her when she was merry,

A long time since.

   INNKEEPER. You always take their side

And yet, you'd think a self-respecting inn

Could have some decent and well-mannered maids!

But no such luck—sullens and sluts, the lot of them!

Give me a stool—I'm tired.

   (He sits, muttering)

Say thirty dinners

And double for the prefect—and the wine—

Best, second best and common—h'm, not bad

But then—

   (Suddenly)

Why do you sit there, staring at the fire,

So silent and so waiting and so still?

   (Unearthly music, very faint at first, begins with the next
     speech and builds through the scene)

   WIFE. I do not know. I'm waiting.

   INNKEEPER. Waiting for what?

   WIFE. I do not know. For something new and strange,

Something I've dreamt about in some deep sleep,

Truer than any waking,
Heard about, long ago, so long ago,
here In sunshine and the summer grass of childhood,
When the sky seems so near.
I do not know its shape, its will, its purpose
And yet all day its will has been upon me,
More real than any voice I ever heard,
More real than yours or mine or our dead child's,
More real than all the voices there upstairs,
Brawling above their cups, more real than light.
And there is light in it and fire and peace,
Newness of heart and strangeness like a sword,
And all my body trembles under it,
And yet I do not know.
   INNKEEPER. You're tired, my dear.
Well, we shall sleep soon.
   WIFE. No, I am not tired.
I am expectant as a runner is
Before a race, a child before a feast day,
A woman at the gates of life and death,
Expectant for us all, for all of us
Who live and suffer on this little earth
With such small brotherhood. Something begins.
Something is full of change and sparkling stars.
Something is loosed that changes all the world.
   (Music up and down)
And yet—I cannot read it yet. I wait
And strive—and cannot find it.
   (A knock at the door)
Hark? What's that?
   INNKEEPER. They can't come in. I don't care who they are.
We have no room.
   (Knock is repeated)
   WIFE. Go to the door!
   (He goes and opens the door)
   INNKEEPER. Well?
   (Strain of music)
   JOSEPH. *(From outside)* Is this the inn? Sir, we are travelers.
And it is late and cold. May we enter?
   WIFE. *(Eagerly)* Who is it?

INNKEEPER. *(To her)* Just a pair of country people,
A woman and a man. I'm sorry for them
But—
JOSEPH. My wife and I are weary,
May we come in?
INNKEEPER. I'm sorry, my good man.
We have no room tonight. The prefect's orders.
JOSEPH. No room at all?
INNKEEPER. Now, now, it's not my fault.
You look like honest and well-meaning folk
And nobody likes turning trade away
But I'm not my own master. Not tonight.
It may be, in the morning—
(He starts to close the door)
WIFE. Wait!
INNKEEPER. *(In a fierce whisper)* Must you mix in this?
WIFE. Wait!
(She goes to the door)
Good sir, the enemy are in our house
And we—
*(She sees the Virgin, who does not speak throughout this
      scene but is represented by music)*
WIFE. Oh.
(Music)
WIFE. *(Haltingly)* I—did not see your wife. I did not know.
JOSEPH. *(Simply)* Her name is Mary. She is near her time.
WIFE. Yes. Yes.
(To the innkeeper)
Go—get a lantern.
Quickly!
INNKEEPER. What?
WIFE. Quickly.
(To Joseph and Mary)
I—I once had a child.
We have no room. That's true.
And it would not be right. Not here. Not now.
Not with those men whose voices you can hear,
Voices of death and iron—King Herod's voices.
Better the friendly beasts. What am I saying?
There is—we have a stable at the inn,

Safe from the cold, at least—and, if you choose,
You shall be very welcome. It is poor
But the poor share the poor their crumbs of bread
Out of God's hand, so gladly,
And that may count for something. Will you share it?
   JOSEPH. Gladly and with great joy.
   WIFE. The lantern, husband!
   JOSEPH. Nay, I will take it. I can see the path.
Come!
   (Music up. Joseph and Mary go. Innkeeper and wife
    watch them)
   INNKEEPER. *(To wife)* Well, I suppose that you must have
    your way
And, any other night—They're decent people
Or seem to be—
   WIFE. He has his arm about her, smoothing out
The roughness of the path for her.
   INNKEEPER. —Although
They are not even people of our town,
As I suppose you know—
   WIFE. So rough a path to tread with weary feet!
   INNKEEPER. Come in.
   (He shivers)
Brr, there's a frost upon the air tonight.
I'm cold or—yes, I must be cold. That's it.
That's it, now, to be sure. Come shut the door.
   WIFE. Something begins, begins;
Starlit and sunlit, something walks abroad
In flesh and spirit and fire.
Something is loosed to change the shaken world.
   (Music up and down. A bell strikes the hour)
   NARRATOR. The night deepens. The stars march in the sky.
The prefect's men are gone. The inn is quiet·
Save for the sleepy servants and their mistress,
Who clean the last soiled pots.
The innkeeper drowses before the fire.
But, in the street, outside—
   (Music, changing into a shepherd's carol)
   1ST SHEPHERD. As we poor shepherds watched by night
   CHORUS. With a hey, with a ho.

1ST SHEPHERD. A star shone over us so bright
We left our flocks to seek its light
   CHORUS. In excelsis deo,
Gloria, gloria,
In excelsis deo.
   1ST SHEPHERD. We left our silly sheep to stray,
   CHORUS. With a hey, with a ho.
   1ST SHEPHERD. They'll think us no good shepherds, they.
And yet we came a blessed way
   CHORUS. In excelsis deo,
Gloria, gloria,
In excelsis deo.
   1ST SHEPHERD. Now how may such a matter be?
   CHORUS. With a hey, with a ho.
   1ST SHEPHERD. That we of earth, poor shepherds we,
May look on Jesu's majesty?
And yet the star says—"It is He!"
   2ND SHEPHERD. It is He!
   3RD SHEPHERD. It is He!
   CHORUS. Sing excelsis deo!
Gloria, gloria
In excelsis deo!
   SARAH. Who sings so late? How can they sing so late?
   LEAH. I'll go and see.
Wait—I'll rub the windowpane.
It's rimed with frost.
   (She looks out)
They're shepherds from the hills.
   WIFE. Shepherds?
   LEAH. Yes, mistress. They have crooks and staves.
Their tattered cloaks are ragged on their backs.
Their hands are blue and stinging with the cold
And yet they all seem drunken, not with wine
But with good news. Their faces shine with it.
   WIFE. Cold—and so late. Poor creatures—call them in.
The prefect's men are gone.
   LEAH. Aye but—the master—
   WIFE. He's dozing. Do as I tell you.
   LEAH. (Calling out) Come in—come in—tarry awhile and
    rest!

SHEPHERDS. *(Joyously)* We cannot stay. We follow the
  bright star.
Gloria, gloria
In excelsis deo!
WIFE. Where did they go? Would they not stay with us?
Not one?
LEAH. Mistress, they did not even look on me.
They looked ahead. They have gone toward the stable,
The stable of our inn.
WIFE. The stable of our inn. And they are gone.
LEAH. *(Excitedly)* Aye—gone but—Mistress! Mistress!
  Do you hear?
WIFE. Hear what?
LEAH. The tread of steeds on the hard ground,
Iron-hoofed, ringing clear—a company
That comes from out the East. I've never seen
Such things. I am afraid. These are great lords,
Great kings, with strange and memorable beasts,
And crowns upon their heads!
INNKEEPER. *(Waking)* What's that? What's that?
Lords, nobles, kings, here in Bethlehem,
In our poor town? What fortune! O, what fortune!
Stand from the window there, you silly girl,
I'll speak to them!
  (He calls out)
My gracious noble masters,
Worthy and mighty kings! Our humble inn
Is honored by your high nobility!
Come in—come in—we've fire and beds and wine!
Come in—come in—tarry awhile and rest!
KING'S VOICES *(Joyfully)* We cannot stay! We follow the
  bright star!
  Gloria, gloria
In excelsis deo!
INNKEEPER. I do not understand it. They are gone.
They did not even look at me or pause
Though there's no other inn.
They follow the poor shepherds to the stable.
WIFE. They would not tarry with us—no, not one.
INNKEEPER. And yet—

WIFE. Peace, husband, you know well enough
Why none would tarry with us.
And so do I. I lay awhile in sleep
And a voice said to me, "Gloria, gloria,
Gloria in excelsis deo.
The child is born, the child, the child is born!"
And yet I did not rise and go to him,
Though I had waited and expected long,
For I was jealous that my child should die
And her child live.
And so—I have my judgment. And it is just.
  INNKEEPER. Dreams.
  WIFE. Were they dreams, the shepherds and the kings?
Is it a dream, this glory that we feel
Streaming upon us—and yet not for us.
  LEAH. Now, mistress, mistress, 'tis my fault not yours.
You told me seek the strangers in the stable
And see they had all care but I—forgot.
  SARAH. Kissing your soldier!
  LEAH. Sarah!
  SARAH. I am sorry, Leah.
My tongue's too sharp. Mistress, the fault was mine.
You told me also and I well remembered
Yet did not go.
  WIFE. Sarah.
  SARAH. I did not go.
Brooding on mine own wrongs, I did not go.
It was my fault.
  INNKEEPER. If there was any fault, wife, it was mine.
I did not wish to turn them from my door
And yet—I know I love the chink of money,
Love it too well, the good, sound, thumping coin,
Love it—oh, God, since I am speaking truth,
Better than wife or fire or chick or child,
Better than country, better than good fame,
Would sell my people for it in the street,
Oh, for a price—but sell them.
And there are many like me. And God pity us.
  WIFE. God pity us indeed, for we are human,
And do not always see

The vision when it comes, the shining change,
Or, if we see it, do not follow it,
Because it is too hard, too strange, too new,
Too unbelievable, too difficult,
Warring too much with common, easy ways,
And now I know this, standing in this light,
Who have been half alive these many years,
Brooding on my own sorrow, my own pain,
Saying "I am a barren bough. Expect
Nor fruit nor blossom from a barren bough."
Life is not lost by dying! Life is lost
Minute by minute, day by dragging day,
In all the thousand, small, uncaring ways,
The smooth appeasing compromises of time,
Which are King Herod and King Herod's men,
Always and always. Life can be
Lost without vision but not lost by death,
Lost by not caring, willing, going on
Beyond the ragged edge of fortitude
To something more—something no man has seen.
You who love money, you who love yourself,
You who love bitterness, and I, who loved
And lost and thought I could not love again,
And all the people of this little town,
Rise up! The loves we had were not enough.
Something is loosed to change the shaken world,
And with it we must change!
    (The voice of Dismas, the thief, breaking in—a rather quiz-
      zical, independent voice)
    DISMAS. Now that's well said!
    INNKEEPER. Who speaks there? Who are you?
    DISMAS. Who? Oh, my name is Dismas. I'm a thief.
You know the starved, flea-bitten sort of boy
Who haunts dark alleyways in any town,
Sleeps on a fruit sack, runs from the police,
Begs what he can and—borrows what he must.
That's me!
    INNKEEPER. How did you get here?
    DISMAS. By the door, innkeeper,
The cellar door. The lock upon it's old.

I could pick locks like that when I was five.
  INNKEEPER. What have you taken?
  DISMAS. Nothing.
I tried the stable first—and then your cellar,
Slipped in, crept up, rolled underneath a bench,
While all your honest backs were turned—and then—
  WIFE. And then?
  DISMAS. Well—something happened. I don't know what.
I didn't see your shepherds or your kings,
But, in the stable, I did see the child,
Just through a crack in the boards—one moment's space.
That's all that I can tell you.
  (Passionately)
Is he for me as well? Is he for me?
  WIFE. For you as well.
  DISMAS. Is he for all of us?
There are so many of us, worthy mistress,
Beggars who show their sores and ask for alms,
Women who cough their lungs out in the cold,
Slaves—oh, I've been one!—thieves and runagates
Who knife each other for a bite of bread,
Having no other way to get the bread,
—The vast sea of the wretched and the poor,
Whose murmur comes so faintly to your ears
In this fine country.
Has he come to all of us
Or just to you?
  WIFE. To every man alive.
DISMAS. I wish I could believe.
  SARAH *(Scornfully)* And, if you did,
No doubt you'd give up thieving!
  DISMAS. Gently, lady, gently.
Thieving's my trade—the only trade I know.
But, if it were true,
If he had really come to all of us—
I say, to all of us—
Then, honest man or thief,
I'd hang upon a cross for him!
  (A shocked pause. The others mutter)

DISMAS. Would *you?*
(Another pause)
I see that I've said something you don't like,
Something uncouth and bold and terrifying,
And yet, I'll tell you this:
It won't be till each one of us is willing,
Not you, not me, but every one of us,
To hang upon a cross for every man
Who suffers, starves and dies,
Fight his sore battles as they were our own,
And help him from the darkness and the mire,
That there will be no crosses and no tyrants,
No Herods and no slaves.
(Another pause)
Well, it was pleasant, thinking things might be so.
And so I'll say farewell. I've taken nothing.
And he was a fair child to look on.
WIFE. Wait!
DISMAS. Why? What is it you see there, by the window?
WIFE. The dawn, the common day,
The ordinary, poor and mortal day.
The shepherds and the kings have gone away.
The great angelic visitors are gone.
He is alone. He must not be alone.
INNKEEPER. I do not understand you, wife.
DISMAS. Nor I.
WIFE. Do you not see, because I see at last?
Dismas, the thief, is right.
He comes to all of us or comes to none.
Not to my heart in joyous recompense
For what I lost—not to your heart or yours,
But to the ignorant heart of all the world,
So slow to alter, so confused with pain.
Do you not see he must not be alone?
INNKEEPER. I think that I begin to see. And yet—
WIFE. We are the earth his word must sow like wheat
And, if it finds no earth, it cannot grow.
We are his earth, the mortal and the dying,
Led by no star—the sullen and the slut,

The thief, the selfish man, the barren woman,
Who have betrayed him once and will betray him,
Forget his words, be great a moment's space
Under the strokes of chance,
And then sink back into our small affairs.
And yet, unless *we* go, his message fails.

    LEAH. Will he bring peace, will he bring brotherhood?

    WIFE. He would bring peace, he would bring brotherhood
And yet he will be mocked at in the street.

    SARAH. Will he slay King Herod
And rule us all?

    WIFE. He will not slay King Herod. He will die.
There will be other Herods, other tyrants,
Great wars and ceaseless struggles to be free,
Not always won.

    INNKEEPER. These are sad tidings of him.

    WIFE. No, no—they are glad tidings of great joy,
Because he brings man's freedom in his hands,
Not as a coin that may be spent or lost
But as a living fire within the heart,
Never quite quenched—because he brings to all,
The thought, the wish, the dream of brotherhood,
Never and never to be wholly lost,
The water and the bread of the oppressed,
The stay and succor of the resolute,
The harness of the valiant and the brave,
The new word that has changed the shaken world.
And, though he die, his word shall grow like wheat
And every time a child is born,
In pain and love and freedom hardly won,
Born and gone forth to help and aid mankind,
There will be women with a right to say
"Gloria, gloria in excelsis deo!
A child is born!"

    SARAH. Gloria!

    LEAH. Gloria!

    WIFE. Come, let us go. What can we bring to him? What
mortal gifts?

    LEAH. *(Shyly)* I have a ribbon. It's my prettiest.
It is not much but—he might play with it.

SARAH. I have a little bell my father gave me.
It used to make me merry. I have kept it.
I—he may have it.
   DISMAS. My pocket's empty and my rags are bare.
But I can sing to him. That's what I'll do
And—if he needs a thief to die for him—
   INNKEEPER. I would give all my gold.
I will give my heart.
   WIFE. And I my faith through all the years and years,
Though, I forget, though I am led astray,
Though, after this I never see his face,
I will give all my faith.
Come, let us go,
We, the poor earth but we, the faithful earth,
Not yet the joyful, not yet the triumphant,
But faithful, faithful, through the mortal years!
Come!
   (Music begins)
   DISMAS. *(Sings)* Come, all ye faithful.
   INNKEEPER. Joyful and triumphant.
   WOMEN. Come ye, O come ye to Bethlehem!
   *(Their voices rise in chorus in "Come, all ye faithful." The
   chorus and the music swell.)*

No Room in the Hotel

by

DOROTHY CLARKE WILSON

Characters:

A Man	A Scrub Woman
A Woman	A Bellboy
A Clerk	A Poetess
A Reporter	A Senator
A Traveling Man	A Senator's Wife

Scene: A dark, curtained stage in a dimly lighted auditorium.

Time: The present Christmas Eve.

Length: About thirty minutes.

(A Man and a Woman come slowly down one of the aisles. They cannot be glimpsed clearly, but the impression is of two shadowy figures in loose flowing garments. The audience probably thinks it is Joseph and Mary, but that will do no harm. In fact, that is exactly what we want it to think. They move down the aisle toward the stage, a little more slowly as they approach it, for the Woman is getting tired. The Man helps her carefully up the steps to the stage, where they stand in front of the curtain.)

Woman. I can't go much—farther. I'm—so tired.

Man. *(Reassuringly)* We're almost there now. Sit down here a minute and rest.

(The Woman sits down on a low bench placed in front of the curtain.)

Woman. *(After a pause, softly)* Bethlehem. I like the name. It sounds soft and kind.

Man. It's a little town. Not like the big city we just left. I could tell that the city frightened you.

Woman. It was the people—all hurrying so fast, not stopping for anything. I kept wondering what they would do if —if we should get in their way.

81

MAN. *(Confidently)* The people will be different here. Most of them are common working folk, like us.

WOMAN. *(Softly)* Bethlehem. I do like it. The hills are soft and curving and friendly, the way they are at home, and the houses aren't so tall they shut out the stars. If—if only the people are friendly, too—

MAN. It's a good country, a kind country.

WOMAN. I hope it will be kind to—*him*. To our son.

MAN. *(Eagerly)* It will be. You'll see. He'll be different from us. I don't want him to grow up just a day laborer like me. I want him to have a chance in life.

WOMAN *(Dreamily)* Sometimes I have a feeling that—that he's going to be a great man, do something wonderful that no one else has ever done. I suppose it's foolish of me.

MAN. It's not foolish.

WOMAN. Maybe every woman has the same dream about her first born. *(Her voice fades away dreamily, and there is a pause.)*

MAN. Are you rested now? The inn is just around the corner. *(He helps her to her feet)* Why—you're frightened! You're trembling.

WOMAN. It's just because it's all so strange. A strange town —strange people—

MAN. I shouldn't have brought you so far from home.

WOMAN. I'm all right now. Let's go. You say there's an inn—?

MAN. They call it a hotel here.

(They move across the stage in front of the curtain and disappear. Presently voices are heard, this time behind the curtain.)

VOICE OF THE MAN. *(Troubled)* You say—no room?

VOICE OF THE CLERK. *(A little curt)* Sorry. Not a room left.

The curtain rises, revealing the lobby of a small town American hotel. At upper left is the inevitable counter type desk, taking up a good deal of space. Downstage, right, facing front, a wooden bench with a shabby leather seat—the type often seen in the windows of second rate hotels. Upstage center a worn divan and several chairs. On rear wall close to desk, a neatly lettered placard bear-

ing the words in large, legible type: BETHLEHEM
HOTEL. CHRISTIAN CLIENTELE ONLY. *Close to
it an office calendar bearing the date Dec. 24. Entrance,
right, to street. Entrance, left, to stairs and other parts of
the building. The atmosphere is that of shabby, bustling,
small-town mediocrity.*

(*The Clerk, a young girl with a slightly pretty but tired
face, is sitting on a stool behind the desk, a popular magazine close to her hand. She has evidently been reading the
latter and is displeased at being interrupted. The Reporter sits at one end of the divan—a young, dapper, up-
to-the-minute person with a pair of alert eyes which do
not miss anything. At the other end of the divan or in a
chair close by sits the Traveling Man, his face hidden behind a newspaper. Over in one corner of the room the
Scrub Woman is down on her knees with a pail and cloth,
washing the floor. The Man and the Woman occupy
the center of the room before the desk. They are obviously foreigners but of uncertain nationality. They are
dark of skin and poorly dressed. The Man wears a long
coat and a close fitting fur cap resembling a turban. The
Woman wears a long dark cape and a shawl or triangular
scarf over her head. She carries in her arms a very young
baby wrapped in a blanket. She cannot understand
English, so she stands bewildered by the conversation between the Clerk and the Man, keeping her eyes, frightened but trusting, on the latter's face.*)

MAN. (*Speaking in broken, difficult English*) My wife, she
tired. Been sick. Got leetle baby.

CLERK. (*Very matter of fact*) Sorry. You'll have to go some
place else. (*She turns away deliberately and busies herself
with her magazine.*)

WOMAN. (*Anxiously*) What does she say? Is there any
trouble?

MAN. She says there's no room. The inn is full.

WOMAN. But—what shall we do?

MAN. (*Placing his hand on her shoulder*) Don't worry.
We'll find something. (*The Man again approaches the desk,
reluctant but determined. His manner is gently courteous and*

dignified.) Ma'am. *(The Clerk does not look up. After a moment he tries again, without impatience)* Ma'am—if you please to leesten—one leetle minute?

Clerk. *(Looking up, frowning. She has been interrupted in the most thrilling part of her story)* What's that? Oh, are you still there? Look here, I thought I told you—

Man. *(Gently persistent)* See! My wife—she small. She take up not much room. Baby only so big. *(Measuring with his hands)* My wife—she been seek. She come long way from here, across ocean. One leetle room for her, what? One small corner?

Clerk. I told you once we haven't any more room. Can't you understand English.

> *(The Reporter is observing the scene with amusement. The Traveling Man has lowered his paper and looks on gravely. The Man removes a roll of bills from his pocket.)*

Man. See. Money. Good 'Merican money. I pay.

Clerk. *(Eyeing the money, uncertainty for the first time on her face)* Wait a minute. I'll go ask the boss.

> [*Exit, left*

Reporter. *(Chuckling)* You've got the right idea, stranger. As Confucius said, "It's the fellow with the dough that gets the bread." *(As the Man stands staring at him)* Don't get me, do you? Well, no matter. Neither would Confucius.

Man. *(Going to the Woman)* Don't be frightened. It will be all right. There must be lots of places. *(He leads her to the bench, down right, and seats her with tender solicitude.)* Sit down here while we're waiting.

Reporter. *(To Man)* Stranger around these parts, I take it. Been long in America? *(Cheerfully, without waiting for the Man in his slow fashion to answer)* I thought not. Well, how do you like our great, free country, wide-open spaces, land of the free, home of the brave, and all that? All ready to jump into our nice, bubbling melting pot, are you? I've often wondered what sensations you fellows have when you're going through the melting process. *(Musingly)* "Confessions of an Immigrant About to Be Dipped." *(Coming to an upright position with a start, a wide-awake look crossing his face. He whips out a notebook and pencil, turns to the Traveling Man for approval, and rising, approaches the Man and his wife, face beaming)* Not bad, what? I say, give me an interview, will you, and we'll share fifty fifty. How about it?

MAN. *(Shaking his head)* Not—understand—

REPORTER. I mean give me some dope about yourself. Who are you? What are you doing here? Where'd you come from and where are you going? *(The Woman draws closer to the Man, fright written on her face)* Scare you, did I? Sorry. That's the way we do things here in America. Fast and furious. You'll get used to it. I'm not a member of the Dies Committee. I'm just a poor newspaper reporter.

MAN. *(Still perplexed)* Not—understand—

REPORTER. *(Waving his hand)* No matter. Forget it. *(Going back to his seat, to Traveling Man)* Good idea, but might have known it wouldn't work. *(Sociably)* Stopping here long, are you?

TRAVELING MAN. Not long.

REPORTER. Ever been in Bethlehem before?

TRAVELING MAN. Yes. A long time ago.

REPORTER. Place has changed considerably, I suppose?

TRAVELING MAN. Not much, all small towns are about alike.

REPORTER. Seen quite a lot of them, have you?

TRAVELING MAN. Yes. I'm a—traveling man.

REPORTER. I thoughts so. When you came in, I said to myself, "There's a man who's seen a lot of the world." In some kind of business, I suppose?

TRAVELING MAN. I used to be. In the hotel business.

REPORTER. So? Well, don't blame you for getting out. These tourist camps have cut in plenty. Look at this joint here. So poor they'd even considered selling the house's respectability for a bank roll. *(Nodding his head in the direction of the Man.)*

CLERK. *(Returning and speaking very definitely)* No. We're full up. Couldn't possibly put you up tonight. *(As the Man still stands hesitating)* Look somewhere else in town, why don't you? Some of the tourist houses aren't so fussy.

WOMAN. What does she say? *(The Man puts his arm about her shoulders, and they converse together in low tones.)*

TRAVELING MAN. *(Rising and approaching the desk)* I say —if it's a matter of space, these people can have my room. It's easy for a single man to find a place, and I'm used to knocking around.

CLERK. *(Wide-eyed, lowering her voice slightly)* Gee, mister, you don't think I really meant that about there being no room, do you? This place hasn't been full since old home week ten years ago.

TRAVELING MAN. Then why—

CLERK. We have our reputation to consider, sir. Our clients are all respectable whites. Why, there isn't a hotel in the county that would take *them* in. *(Nodding toward the couple)* I'll bet you wouldn't want to sleep in a room after 'em yourself.

TRAVELING MAN. *(Earnestly)* But—you may be making a big mistake. You may be turning away really important people.

CLERK. We would be if we took *them* in. Maybe you haven't heard, but tonight we've got important people coming. *(Reporter looks up, interested.)*

TRAVELING MAN. That's what I thought, too. I wonder— could I talk to the manager?

CLERK. You wish to make a complaint?

TRAVELING MAN. No, no. I just want to tell him about an experience I once had and maybe keep him from making the same mistake.

CLERK. Sorry. He's busy now.

TRAVELING MAN. I wouldn't take long. Just a minute—

CLERK. He's terribly busy. *(The Traveling Man returns to the divan, and as soon as his back is turned, the Clerk and the Reporter exchange a significant glance. The latter taps his head.)*

MAN. *(Slowly)* My wife—she stay here while I find place? *(The Clerk is nonplussed at the idea but does not know what to answer)* She tired. She come long way.

REPORTER. *(Cheerfully)* Sure! Of course you can leave your wife here. It's a free country and a hotel lobby's a public place.

CLERK. *(Weakly)* Why—I—I suppose so—

MAN. *(Seating the Woman on the bench, right.)* I'll be back. Just sit here and wait.

WOMAN. *(Clinging to him)* Don't leave me—alone—

MAN. I must. We have to find a place to stay or a car to

take us further on. There's the child, you know. *(The Woman settles back.)* Don't be frightened. This is the good country, the great, free America.

WOMAN. *(Quietly, looking down at the sleeping child)* I wait.

(The Man goes out, right. During the last of the preceding scene the Bellboy has entered and stands lounging against the desk. He is of very colored lineage.)

BELLBOY. *(To Clerk, nodding toward the couple)* Niggers?

CLERK. You're color blind.

REPORTER. *(Pleasantly)* How the iron pot loves to call the copper kettle black!

BELLBOY. What are they then if they ain't niggers?

CLERK. That's the least of my worries. What I'm worrying about is whether she's still here when the senator and his wife pull in.

REPORTER. Ah, then Senator and Mrs. Fairweather *are* planning to spend Christmas in Bethlehem!

CLERK. *(Hastily)* But it's entirely confidential.

REPORTER. Oh, of course. Let's see, Bethlehem is the senator's home town, isn't it?

CLERK. Yes. He owns half the place. Has a big house up Main Street, but they don't open it up very often. For a short visit like this they always stop here at the hotel.

TRAVELING MAN. Fairweather. I've heard the name.

REPORTER. It's in the papers plenty right now. He's the one who's said to be sponsoring the anti-alien bill. It's still in committee, but we're expecting it to break any day now. By the way, boy, where's the telephone?

BELLBOY. This way, boss.

CLERK. *(Worried)* The senator is especially anxious to avoid publicity just now. You—you aren't going to call any reporters?

REPORTER. What do you take me for? Do you think I'm the man to hand over a piece of confidential information to *a reporter? (He follows the Bellboy, right. Reporter, thrusting his head back again.)* No, ma'am! A scoop like that goes only to the city editor!

(The Clerk again looks worried. The Bellboy returns, leaning negligently against the counter.)

CLERK. Who'd he call? Could you hear?

BELLBOY. Long distance, that's all I know. Who is he?

CLERK. (*Consulting the register*) Name, Smith. Residence, New York City. Occupation, Publicity Expert. (*Brightening*) Well, at least he isn't a newspaper reporter.

BELLBOY. You say New York City? I've got a mammy lives in New York City.

CLERK. (*Curtly*) You don't say! (*Turns her back on him.*)

BELLBOY. (*Wistfully*) I s'pose you'll be going home on Christmas.

CLERK. What's that to you?

BELLBOY. Oh—nothin'. Only I—I ain't never been away from home on Christmas before. I was just hopin' there'd be somebody around to talk to.

CLERK. If you don't quit your impertinence, you'll be losing your job.

(*The Clerk turns again to her story, becoming deeply absorbed. The Bellboy saunters to the entrance, right. Meanwhile the Scrub Woman has finished with the part of the room she has been cleaning and gone out, left. She now returns with a fresh pail of steaming water and approaches the corner occupied by the Woman. She gazes at her curiously, and her eyes light with that luminous sentimental softness which some women always show at sight of a baby. She comes closer and reaches a tentative finger toward the bundle. The Woman smiles and lifts the blanket. The Scrub Woman's face wrinkles up in delight, and the two exchange diffident smiles.*)

SCRUB WOMAN. Pretty little tyke, ain't he? How old is he? (*The Woman smiles blankly*) I said how old— Mercy me, you don't understand no English, do you? (*They look at each other a moment, dismayed by this insurmountable barrier, then the faces of both women turn again to the baby. Here they have a common ground. They can converse without language.*) Bless me, he's wakin' up! The cute little tyke! Ain't even cryin'. Mine used to wake up like that, too, all smiles. Look at that! Ain't he cute? (*The two women look at the baby, then at each other, smiling appreciatively like two old friends.*) There! He's suckin' his little fist. He's hungry. I wish I had somethin' to give 'im. I ain't got noghin' but a mite of candy. (*She feels in the pockets of her apron and pulls out a small*

*wooden box shaped like a tiny chest. She opens it and offers
it to the Woman, who shakes her head. The Woman takes
from beneath her cape a bottle of milk wrapped in a cloth.
She unwinds it, feels its warmth ,and starts to put it inside her
dress to give it further warmth)* Here! Let me feel. *(The
Scrub Woman takes the bottle, laying the box down carelessly on the edge of the bench)* Oh, it's much too cold! He'll
be havin' the colic. Wait! I'll fix it. *(She takes the bottle to
the pail of hot water, and very carefully lowers it into the
water. The two exchange understanding smiles.)*

CLERK. *(Looking up from her magazine and frowning as
she notices for the first time what has been going on)* You'd
better get that floor done. We're expecting important people.

*(The Scrub Woman bends to the pail, washing the floor
with one hand while holding the bottle with the other.
Presently she removes the bottle, wipes it on her apron,
tests it on the back of her hand, and gives it to the
Woman. She leans over, watching the baby for a moment,
then reluctantly returns to her floor washing.)*

REPORTER. *(Returning, breezily)* The telephone service in
these small towns isn't so hot, but I got them—finally. *(He sits
down again at the other end of the divan from the Traveling
Man.)* Staying here over the holidays?

TRAVELING MAN. I'm not quite sure—yet. *(His glance
travels again to the Woman sitting stolidly on the bench. Of
the three other occupants of the lobby he alone has watched
the little scene between the Woman and the Scrub Woman
with interest.)*

REPORTER. *(Easily)* Don't let those foreigners play on your
sympathies, stranger. People like them wouldn't know what
to do with a soft bed, anyway.

TRAVELING MAN. It's dangerous business—turning people
away—

REPORTER. It would be more dangerous taking them in.
Even a backwoods hotel like this couldn't risk its reputation.

TRAVELING MAN. *(Earnestly)* I'd like to tell you about an
experience I had once— a long time ago—when I was in the
hotel business.

REPORTER. *(Suddenly alert)* I believe there's a car stopping
outside. Pardon me, sir. You were saying—

TRAVELING MAN. *(Disregarding the interruption)* One night a couple came to my hotel seeking shelter. There were crowds in the town that night, and the hotel was nearly full, but not quite. I had a few rooms left, but I was keeping them, for I expected more important people. So I turned them away— this man and woman—

REPORTER. I wonder if it's the senator. Oh—oh! I should say not. Look who's coming! No senator ever looked like that. Sorry sir. Tell me your story later.

(The Poetess enters, followed by the Bellboy carrying her bag. She is young, pretty, breezy, and ecstatic. She pauses halfway to the desk and casts about her a glance so all encompassing that we know immediately she has seen everything—and nothing. She is all prepared to enthuse, so she enthuses.)

POETESS. How perfectly quaint! *(She approaches the desk)* Is this really Bethlehem?

CLERK. Yes, ma'am. *(Pushing the register forward)* Right here, please.

POETESS. *(Disregarding the book, in a burst of frankness)* I suppose you'll think I'm silly, being so excited, but this is a real adventure for me. You see, I've been wanting to come here for years, every Christmas.

CLERK. Yes, ma'am. If you'll please sign on this line—

POETESS. *(Finding the prosaic response unbearable, turns unconsciously toward the Reporter, who has been listening with his usual attentive ear for other people's business)* This really is Bethlehem, isn't it?

REPORTER. *(Rising gallantly)* It certainly is, Miss—

POETESS. Curtis. Gwendolyn Curtis. *(She looks at him hopefully to see if the name strikes a responsive chord)* You—you may have heard of me. I write things. Poetry, mostly.

REPORTER. *(Trying hard to remember)* The name does sound familiar. That's a coincidence, because I'm a writer, too.

POETESS. *(Eagerly)* Poetry?

REPORTER. Oh, no. Just newspaper stuff.

POETESS. *(Disappointed)* Oh! I thought if you wrote poetry maybe you came here for the same reason I did.

REPORTER. And why is that, if I may ask?

POETESS. Well, once when I was a very little girl I saw the name "Bethlehem" on the map, and I began thinking even then that if I could just come here for Christmas, I could—well, sort of get the real meaning of the day so I could write about it. You understand what I mean?

REPORTER. *(A little out of his depth)* You mean the combination of Bethlehem and Christmas might—might sort of inspire you—

POETESS. *(Eagerly)* That's it. I love to write poems about Christmas, only none of them have seemed to—well, to get at the heart of the thing. They've been all shiny balls and tinsel. But now—just to be here—in this little town called Bethlehem —*(To Clerk)* Do you suppose there are any sheep near here?

CLERK. *(Indifferently)* I'm afraid not, ma'am. The farmers around here go in mostly for hogs.

POETESS. *(Somewhat dampened)* Oh! Well, at least there are stables and stars—and maybe babies.

REPORTER. *(Helpfully)* Sure! There's one of them over there. *(He points toward the Woman. The Poetess turns eagerly in her direction and frowns.)*

POETESS. Is—that the kind of people you have here in Bethlehem?

CLERK. *(Eagerly)* Oh, no, ma'am. We don't. She's just waiting here for her husband to find a place to stay. I had to tell him there weren't any rooms. You see we couldn't have people like that stopping at our hotel.

POETESS. I should think not. You're sure the rooms are clean?

CLERK. Oh, yes. As clean as scrubbing can make them. We hire a woman who does nothing else.

POETESS. *(Looking disapprovingly at the Scrub Woman)* So it seems.

REPORTER. They have them in the city, too. The reason you never see them is that they come out after dark, like bats.

POETESS. Well—it's only for one night, anyway. *(Signing)*

CLERK. *(To Bellboy)* Take the lady's bag up to Two Fourteen. And hurry back. The senator may be coming any time. *(The Bellboy picks up the bag and goes out, left, the Poetess following.)*

POETESS. *(Offstage)* What! No elevators?

REPORTER. *(Turning to Traveling Man)* Now sir—you were saying—sorry we were interrupted.

TRAVELING MAN. I doubt if you'd be interested in the story. *(He turns again to his paper, and the Reporter, a bit crestfallen but recovering quickly, gets up and saunters to the entrance, right. The Scrub Woman again approaches the Woman.)*

SCRUB WOMAN. Poor little tyke! Gone fast asleep again. I'll bet you got a cramp in your arm. Here! Let me take 'im a minute, while you get a mite of rest. *(She sits down beside the Woman and takes the bundle, crooning delightedly as only a woman who has known and loved children long and tenderly can do.)*

REPORTER. *(After an interval)* Ah! Here's the senator now!

CLERK. *(Going quickly off, left)* Sam! Quick! Hurry up! *(The Bellboy re-enters)* The senator's here. Get his bags—quick! Don't keep him waiting.

BELLBOY. Yes, *ma'am.*

(The Bellboy saunters slowly to the entrance, right. Presently Senator Fairweather and his Wife enter, followed by the Bellboy, weighted down with luggage. The Senator is a very ordinary looking man with a worried, harassed face. One suspects that the slightly bombastic manner he affects is to convince himself as much as other people that he is in reality an important person. The Senator's Wife, however, makes up for all her husband's shortcomings. She was born to a position of importance and knows it. They approach the desk without even a casual glance at the other occupants of the lobby. The Scrub Woman hastily gives back the baby and returns to her scrubbing.)

SENATOR. You received my telegram, I presume?

CLERK. Yes sir. We have everything all ready for you, sir. Would—would you like to see the manager, sir, before you go up to your rooms?

SENATOR. No. It isn't necessary. *(He signs the register.)*

SENATOR'S WIFE. *(Shivering)* I'd forgotten what a bleak place this is. I believe we should have opened the house, James.

SENATOR. No, no, we're wasting enough time as it is. I

ought to be back in Washington this minute, with that bill coming up next—*(He stops himself just in time and looks around warily. The Reporter springs to his feet, blandly smiling.)*

REPORTER. Why, Senator Fairweather, what a piece of luck!

SENATOR. *(Eyeing him closely)* I—don't seem to remember—

REPORTER. Oh, you wouldn't. I only met you once, but I've followed your career with much interest. Believe me, I've quoted you on more than one occasion, Senator.

SENATOR. *(Pleased)* Have you? Well, that's flattering, Mr.—

REPORTER. Smith, Now about that bill, Senator, that anti-alien bill that's coming up next week—

SENATOR. *(Sharply)* How do you know it's coming up next week?

REPORTER. But I thought you just said so.

SENATOR. Oh—well, maybe I did, but it's entirely confidential.

REPORTER. Oh, of course. But people will know about it, anyway, now that the committee has reported favorably.

SENATOR. Who told you that?

REPORTER. Oh, nobody. But how could it be otherwise with a man of your influence on the committee?

SENATOR. Well, it's not absolutely decided yet, but just between you and me—and here's hoping there are no reporters listening—it's going through.

REPORTER. *(Eyes gleaming)* That *is* news.

SENATOR. It's time the people of this nation were waking up to the dangers from the foes right here in our midst. *(The Reporter half turns his back and begins scribbling hastily.)* It would be a good thing if we could ship every alien in the country, English speaking excepted, back where he came from. But since we can't do that, we'll do the next best thing. We'll keep any more from coming. And we'll take every measure possible to protect our sacred institutions of liberty and democracy from the subversive influences of these inferior races which we have carelessly permitted to reap the benefits of our Anglo-Saxon heritage.

REPORTER. Hear, hear!

SENATOR'S WIFE. James, no political speeches. We're in Bethlehem, not Washington, and it's Christmas. We have at least a dozen charity baskets to attend to, and—(*Her face suddenly freezes*) James! Who is that woman? (*The Senator's glance follows her, and they both stare at the Woman.*)

CLERK. (*Weakly*) I can explain—

SENATOR'S WIFE. James, I've made up my mind. We're not staying here. Even if it is only for one night, we're opening the house.

SENATOR. Now, now, my dear—

SENATOR'S WIFE. I can stand almost everything about a country hotel—bad beds, leaky faucets, poor food, even—even scrub women doing their work under your feet. But I simply draw the line at staying under the same roof with—with—

CLERK. The lady—I mean the woman, ma'am—isn't staying. She's just sitting—

SENATOR'S WIFE. (*With withering sarcasm*) Apparently.

REPORTER. The fact is, Senator, the woman came here with her husband a few minutes ago, and the two of them wanted a room. The clerk refused them.

SENATOR'S WIFE. (*With more approval*) I should think so.

CLERK. (*Relieved*) That's the way it was, ma'am. You see—

REPORTER. She told them the hotel was full.

SENATOR. This place full! That's a good one.

REPORTER. Then the man went out to find another place and left the woman here. There really was nothing the clerk could do.

SENATOR'S WIFE. Well, I hope you sterilize the place thoroughly.

SENATOR. You say there was a man. Did he look—threatening?

REPORTER. (*Doubtfully*) Threatening, Senator?

SENATOR. I have to be careful. A man in my position—

REPORTER. No. This man looked perfectly harmless.

(*The Poetess enters, left. She has lost her ecstatic rapture. She carries her suitcase and a key, which she lays on the desk.*)

POETESS. I'm checking out. (*To Bellboy*) Here, boy, call me a taxi.

[*The Bellboy goes out, right.*

CLERK. B-but—you just came, ma'am.

POETESS. And now I'm just going. I couldn't spend even

one night in this place. The beds are terrible, and the radiator rattles, and there isn't even a private bath.

CLERK. There's only one private bath, ma'am, and of course the senator—

(But the Poetess is already on her way to the door.)

TRAVELING MAN. *(Interposing himself gently)* So—you're going away without finding what you're looking for?

POETESS. I was a fool. There's no beauty nor romance here —nothing to remind one even remotely of the first Christmas.

BELLBOY. *(Returning)* Taxi's gone now, ma'am. You'll have to wait.

(She sits down in one of the chairs impatiently. Presently the Man enters, right. We had almost forgotten since seeing him last that he is so tall and imposing in appearance, that he moves with such a peculiar dignity and grace, like a man accustomed to the long, flowing garments and fresh, outdoor vitality of another mode of life. The occupants of the lobby feel this and stare at him curiously. The Man goes straight to the side of the Woman with scarcely a glance for the others. It is as if the two were alone together in an otherwise untenanted time and space. The Woman looks up questioningly.)

MAN. I've been all through the town. I've asked people everywhere. I can't find a place.

WOMAN. *(Making no move except to tighten her arms about the bundle)* What shall we do?

MAN. I—don't know—yet. I must—think.

(He stands very still in that deep, aloof concentration which men of certain races are able to attain. The others in the lobby watch him curiously.)

SENATOR. *(To Reporter in a penetrating whisper)* Do you think he could have followed me?

REPORTER. Very unlikely.

SENATOR. European, do you think?

REPORTER. Acts more like an easterner. Syrian, maybe.

SENATOR's WIFE. *(Sharply, to Clerk)* Well—aren't you going to do something? Why don't you tell them this is a respectable hotel and not Ellis Island?

(The Scrub Woman approaches the Man.)

SCRUB WOMAN. What's the trouble? Can't find no place to

put you up? You can stop at my place if you want. It ain't much. Just one room in an old shack out behind the hotel. But I got an old couch I can put her on.

WOMAN. What is it? What does she say?

MAN. She says she has a place where we can stay. *(To Scrub Woman)* Not me. I sleep out—in straw—anywhere. But she been seek. She small—she not take much room—

SCRUB WOMAN. Come along. There's room. My little grandson, he can sleep on the floor one night. He won't mind. He's been a-hankerin' for some company for Christmas.

MAN. I pay money—

SCRUB WOMAN. Lan' sakes, what do you take me for! I don't want no money. Come along now.

[*She goes out, right, and the Man and Woman follow.*

SENATOR'S WIFE. Well—you'd better get the place disinfected at once. *(To the Bellboy)* Here, boy. Get a dustcloth and wipe off that seat. And find something to spray the room with.

BELLBOY. Yes, ma'am *(He takes a large dirty handkerchief from his pocket and goes to the seat, dusting it with generous but superficial gestures.*

SENATOR. I'm still not satisfied he wasn't following me. These foreigners are a vindictive lot. No good in any of them.

BELLBOY. *(Picking up the wooden box)* That woman, she went off and left a box.

REPORTER. That reminds me, I have a telephone call to make.

SENATOR'S WIFE. Come, James, let's get to our rooms.

(The company all start to move their separate ways, when the Traveling Man suddenly speaks in a voice so vibrant and compelling that every person stops short and looks at him.)

TRAVELING MAN. *Let me see that box.*

BELLBOY. Y-yes sir. *(He takes it to him rather gingerly, as if the Traveling Man's attitude had endowed the thing with extreme and possibly sinister importance.)*

TRAVELING MAN. *(Holding the box and studying it)* A very unusual little box.

SENATOR. *(Terrified)* C-could it be a—*bomb?*

SENATOR'S WIFE. *(Eagerly)* An antique, do you think?

POETESS. *(Putting down her suitcase)* How romantic! Do you suppose it's full of crown jewels?

REPORTER. Open it up, stranger. Bet you ten to one it's a pack of Camels.

SENATOR. No, no! For heaven's sake! Listen to it first and see if it ticks!

SENATOR'S WIFE. James, don't be absurd. I believe that's a valuable antique, and if it is, I'm going to—*(Stops warily.)*

CLERK. *(Nervously)* Maybe I'd better show it to the manager.

(The Traveling Man quietly opens the box and looks inside. There is a breathless pause of expectancy. The Senator puts his hands over his ears as if expecting an explosion, then draws his breath in relief as nothing happens.)

POETESS. *(Breathlessly)* What is it?

REPORTER. Camels or Chesterfields?

CLERK. If it's anything of value, I really must report it. It's against the rules—

TRAVELING MAN. *(He suddenly lifts his eyes and sweeps them about the little group. His voice, though still quiet, has a compelling quality)* Have any of you ever traveled in the east? *(He looks around, and they slowly shake their heads. He continues dreamily.)* Seen visions of its ancient grandeur rising from the smoke of an Arab campfire, watched its caravans come swaying through the desert, loaded with perfumes and spices, breathed the heavy fragrances that hang brooding, like spirits of the past, over its temples and its tombs? *(Again they shake their heads, caught in the spell of the pictures he has conjured.)* No? But perhaps you have heard of a certain substance known as —myrrh?

POETESS. *(Breathlessly)* Myrrh!

SENATOR'S WIFE. *(Puzzled)* Myrrh?

REPORTER. Myrrh. I seem to have heard the name.

TRAVELING MAN. It is a substance with a venerable and interesting history. From ancient times it has been used as a perfume, a medicine, and an embalming agent. It is both rare and costly. Priests were anointed with it back in the time of Moses. In the days of Solomon maidens wore it as a bag of fragrance beneath their breasts. And according to the old tradition it was one of the gifts brought by the Wise Men of the east to the Christ Child.

POETESS. *(Dreamily)* "And they presented unto him gifts, gold and frankincense, and myrrh."

REPORTER. That's where I heard it. In Sunday School.

SENATOR. All very interesting, but we hardly have time—

TRAVELING MAN. *(Continuing imperturbably)* It is a resinous gum exuding from the bark of a small, scrubby tree, and it occurs in pieces of irregular form, varying from a pale, reddish yellow to reddish brown in color. *(As he speaks he takes a small object from the box and holds it up.)* Like this.

......*(The Traveling Man has been working them up to a state of suspense and excitement, and now that the climax of his little act has come, they are duly excited, without knowing exactly why. They gather around, look at the object curiously and peer into the box.)*

POETESS. *(More stirred than the rest)* You—you really mean that is myrrh—there in that box?

TRAVELING MAN. It looks very much like it.

REPORTER. But—people don't go lugging priceless oriental stuff around country hotels. There's something blamed queer. Who could have left it there?

TRAVELING MAN. Who, indeed?

POETESS. Who but that woman—and her child?

SENATOR. I knew there was something queer about those dirty foreigners. They aren't what they pretended to be. I shan't rest easy until they're out of this town, and I mean to—

POETESS. *(Suddenly taking the center of the stage)* Listen, all of you! Are you blind? Can't you see what this means? It—it's unbelievable, I know. It's a miracle, but who are we to say miracles can't happen? *(They stare at her uncomprehendingly.)*

REPORTER. What are you talking about?

POETESS. It couldn't be just coincidence, could it? A man and a woman and a child—coming to Bethlehem on Christmas Eve—and bringing a box of myrrh?

REPORTER. By Jove, the girl's got something there!

SENATOR. Young woman, are you trying to make us believe there's something—something uncanny about this place?

SENATOR'S WIFE. *(Her imagination kindling)* It is—a curious coincidence. But of course it couldn't be—

POETESS. *(Now transformed into a flame of enthusiasm)* Why not? Why couldn't it happen to us as much as to other people? Literature is full of stories of its happening. Almost every nation has its legend of the Christ Child coming back to earth on Christmas Eve. Who are we to say they are all untrue? Things happen every day that people can't explain.

REPORTER. Sure. Look at Ripley's "Believe It or Not"!

SENATOR'S WIFE. *(Her eyes wide with excitement)* But—suppose it were possible suppose they could visit the earth again—surely they wouldn't choose to appear as—as dirty, ignorant foreigners!

TRAVELING MAN. *(Quietly)* You forget that the Christ Child was not of Anglo-Saxon parentage. He was a Syrian Jew, his father was a manual laborer, and he was born in a stable because there was no room for him in the—hotel. Just as there is no room tonight.

POETESS. But—we didn't know—

TRAVELING MAN. Neither did they know then. They were just a man and woman—wanting shelter.

POETESS. How terribly that innkeeper must have felt—afterward—when he found out!

TRAVELING MAN. Yes. *(Slowly and thoughtfully)* There is an old legend that he still walks the earth—sometimes—trying to keep others from making the same mistake he did.

SENATOR. It's preposterous. It's—incredible! But—by Jove, I believe it's true!

SENATOR'S WIFE. I felt all the time there was something unusual about them. You know, James, I've always been a little—occult.

SENATOR. Well, if such things can happen, it's logical to suppose they might happen to us. After all, if the—the Holy Family wanted to put in an appearance, it's natural they should choose important people.

POETESS. *(Softly)* Just think! They were right here in this room—sitting on this very seat. *(She hovers over the bench.)*

SENATOR'S WIFE. *(Suddenly)* Yes, and where are they now? Out in some hovel with that ignorant scrub woman. It isn't respectable. What would people say if they knew? James, we must do something.

SENATOR. Yes, my dear. But what?

SENATOR'S WIFE. Why, get them in a decent, respectable room, of course. That poor tired woman and that little baby! Probably the place they're in is no better than a stable. We'll put them in our suite, James. *(To Bellboy)* Do you know where that woman lives?

BELLBOY. Y-yes, ma'am. *(His eyes are wide)* Gosh, ma'am, d-do you really think that was—*Him?*

SENATOR'S WIFE. *(Quelling his intimacy with a glance)* Take me there immediately. *(To Clerk)* And see that everything is made ready in our suite. You'd better put a crib in and have a nice hot lunch taken up. The very best of which the hotel is capable.

CLERK. Y-yes, ma'am. *(She goes out left, hastily.)*

POETESS. I'm going, too. I wouldn't miss it for anything.

SENATOR'S WIFE. You'll come, of course, James. It's your place, being a senator. Almost like giving an official welcome to a foreign dignitary. *(They all start for the door right but before they reach it, the Scrub Woman enters, and they retreat. Without noticing, she goes at once to her pail. Senator's Wife, breathlessly)* Where are they? Where did you take them?

SCRUB WOMAN. *(Flustered and a little frightened)* Them?

POETESS. The man and woman and—and child. Where are they?

SCRUB WOMAN. Gone.

SENATOR'S WIFE. Gone! Didn't you take them home with you?

SCRUB WOMAN. Yes'm. But they didn't stay. The man, he was anxious to get along. I found a man with a car he could hire. I seen 'em get into it myself and drive off.

SENATOR'S WIFE. But—where were they going?

SCRUB WOMAN. The man said as how he'd got a brother what's got a farm over in the next county. That's where they was bound for. They're goin' to build 'em a little house and keep hens.

SENATOR'S WIFE. *(Dazedly)* Keep—hens—

POETESS. Don't you understand? They've just—gone, that's

all. Of course they had to go that way—quietly, mysteriously —as they came. (*Radiantly, to Scrub Woman*) Do you know who it was you befriended tonight?

SCRUB WOMAN. (*Shaking her head*) I didn't ask no names. I just knew they needed a place to sleep. And there wasn't no room for 'em here. (*Without waiting for further explanations, she returns to her pail. She picks it up, gathers up her other cleaning implements, and goes out, moving with the same slow, patient stolidity which has characterized all her movements.*)

POETESS. (*Gazing after her sadly*) Poor stupid woman! And here she's been in actual contact with—with Divinity, and didn't even recognize it!

REPORTER. (*Dryly*) At least she came in contact with it. That's more than any of us was willing to do.

SENATOR. (*Severely*) This isn't a time for levity. We've all been through a deeply emotional experience. We've been privileged to witness a miracle. Out of all the millions to whom this thing might have happened, we are the ones chosen. It should make us thoughtful. It—it should change our whole lives.

POETESS. (*Eagerly*) Oh, it has! It's changed mine.

TRAVELING MAN. (*Face lighting*) If you really mean that—

SENATOR'S WIFE. Of course we mean it.

POETESS. I know I'll be able to write so much better poetry —perhaps even make the best magazines. My mind is so full of new ideas I can hardly wait to write them down.

TRAVELING MAN. (*Disappointed but turning hopefully to the senator*) You mean, Senator, you'll be changing your position on this anti-alien bill?

SENATOR. I'll—what? What's that?

TRAVELING MAN. (*Quietly*) Were they not aliens—this man and woman and child?

REPORTER. That's right, Senator. You'll have to change your mind about all aliens being such a bad lot. That is, if you're really consistent. After all, it might be embarrassing to find you'd deported the Holy Family as seditionists.

SENATOR. (*Testily*) Nonsense. This is an isolated instance, having no bearing whatever on the practical problems facing the country. Our business is to safeguard this democracy which is our precious Anglo-Saxon heritage, and to do so we must eliminate all these impure strains which have so insidiously crept in.

Reporter *(Musingly)* In other words, destroy the democracy.

Senator. What's that?

Senator's Wife. James, I've made up my mind. After this experience we can't just keep on observing Christmas the way we have. We—we've got to make some real sacrifices this year.

Traveling Man. *(Turning to her eagerly)* Yes?

Senator's Wife. *(To all the company)* I—I'm going to give twenty charity baskets this Christmas instead of ten!

(The Traveling Man turns slowly away. His head bows. He stands motionless holding the little box.)

Senator. Very good, my dear. *(He taps the desk nervously)* Now if that clerk would only come back—

Bellboy. *(To Poetess)* Your taxi's waiting, ma'am. Shall I say you don't need it now?

Poetess. Certainly not. There's no reason to stay now. How lucky this all happened before train time! Now I won't have to sleep in that awful room. I can spend Christmas in comfort, in my New York apartment.

Bellboy. *(Eagerly)* You—honest to gosh—goin' to be in New York—tomorrow mornin'?

Poetess. *(Coldly)* Yes. Why?

Bellboy. *(Eagerly)* I got an old mammy livin' in New York. She's all alone this Christmas. There's just her an' me. D-do you s'pose—

(The Traveling Man turns with interest.)

Poetess. *(Impatiently)* Well?

Bellboy. Could you maybe call 'er up an' wish 'er Merry Christmas for me an' tell 'er I'm all right an' hopin' she's the same? It—it wouldn't take but a minute, ma'am.

Poetess. Well, of all the—I could have you discharged for this. *(Turning to the others)* The insolence of the boy!

Bellboy. Yes, ma'am. *(He hastily picks up the suitcase)* Your taxi's waitin', ma'am.

Poetess. Good night, everybody. Merry Christmas! Watch for my poems, won't you?

[*She goes out, right.*

SENATOR. Ah, here's the clerk. *(Severely)* you've kept us waiting.

CLERK. *(Excitedly)* The rooms are ready, sir. I've had the crib taken up—

SENATOR. We won't be needing the crib. The parties have —er—moved on. We'll be occupying the suite ourselves. Where's that boy gone? *(As the Bellboy re-enters)* Here! Take our bags up.

BELLBOY. Yes, boss. *(He is again the obsequious and dutiful servant.)*

SENATOR. *(Turning)* I—er—think we'd better not advertise this little experience, gentlemen. My—er—my public might not understand. And if the notion ever got around that I was a bit queer— It doesn't do to mix religion and politics.

SENATOR'S WIFE. Come James. The baskets!

SENATOR. Yes, my dear. *(They go out, left. To Clerk)* Tell the manager I'd like to see him in my suite.

CLERK. Yes sir.

[She goes out, left.

REPORTER. *(Drawing a deep breath)* Well! And I thought a small town would be a dull place on Christmas Eve. Will *this* be a story! *(He starts writing furiously)* Nobody will believe it, of course. I'm not sure I do myself. But if it isn't front page stuff, I'll swallow my typewriter!

TRAVELING MAN. *(Slowly, to himself)* I think now I— understand.

REPORTER. *(Idly)* What's that? What do you understand?

TRAVELING MAN. Why the world hasn't changed more in the last two thousand years. Why there are still wars and hatreds and oppressions and class struggles and racial bitternesses twenty centuries after the Dream of a new way of Love was born in the hearts of men.

REPORTER. *(Curiously)* Why?

TRAVELING MAN. Because—its senators and its hotel keepers and its poets are still not as wise as its scrub women.

REPORTER. And—its reporters, possibly?

TRAVELING MAN. Possibly. You know best about that.

REPORTER. And it's the senators, not the scrub women, who shape the world's destiny.

TRAVELING MAN. No. You're wrong. There was a scrub

woman in that other Bethlehem, too. There must have been. If there hadn't, the Child wouldn't have had even his stable and his pile of straw. And she did far more to shape history than King Herod with his selfish, petty little nationalism ever did—or that Roman senator for whose sake the last room available was left empty. *(After a pause)* Don't worry, my friend. As long as there are a few scrub women with simple human friendliness in their hearts, the Dream is safe. It will come surely to fulfillment. The pity is that it must come so slowly.

> *(The Scrub Woman enters. She looks around carefully as if she had lost something. She even gets down on her knees and peers under the bench where the Woman sat. The Bellboy enters, left.)*

REPORTER. *(Hastily scribbling on a bit of paper)* Here, boy, call this number for me, will you, long distance, and get this party for me on the wire.

BELLBOY. *(Taking the paper)* Yes, boss.

[*Goes out, left.*

TRAVELING MAN. *(To Scrub Woman)* Lose something, did you?

SCRUB WOMAN. *(Rising painfully to her knees)* Yes. You ain't neither of you seen a box, have you? A little wooden box?

TRAVELING MAN. *(Holding out the box)* Is this it?

SCRUB WOMAN. *(With relief)* That's it. *(She takes it and opens it, regarding the contents with satisfaction)* I keep a bit o' hard candy in it for my little grandson. His pa can't afford him no sweets.

TRAVELING MAN. I knew it was yours. I've been saving it for you.

(She smiles and goes out, clutching the box.)

REPORTER. *(In amazement)* Well, I'll be—! But you said it was—

TRAVELING MAN. No. I only said it looked very much like it. It did.

REPORTER. But you knew all the time.

TRAVELING MAN. Yes.

REPORTER. What's the idea? Are you a practical joker or

just plain liar? You don't look like a man who goes around deceiving people.

TRAVELING MAN. There was no deception.

REPORTER. There wasn't! Didn't you make us all believe—

TRAVELING MAN. *(Quietly)* That Divinity visited this hotel tonight and was refused admittance. Which was true. Is there not divinity in every one of us, and are we not therefore all brothers? Wherever there is a human being in need, a human body oppressed, a human soul obscured, there for us is the challenge of the Divine Presence.

REPORTER. *(After a pause, slowly)* You—seem to know a great many things. Who are you, anyway?

TRAVELING MAN. I told you. I'm a traveling man. I used to be—in the hotel business. But I'll have to be leaving you now. I must go up to my room and pack.

REPORTER. You mean you're not staying here for Christmas?

TRAVELING MAN. No. My work here seems to be finished. Good night.

[*He goes out, left.*

REPORTER. *(To himself)* Gosh, what a story! It—it's tremendous! *(Scribbling)* "Well-known Senator the Victim of Supernatural Hoax!" "Noted Poetess and Society Leader Featured in Strange Christmas Eve Joke!" "Bethlehem Again Makes the Headlines!" *(He stops writing, stares thoughtfully into space, then deliberately tears up the paper)* No use, Smith. You can't write about a thing like this. People would laugh and shake their heads and joke about it over their breakfast and—and go right on acting as if nothing had happened. It—it's no good to write. Darn it all, Smith, you've got to do something! *(Rises with determination.)*

BELLBOY. *(Appearing, left)* Line's busy, boss.

REPORTER. *(Rousing)* What's that? My call?

BELLBOY. I say line's busy. Shall I keep on callin'?

REPORTER. *(Staring at him but obviously not seeing him)* No. No, you needn't call. I—I've got to think this thing through. *(Walks thoughtfully)* It's—it's going to mean even more than I thought at first. Being careful, for instance, what sort of stuff I turn out, chasing up the unpopular sides of stories. Even—even doing something right away to help stop that anti-alien bill. *(Lifting his hands to his head in a gesture half dismayed, half exultant)* Gosh, Smith, old boy! You—you haven't even begun to find out what you've let yourself in for!

BELLBOY. Here's your money, boss. Gee, but that New York op'rator sure sounded like home!

REPORTER. *(Looking at the colored boy as if he recognized him for the first time as a human being)* You—you're homesick, aren't you, boy?

BELLBOY. Yeah. *(His voice chokes)* Guess I am, boss. First time I ever been away from home on Christmas. And—and white folks don't somehow treat you like people.

REPORTER. Here! Take this and call your mother up. Wish her a merry Christmas.

BELLBOY. Gee, boss! *(His eyes shine.)*

REPORTER. And after you get through work, come up to my room. I'll get some eats and stuff, and we'll do some celebrating together. I'm all alone, too, and you can make believe I'm your big brother.

BELLBOY. *(Speechless with delight)* Gee, boss—

REPORTER. I didn't say boss. I said—brother.

(He holds out his hand to the Bellboy in a fraternal gesture as the curtain falls.)

It's Easter, Dr. Jordan

or

"...and Try His Works to Do"

by

SHERWOOD KEITH

A four part, reverent, modern Easter story based upon experiences which came to a young graduate nurse and a promising young surgeon.

The lighting is important. The "acting area" should be lighted by spotlights and the remainder of the "set" should be absolutely dark. Into this spotlight the two characters "fade in" and "fade out" (as designated in the dialogue) to denote the reading, the four parts of the play, and the passing of time.

Organ music befitting Easter and the mood of the play may be used to good advantage at the beginning, between each part; and at the conclusion of the play, the hymn, "There Is a Green Hill Far Away," sung by massed choirs and congregation is a suggestion.

Characters:

> JEAN, an attractive nurse
> DOUGLAS, a young doctor, clean-cut, good looking.

SETTING: No scenery required except regular decorations for Easter.

LENGTH: About thirty minutes.

SCENE I
(Ten-second organ prelude.)

JEAN. *(Coming into spotlight)* For some strange reason, it was my lot to stand beside a tall, cool man, at the first roll call and assembly of young internes and student nurses, at the beginning of training at the great San LaFarre Memorial Hospital in the big city. He answered the roll call to the name of Douglas Jordan, with a feeling of great self-confidence, and I was duly impressed. This impression lasted all through the five long years of training, as I worked with him; serving sometimes as his left hand, sometimes as his right hand and even sometimes as both his hands. On a rare Sunday afternoon of our fifth and last year at the hospital, rare because it was Easter Sunday and also because we both had been relieved from duty for the remainder of the day, and had a chance to wear civilian clothes, I met him coming along one of the corridors.

DOUGLAS. *(Entering)* Hello, Jean!

JEAN. Did you have a nice rest?

DOUGLAS. What do you mean?

JEAN. This morning, in Chapel. If you would go to bed nights, you'd be able to stay awake when you should.

DOUGLAS. I wasn't asleep, just doing some heavy thinking, that's all. I was wondering what in the wide world people— Oh, never mind. Say, have you a date for tonight?

JEAN. Not a date, but definitely an engagement.

DOUGLAS. I might have known I'd be too late in asking you out.

JEAN. I'm going to attend the Easter Vesper Service and organ recital.

DOUGLAS. Oh, sure, of course, you've got one on, too.

JEAN. What?

DOUGLAS. A new hat, that's why you're going, isn't it?

JEAN. You mean, to show it off? Do you think that's why I'm going?

DOUGLAS. Well—no—maybe not, but that's what I was thinking about in Chapel, for one thing. Think of the actual millions of dollars spent on clothes for the Easter parade.

JEAN. Are you by any chance giving me a lecture because of this cheap little insignificant bonnet of mine, Mr. Jordan?

DOUGLAS. No—but I do get upset and then some, when I think of the good that those millions would do, if given to churches and hospitals. Think of the clinics, children's clinics that could be in operation. Believe me, when I get out on my own—

JEAN. Are you going to be a minister or a surgeon?

DOUGLAS. I'm serious!

JEAN. I know you are, and I daresay you're right. *(Pause)* Just think, less than three months to go, then the world will know you, not as Mr. Jordan any more, but as Dr. Jordan. I think you'll do right well with that name, too.

DOUGLAS. I intend to do better than that—

JEAN. Conceited!

DOUGLAS. Stop kidding, will you?

JEAN. All right, I'm sorry. Have you made any plans as to what you're going to do, yet?

DOUGLAS. Nothing definite. Of course I'd have to start in practicing in the smallest sort of way, until I can get enough money and recognition together to organize a children's clinic of my own.

JEAN. That would be grand, Doug.

DOUGLAS. What do you mean, would be? It will be grand when I can really get going.

JEAN. It's certainly a praiseworthy ambition.

DOUGLAS. It's something, really the one big aim I've had, to have a clinic of my own some day. When that day arrives, I know I'll be doing a little bit of good for some people and that's all I want.

JEAN. That's all anyone should and could want, isn't it?

DOUGLAS. I suppose so—but look here—what about you?

JEAN. What about me?

DOUGLAS. What are you going to do as a top-ranking graduate nurse?

JEAN. Just this—the best I can and all I can, in my profession, and for it. No particular plans yet.

DOUGLAS. I know, but—

JEAN. There aren't any buts and I must run or I'll be late for Vespers. I'd ask you to run with me if I could be sure you wouldn't go to sleep during the service.

DOUGLAS. No, I guess I'd better not go.

JEAN. What's the matter—afraid you'll see too many new hats?

DOUGLAS. Yes, I guess so, something like that. I—I've got some more thinking to do. Tell you what—I'll meet you by the South gate, near the parsonage, after the service and we can take a walk, maybe.

JEAN. All right, if you'll let me tell you about the service.

'DOUGLAS. Tell me anything you like.

JEAN. Good-bye for now, then—

DOUGLAS. Cheerio!

(They move in opposite directions out of the spotlight. Ten-second organ interlude.)

SCENE II

JEAN. *(Coming into spotlight)* And so it was that, in less than three months, Douglas Jordan, the most professionally talked of interne and certainly by far the most prominent ranking member of his class, was graduated and sent forth into the world, to make it, at least physically speaking, a happier place in which to live, for all those people who were to come to him for advanced surgical help and care. Following graduation, I was immediately sent on a case in the South which proved very confining. It was nearly two years later that I was transferred back to New York and I could once more renew acquaintances with many of my classmates. One of them was carrying a rumor that Dr. Douglas Jordan was in New York to give up the medical profession. There were other tales concerning him, which we all tried hard not to believe. The day before Easter I went out alone to do some shopping. I stopped at an intersection and waited for the lights to change. *(Douglas moves into spotlight)* Hello, stranger! Remember me—you know—the little girl that used to pass you instruments at an operating table?

DOUGLAS. Jean! How are you? Say, but it's great to see you. What are you doing here, in New York, I mean? Where have you been? My, but you look grand! How long have you—

JEAN. Just a minute, not so fast, if you please.

DOUGLAS. Forgive me, I'm sorry, but how are you, anyway?

JEAN. I'm fine, Doug, and you?

DOUGLAS. Me—why I—I'm all right.

JEAN. Are you?

DOUGLAS. Sure, really—but say—how come you're in New York?

JEAN. How about you answering your own question first.

DOUGLAS. You mean, why am I here? *(She nods)* Oh no, that's a long story.

JEAN. It wouldn't be the first long one you've told me.

DOUGLAS. Yes, that is true enough, but—

JEAN. I insist!

DOUGLAS. Well look, have you an engagement? I mean, are you in a hurry?

JEAN. Not especially, just shopping around for a—a few necessities.

DOUGLAS. Necessities? They wouldn't be Easter finery, by any chance, would they?

JEAN. Yes, Dr. Jordan, now that you've asked, I'm looking for a new hat, shoes, gloves, bag, coat, and dress!

DOUGLAS. I see, then perhaps I'd better not detain you further. (Crosses Jean.)

JEAN. Don't be silly, Doug. I'm sorry I spoke so sharply to you, but I didn't like the tone you used on Easter finery, either. Can it be that you're still bitter about the way people spend money for clothes at Easter time?

DOUGLAS. If I am, don't you think I've a right to be? You don't see any new clothes on me, do you? Do you know why?

JEAN. Well—I suppose it's—

DOUGLAS. I'll tell you, then you won't have to suppose any more. It's because I've used my money where I thought it would do some good; every single penny I could scrape together, and believe me they've amounted to precious few. I came out of that hospital, on the day of graduation, with a white scroll clutched in my hand, that I believed meant something. If they had written "the Good Samaritan" on it instead of Dr. Douglas Jordan it couldn't have meant more to me.

JEAN. I know that.

DOUGLAS. I went into a small town on the outskirts of a great city in the Middle West. I rented a two-room flat. I lived in one and had the other turned into my idea of a doctor's office. I had a nice, large sign made, and hung outside, in black and gilt lettering, which read Dr. C. Douglas Jordan, Surgeon. Under that it read Children's Health Clinic. My entire savings had dwindled to $11.53. I had circulars printed, and delivered them at night myself—went from door to door with them.

JEAN. That must have helped considerably.

DOUGLAS. It did. Poor people came in droves to the office, and I took care of them, made them well and happy.

Jean. I'm so glad; that must have made you happy, too.

Douglas. It did, until—

Jean. Until what?

Douglas. *(Bitterly)* Until I found that I was all alone. That no one was behind me, that no one who could pay for an operation or even a treatment ever came near the office. Everything was fine until I had no more pennies and no credit with which to buy medicine and bandages for those poor people who really need help. Do you know something? I even went so far as to sell or pawn every last thing I could possibly do without and many of my instruments, in order to finish cases I had started. Even the black frame for my degree that my roommate at the hospital gave me went for a roll of bandage. Isn't that funny? Why aren't you laughing—the others did!

Jean. When?

Douglas. When I borrowed money to take me to New York.

Jean. You mean, you quit?

Douglas. Quit? Sure I quit. What would you have done?

Jean. I don't know, Doug—I'm sure—but what are you doing now?

Douglas. Looking for a job; know where I can find one?

Jean. Have you been over to the hospital?

Douglas. What would I find there, do you suppose. No, that's not the kind of job I want. One try at that kind is enough. I'm looking for a job that will give me a pay check each week, and perhaps even a thank you, as well.

Jean. You're through with medicine then? You're going to be a traitor to the doctor's oath?

Douglas. I wonder if it's I who would be the traitor after what I've done for others.

Jean. Yes, Doug, it would be you.

Douglas. It's easy for you to talk, Jean; you're on your way to buy yourself clothes for Easter.

Jean. Yes, that's right—and it will do me good. I'll tell you why. At Easter time, a newness of life is almost universal. The Resurrection of Christ symbolizes a newness of spiritual life—the springtime symbolizes a newness of life in nature and in this earthly living. Don't you see what I mean?

Douglas. Yes, I see what *you* mean. That's fine for *you!*

Jean. Oh, give this Easter time a chance to renew your

spirit and your courage, will you? Remember, Dr. Jordan, there are many people still counting on you. Won't you come over for dinner this evening and join the old crowd again? Dr. Rositer and Dr. Williams and Dr. Roberts will be there, and maybe some others.

DOUGLAS. Thanks, Jean, that's very nice of you, but I can't come, not tonight. I have a date with a young lady I've recently met and I think I really should keep it.

JEAN. Of course, and good for you. But do come over and see us soon, won't you?

DOUGLAS. Never can tell. Remember me to the gang anyway, will you?

JEAN. I surely will. Good-bye for now and good luck always, Doug.

DOUGLAS. Yes, thanks, Jean, good-bye.

(Again they walk in opposite directions, out of the spotlight. Organ interlude.)

SCENE III

JEAN. *(Returning into the spotlight)* Shortly after this accidental meeting with Dr. Jordan, it was my good fortune to be sent to Chicago, to assist a noted surgeon and scientist in medical research. I had been there about eight months, when one day Dr. Rositer, a friend of mine and an old chum of Doug's came into the laboratory and we had a fine chat. He told me of Doug's marriage to a very lovely and a very wealthy girl. He also said that Doug has set himself up in a luxurious office on Park Avenue, and at last had an opportunity to do all he'd wanted for others. After that, whenever I'd receive letters from my old friends, there would be glowing reports of his success. I gathered that Dr. Jordan was on his way up the ladder, and I was glad. Three years to a day, since my last meeting with Dr. Jordan, I was walking through a Fifth Avenue shop—I had gone to New York for a short vacation—and I found myself thinking of him, when suddenly—

DOUGLAS. *(Walks across and nearly runs into Jean)* I beg your par—Jean! Is it you, or am I seeing things?

JEAN. Why, it can't be Dr. Jordan. I was just thinking about you.

DOUGLAS. And I was thinking about you, too, not an hour

ago and of our first meeting. It was three years ago this very day, wasn't it?

JEAN. That's right, the day before Easter. How are you? May I still call you Doug, or must the Park Avenue surgeon be addressed only as Dr. Jordan these days?

DOUGLAS. Don't be silly. I'm feeling great, and so are you by the looks.

JEAN. Thank you, I am. Are you still opposed to my getting a new hat for Easter?

DOUGLAS. Certainly not; as a matter of fact, my wife is shopping for the last few necessities to complete her Easter apparel.

JEAN. Did you say necessities?

DOUGLAS. You haven't forgotten the subject of that discussion three years ago, have you?

JEAN. No, I haven't, and Easter necessities was not entirely the subject of our discussion. It was you, I believe.

DOUGLAS. I guess you're right, at that.

JEAN. Things have changed for you since then, haven't they?

DOUGLAS. Most definitely, Jean. I'm sitting on top of the world and have everything anyone could ask for. A lovely wife, a nice home, a swimming pool, servants, two cars and I've just purchased two of the smartest polo ponies you've ever laid eyes on.

JEAN. Have you?—that's fine.

DOUGLAS. You must come out and see them. They cost a small fortune, but they're worth it, genuine thoroughbreds, both of them.

JEAN. Tell me, Doug, how is your clinic going?

DOUGLAS. Clinic? What clinic?

JEAN. Why, the one you always talked about having for poor children? Haven't you established one yet?

DOUGLAS. No, and I guess I never will—too busy now to do anything *well*, what with so many clubs to attend, golf and riding in the mornings, more golf and gymnasium work in the afternoons, and the evening date book is full for months ahead, I notice. It's a pretty mad whirl, but what can I do? You see—

JEAN. Yes, I see. It's too bad you couldn't follow your ambition—in regard to the clinic, I mean. Remember how we all joked with you about that in training?

DOUGLAS. Yeah—I should have joked right along with you, I guess.

JEAN. Oh no! You see, we were really serious. We believed in you, and expected great things. So the joke's on us, after all.

DOUGLAS. Well, I'm where I want to be and I've no time to do any charity work. My office hours are full to overflowing with people who appreciate what's done for them and are willing to pay well for my professional services.

JEAN. Yes, I can well imagine.

DOUGLAS. By the way, Jean, what are you doing?

JEAN. Why, I—

DOUGLAS. What I mean to say is that I always liked your work, and if you'd like I can arrange to have you come into my office as one of the assistant nurses, or I might even put you in as my receptionist. I'm sure we could arrange your salary to suit you, and—

JEAN. Thank you, Doug, but I couldn't possibly. I have an excellent position in Chicago that keeps me busy and happy.

DOUGLAS. Well, I only thought—

JEAN. Of course, and thanks loads.

DOUGLAS. I—er—I wish I could invite you out to dinner some night this coming week, but we're full up I'm afraid—and I don't know whether we have a free night the following week or not, but you must come down to the office, anyhow. Come down tomorrow.

JEAN. Tomorrow's Easter Sunday.

DOUGLAS. I know, but Sunday afternoons are about the only time I get to check up on things. Won't you come?

JEAN. I'm afraid I can't, not tomorrow. The Easter services have always meant a great deal to me. Have you forgotten I always attend them?

DOUGLAS. That's right, you did used to, and then you'd tell me all about them afterwards. I'm going tomorrow morning with my wife, to the church near the hospital.

Jean. Fine, I'm going there, too. I'll look for you. I'd like to meet your wife.

Douglas. Which reminds me that *I've* got to meet her. *(Looks at watch)* I'm late now, so I'm afraid I'll have to say good-bye and run.

Jean. Of course, wives are pretty important. It's been nice to see you again, Doug, even for a minute.

Douglas. It surely has been good to see you; and look, if I shouldn't see you again this trip, let's meet in New York two years from today next time, instead of three.

Jean. All right, it's agreed. You don't need any good luck it appears, so I'll just say good-bye.

Douglas. Good-bye, Jean.

(They cross out of spotlight. Organ interlude.)

Scene IV

Jean. *(Moves into spotlight)* What an unfortunate and terrible experience it is, to lose the respect for someone of whom you once thought a great deal. I shared this experience with many others after this chance meeting with Dr. Jordan. But when a man so loses himself in a completely wrong sense of values, his much needed help must come from our heavenly Father and not from mortal man. Therefore, realizing that I could materially do nothing for him and could give him no more than my earnest, heartfelt prayers, I returned to my position in Chicago. The research was completed nearly two years later. I returned to New York and was immediately placed as head supervisor of nurses on the third floor of the great San LaFarre Memorial Hospital, the institution where I had completed my training seven years ago. *(Douglas moves to edge of spotlight with back to her.)* As was customary there, it was my duty to be the first to greet new patients of that floor. One late afternoon as I approached the waiting room at the end of the main corridor, a man standing at one of the windows turned toward me.

(Douglas turns slowly to face her.)

Douglas. Hello, Jean.

Jean. How do you do.

DOUGLAS. What's the matter, have I changed so appreciably that you don't recognize your old friend Doug Jordan?

JEAN. Douglas Jord—why hello, Doug. Forgive me, it's rather dark in here and for a minute I—

DOUGLAS. Oh, that's all right. I understand. I sent for you. Evidently they didn't tell you.

JEAN. Why—no, they didn't. But what are you doing here? I heard that you'd left New York for a while.

DOUGLAS. And you're surprised to see me back so soon, is that it? In a way I'm surprised to be back myself, and yet there's no place I'd sooner come than the San LaFarre.

JEAN. You mean—

DOUGLAS. Yes, as a patient. A slight heart disorder of some sort, it appears. I'm here for observation for a time.

JEAN. Oh, I'm terribly sorry to hear that.

DOUGLAS. Don't say that, Jean, please.

JEAN. Why, what do you mean? I *am* sorry that—

DOUGLAS. Please! When you say that, it spells pity to me, and believe me I've had enough of that. That's one of the biggest reasons I went away, to get away from people who have been pitying me and feeling sorry for me, even a long time before the tragedy occurred.

JEAN. What tragedy, Doug?

DOUGLAS. Don't you know?

JEAN. Why no, you see I've only been back a short time and I—

DOUGLAS. My wife was trampled and killed by two of my polo ponies.

JEAN. Oh, Doug, when?

DOUGLAS. Five months ago, and she left behind a sickly little year-old baby boy, who finally died, three months ago. I lost my wife and then my son almost together. That was terrible, but that wasn't the tragedy. The tragedy was me, because today I could have my wife and a perfectly normal, healthy son, if I hadn't turned my back on them and on myself. I had to have servants, cars, a polo string and clubs to make me happy. I had to let other people worry and work hard and deprive themselves of things they needed, so that they could pay my exorbitant fees for even my office calls, in order that

I might pay the membership dues at another club. I had to ruin my wife's health, so she was too weak to hold her son, my son, in her arms, to say nothing about trying to hold a couple of excited ponies. Now do you see what I mean by tragedy?

JEAN. But Doctor, I—

DOUGLAS. Doctor! Ah yes, there's the *real* tragedy! I'm a doctor, that's what it says on my degree. Speaking of that, it's hanging in my office in a solid gold frame. I'm afraid that's where the value is now! In the frame, not the degree.

JEAN. Doug, I'm terribly sorry I didn't know about all this before. I might have been of some help.

DOUGLAS. No, Jean, no one could have helped but me, and I failed miserably. You have always tried to help me, but I wouldn't let you or anyone until it was too late. And now no one wants to help me; they're all too busy pitying me. What about you?

JEAN. What *about* me? Do you expect help from me?

DOUGLAS. Well, no, I don't exactly expect help from you and I wouldn't blame you if you refused. It's a little late for me to deserve help from anyone.

JEAN. What sort of help are you looking for, Doug?

DOUGLAS. I don't really know, Jean. I feel away from everything, almost lost.

JEAN. You've lost yourself, haven't you?

DOUGLAS. Lost myself? Yes, I guess that's about it.

JEAN. Then I can't help you; nor can anyone else that you know.

DOUGLAS. What do you mean?

JEAN. I mean just this, that if you've lost yourself, by your own doing, you've got to find yourself, by your own doing. In helping you to accomplish this, there is someone, whom you once knew—I'm afraid you've forgotten Him entirely for a long time—but He is waiting, I'm sure, for you to come to Him and ask His guidance.

DOUGLAS. Who is that, Jean?

JEAN. Oh, Doug, don't be so blind. Have you forgotten or don't you realize that tomorrow is Easter, the day of Christ's resurrection?

DOUGLAS. Do you mean—?

JEAN. Yes, Doug. He is the one, our risen Lord, who can help so very much if you'll only go to Him, if you'll only let Him know by what you do that you really want His care.

DOUGLAS. I—believe you're right. Yes—it's not material, earthly help I need or want, it's something more than all that. But what do I—I mean—how can I let Him know—

JEAN. That you need him? Pray to Him, Doug, and live the kind of life that Douglas Jordan as an interne lived, right here in this hospital. You can, if you will. It's never too late.

DOUGLAS. Thank you, Jean, I'll try to think through what you've said today.

JEAN. Good for you. Now I must go. The nurse will show you to your room right away. Good night, Dr. Jordan. By the way, there's a Bible on the night table by your bed.

DOUGLAS. Good-night, Jean, and thanks again. (*Jean moves out of spotlight. Douglas pauses a moment, then faces the audience.*) The nurse showed me to my room which overlooked the East River and beyond, and then brought in my supper tray. She returned for it shortly after, then she said good-night and I was left alone. I picked up the Bible from my night table and fingered through it. Every now and then I would stumble on certain passages that were once familiar to me. Then I drowsed and my whole life seemed to pass in review, and I was deeply shaken. With the first ray of morning light, I awakened to find the Bible still clutched in my hand. I arose to take notice of a passing tugboat on the river. How quietly and serenely it moved. The night street lamps went out on the Queens Bridge and on both sides of the river. All at once a great calm seemed to overtake me as I watched the Easter dawn and then the sun arise into the heavens, making the swirling waters sparkle in blue and gold. I was caught spellbound and felt a strange newness of spirit stir within me. (*Organ plays very softly one verse of "There Is a Green Hill Far Away."*) Suddenly from the distance an organ was playing, and I realized the student nurses were at early morning Chapel. (*As the organ begins the second time, Douglas quietly, and more or less to himself, begins first to hum the hymn with the organ, then gradually sings the words. The organ stops playing and after a pause Douglas says)*—And try his works to do—

JEAN. *(Moving into the spotlight)* Good-morning. It's Easter, Dr. Jordan.

DOUGLAS. Yes, Jean, it's Easter!

JEAN. How do you feel this morning?

DOUGLAS. How do I feel? I wish there were words that could tell you and everyone how I feel.

JEAN. Like a new man?

DOUGLAS. Yes, Jean, like a new man, not only physically but mentally and spiritually as well. And I'd like to do something now, if I may. It's been a long time since I offered a prayer, but maybe if you're here with me, well at least I can try—*(Douglas kneels on one knee facing audience. Jean stands close behind and to his side and puts her hand on his shoulder. She bows her head as Douglas with head high prays.)* Our Heavenly Father, I come to Thee this day and humbly offer myself, Thy poor wretched servant, into Thy keeping. May it be Thy will to forgive the wrong and sin I have committed. Give to me, oh God, the newness of spiritual life, which this day commends and may I, with Thy loving care, go out into the world to give help and to teach men the lesson of Thy Son's resurrection even as I have learned it. I pray that I may be worthy again of the oath of my profession. Give me Thy richest blessing and the boundless strength and opportunities, that I may in this newness of life that is mine always and ever —try Thy works to do, for the honor and glory of Thy Son, our Lord Jesus Christ. I ask it in His name. Amen.

JEAN. Amen. *(After a brief pause Douglas rises, turns to Jean and as she holds out her hands to Douglas.)* That was a fine prayer, Doug, and I know that from now on I shall be terribly proud of Dr. Jordan.

DOUGLAS. I meant it, Jean; thanks to you for showing me the way.

JEAN. I think it is Easter that has shown you the way to God.

DOUGLAS. Then from now on every day shall be Easter, not only for Dr. Jordan himself, but for all those little children who visit his new clinic.

JEAN. Clinic? You mean, Doug, you're actually going to have one?

DOUGLAS. Yes, Jean, I really want that children's clinic now.

JEAN. Oh, it really is Easter, Dr. Jordan.

(Douglas and Jean take each other's hand, and as they face the audience and step back two or three paces, the organ plays an introduction to the hymn, "There Is a Green Hill Far Away." This is the cue for the massed choirs and congregation to rise and join with Douglas and Jean in the singing of the first verse. At its conclusion the play ends.)

CURTAIN

The Symbol of a Cross

A Religious Drama

by

MATTIE B. SHANNON

Characters:

ABDIEL, a carpenter. A man of about forty. He has a strong body and a thoughtful face.

PATRICIA, his wife. A beautiful Greek woman who feels she has married beneath her station in life and longs for wealth and position.

LOIS, their daughter. A girl of about twenty years, lovely in body and spirit.

REUBEN, their son. He is about eighteen years old. An easily led, impulsive lad who is a helper in his father's shop.

CHLOE, a maid servant.

CAIUS, a Roman official.

PHILLIP, a disciple of Jesus. Young and with a strong, forceful manner.

LENGTH: About twenty minutes.

SCENE I

TIME: A spring morning in the year A.D. 30.

SCENE: A small garden just outside the shop and home of Abdiel, the carpenter.

(The little garden is bright with sunshine and fragrant with spring flowers. Chloe enters from the right. When she is about center, Patricia enters at right and calls sharply.)

PATRICIA. Chloe!

(Chloe pauses with a frightened start and turns, facing Patricia.)

PATRICIA. Must I rush through the house and shop after you because you either do not listen or do not care to obey my commands?

CHLOE. *(Apologetically)* I beg—

PATRICIA. Aye. You are ready enough of tongue when it is time for excuses. Tell me, did you not hear me say that we are expecting a visit from a Roman official this morning and I wish everything to be tidy?

CHLOE. I am now on my way to get the water jars and—

PATRICIA. Why are you so late going to the well?

CHLOE. I but stopped a few moments to help Lois with her task.

PATRICIA. And is serving my daughter Lois more important than serving me? Go back into the house and fix the rugs as I bade you and then go to the well.

(Chloe bows, turns and hurries through exit at right. Patricia turns as Reuben enters from the right.)

REUBEN. *(Smiling)* Well, my dear mother, what brings the frown of displeasure to your brow so early this morning?

PATRICIA. The stupidness of a village servant!

REUBEN. *(Putting his arm around Patricia and leading her to the bench where they are seated)* Come, my mother! I doubt if there be a carpenter's wife in Jerusalem or all this country around about who has even a village servant!

PATRICIA. You know it is only because I am not strong and the girl was a waif whom your father would befriend. Let me tell you this; if your father spent less time dreaming he is a craftsman in wood and thought more of material things I might have a slave from Jerusalem.

REUBEN. *(Patting Patricia's hand)* Mother, you know father is really more than just a carpenter. He has the soul of an artist. And did he not win the award? Did not his model of a cross win—although many of them were placed before the mighty Pilate for his approval?

PATRICIA. Aye. But did I not spend hours persuading him to make the model?

REUBEN. Aye. But now it seems to me that you are assured of a regular income. *(Rising and mocking the manner of the expected Roman official, his head thrown back and his hand at his chest.)* This very morning Caius, the great official from the court of Pilate, visits this humble home to receive the signature of Abdiel; a signature to a contract in which Abdiel promises to make the crosses for the punishment of Rome's criminals during the year. That, my mother, should provide some ready gold. *(Footsteps are heard just outside the entrance at right and Reuben turns, facing the right as he bows)* And here is the master carpenter now! *(Abdiel enters and pauses just inside right entrance. He smiles at his wife and son but his face immediately resumes its expression of thoughtfulness.)*

REUBEN. Have you come here to wait in the garden, father? 'Tis a much more pleasant place than the musty old shop.

ABDIEL. I will wait here for a short while, my son.

REUBEN. Well, I will hurry and do the errand you gave me. I hope I will be back in time to look upon the grandeur of Rome when Caius arrives in all his glory.

(Reuben exits at left. Abdiel moves to the bench and is seated at left of bench, facing toward the shop which is visioned just off the platform at the right.)

ABDIEL. *(Sighing deeply)* I seem not to be able to work until this matter is settled.

PATRICIA. And pray what do you mean by that statement, Abdiel? The matter is settled. You won the contract. Caius brings the parchment for your signature this morning. That's all there is to it.

ABDIEL. Nay, my wife. That is not all. To me it is not all. Signing that contract means that day after day I will labor with no joy in my task; with no pleasant thoughts as I run the adz over the rough wood and vision what my hands will create from it. I—

PATRICIA. It should be pleasant to think of the gold that will be yours. It should be pleasant to think that your wife and children may have a few luxuries. There is an added advantage in this work; you cannot *give* the crosses away. I happen to know that is what you have done with many things you have made in the past.

ABDIEL. But, my dear wife, it was real happiness to give a chest to a little maid in which she might keep her bridal clothes and to present a box to a young widow that she might place therein the treasures of her loved one who had passed beyond.

PATRICIA. Well, you will have no time for such generosity now. When one contracts with Rome, one lives up to the letter of the law.

ABDIEL. Aye. I know.

PATRICIA. You must have ambition, Abdiel. You will become well known. You will be asked to make articles even for the palace. You will have to employ help. You will be the richest carpenter in or near Jerusalem. Think how fine it will be;—wealthy like Marius who had the contract these many years and now—he needs to work no more. Think of it, Abdiel!

ABDIEL. *(Not unpleasantly)* I need not think of that, my wife. You do it for me.

PATRICIA. *(Tossing her head)* 'Tis well that someone in this family thinks of those things!

ABDIEL. *(Placing his hand over hers)* You are a good wife to me, Patricia. Perhaps I am just a dreamer. *(He rises and stands, looking off right)* I have been so happy in that little shop, making things to help people to live; lintels for village houses, cradles for new babies, benches, tables—and sometimes, toys for the little ones to whom Lois loves to tell stories. And now—I must make crosses on which people will *die*. I—

(As he stands, looking off right, his expression changes and he becomes quiet. Patricia looks at him questioningly.)

PATRICIA. What is it, Abdiel? You look—

ABDIEL. Someone has entered the shop and I—

PATRICIA. *(Straightening her headdress)* Is it Caius?

ABDIEL. Nay. *(Moving forward toward the right)* 'Tis a young man who wears the simple robe of a peasant. I will inquire what he wishes.

PATRICIA. Oh, a *peasant!* Well, dear Abdiel, I beg you, do not promise to carve him a gift, no matter what his need. You are now master carpenter to Rome and will have no time except for the making of what Rome desires.

(Abdiel moves off platform at the right. Patricia rises, straightens her draperies and is about to move forward when Lois enters from the left. Lois is smiling sweetly and her head is bowed as though she is thinking deeply. She does not see her mother at first and is startled when Patricia speaks.)

PATRICIA. Well, Lois!

LOIS. *(Turning toward Patricia who resumes her seat on the bench)* Oh, mother, I was thinking so deeply that I did not see you! I—*(She moves toward her mother)* Oh, mother dear, something wonderful has happened to me this morning!

PATRICIA. Perhaps you have seen Phillip of Bethsaida?

LOIS. No, mother. I have not seen Phillip although I have heard that he is near. Mother, I can find no words in which to tell you. I—*I have seen Jesus!*

PATRICIA. And is it so wonderful that you have looked upon a carpenter from Nazareth?

LOIS. Why, Mother, you have heard me say how I have *longed* to see Him! You know how Phillip has told me of Him. You know that I believe Him to be the promised Messiah. *(She goes to Patricia and is seated beside her)* May I tell you what happened, Mother?

PATRICIA. *(Coldly)* My child, as your mother I have never refused to listen to anything you have had to tell me but this has no interest for me. Even were I not a Greek and if I had been trained in matters of your father's religion, I fail to see how this Man—this simple village Carpenter—could be your Messiah.

LOIS. I know how you feel, Mother. Did I not have the very same feeling of distrust and unbelief when—*(She pauses, overcome with emotion.)*

PATRICIA. I will finish for you. You had the same feeling when Phillip, who had already asked your Father for your hand in marriage, left all to follow—this Nazarene. An impossible happening!

LOIS. I know, Mother. So it seemed to me at the time and I was very hurt, even doubting if Phillip really loved me but now—

PATRICIA. Aye? Now?

LOIS. *(With quiet intensity of feeling) Now I know Phillip is right!* Phillip and I may have our happiness sometime but now—Jesus *needs* Phillip and he must serve the Master.

PATRICIA. My child, how can you get beyond the fact that this Man is a Carpenter from Nazareth?

LOIS. Mother, when Phillip saw and heard Jesus, he believed in Him. Phillip found Nathanael and said unto him, "We have found him, of whom Moses in the law, and the prophets did write, Jesus of Nazareth."

And Nathanael said, "Can any good thing come out of Nazareth?" Phillip said, *"Come and see."*

Mother, Phillip and Nathanael followed Jesus because they

have truly seen Him — seen Him as He is — *the promised
Messiah.* *(She rises in intensity of emotion and moves to
center.)* I, too, have seen Him! I do know.

(She turns toward Patricia.) It seemed at first so simple a
happening. I was sitting with the children in the field, near
to the Bethany road. He passed by. The children had been
clamoring for a story. Suddenly they were quiet. Rising, they
pressed close to the Stranger who seemed to draw them with
invisible chords of love. Tenderly He touched their heads,
while His eyes smiled into mine. Young Timothy, standing
near me, whispered, "It is *Jesus!* I saw Him yesterday."

So sweetly Jesus spoke to us, talking of God as a kind,
heavenly Father, Who loves us as His children.

PATRICIA. A strange doctrine! Greece has no such god.

LOIS. Strange—but very comforting. For the first time since
Phillip left me there is a sense of peace in my heart. I have
seen neither signs nor wonders. I have not witnessed the
miracles of which they tell but I—I *have seen Jesus!* I understand why Phillip left all to follow Him. I understand *now.*

PATRICIA. You have always been a strange child; a dreamer
like your father. As sensitive of soul as he who dislikes to
make crosses for which Rome will pay him well because—
bah! his reasons are too silly!

LOIS. Mother, I understand my father's thoughts. I would
not like to make crosses. They are forever the symbols of sin
and suffering.

PATRICIA. To me it is but silly reasoning. Your father will
be paid well in the gold of Rome.

LOIS. *(Looking toward the right)* Here comes Father now!
*(She moves toward Abdiel who enters from the right, with a
smiling face and extended hands)* O Father, I have much to
tell you! I—*(looking up into Abdiel's face)* What is it, Father?
You look perplexed.

ABDIEL. *(Taking her hands in both of his)* I have had a
strange visitor—a young man of perhaps thirty—and he has
given me reason for thought. He was a carpenter.

LOIS. A *carpenter?*

ABDIEL. Aye. We talked together of our trade. Somehow
—my heart was opened to him. I even told him of this contract with Rome and—

PATRICIA. You discussed it with a passing peasant?

ABDIEL. *(Quietly)* He was not a common peasant. He was of the line of David, and, somehow, the simple things he told me have sunk deeply into my remembrance. It is as though I could never forget them.

(Lois' face expresses joy.)

I was thinking of the gold the contract with Rome would bring me, and, as though to read my thoughts, the Stranger softly said, "Lay not up for yourself treasures on earth, where moth and rust do corrupt, and where thieves break through and steal:

But lay up for yourself treasures in heaven, where moth and rust do not corrupt, and where thieves do not break through and steal:

For where your treasure is, there will your heart be also."

LOIS. Father, that Stranger was—*Jesus! I know it.*

ABDIEL. *Jesus! Aye. I believe it!* The One I have longed to see. I knew it was so wonderful a Man. It *was* Jesus!

LOIS. It must be so, father. I met Him just a while ago and—

ABDIEL. Aye. It was. I know it. Did not my heart burn within me as we talked. *(Chloe enters from the right.)*

CHLOE. Your pardon, my master. The Roman official is here.

(Chloe is immediately followed by Caius who enters in a quick, arrogant manner. Patricia rises and all turn, facing him.)

CAIUS. *(Extending a parchment roll toward Abdiel)* Here, Abdiel, is the contract. I have no time for loitering. Sign it.

ABDIEL. I—*(He hesitates but seems to gain confidence)* I appreciate the honor but—kindly say to Pilate that I do not care to sign the contract.

PATRICIA. *Abdiel!*

CAIUS. *(In great anger)* You dog of a Jew. So! You spurn the favor of Rome. I could hang you on the very cross you have made!

ABDIEL. I mean no offense, I assure you. I mean no offense to Pilate nor to Rome. The cross I made is yours but I—I care not to make others. I care not to make crosses.

CAIUS. *(Throwing the parchment at the feet of Abdiel)* So!

See to it that you do not starve of your impudence. "I care not to make crosses!" Bah!

(Turning quickly, Caius stamps through the right exit.)

PATRICIA. *(Moving forward to Abdiel who stands at center front)* Abdiel, have you lost your reason? Is your mind completely gone?

ABDIEL. *(Strongly)* Nay. I have found my reason and my mind is clear. I have seen Jesus. I care not to help men to *die*. Hereafter I will be busy helping them to *live*.

SCENE II

TIME: Sunday afternoon, April 9, A.D. 30.
SCENE: The same.

(Patricia is seated on the bench at center. Lois enters from the left.)

LOIS. Oh, my mother, I have heard such strange rumors in the village; rumors that Jesus' enemies are plotting against Him and that He is to be taken.

PATRICIA. *(Showing little interest)* And why should that trouble you? What is this Jesus to you?

LOIS. *(Going toward Patricia with extended hands)* Mother! He is our Messiah! You know that is what we must believe.

PATRICIA. If He indeed be the Chosen of your God, Jehovah, surely naught can harm Him.

LOIS. *(Sitting beside Patricia and taking her hand)* It all seems so—so *strange*. Oh, I wish I might talk with Phillip! I wish father and Reuben would return. It is unusual for them to stay in the city after the Feast of Passover. I do so long for news.

PATRICIA. The news will come in good time. Your father and Reuben are visiting in your Uncle's home. *(Looking down at Lois' arms)* Lois, where are the two bracelets your Uncle sent you; the ones he purchased in Greece. You did not give them to me to place in the box and you are not wearing them. They are too valuable to let lie around.

LOIS. *(Hesitatingly)* Mother, they were mine, were they not? Truly mine?

PATRICIA. What a strange question! Your Uncle gave them to you. Of course they are yours.

LOIS. Mother, it is hard to tell you this. I meant to tell you before. I—I was not unappreciative of my Uncle's gift but—mother, Phillip told me of the great work that Jesus and His disciples do among the sick and needy and so—well, I gave Reuben the bracelets and asked him to give them to Jesus while he was in Jerusalem.

PATRICIA. *(Rising angrily)* So! What next! Am I indeed possessed of a family that—

LOIS. *(Rising also)* Mother, I beg you, do not be angry. I must help Jesus. I *must.*

PATRICIA. What strange power does this Man possess? Is He a conjurer—a hypnotist? Your father talks to Him and will not make crosses for the gold of Rome. You speak with Him and send Him the only valuable things this family owns. Are you both *mad?*

LOIS. Nay, mother. Believe me, we are only trying to put first things first, according to the teaching of the Master. Phillip has told me so much of His teaching and since I have seen Jesus all these things of which I have heard return to me.

PATRICIA. Strange teaching, indeed! It leads you to give your bracelets to help get a throne for a Galilean Carpenter. *(Her voice rises)* Your Uncle must be told what has become of your Grecian bracelets.

(Reuben and Abdiel have entered from the left, unseen by Patricia and Lois. As Patricia ends the foregoing speech, Reuben steps forward, holding the bracelets in his extended hand.)

REUBEN. *(In dull, lifeless tones)* The bracelets are here, mother.

PATRICIA. *Here?* At least one member of the family has understanding.

LOIS. *(Going forward)* Oh, Reuben, why did you not give them to Jesus?

REUBEN. *(Clenching his hands over the bracelets)* The Christ is *dead!*

LOIS. *Dead?* The Christ is *dead? (Turning to Abdiel who stands with bowed head)* Father, tell me it isn't true! It *can't* be true!

ABDIEL. *(Taking her hands in his)* I wish I could deny it, child. It is indeed true. I—I saw Him crucified on Calvary.

LOIS. *(Moving back until she sits on the bench at rear)*
Dead. Dead. *Jesus.* How can it be? And *crucified,* did you
say, father?

ABDIEL. Aye, my child.

LOIS. How *could* they do that to Him? And *who,* father?

ABDIEL. The chief priests and scribes plotted against Him,
fearing His power with the common people. Judas Iscariot
betrayed Him.

LOIS. Oh!

ABDIEL. He was arrested. He was taken before Annas,
Caiaphas, and then Pilate, charged with blasphemy. He made
no defense.

PATRICIA. Pray, what defense could He make? It was common knowledge that—

REUBEN. Mother, I beg that you speak no further. Strange
things have happened and stranger things may yet happen.

PATRICIA. *(Rising) You,* too, my son? Surely your belief
in this Man is gone *now.* He has died as a *criminal.*

REUBEN. There is much that we cannot understand but
let me tell you this; were it not for this Man, your *son* would
be a *criminal*—a *thief.*

ABDIEL. Aye. Tell your mother, my son.

PATRICIA. *(Sitting as before) What?* My *son*— a *thief?* No!
*(Abdiel moves to bench and is seated beside Patricia, placing
    his hand over her clenched ones.)*

REUBEN. I am *not* a thief, mother, but—were it not for this
Jesus, I should have been—*just that!* There were two thieves
who hung beside Jesus on Calvary.

PATRICIA. *(Sobbingly)* Oh!

REUBEN. *(Turning toward Lois)* Sister dear, try to understand as I tell this. *(Lois smiles tearfully at him)* You know
that I shared our dear mother's bitterness of heart when father
refused to sign the contract for the making of Rome's crosses.
It seemed so easy a way to make gold. I brooded over it. I—I
felt angry with you because you seemed to appreciate the
stand father had taken and I—well, when you gave me the
bracelets to take to Jesus—*(he pauses, finding it hard to proceed.)*

LOIS. *(Softly)* Yes, Reuben? When I gave you the bracelets
for Jesus?—

REUBEN. I determined to sell them and keep the money. I—

PATRICIA. *(With a sob)* My son!

REUBEN. *(Giving his mother a tender look)* I found a man who would buy them and made arrangements to meet him. I heard rumors of Jesus being taken. I gave it little thought —*then*. Three days ago I left father at my Uncle's and raced across Jerusalem to meet the man at the city gate. The city was filled with confusion. Crowds had gathered. Jostling crowds. Suddenly I wished to see what they were seeing. My hands clenching the bracelets, I pushed through the mob. I heard a man say, "Ha! The Galilean King goes to be crowned on Calvary!" And—suddenly, I *saw Jesus*. He was stumbling along the dusty road bowed beneath the weight of a—cross. He turned and seemed to look straight at me. I remembered, —in a second, it seemed—all that I had heard of Him. As He looked into my eyes, I felt *cleansed*.

LOIS. Oh, Reuben!

REUBEN. *(Very intensely)* I sank into the dust of the roadside. I held the bracelets toward Him, scarcely realizing what I was doing, but knowing, deep in my soul, that I could not be a thief.

He smiled at me. I heard Him say softly, "You *have* given me a gift—*the gift of repentance.*"

PATRICIA. He *knew?*

REUBEN. Aye. He seemed to read my very soul. A soldier cried out, "Move along, you King of the Jews!" And then—I followed Jesus to Calvary. *(Lois is sobbing softly. Patricia sits with bowed head. Reuben moves toward the left and Abdiel rises and moves toward the center as he speaks to Reuben.)*

ABDIEL. My son, I know your heart is heavy as are all the hearts of those who loved and believed in the Master but I tell you this; a temptation *overcome* strengthens the soul. Grieve not because of the temptation but rather glory in the fact that you were able to overcome through the strange power of Jesus. In His eyes was the truth that called men to perfect manhood. He had something that brought people joy even in the midst of poverty and suffering. What was it?

LOIS. My dear father, was it not *faith in the power of a divine being* that Jesus gave us? Shall we not think of that even though He is dead?

(As she is speaking Phillip enters from the left. His face is bright with joy.)

PHILLIP. *(With hands extended toward the group)* Nay! Jesus is not dead! *Jesus lives!*

(Patricia, Abdiel, and Reuben face Phillip. Lois runs to him, taking his hands in hers.)

ABDIEL. What, Phillip? What say you?

LOIS. *Jesus lives?*

PHILLIP. Aye. He lives. He lives again.

ABDIEL. Praise be to Jehovah!

LOIS. Oh, Phillip, He has shown His power! *(Turning her head toward Patricia who has not joined the group at center)* Do you hear, mother? *Jesus lives again!*

PATRICIA. And no doubt we are listening to an idle tale.

PHILLIP. Not so, my friends! Jesus has been *seen, alive!*

LOIS. Tell us of it, Phillip.

PHILLIP. The women with spices sought the garden early. They found the stone away from the door of the tomb. They met Jesus alive and worshipped at His feet.

ABDIEL. Praise be to God!

PHILLIP. There was an angel at the tomb.

LOIS. An angel?

PHILLIP. Aye. An angel with a message that we would see the Master in Galilee! Come, Abdiel! Come, Reuben! We must find the disciples and seek our Lord!

ABDIEL. I will come at once. *(Turning to Reuben who has stood quietly listening to all that has occurred)* Reuben, are you not coming with us?

REUBEN. *(Looking at his father with a strange expression)* I cannot come. You know not all.

ABDIEL. What can you mean, my son? This is not the time for hesitation. What disturbs you when our hearts are filled with joy unspeakable?

REUBEN. 'Tis hard to tell of it.

ABDIEL. Speak, my son.

REUBEN. 'Tis this, father. 'Tis—the cross on which Jesus died was made by *you and me.*

ABDIEL. *(Tenderly)* My son, grief and worry have upset you. How *could* you know that?

REUBEN. I *do* know it.

PHILLIP. But *how,* Reuben?

(Abdiel moves close to Reuben and places his arm across Reuben's shoulder.)

REUBEN. The morning Caius came for the cross I was in the shop early. *(Looking up into Abdiel's face)* I had a strong feeling of pride because the cross I helped you make had won the contract, father. I thought of the many others we would make for the gold of Rome. Suddenly, as I moved my hands over the wood, I remembered how many artisans place their mark on things they make and so I—

ABDIEL. You *marked* that cross?

REUBEN. Aye, father. Where the upright and the cross beam met I carved a symbol, a small cross, deep into the wood. *(His hand presses against his eyes.)* Father, the cross Jesus carried to Calvary bore that mark. I saw it. *(A sob chokes his words)* I saw it as I stood by the roadside and He— *(He turns, walking toward the rear. Abdiel turns also, his head bowed.)*

ABDIEL. I *made His cross; the Master's cross.* Oh, Jesus, forgive me! *(Turning to Phillip)* Go, Phillip, I cannot go with you to seek the Christ whose cross I made.

PHILLIP. *(Placing his hand on the shoulder of Abdiel)* Nay, my friend. You did not make His cross. I know that. All of us who sinned, who betrayed, who denied, even we who were indifferent to His message—*we made His cross!* But hear you this—*I know we are forgiven. If we are repentant. The cross is to be forevermore a symbol of divine love and forgiveness.* Did not the angel mention Peter especially? It was this the women told. The angel said, "Tell the disciples—*and Peter* that He goeth before you into Galilee." And Peter—*denied Him.*

ABDIEL. *(Facing front and standing at center)* Is it indeed so? I see it now! Jesus has shown His power, not only over death, but His power to forgive sin. Truly He is the Son of God!

PHILLIP. Aye. And He is the way to life everlasting.

PATRICIA. *(Moving to center and standing beside Abdiel, almost overcome with emotion)* If He be truly risen, I—I, too, believe!

THE END

The Cloth of Sendony

An Easter Play

by

ELIZABETH H. EMERSON

Characters:

JOSEPH OF ARIMATHAEA, *a wealthy Jew in the prime of life, a collector of rare cloth, a member of the Sanhedrin.*

SUSANNAH, *niece of Joseph, of marriageable age.*

DAVID, *a friend of Susannah's, who comes into great wealth.*

NICODEMUS, *a Pharisee, member of the Sanhedrin, an old man.*

JAIRUS, *a synagogue ruler from Galilee.*

JUDITH, *his twelve-year-old daughter.*

SERVANT, *in the house of Joseph.*

MESSENGER *from Caiaphas, the high priest.*

THREE TO FIVE PRIESTS, *the temple guard.*

SCENE: A room in the home of Joseph of Arimathaea, just outside Jerusalem.

TIME: Passion Week.

LENGTH: Three acts. About one hour.

ACT I

Scene 1

TIME: *Saturday night before the Passover.*

(Susannah is seated on a stool and is doing needlework. She is a beautiful girl and is dressed in a richly embroidered costume. Joseph, also richly garbed, enters and stops inside the doorway, looking at Susannah as if he enjoys the picture. He carries carefully the Cloth of Sendony.)

JOSEPH. Thou are working again, Susannah? Why dull thy bright eyes and prick thy dainty fingers? If thou art lacking in fine pieces for the home thou wilt call thine own some day, why, it may be I'll give thee this. *(His eyes shine and he handles the cloth as if he loves it very much.)*

SUSANNAH. Oh, Uncle, may I see? *(He spreads it over her lap)* Where didst thou find such a prize?

JOSEPH. Long ago in Arimathaea I bought it, and a pretty price I paid for it, too. How it came into the possession of the maid who sold it to me I do not know, but I believe it came originally from India. "Cloth of Sendony," they call it. Threads of gold are woven with fine linen. *(He feels its texture.)*

SUSANNAH. But I have never seen it before.

JOSEPH. I have kept it well hidden, I assure thee. Such pieces become more valuable with each passing day. Strange, is it not, that I, who have gone everywhere looking for the best, should find my greatest treasure at my very door?

SUSANNAH. Is it really finer than all the others?

JOSEPH. I count it so, and, although I would not have thee repeat what I speak, there is none wise enough in the knowledge of cloth to dispute my word.

SUSANNAH. *(Lifting it in her hands)* Oh, it is lovely, Uncle. What is to be its use?

JOSEPH. I do not know that it has one, unless beauty be a use. But I have thought that I might find no better thing to do with it than to bestow it upon my niece on the day she weds.

SUSANNAH. Oh, no, Uncle, already my chests are full of the beautiful things thou hast brought to me from all over the world. This should serve some nobler purpose.

JOSEPH. I doubt if there be one.

SUSANNAH. *(Confused)* My betrothal may be long in coming, Uncle.

JOSEPH. Not if David has his way.

SUSANNAH. He hath not spoken to thee?

JOSEPH. Not in words, but I can read the signs.

SUSANNAH. Uncle! Thou art not anxious to have me leave thee?

JOSEPH. Ah, my child, that will be a sad hour for thy uncle, and I do not wish to hasten it. Thou art as a daughter to me, Susannah. *(He takes the cloth and drapes it over the chest at the back of stage, so that it falls in graceful folds, being careful that it does not touch the floor. He returns to a seat near Susannah.)*

SUSANNAH. And thou art a father to me, for I have never known any other. Always I have held thee first of kin, even when I was a little child and thou didst live among thy vineyards and olive orchards in Arimathaea. I loved to visit in thy home when the luscious grapes ripened and the smell of the sweet wine was in the air. How are the vineyards now, Uncle?

JOSEPH. They are the same as then, but now they are cared for by a steward. I do not often go to Arimathaea. Once a year, perhaps. The steward tends the vines, prunes the olive trees, employs the pickers, pays the wages, oversees the wine-press, and, when the season is over, sends the profits to me. Ah, Susannah, it is those very vineyards and orchards that make it possible for us to enjoy such a home as this; to purchase pieces of cloth like this; to delight my eye with the most skillful work of men's hands.

SUSANNAH. Always I am in the homes of the wealthy. Either I am with thee here, or I am with my Aunt Joanna in Tiberias. Her home is like a palace.

JOSEPH. And well it may be. King Herod is generous to his stewards and Joanna's husband is a favorite steward, I understand. But I could never see why a woman of Joanna's standing would follow Jesus of Nazareth about Galilee.

SUSANNAH. There were many in the company.

JOSEPH. But they were not of her station.

SUSANNAH. They were of all kinds.

JOSEPH. So I learned. Joanna should not have taken thee into such a company, even if she, herself, must go. I have never told thee, Susannah, but it was for this reason that I went to Galilee to bring thee here. When I learned that the notorious Mary of Magdala was actually in the same company with my sister's child, following a wonder-worker about Galilee, I lost no time in going for thee and bringing thee here.

SUSANNAH. (Resuming her needlework and becoming reflective) My aunt Joanna meant no wrong in taking me with her, and I cannot think that she did a wrong, Uncle, for during that time I learned a great deal. It is something I cannot explain, but to be in the presence of Jesus of Nazareth day after day, to see the way his love for the people seemed to make him able to help them, to hear him telling stories at the close of day—Oh, Uncle, it was truly wonderful and I shall never forget it!

JOSEPH. But I am glad I have thee safely here. Thou art young. Jesus has stirred up much opposition. Either he has made extravagant claims for himself, or his friends have made them for him. There is such hatred of him that even the Pharisees and the Sadducees are consulting about the best way to bring charges against him.

SUSANNAH. But he has not been in Jerusalem for many months.

JOSEPH. Not since the festival of Tabernacles. But it was not the fault of our ruling body that they did not arrest him then. And since that time they have been seeking him out and laying traps for him. I hope that he may be too keen for them, for I cannot see that he does harm. But it is a time for us to remain quiet and to keep well out of any disturbance that may come.

(*Enter* Servant.)

SERVANT. A messenger, master.

JOSEPH. From whom, pray? Dost thou know him?

SERVANT. Sir, he looks the same that once came from thy steward in Arimathaea.

JOSEPH. Ah, some trouble brewing. Send him within. No, I shall speak to him outside.

(Joseph *leaves and the Servant follows, but returns at once.*)

SERVANT. A guest is waiting.

SUSANNAH. A stranger?

SERVANT. I have admitted him often.

SUSANNAH. Admit him now.

(Servant *opens the door and admits* David. *He is a hand-some youth, very gracious in manner. As the* Servant *leaves,* Susannah *rises and takes a step toward David.*)

DAVID. Peace be unto thee.

SUSANNAH. Ah, David, it is thou. My uncle hath but stepped outside to speak with a messenger. Didst thou not see him?

DAVID. (*Bowing and standing at a respectful distance*) I saw him, Susannah, and he promised soon to join me here.

But I can endure the delay. Moments alone with thee are rare. And I must tell thee—I have good news.

SUSANNAH. Good news for me, David?

DAVID. I hope thou wilt take it so. But it is to thy uncle I should rightly speak. Ah, he is here.

(Joseph enters. He goes to David and kisses him first upon the left cheek and then the right.)

JOSEPH. Thou art welcome, David.

SUSANNAH. *(Picking up her work and going out)* David wishes to speak with thee, Uncle.

(Both men stand looking after Susannah.)

DAVID. It is of Susannah I would speak to thee. Since I have no near of kin to represent me, I myself must come. For many months I have desired to ask for her in marriage. But with nothing to offer save my good name—

JOSEPH. Thy name is indeed above reproach. I knew thy father well.

DAVID. A great fear has consumed me—a fear lest some other step in before me, taking the fairest of women from me—

JOSEPH. My wealth is sufficient—

DAVID. But now all is different, for I have received an inheritance. My dead father's brother lived for many years in Rome. He had great wealth, but he was not blessed with offspring. I am his first of kin, and he has left his riches to me. If I have found favor in thy eyes, there is no need for further delay. I can give to thy niece a home such as this and a life suited to a relative of the great Joseph.

JOSEPH. This is, indeed, good news. Thou are a worthy youth, and to thee I can safely intrust Susannah, who is to me as a dearly beloved daughter. When the Passover season has passed, come to me for the betrothal vows. But stay, thinkst thou Susannah dost favor thee?

DAVID. For answer to that question which has long tormented me, I have only the light in her eyes and the smile with which she greets me.

JOSEPH. I think that thou hast judged rightly, David.

DAVID. Thy words bring happiness to my heart. After the Passover I shall see thee again. *(He bows, placing his hand upon his heart)* Peace be with thee.

JOSEPH. And with thee, my son.

(David *leaves and* Joseph *takes from the chest an account book. It is made of two boards, hinged together, covered with figures. He sits and bends over the book. Susannah enters and goes to him.*)

SUSANNAH. Thou art puzzled, Uncle. May I help thee?

JOSEPH. Not today, child, though I am somewhat troubled. The messenger from Arimathaea brought me no good news. The workers in my olive orchards are complaining that their wages are not enough. The steward sends me word that there will be rioting if I do not make peace with them. They complain, too, that their hours are too long. This sudden senseless outbreak annoys me. And I cannot leave Jerusalem now at the time of the Passover to reason with them.

SUSANNAH. Wilt thou increase the pay, then?

JOSEPH. To increase the pay of each by even a little would decrease my profits by much. I cannot do it. And why do they ask it? They live well enough. But come. Well I know thou art concerned about nothing save the visit of David. Shall I tell thee of our talk?

SUSANNAH. I could guess his purpose.

JOSEPH. (*Smiling*) David is a most worthy youth. If he had come asking for thee in marriage, bringing nothing except his good name and his upright life, I could not have refused him.

SUSANNAH. He spoke to me of good news. What was it?

JOSEPH. An inheritance, a large inheritance, from a deceased uncle. And I must tell thee that it is a great happiness to give my niece to one so well able to provide for her. I am right, am I not, in thinking that thou dost favor David?

SUSANNAH. (*Failing to show the joy her uncle expects*) Yea, Uncle, he has long been my friend. There is no other so good among the young men I know. I think he loves me well.

JOSEPH. Then thou art wholly happy?

SUSANNAH. I—I think so, Uncle. I am very glad that David has come to thee. There is just one thing—I almost wish that David had not come into this great inheritance. I suppose he thinks that money and all that it can buy are needful for me. True, I have always had these things. But I had thought—I've known for long that David loved me—I had thought that we might be happy without it. I have pictured us living in

some quiet street among the poorer people, helping them to
live better. Now, I suppose my home will be such as this,
with servants to do my bidding, and all of David's wealth
making my life smooth and easy.

JOSEPH. Thou art a strange child, Susannah, crying for
poverty when thou hast no idea of its meaning, or of the
limitations it would place upon thy life. Put all unhappy
thoughts from thy mind, and prepare for thy betrothal. It
will be arranged before many weeks have passed.

SUSANNAH. Yea, Uncle.

(Servant *enters*)

SERVANT. Guests are waiting.

SUSANNAH. *(Rising quickly)* Guests? Who can come at
this hour?

SERVANT. Thy pardon, master, but he is the same that came
at the Passover before this one.

JOSEPH. Jairus of Galilee?

SERVANT. It is he. A little maid is with him.

JOSEPH. Make haste to admit them.

(Servant *goes out.*)

SUSANNAH. It is Judith, she that was restored by Jesus of
Nazareth.

(Servant *shows in* Jairus *and* Judith. Susannah *goes to*
Judith *and they embrace.* Joseph *and* Jairus *greet each
other.*)

JOSEPH. Welcome, Jairus, to our home.

JAIRUS. Peace be to this house.

JOSEPH. *(Turning to* Judith) And this is thy daughter?

JAIRUS. My Judith.

(Judith *steps to* Joseph *and lifts his hand to her heart.*)

JOSEPH. We rejoice to see thee. Thou wilt remain with us
for the Passover. Susannah, take the child and bid thy servant
give her every care. *(Servant appears with roll of baggage and*
Joseph *addresses him.)* Go, make ready the best room; ask the
servants to prepare food; and see that the donkeys are cared
for. (Susannah, Judith, *and the* Servant *exeunt.* Joseph *points
to a seat.)* Sit thou there, Jairus. Four days upon the beasts
is a tiresome journey.

JAIRUS. Yet we stopped often for rest. Judith has never gone
so far from her home and I was careful not to overweary her.

JOSEPH. The child seems young for such a trip. How old is she?

JAIRUS. Judith hath passed her twelfth birthday. At that age I have brought all my sons and daughters to the Passover here. It seems to me the right of every Jewish child, while yet a child, to come once to our beloved Jerusalem for the observance of the sacred feast.

JOSEPH. Yea, at such an age my father first brought me from Arimathaea. I remember yet the wonder of that first visit, and the pride of race I felt as I saw the impressive ceremonies in the temple.

JAIRUS. Judith's eyes have been wide with wonder all the way. Indeed at this time of year even I who have been over the road many times yet marvel at the beauty of the hills and fields carpeted with flowers of every color.

JOSEPH. Yea, truly Jehovah led our fathers to a beautiful and favored land. Didst thou note how the grain fields and orchards fare?

JAIRUS. I have never seen a better promise of harvest. The wheat, I think, will yield forty- or sixty-fold if the drought come not.

JOSEPH. Where didst thou spend the Sabbath? Thou must have been near at hand, for the day has but passed.

JAIRUS. We have but come from the home of Mary and Martha and Lazarus in Bethany.

JOSEPH. The Lazarus who is reported to have been raised from the dead?

JAIRUS. The same. Dost thou know him?

JOSEPH. Nay, my business does not bring me into dealing with the humbler folk. Of what sort is he?

JAIRUS. He is a silent man. He goes about his work of gardening, seldom speaking. Yet quiet goodness shines from his face and he is well-liked by his neighbors. It is not strange that Jesus of Nazareth loves him.

JOSEPH. What about this Jesus? Hast thou seen him often?

JAIRUS. Yea, and he comes to Jerusalem tomorrow with a large company of friends.

JOSEPH. He comes to Jerusalem at the time of the Passover?

JAIRUS. So he has determined, much against the will of his closest friends.

JOSEPH. It is not to my liking, Jairus, that he should come at this time. The feeling here is very bitter against him. His coming will but make a disturbance in the city. A messenger should be sent to warn him, that he may turn back.

JAIRUS. I think a messenger would not turn him back. His mind is made up.

(Servant *enters.*)

SERVANT. Nicodemus would see thee.

JOSEPH. Bid him enter. (Servant *exits. To* Jairus) Nicodemus is a dear friend. He has no family and he is almost as one of us.

(*They stand as Servant shows in* Nicodemus.)

NICODEMUS. Peace be to this house.

(Joseph *greets* Nicodemus *in usual way.*)

JOSEPH. Welcome, Nicodemus. Our friends have but arrived from Galilee to observe the Passover—Jairus and his daughter. Thou knowest Jairus?

NICODEMUS. (*Placing his hand above his heart*) Peace be unto thee.

JAIRUS. And unto thee.

NICODEMUS. The fame of the restoration of Jairus' daughter has gone far. It chanced that I traveled in Galilee on the very day the child lay sick. I heard the uproar as I passed thy house and, making inquiry, I learned of Jairus' sad loss. Then I saw the Healer enter the house and afterward heard the sounds of great rejoicing. Is the child now well?

JAIRUS. Aye—and well content. Jesus has no follower who is more devoted to him and our debt to him is very great.

JOSEPH. (*Addressing* Nicodemus) Jairus tells me that Jesus is on his way to attend the Passover.

NICODEMUS. (*With a look of concern*) That is not wise. There is already trouble enough. Thou hast known, Joseph, of the attempts to bring charges against him. I fear for his life if he comes here now.

JAIRUS. Jesus' life has been endangered in Galilee, but he quietly walks away from the angry crowds. He seems to feel some force drawing him to Jerusalem.

NICODEMUS. Thinkst thou that he trusts to some magic to deliver him from a Jerusalem mob? Or does he know the strength of these enemies who can so quickly arouse people

against him? A handful of his fellow townsmen in Galilee is
far different from a mob here, stirred up by the leaders of the
Sanhedrin.

JAIRUS. Art thou not a member of that weighty body? And
thou, too, Joseph?

JOSEPH. Thou art right. We occupy seats in the Sanhedrin,
but our voices can scarcely be heard among the loud ones of
the powerful few who have set their minds on making away
with this man. They rule the body.

JAIRUS. But surely you can speak in his behalf. Your words
are not without weight.

NICODEMUS. Thou knowest not these headstrong men.
Pharisees and Sadducees hate each other, but they have joined
in their attack upon Jesus. It is useless for us to jeopardize
our positions in order to speak in behalf of this man about
whom we scarcely know what we think.

JAIRUS. Dost thou know him well?

NICODEMUS. Two Passovers ago I spent an evening in his
company. His words were confusing. He spoke of being
born again—I know not what he meant. Perhaps if I had been
more in his company—but my duties kept me, and it has
been needful to remember my position in the Sanhedrin.

JOSEPH. I, too, have felt that I must preserve the good
name I have. My acquaintance with the man has been limited
to some hours spent at the outer edge of crowds. Once I
heard a lengthy discourse given to a large group on a mountainside. The words he said then have never left me, and I
have found myself trying to repeat them—and wanting to de-
termine my conduct by them. Yet that is a difficult thing. He
seems to care little for much we Israelites have always cherished, and he places no high value on law observance. Nicodemus, thou art a Pharisee, and well-versed in the law. How
dost thou think of his light treatment of its keeping?

NICODEMUS. I am a Pharisee, but not of the stricter sort.
In the Sanhedrin are men who will stand quibbling all the
day and half of the night as to the burden a man may lift
on the Sabbath, but will not lift so much as a finger to help
a man who has fallen among thieves on the Jericho road. It is
against such extravagances of the law that Jesus speaks. His
test of action is the need of man.

(Susannah *and* Judith *enter and stand quietly, waiting to be addressed.)*

JAIRUS. Thou speakest truth, Nicodemus.

JOSEPH. *(Noticing the girls)* Thou wouldst speak with me, Susannah?

SUSANNAH. Yea, Uncle, if I may. I am greatly troubled. Judith has told me that Jesus is on his way to Jerusalem. Only today thou didst tell me that it would be unsafe for him to come here. Wilt thou not send him warning and ask him to turn back?

JOSEPH. We have already spoken of it. Jairus thinks that a message will not avail. Judith, what sayest thou? Thou art his friend.

JUDITH. I think as my father. I heard him say that he must needs come to Jerusalem.

SUSANNAH. He must not come! It may mean his death!

JOSEPH. A trusted messenger shall be sent. That can do no harm. Rest in peace, Susannah.

NICODEMUS. *(Going to* Judith *and placing his hand upon her head)* Is this thy child, Jairus?

(She smiles into his face.)

JUDITH. I am Judith.

NICODEMUS. *(Reverently)* One to whom the servant of Jehovah hath given life! The Lord bless thee and keep thee.

CURTAIN

Scene 2

TIME:—*Afternoon of the first day of the week.*

(Susannah *and* Judith *enter.* Judith *is much interested in the things the room contains. She goes here and there, examining this and that.)*

JUDITH. Is not thy uncle a very rich man?

SUSANNAH. All that he touches seems to prosper.

JUDITH. My father says that he has gone all over the world gathering these beautiful things. *(She notices the Cloth of Sendony and goes to it.)* Oh, this is the most beautiful of all!

SUSANNAH. Is it not? It came from India. My uncle calls it Sendony.

JUDITH. What use will thy uncle make of it?

SUSANNAH. Oh, Uncle does not think of use. It is enough for him if a thing pleases his eye. He spoke of giving it to me on the day that I am married. But my chests are full of his presents. Come, let me show thee.

(The girls go to the chest. Susannah carefully takes the cloth from off the chest and folds it, placing it on a stool beside her, before she opens the chest and pulls from it other pieces of bright cloth, but Judith is more interested in the remark Susannah has made.)

JUDITH. Oh Susannah, are thou betrothed?

SUSANNAH. *(With radiant face)* I shall be very soon, Judith.

JUDITH. Oh, I am so happy for thee. Is he a very wonderful man?

SUSANNAH. He is David, son of Jacob, the scribe.

JUDITH. And dost thou love him very much?

SUSANNAH. Very much, Judith.

JUDITH. Of course I am but a child, but when I have a husband I want him to be a very good man—as good as my father.

SUSANNAH. David is a good man. *(She muses for an instant, then changes the subject.)* Now wilt thou tell me all that has happened since I saw thee? My uncle is most kind and generous, and I am happy here with him; but I have sorely missed thy companionship and that of my dear Aunt Joanna. And Jesus, has thou been with him often? Has there really been all the trouble of which we have heard?

JUDITH. Oh, greater crowds than ever have been around him. He has made a great many sick people well.

SUSANNAH. But there are people who do not like him?

JUDITH. There are and they will not let him alone.

SUSANNAH. Hast thou seen any of his enemies?

JUDITH. One day when my father and I were in a crowd listening to Jesus a little group of Pharisees came to question him. They were tall and stately and had so much dignity *(she imitates them)* looking from side to side and listening so closely to all that was being said. I made myself as small as possible to get through the crowd—

SUSANNAH. *(Smiling)* Thou art not very big, Judith.

JUDITH. I reached the side of Jesus just as they came to him from the front, for the people had fallen back to let these great ones enter. And what dost thou think was the question they asked Jesus after all their trouble to get to him? (Susannah *shakes her head*) Why, they wanted to know why his disciples did not wash their hands before eating! I could but laugh! I know there is such a law, because my father is very careful to observe all the fine points of the law. But thou knowest as well as I that many people cannot keep this rule. And how could Jesus and his friends always go through that long ceremony when they are living out of doors and often getting their food from the grain fields by the roadside?

SUSANNAH. I believe that Jesus thinks about more important things than that.

JUDITH. Once I heard him say that the Pharisees strained their drink lest they swallow a tiny gnat, but could swallow a camel with no trouble at all. Well, this was the gnat. And then he told these men about the camel. He quoted to them one of their own laws which really does make a difference— the one about honoring father and mother—and showed them that they not only do not keep the law, but that they even tell falsehoods to avoid it.

SUSANNAH. What did they say?

JUDITH. Oh, there was nothing they could say, and they slipped away very quietly, but they were careful not to lose a single little bit of their dignity.

(Both laugh.)

SUSANNAH. Art thou fearful for the safety of Jesus if he should come to the Passover?

JUDITH. *(With reverent simplicity)* Nay, Susannah, I am not afraid. I know what he did for me. Can he not as well care for himself?

SUSANNAH. Nevertheless I am glad that my uncle and thy father sent him warning. Perhaps he will turn back into Galilee or Samaria until all is quiet again. *(There is a noise outside, as from far away. Voices are calling. There are snatches of song. The girls listen.)* What can that be?

JUDITH. How much noise they make!

(The singing becomes distinct. A hymn of praise is sung

joyously by a chorus behind scenes, gradually coming nearer and nearer. The girls go to the window excitedly.)

SUSANNAH. Could it be a company coming to the Passover?

JUDITH. We did not sing as we came.

SUSANNAH. *(Thoughtfully)* And their singing is beautiful, as if they were very happy.

JUDITH. I cannot see. *(She runs for a stool to stand upon)* Oh, some are Galileans.

SUSANNAH. There are children, too. They are carrying fig and palm branches.

JUDITH. *(Grasping Susannah's arm, and hesitating a minute to be sure)* Susannah, it is Jesus! He is riding upon a donkey! Look! The crowd is growing. The Jerusalem people are coming to meet him.

(At this point the music is most distinct and the girls join in, snatching the shawls they wear and waving them excitedly from the window. The music gradually fades away, and the girls turn from the window.)

SUSANNAH. They are going on into the city. What will happen to Jesus there? Either the message did not reach him or he did not heed it. He is here, so near to us. Oh, I am afraid of what may come!

JUDITH. But didst thou not see how the people love him? They scattered palm branches in front of him and spread down their cloaks for his donkeys to pass over. Why, I thought they treated him like a *king!*

CURTAIN

ACT II

Scene 1

TIME:—*Wednesday evening.*

(Susannah is busy with her needlework as David enters.)

DAVID. Thou art alone?

SUSANNAH. Yea, my little friend Judith is weary with her first visit to the great city and has gone to rest. My uncle and his guest, Jairus, have gone to Bethany at the invitation of

Lazarus. They were to meet Jesus there. They are anxious for his safety—at least Jairus is anxious. He thinks Jesus does not realize how strong his enemies are. Hast thou seen him, David?

DAVID. Yea, I have seen him. I want to talk with thee, Susannah. *(They are seated)* It is a long story, I fear, but if we two are to wed, I want that thou shouldst know it. Thou knowest somewhat of my life. My father was a scribe, learned and respected of all men, a devout Jew. I have told thee how, before his sudden death, he lost almost the whole of his possessions, leaving me, his only child, a poor youth. But I had other wealth than money, for I have always observed our rules, revered my father, honored my mother—in fact, I have kept the law to the letter. I have studied, too, the prophets and all the holy writings, and my father taught me much. But with all my learning there are things about our religion that I do not understand.

SUSANNAH. I, too, am often puzzled by the words of the rabbis.

DAVID. This ceaseless argument of Pharisee and Sadducee about the resurrection: Pharisee, with never-ending words, prating of eternal life; and Sadducee saying that there is no such thing, that when this life is done, all is over. When Jesus of Nazareth was teaching in and about Jerusalem, he often used the words, "eternal life." I used to search out the places where he was speaking to hear what he would say. Eternal life! What did he mean? I wished to talk with him, but I never reached the point of doing it, and before I knew it he had gone away. But the question stayed in my mind. And so, today, when I learned that he had returned to Jerusalem, I determined to seek him out.

SUSANNAH. And thou didst find him?

DAVID. That was not hard to do. I pressed through the crowds around him and gained his ear. "What shall I do to have eternal life?" I said. But he seemed not to understand me, and he began to question me about my early life. I half wanted to turn and go away—it was no matter of his how I had lived, for I was an utter stranger to him—but something in his smile held me and I answered that I had kept the law from my youth.

SUSANNAH. Thou hast indeed, David.

DAVID. His next words were stranger yet, and they angered me. He bade me sell all I have, give to the poor, and follow him! "How does he know of my recent inheritance?" I thought. He continued to speak: "How sayest thou, 'The law and the prophets I have kept'? For it is written in the law, 'Thou shalt love thy neighbor as thyself,' and behold many of thy brethren, sons of Abraham, are clad in filth and dying of hunger, and thy house is full of many good things, and nothing at all goes out to them."

SUSANNAH. *(very eagerly)* What didst thou say, David?

DAVID. I turned and walked away. What else could I do?

SUSANNAH. Without the answer to thy question?

DAVID. I wish I had not asked it.

SUSANNAH. I, too, often heard him use those words. Eternal life! Life after death, I suppose. Yet I think he talked more of life here. Said he more to thee?

DAVID. Not to me, but I heard him speak to someone near him, and I thought he said, "It is easier for a camel to go through a needle's eye than for a rich man to enter into the kingdom of heaven." *(Rising)* I tell thee, Susannah, that man knows nothing of what wealth can mean to one who has not had it. To struggle with poverty for years, with all the deprivations it means, and then suddenly to be lifted into a place of influence, and best of all to feel myself able to ask for the hand of the woman I love—this is indeed life. My future glowed before me. Then came this foolish teacher, ordering me to give away all I have. Why I ever listened to him I cannot tell!

SUSANNAH. But he speaks with authority.

DAVID. Yea, too much authority. If I could only forget him and his foolish advice. *(He walks about, much agitated)* But his words ring in my ears. I cannot sleep. I shut my eyes and visions of naked, hungry people come to me. *(He sits down near* Susannah*)* Help me, Susannah. Help me to forget all that he has said. This is why I came to thee. I thought that if I told thee all and looked again into thy beautiful face, feeling the assurance that thou art soon to be mine, I could forget his words.

SUSANNAH. *(Speaking as if to herself)* And I have tried so

hard to remember his words! Art thou sure thou shouldst try to forget? It may be that thou shouldst remember them, treasure them in thy heart—obey them.

DAVID. *(Starting up angrily)* What? Thou speakest so? Thou, who hast never known a day of poverty? Thou, always the favored of thy rich kinsmen—with every wish and need supplied out of their abundance?

SUSANNAH. *(Speaking very quietly)* It may be that I have not the right to speak, but I, too, would tell thee all that is in my heart.

DAVID. Yea, Susannah, I would hear thee. (David *is seated again.*)

SUSANNAH. As thou knowest, I, too, have neither father nor mother. The greater part of my life I have made my home with my Aunt Joanna in Tiberias.

DAVID. She that is the wife of Herod's steward?

SUSANNAH. The same. Their home is one of wealth and beauty. As thou sayest, I had every wish granted—every wish that money can buy. But money cannot buy all things. It cannot buy health. My aunt had suffered from a grievous illness. She heard of the Healer and his great deeds. Half against her husband's will, she went to him and was healed. It was after that that she sometimes took me with her and we joined the little band of followers of Jesus. He was going from village to village, helping those in need and talking to all who would listen to him. Sometimes he would grow careless of his own needs in his eagerness to serve others, and it was our work to prepare such food as we could find, bind up his tired feet, and in every possible way help him to carry on his work.

DAVID. I do not like to think of thee doing the work of a servant.

SUSANNAH. During those weeks I learned many things, David. I, always, sheltered from the unpleasant, heard the horrible cries of maniacs. I saw the hideous sores of lepers. At first I stood far away from scenes of misery, but later I learned that there is joy in binding up a wound, in helping someone back to life and health. I listened, too, to the stories Jesus told his disciples, and the little talks he often gave as we sat about him. And I learned that he does not care for the things I had been taught to treasure. He even seems careless about such things as houses and jewels and rich clothing. Since I have known him, all this *(she waves her hand about the room)* seems rather useless and foolish. Forgive me, David, that they coming into great wealth means so little to me. I could live happily with thee without it.

DAVID. But thou wilt not. Let us put aside all this disturbance of our happiness and plan our life together. Already my possessions are as great as thy uncle's and I am but a young man. I am not one to squander or to bury what I have. My mind is full of ways to increase my wealth and make it grow into such a fortune that the lords of Jerusalem will be saying, "David is the richest man in the city, and Susannah, his beautiful wife, is to be envied of all women." (Susannah, *with a frightened cry, rises quickly and steps away from him.* David *also rises, and steps toward her)* Susannah! What have I done?

SUSANNAH. *(Very slowly and thoughtfully)* Thou hast done nothing, David. Not what thou hast done or said, but what thou art is building a wall between us. It is a high wall. We cannot scale it to reach each other.

DAVID. I do not understand thy meaning.

SUSANNAH. I thought I knew thee. I loved thee for thy good life and thy steadfast keeping of the law. I dreamed of a life of quiet happiness with thee. When I learned of thy wealth, I rejoiced because I knew that we could do much together to make it possible for others to live better lives. That was my dream of eternal life for us. I see now that it is only a dream —one that cannot be fulfilled. My thought is not thine. Thine is not mine.

DAVID. And dost thou think this foolish dream will destroy a love such as ours? I wish that I had never seen this Jesus of Nazareth! I wish that thou hadst never seen him.

SUSANNAH. But I have seen him, and thou hast seen him, and what a difference it has made! I must go my way, thou must go thine. Together we would find no peace.

DAVID. *(Slowly, with rising anger)* Perhaps thou art right. "Sell what thou hast and give to the poor!" Become one of them! Wear their filthy rags! Eat their poor food! Live in their hovels! See my wife in the position of a slave! No, not for life here or hereafter will I do that! Farewell. *(He turns to go.* Susannah *runs to him and touches him. He stops, astonished.)*

SUSANNAH. Go, but not in anger, David. *(Her look quiets him and the anger melts from his face. He takes her hand, lifts it to his breast, then to his brow, and goes. She stands looking after him with all her sorrow in her face. The light softens. As* Susannah *starts to leave, she meets a* Servant *who is entering the room)* Wilt thou say to my uncle that I have retired?   *Exits*

SERVANT. Aye.

(The sound of voices comes from the door opposite and the Servant *crosses stage and admits* Joseph *and* Jairus.)

JOSEPH. *(To* Servant) Wilt thou call my niece?

SERVANT. She but asked me to say that she had retired, master.   *Exits*

JOSEPH. Ah, the hour is late, but I am far from sleep.

JAIRUS. Nor can I think of rest. The events of this night will never leave my mind.

JOSEPH. Aye, its pictures are painted in deep colors. They will remain. Lazarus prepared a great feast.

(They are seated.)

JAIRUS. I think it is Martha who deserves the credit for the feast. Martha is a masterhand at the preparation of good food. And she is devoted to Jesus.

JOSEPH. It was a company of his friends. I know not why I was invited.

JAIRUS. Art thou not his friend?

JOSEPH. I hardly know. Tonight I felt so. I wished that I might, in truth, become a friend of one so exalted in spirit. Of all the sacred writings, I have read most and loved best the works of the prophets. Tonight this Jesus reminded me much of Hosea, the prophet of tender love and forgiveness. I felt myself changing under the gaze of his clear eyes and the sound of his musical voice. If I could feel assured of what he is, even yet I might make my influence felt in his behalf. But I am puzzled, perplexed—

JAIRUS. These questions did not seem to concern Mary. Her

act of loving devotion was a beautiful thing. I shall never forget the strange hush which lay over the group.

Joseph. I wonder that Judas dared to speak. He is a disciple, is he not?

Jairus. He is, but I do not trust him.

Joseph. That was a stern rebuke he received.

Jairus. He carries the money bags.

Joseph. Thou dost not think—

Jairus. *(Becoming much agitated, rising, walking about)* I know not what I think. I only know that to me the face of Judas seems dark and troubled, as if some struggle were going on within him. He is ever thinking of money, money, as if that were the greatest thing in the world. How can he have been so long with Jesus and learned so little of his teachings about life's true meaning? Where was he when Jesus told the story of the rich man and the beggar? When he said one cannot serve God and money? When he asked the rich young ruler but a few days since to sell all he had and give to the poor? Why, I have only now and then been in his company, but I know, beyond a doubt, that *love,* not money, is the thing that Jesus calls the greatest. (Joseph *looks astonished and* Jairus *suddenly stops, dismayed at his blunder)* Ah, I had forgotten that thou art a man of wealth, Joseph. Forgive my impetuous speech, which, I fear, wounds a friend in his own house. The truth is, I am consumed with fear of what may come to Jesus through the hand of Judas, and such fear almost upsets my reason.

Joseph. *(Placing his hand on* Jairus' *shoulder)* Thou art forgiven, my friend, for a wrong thou didst not intend is no wrong. But thou art weary and the hour is late, go to thy rest. The servant will see that thy needs are cared for. Peace be with thee.

Jairus. The peace of Jehovah be with thee.

Jairus *exits*

(Joseph *is left alone. He sits down and bows his head in his hands, then lifts it and speaks very distinctly and thoughtfully.)*

Joseph. *Love,* not money!

CURTAIN

Scene 2 (Optional)

TIME.—*Before daybreak on Thursday morning.*

SCENE.—*This scene, if included, may be played in front of a plain curtain (possibly in front of the front curtain if space permits), or the stage may be set to suggest a court of the temple, with two or three large pillars and steps leading to other parts of the temple. Three priests (if more characters are desired, other priests may be added and speeches adjusted accordingly), composing the temple guard, are sitting and lying about. Two are in conversation. Very dim lights should suggest an early morning hour, or the only lighting may be that from torches carried by the priests.*

FIRST PRIEST. Whatever is done must be done today.

SECOND PRIEST. There can be no slipping this time.

FIRST PRIEST. It must be done quietly. We want no trouble with Pilate.

SECOND PRIEST. Thou lovest Pilate so well?

FIRST PRIEST. Thou knowest how well I love any Roman. But under Pilate we wear our hated shackles loosely. I've no desire to feel them tightened. This wretched uprising of Barabbas threatened to lose us our power. Another riot and we proud Israelites may be slaves in fact as well as in name.

SECOND PRIEST. Thinkest thou the Pharisees can be relied upon?

FIRST PRIEST. They hate this impostor enough—some of them. But the number of those who declare this Jesus to be the Messiah grows daily. When I am not too angry at their impudence, I laugh at their folly. Messiah indeed! (*He laughs noisily*) Looked he not like a king as he rode into Jerusalem on the donkey—with that crowd of long-haired Nazarenes following him?

SECOND PRIEST. But in seriousness, they say that Nicodemus, the Pharisee, holds that Jesus may be the Messiah.

FIRST PRIEST. I have my eye upon Nicodemus. I have never forgotten that he defended Jesus at the festival of Tabernacles.

THIRD PRIEST. Defended him?

FIRST PRIEST. Mildly, it is true.

THIRD PRIEST. Joseph, too, Joseph of Arimathaea, is not wholly to be counted upon, I think.

FIRST PRIEST. What knowest thou of him?

THIRD PRIEST. Little, except that he is a friend of Nicodemus. And I have noted his silence in the Sanhedrin.

FIRST PRIEST. There may be others in the Sanhedrin who sympathize with these.

THIRD PRIEST. They will not dare to speak, or if they do their voices can be drowned.

FIRST PRIEST. Think you Judas can be relied upon to do his part?

SECOND PRIEST. Double the pay if there is doubt.

THIRD PRIEST. I trust him. Listen. Someone enters.

(Joseph *approaches. The* Priests *who have been talking peer through the darkness.*)

FIRST PRIEST. Who comes?

JOSEPH. I, Joseph of Arimathaea.

FIRST PRIEST. How now, Joseph, what brings thee forth at this early morning hour?

JOSEPH. It is worth any man's effort to rise early to see the dawn on a morn such as this, and to watch the dome of the temple catch the first rays of the sun. But it is a matter of business that brought me here. I wish to relinquish my place at the money-changer's table.

FIRST PRIEST. What? Do my ears hear aright? Thou, Joseph, dost wish to give up the place held by thy fathers these many generations? Have thy profits been too small of late?

JOSEPH. The profits are well enough, even when one subtracts what finds its way into the coffers of the priests.

FIRST PRIEST. Oh! So thou art envious of us, and would deny to Jehovah's priests their rightful share?

JOSEPH. I envy no man his money. If there be one who carries about with him a conscience with which he can sleep, I envy him.

FIRST PRIEST. How long, pray, has this disease of the conscience afflicted thee? I've seen thee sit through many a Passover and rake the profits from the changer's table into thy money pouch. Ha! Joseph of Arimathaea with a conscience!

(*All laugh except* Joseph.)

JOSEPH. Scoff as you will—today I do not sit at the changer's table! Farewell. (*He turns to leave.*)

THIRD PRIEST. Joseph, I hear thou art a friend of Nicodemus.

JOSEPH. (*Turning*) Nicodemus is worthy of the friendship of any honest man.

THIRD PRIEST. And I have been told that he is a friend of Jesus of Nazareth.

JOSEPH. And if he is?

[*He leaves*

(*The* Priests *rub their hands in amusement.*)

FIRST PRIEST. They are a goodly pair. Think you they will use their influence with other members?

SECOND PRIEST. They will not speak out. Even now Joseph answered thy taunt with an evasion.

THIRD PRIEST. What meant he by a conscience?

FIRST PRIEST. 'Tis my opinion that this Joseph, and Nicodemus also if the truth were known, have secretly been in the company of this Jesus of Nazareth. They savor of his teaching. Why, I have heard that after they have been with him some wealthy men have actually sold their possessions and given away their money. Our charge against him must, of course, be blasphemy, or disturbance of the peace. But between us here, we know right well that he is a dangerous character, with his talk of all men being brothers and the giving up of wealth.

SECOND PRIEST. Silence! Who comes here? (*He swings his torch in the face of the visitor.*)

(David *enters. His face is hardened.*)

DAVID. Forgive my coming upon you at this early hour, but I would speak with you who have the care of the temple. I am David, son of Jacob of Jericho, some time since gone to his fathers.

FIRST PRIEST. Yea, I knew Jacob of Jericho, a noble scribe. What service can I render to his son?

DAVID. My father died a poor man. But in Rome he had a brother who had no offspring. He had great riches and vast lands. I have but lately come into this inheritance, for I am his only heir. I would not let it diminish in my hands, but rather make it grow into a vast fortune. I have heard that in the temple on feast days there are ways by which a man may, if he have the necessary funds by which to start, increase his wealth most rapidly. I know little about these things and I have come to you.

Second Priest. *(To others)* Is not his coming most fortunate?

Third Priest. (To First Priest) Thinkest thou he is too young for such a post?

First Priest. *(Disregarding questions)* Even today, David, there is opportunity for thee to try thy hand. Just now a changer of money came saying he would not occupy his table today. Hast thou shekels?

David. Many.

First Priest. Then today, if thou wilt, take thy place at the second table in the shelter of the porch, and change the foreign coins of visiting Jews into our coin. Only the shekel is acceptable as an offering in the temple. Display thy piles of coins and cry thy wares. And for a foreign coin, give half its worth in shekels. Thy fellow changers will do the same. *(He stops, noticing the alarm he has given* David.*)* Open not thy eyes in so great astonishment. It is the custom. The Jews of Alexandria and Rome are not in poverty. They may as well leave some small part of their wealth in Jerusalem. And besides, they expect it.

David. And all that I make is mine?

First Priest. Ho, thou thinkst to increase thy store too fast! Half of thy gain goes to the council of the priests. That, too, is the custom.

David. *(Thoughtfully)* Thou sayest at the second table? *(He pauses, then speaks with determination)* The third hour will find me there.

(David *leaves and the* Priests *are quiet until he has gone, then they all join in subdued laughter.*)

Second Priest. What youth!

First Priest. Such innocence!

Second Priest. I think he never in all his life took more than his due of any man.

THIRD PRIEST. (*To* First Priest) Art thou not ashamed to claim half he makes? No changer ever handed over more than a third of his earnings.

FIRST PRIEST. He must pay something for his youth and innocence. He has a long time in which to gather shekels, and, if I mistake not, when he learns the ways of men, he will gather many. But we linger too long here. To your duties: (*All stand, and he touches each as he assigns the tasks. The light increases.*) Thou to the slaying of the morning sacrifices. Thou to laying the wood upon the altar and kindling the fire. I shall attend to the lighting of the lamps. The great city is beginning to stir. I hear the tramp of feet approaching the temple. Jehovah must be worshiped with offerings and song. Away to your ablutions.

(*They start to leave the stage as the curtain falls.*)

ACT III

Scene 1

TIME.—*About sundown on Thursday.*

(Susannah *and* Judith *sit near the front of stage, in the room of* Joseph's *house used in other scenes.*)

JUDITH. Father says that the Passover is a time of great joy in Jerusalem.

SUSANNAH. Nowhere can the lamb be rightly blessed but in the great temple.

JUDITH. (*Clapping her hands in excitement*) Oh, I am so happy to be here with thee! (*She notices the look of sadness on Susannah's face and puts her arms about her*) But thou art not happy, Susannah, and that makes me sad.

SUSANNAH. Happy? No, but since the early morning when I saw and talked with Jesus, I am content. Was it not strange how he understood my trouble almost before I spoke? And he remembered David, too. So many come to him with questions and griefs. How can he remember them all? And yet I wonder if he ever forgets anyone. "Ah, yes," he said, "that noble youth who had kept all the law. He thought that was enough, but I saw that his wealth was too dear to him, and he left me resentful and sorrowful." (*Slight pause*) And dost thou know, Judith, I have wondered whether David might ever have loved me as much as his possessions? (Joseph *enters. Both girls rise and go eagerly to meet him*) Hast thou the lamb, Uncle?

JOSEPH. With the priest's blessing. Already it is roasting by the fire.

JUDITH. And the blood? Hast thou sprinkled the doorposts?

JOSEPH. Doorposts and lintels, child.

SUSANNAH. I love the old customs, Judith. I love to remember all the old stories and to hear them told every year at the Passover feast. Uncle, art thou very sure there is not the least crumb of leaven in the house?

JOSEPH. Why, a sparrow would starve if the life of it depended on the leaven it could find here. What of the dishes? Are they cleansed for the feast?

SUSANNAH. Judith and I have prepared them with our own hands, Uncle. We could not trust such a work to the servants.

JUDITH. Who will tell the Passover story tonight?

JOSEPH. There is a tradition that the oldest of the group recite the tale of Israel's deliverance from Egypt. Nicodemus shares our feast tonight and I have asked him to tell the story.

(Servant *admits* Nicodemus *and* Jairus, *and all turn to them.*)

NICODEMUS. Peace to you all.

JAIRUS. Has the rumor reached you?

JUDITH. *(Running to him)* What rumor, Father?

JAIRUS. *(Turning to* Joseph) Surely thou hast heard that there is a plan to arrest Jesus tonight?

JOSEPH. Yea, the word came to my ears while the lambs were being slaughtered in the temple, but I put no faith in its truth. Why should they take him at night? He has been all day in the temple.

JUDITH. But dost thou believe it, Father?

JAIRUS. I cannot tell what I believe, my child. I only know that I see no way to protect him, since he heeds no warnings and talks freely in all Jerusalem.

SUSANNAH. Would that he had turned back into Galilee.

NICODEMUS. *(To* Joseph) Didst thou see him so quickly

change the temple court today from a place of merchandise
to one of worship? With nothing save a few small cords in
his hand, he sent them all before him—sheep, oxen, cattle,
merchants, money-changers—as if he had the power of an
army with banners.

Joseph. But think you such an act did not further inflame
the wrath of those who wish to make away with him?

Nicodemus. I am sure it did so. And he must have known
that it would. His heedlessness is strange.

Judith. Father, may I speak? I think I know why Jesus
does not seem afraid. *(All eyes are upon her.)* I think that
Jesus does not care so much for life as we do. I heard him
say once, "He that loseth his life shall find it." And another
time he said, "For the son of man himself hath not come to be
served, but to serve."

Jairus. And dost thou understand these words, child?

Judith. Nay, Father, not altogether. But I think there are
certain things that Jesus must do and say, and if people
treat him very badly because of them, even if they should
kill him, he would not care.

Nicodemus. *(Weighing the thought)* There are men like
that—prophets of old.

Jairus. *(Turning to the men; the girls step back)* I saw a
strange sight today in the temple. I stood near the money-
changers' tables—by the second in the court. I noted the youth
at the table—a fine, handsome man he was, but not accustomed to the place. (Susannah *listens intently.*) Sometimes
he seemed to hesitate about the change, and once I saw a
poor woman come to get her shekels, so that she could buy
doves for her sacrifice. The little foreign coin she carried
could not have been worth more than two shekels, but I saw
him press five into her hand. Later, when a proud Roman
Jew approached him his face grew hard and he charged him
twice the worth.

Nicodemus. How fared he when the storm broke?

Jairus. His table was upset, the same as the others, and his
coins rolled over the floor. Like all the rest he stopped to
gather them. But Jesus saw him, went to him, and touched
him. He arose, and for one long moment they looked in silence

into each other's eyes. When the young man went away, leaving his coins for any who might gather them, no one could have said which face showed the greater sadness.

JOSEPH. A handsome youth, thou sayest?

JAIRUS. So he was, and if I mistake not, new at the work.

JOSEPH. A money-changer's table has no equal as a place to double one's possessions. Some newly rich man, it may be, eager to grow richer.

SUSANNAH. *(Trembling with excitement, taking her uncle's arm)* Uncle, dost thou think—

JOSEPH. *(Ignoring her question)* Go, Susannah, Judith, search the sky for the first three stars of Passover night.

(They move to the window, Judith *happily, and* Susannah *sadly and slowly.)*

JUDITH. *(Clapping her hands)* I see the first!

JOSEPH. After our meal at the house of Lazarus last night, Jairus, didst thou not speak of doubting the faithfulness of Judas?

JAIRUS. Yea, I put no confidence in the man.

SUSANNAH. *(To* Judith, *who is not listening to her)* Thinkest thou that the young money-changer could have been David?

JUDITH. Look, Susannah, there is the second star. Just a little point of light.

JOSEPH. Let me tell thee, Jairus. At an early hour when all our house was still, I arose and went to the temple to speak on a matter of business with the priests who guard it. They are the leaders in this opposition to this harmless man. As I drew near, their voices were loud and I could not but hear these words, "Think you Judas can be relied upon to do our will?" My friend, if trouble comes this night, it will be through a faithless disciple.

SUSANNAH. *(To herself with a sigh)* Jesus must have thought that David might change.

NICODEMUS. And it is said that Jesus and his disciples eat the Passover together this night. Will Judas be present? A traitor at the Passover supper!

JUDITH. *(Turning to the men)* The third star is in the sky. Listen!

(The temple trumpet calls loud and long and all are silent.)

JOSEPH. (*Speaking very impressively and leading the way with great dignity*) The temple trumpet calls to the Passover feast. Let us go to the room made ready.

(*The drop of the curtain indicates the passing of the time for the eating of the feast. As the curtain is raised, the clear voice of Judith is heard reading in the next room.*)

JUDITH.

"Who remembered us in our low estate;
And hath redeemed us from our enemies:
Who giveth food to all flesh;
O give thinks to the God of Heaven";

ALL. "For his mercy endureth forever."

(*The ceremony is finished. The men enter, gathering their robes about them and fastening them in their girdles. They carry walking sticks and walk toward the door as* Joseph *speaks. They are followed by the girls.*)

JOSEPH. In this manner did the children of Israel go forth out of Egypt.

SERVANT. (*Appearing at the door*) A messenger from the great Caiaphas. He begs me to say that he is in haste.

JOSEPH. What? A message from the high priest at this hour of the night? Admit him quickly. (*To the others*) What can be the meaning?

JAIRUS. The worst, I fear.

(Messenger *enters and hands scroll to* Joseph, *who reads it and hands it to* Nicodemus.)

JOSEPH. A meeting of the Sanhedrin! A meeting at once. Thou, Nicodemus, and I are summoned to appear.

MESSENGER. Is there a reply, sir?

JOSEPH. Go, report to the high priest that we are on our way.

The Messenger *leaves*

SUSANNAH. (*In great fright*) What does it mean, Uncle?

JOSEPH. That Jesus has been arrested and taken before Caiaphas. (*He embraces* Susannah *tenderly*) I must leave thee, Susannah. I entrust thee to the care of my friend Jairus. Do not weep.

SUSANNAH. But thou wilt come again when the meeting is over?

JOSEPH. Ah, who can foretell the matters of this night? Or when thy uncle may come to thee again? *(He starts to go, but she restrains him.)*

SUSANNAH. Dost thou think the Sanhedrin will condemn a man who has done only good?

JUDITH. I do not think so, dear Susannah.

JOSEPH. Would that I had the hope of youth. *(To both)* But thou dost not know the Sanhedrin.

SUSANNAH. But thou and Nicodemus?

JOSEPH. What are two among seventy?

SUSANNAH. And if the Sanhedrin condemns a man, then is there no way to save him?

JOSEPH. With Pilate, the Roman governor, rests the final word. *(He kisses her hand, and he and Nicodemus leave.)*

(The three remaining look after them in silence, Susannah quietly weeping. Jairus begins to walk about, trying to make some plan in his mind.)

JAIRUS. I cannot stay here. You are safe here with the servants. It may be that the words of witnesses might turn the tide. I must go. Surely we can gather together a host of those he has helped and go to Caiaphas to bear testimony to the goodness of Jesus.

JUDITH. Go, Father. Go quickly.

JAIRUS. *(Tightening his girdle and picking up his staff)* Have no fear, and Jehovah grant you hope and peace. *(He hastily bids them farewell and leaves.)*

(Susannah and Judith drop disconsolately upon seats and are silent for a long pause.)

SUSANNAH. The minutes are like hours.

JUDITH. If someone would but bring us word.

SERVANT. *(Entering)* David seeks admittance.

SUSANNAH. *(To Judith)* David, whom I thought never to see again! *(To Servant)* Admit him.

JUDITH. It may be that he brings us news.

DAVID. *(Entering in haste and excitement)* Susannah! Dost thou know that they have taken Jesus prisoner?

SUSANNAH. *(Standing very still and with great dignity)* I know.

DAVID. But dost thou not care? I thought to find thee in an agony of tears.

SUSANNAH. What is it to thee if my tears are stayed? What is it to thee that Jesus has been taken? Thou dost not care.

DAVID. *(Stepping nearer)* Speak not so, Susannah. Let me but tell thee all. When I left thee, bitter anger filled my heart. I determined to make every coin I have yield two. I went to the temple—

SUSANNAH. *(Scornfully)* And became a money-changer—

DAVID. I know that I merit thy scorn—

SUSANNAH. Not scorn, David. Pity.

DAVID. But it was well that I went to the temple, for there Jesus found me. He looked into my eyes, held me with his gaze of sorrow, and Susannah, as truly as ever he opened the physical eyes of blind Bartimaeus, so he has given me sight of the spirit—

SUSANNAH. *(Hopefully and joyously)* And wilt thou try to save him?

DAVID. If thou canst tell me one thing that I may do to save him from the mob that now awaits the word of Caiaphas and the Sanhedrin—speak, Susannah!

SUSANNAH. *(Her face alight with love and understanding)* Then, go, David, beloved. Find Jairus and the company of people who would witness to the goodness of Jesus in healing their bodies, and cry aloud that he has healed thy soul! *(He presses her hand to his heart, lifts it to his lips, and goes out quickly.)*

(Susannah *stands smiling through tears.*)

CURTAIN

Scene 2

TIME.—*Late afternoon of the day of the crucifixion.*
   (The room is empty. The light is subdued. The Cloth of Sendony is still upon the chest. Just after the curtain is raised, Joseph *and* Nicodemus *enter. They look haggard, dusty, worn. Their voices show great weariness.* Joseph *summons his* Servant, *who enters at once.)*

JOSEPH. My niece—where is she?

SERVANT. She sleeps, Master.

JOSEPH. That is well. Go. (Joseph *and* Nicodemus *sink upon seats*) Would that I had a conscience such as Susannah's. She bears no load of guilt.

NICODEMUS. Thy guilt is no greater than mine, Joseph.

JOSEPH. But thou didst speak in the Sanhedrin. I kept silent.

NICODEMUS. Too late, I spoke. Only once did I lift my voice and that but feebly. Why did I not cry aloud? Proclaim his innocence? Yea, more, proclaim my belief in him as the Messiah, for such I now think he was.

JOSEPH. *(Slowly)* Yea, there on yonder hill hangs a prophet of Jehovah. And to think that I was silent! *(The last words are spoken loudly.)*

NICODEMUS. Dost thou not care that the servants hear thee?

JOSEPH. Nay, I care not. I would cry out my sin before all the people—but they would not believe what fear has made of me. I pass along the streets of Jerusalem and draw my costly garments close about me, and they say, "There walks the rich Joseph of Arimathaea. His coffers burst with the shekels he draws from his olive orchards and vineyards. He goes over the world collecting the rarest of cloth. His house is filled with the treasures of Egypt and Rome. No one in all Palestine is so learned in the values of the creations of men's hands." *(Bitterly)* And they never guess that under the finely-woven coat there is the heart of a coward. A coward who was afraid to speak for the greatest of Jehovah's prophets; that even in the Sanhedrin, when he had his last chance, his lips were sealed by fear—fear of losing his place, his power, his possessions! *(With a sweep of his hand he indicates his possessions in the room)* A craven, sniveling coward!

NICODEMUS. It avails nothing to call thyself names, Joseph.

JOSEPH. Then let others do it. They tell me that the friends of Jesus have gone into hiding, scattered over all the country, lest they suffer a fate like his. *(With sudden resolve)* Come, I am done with secrecy. Let us go into the crowds and proclaim that we are friends of this man they call a criminal. Let them do with us as they will.

NICODEMUS. Wilt thou not see thy niece, then?

JOSEPH. Nay, I cannot look into her eyes. She trusted me

to use my power. *(He starts out, but* Nicodemus *pulls him back.)*

NICODEMUS. Stay, Joseph, this feverish haste is not like thee. Thou art mad with regret and grief. If we think, it may be there is yet some service we can render—

JOSEPH. *(Scoffingly)* Service to the dead?

NICODEMUS. *(Thoughtfully)* Yea, service to the dead. It may be of little worth to give the body its last care, but hast thou thought that on the morrow, outside the city—

JOSEPH. Aye—the hungry vultures! Come! Haste! Let us beg the body from Pilate! I have a tomb newly built—

NICODEMUS. It lies within thy garden, does it not?

JOSEPH. Aye. And for the body there must be wrapping. *(He looks about and his eyes fall upon the Cloth of Sendony. He moves toward it, but hesitates, then takes it in his hands. As he speaks it is clear that his thought changes to the cloth itself. His eyes gleam again as he feels its texture)* Of all that I have gathered, this is the most precious. Sendony! Threads of pure gold are woven with fine linen. *(He holds it up)* See how it shimmers in the light. Take it in thy hands, Nicodemus. Feel the weight of it. *(He looks up at* Nicodemus, *who, amazed at his friend's sudden change, makes no move to take it.* Joseph, *seeing* Nicodemus' *face, comes to himself, and the cloth falls to the floor. He speaks with deep contrition.)* I thought that my heart had learned repentance. But thou seest how the very touch of the cloth makes me forget all else. Verily, Nicodemus, "It is hard for a rich man to enter into the Kingdom." *(He pauses and shows by his attitude that the cloth is to him a symbol of all of his possessions, and that a decision to give it up will mean for him a relinquishment of his old life centered about the acquiring of material things.)*

NICODEMUS. *(Picking up the cloth and handing it to* Joseph. *Light falls upon them)* Thou wilt use this as a burial robe?

JOSEPH. *(With high resolve)* Aye, not only for his body, but also for my weak, grasping, cowardly soul. Susannah said the Sendony should have some noble purpose. Let us haste to Pilate.

CURTAIN

Scene 3

TIME.—*Early morning of the day of the resurrection.*

(Susannah *stands at window looking out. Her face is lighted as by the rising sun.* Joseph *is again well groomed. There is a spirit of calm strength in his face, as he watches* Susannah. *He sits quietly, a sharp contrast to his attitude in the last scene.*)

JOSEPH. What art thou seeing, my child?

SUSANNAH. The sun rising over the city. I never saw the promise of a fairer day.

JOSEPH. And thou art thinking—

SUSANNAH. *(Coming to him and sitting at his feet)* Of many things, dear Uncle. Of all that thou hast told me of how Jesus died—of the words he said upon the cross, especially those words of forgiveness. They are beautiful words.

JOSEPH. Very beautiful, my dear.

SUSANNAH. It is strange, Uncle, that at last when I fell asleep, after all the hours of vigil, I did not dream of his death, but of his *life*. Little scenes out of the time I knew him best flitted before me. I saw him lift a laughing child high in his arms. I saw him bending over a poor cripple by the roadside. I saw him teaching beside the sea. In sleep I felt, as Judith feels always, that I need not weep for his death. And even now I feel his life more than his death.

JOSEPH. I did not heed his words while he lived, but when I saw him die—

SUSANNAH. Tell me Uncle, why didst thou not wake me when thou camest for the cloth?

JOSEPH. I knew thy great need for rest, my child, and I could not think then that thou wouldst forgive me for my cowardice. Furthermore, I did not come for the cloth. I sought my home as refuge in despair and shame and great weariness. It was Nicodemus who made me see there was yet something to be done. It was a very small thing to do, Susannah, to care for the body of Jesus.

SUSANNAH. It was a very beautiful thing, Uncle.

JOSEPH. It did not atone for all that I had left undone, but, strangely, it has brought peace to my soul. The old restlessness and yearning for possessions seem to have gone. Nico-

demus knew Jesus much better than I, and that night as we
sat together in the garden after we had done what we could,
he told me again of how he sought him out by night and
learned those words, "Ye must be born again." They ring in
my ears. Truly, Susannah, I feel a new man today. I have
been thinking of all the long journeys I have taken, seeking
to gain. It may be that I shall now take other journeys, seeking to give.

SUSANNAH. Thy wealth?

JOSEPH. Yea, that may be. But I was thinking of other
things—ways in which I might carry to the people the *love*
of Jesus. I saw it, Susannah, on the cross—and I must tell
others of it.

(*The* Servant *admits* David, *who stands in the doorway
    radiant.* Joseph *and* Susannah *rise quickly to meet him.
    At the same time* Judith *enters from opposite side.*)

SUSANNAH. David! Speak! Thou hast some glad message
for our troubled hearts.

DAVID. Aye, I speak gladly. Jesus is not dead. He liveth!

SUSANNAH. Not dead? What dost thou mean?

JOSEPH. With mine own hands I placed his body in my
tomb.

DAVID. Yet I tell the truth. I have spoken with those who
have seen him.

JUDITH. *I* believe thee, David.

JOSEPH. I cannot doubt thee, but neither can I understand
what thou dost say.

(Jairus *enters and* Judith *runs to meet him, placing her
    arms about him.*)

JUDITH. Father! Tell me it is true! Jesus is not dead!

JAIRUS. Nay, the tomb could not hold the Son of Jehovah.
It is rumored that he goeth into Galilee. Come, Judith, make
haste. Gather thy possessions. Prepare for the journey. Let
us go to join him on the way.

(*They go quickly, the others looking after them.*)

SUSANNAH. (*With slow emphasis*) They go to find Jesus.
(*To her uncle*) Wilt thou, too, go to look for him? (*To* David)
And thou, David?

JOSEPH. Nay. (*He speaks slowly and his words are full of
meaning*) I think that I have already found him.

DAVID. (*Meditatively*) "Love thy neighbor as thyself," said he, "if thou wouldst have eternal life." *(He pauses; then, turning to* Susannah, *he speaks with strong conviction and determination.)* Nay, Susannah, I shall not go into Galilee to find him. With thy help I shall find him here.

Joseph. I thought that I had a good life because I knew the value of a piece of cloth, until I gave my priceless Cloth of Sendony to wrap his body—*(He suddenly stops, and the old look of desire comes into his face. Suddenly he summons his* Servant, *who appears at once.* Susannah *and* David *stand together, looking at him in wonder.)* Go thou quickly to my garden. Look within the tomb where Jesus of Nazareth was buried, and if thou canst find it bring me—*(He breaks off again, realizing what he is saying.)* Nay, nay *(dismissing* Servant *with a gesture)* I have no commission for thee. *(A smile lights his face as the* Servant *goes. A soft light falls upon him.)* Let the soldiers who guarded the tomb cast lots for the Cloth of Sendony. I saw them do it for the garment Jesus wore to his death. Henceforth my treasures will be not those made by the hands of men. They shall be love—forgiveness—service to men.

CURTAIN

Where Love Is

Dramatized from Tolstoy's Story
"Where Love Is, There God Is Also"

by

IDEN PAYNE

Characters:

MARTIN AVDYEITCH, *an old shoemaker*
GERASIM, *a merchant*
A YOUNG WOMAN, *a stranger*
STEPANUITCH, *an old soldier*
AN OLD APPLEWOMAN
ILYA, *a boy of twelve*

PLACE: Russia.

LENGTH: Thirty minutes.

SCENE: *The cellar in which Martin lives and works. Martin's cellar is a small room with a window at the back (Right Center), through which, as the pavement is raised, one sees only the wall and the feet of the passers-by. Near the window to the Left of it is the door, to which one descends from the street by four or five steps. On the Right is the stove. The corner above the stove is dark and littered. Clothes hang on a line drawn across it. At Left Center there is a rough table with a chair behind it. Martin's shoemaker's equipment is near the window. To the Right of the window is a shelf on which are several pairs of boots already repaired. Left of the door is another shelf with several small objects, including a Gospel and a small lamp with reflector. An ikon is in the corner above the bed.*

(*When the curtain rises Martin is discovered at work. Feet pass the window. Martin looks at them eagerly, but appears to be disappointed. He resumes his work. Presently the door opens and* Gerasim, *the merhcant, enters. He turns, as each character does on coming in, towards the ikon, bows and makes the sign of the cross.*)

MARTIN. I am working at your boots now, gracious sir, but you come before your time.

GERASIM. Of course I know that, shoemaker. Wouldn't do to forget one's appointments. No. Truth is I've had to change my plans. Ready or not, I must have my boots this evening.

MARTIN. Nothing easier, gracious sir. You shall have them, and they'll be repaired.

GERASIM. *(Puts his walking stick on table Left Center)* I would have been glad to give you longer, but I have settled my business before I expected—and a good price I'm to be paid for the timber—Praise be to God for His mercies! Now I'm all impatience to be gone, and that peasant—what's his name?—Dutlof—is driving into the city to-morrow. At dawn he sets out.

MARTIN. You shall have your boots, never fear.

(Feet pass the window—Martin observes them.)

GERASIM. *(Laughing)* People pass by your window, and all you see is their feet.

(He walks across the room to the stove.)

MARTIN. And yet I know them, more often than not. I recognize them by their boots, you see. There are few pairs in this district that have not been in my hands once and again. Through the window I often recognize my work. (Gerasim *laughs. Feet pass the window)* That's Stepanuitch, that old pair of felt boots. He's come out to shovel the snow. An old soldier he is of Nicholas' time. The merchant above gives him a home for Christ's sake, and Stepanuitch helps the dvornik a little. That's all he can do, he's so feeble. He's a tiresome old gossip—always tells what he had to do in the army—how he quenched his thirst with snow—but there—one feels sorry for him, so old and decrepit.

GERASIM. Wouldn't call you a youngster, shoemaker!

MARTIN. *(With a shrug)* I—Oh I— (Gerasim *crosses to door Left Center)* When would it suit the gracious sir to come for his boots?

GERASIM. *(Consulting his watch)* Well, I have one or two calls to make. Doesn't do to give offense by neglecting people. I'll be back in less than an hour.

MARTIN. I shall be ready.

GERASIM. That's as it should be, shoemaker. When I told the innkeeper I wanted my boots heeled, "Go to Martin Avdyeitch," he said, "the cobbler in the cellar yonder. He's a faithful workman," he said. "Uses good leather; doesn't charge too much; and he always keeps his word. If he can finish a job by a certain time, he'll take it; otherwise he'll not deceive you, he'll tell you so beforehand."

MARTIN. (Puzzled) How could we get on if we didn't stick to our promises? Everything would be topsy-turvy if we didn't do that.

GERASIM. All the same the innkeeper knew it was something to boast about. "He's a good man, Martin Avdyeitch is. He always has plenty of work."

MARTIN. No use complaining! Yes, I have work, God be thanked. But a good man?—no—that's not so. I have many things to repent. When I was younger I would drop into a public house on a holiday, and drink tea. Yes, and vodka too, many a time. Perhaps some acquaintance would be there, and we'd drink together, and when I left—I don't say I'd be drunk, but I'd be happy; talk nonsense; sing a bit; and maybe shout abuse at a passer-by. That's sinful. (Sighs) But there's much worse than that in my life.

GERASIM. What was that, shoemaker? (He sits Center) Or perhaps you'd rather not speak of it?

MARTIN. I was ungrateful to God, gracious sir. I fell into despair, and complained of God. It was like this. When my wife died, she left me one child, a boy, my Kapitoshka. He was only three years old. We'd had children in our early days, but they'd died young. My Kapitoshka was all I had left. He grew older. He began to help me with my work. We were happy together, my Kapitoshka and I. But sickness fell upon him. He took to his bed. In a week he was dead. No, I had no luck with children. In my despair I turned against God. I even prayed I might die. (He shakes his head and sighs) Ekh! Ekh!

GERASIM. But you escaped your despair, shoemaker? You're not that way now, I can see.

MARTIN. No indeed, I thank the holy name of God. It was this way. A pilgrim came to these parts. An old man he was—many a day he'd been a wanderer. He found me all sunk in melancholy and he spoke to me plain. "You don't talk right, Martin," he said. "We must not judge God's doings. The world moves, not by our skill but by God's will. Do you know why you are in despair? It is because you wish to live for your own happiness." "What should we live for?" I asked him. "We must live for God, Martin," he said to me, "God gives you life, and for His sake you must live. When you begin to live for Him, you will not grieve over anything, and all will seem easy to you." That set me thinking. I took to reading God's words, and bit by bit my heart has grown easier. That was the way of it, gracious sir.

(Martin *peers up at the window as feet are seen to pass.*)

GERASIM. Are you looking for somebody, shoemaker?

MARTIN. I thought it might be . . . a stranger. (*He rises and goes to the window*) But no. . . . It's that woman who's been staying with Maria Davidovna. Dear me, how pale she looks!

GERASIM. (*Looking at his watch*) This won't do. Here am I listening to your gossip, shoemaker, instead of making my calls. I'm to blame though—asking you questions. But the tongue, you know, the unruly member. Now don't forget my boots.

MARTIN. (*At the window*) They shall be ready. (Gerasim goes out) Dear! Dear! (*He hesitates; and then, making up his mind, crosses hastily to the door; opens it; goes up one or two steps and calls.*) Hey! Good woman! Why are you standing there in the cold with your child? Come into my room where it is warm. You can manage much better here. This way. (*He steps back into the room. A thinly clad woman is seen on the steps holding a baby wrapped in a shawl. She descends to the door and then stops*) Come now. Why do you hesitate? (*She comes into the room*) That's right. Nearer the stove now. You must sit down awhile. You can warm yourself, and nurse the little one.

THE WOMAN. I have no milk for him. I myself have not eaten since morning.

MARTIN. (*Shaking his head*) To think of that now! We must see what can be done about that. It's well I left the cabbage soup in the oven after I'd had my dinner. (*He opens the oven door; brings out cabbage soup; and pours some into a bowl)* You must sit down and eat, good woman. No use to go hungry. I will mind the little one. You see I once had children of my own: I know how to handle them. *(He takes the child)* See, I'll lay him on my bed. Poor little fellow, he's tired out with weeping. The tears have dried on his cheeks. *(The* Woman *breaks into sobs)* T'ck! T'ck! T'ck! This will never do, you know. Come here! Sit down and eat. *(The* Woman, *still weeping, crosses herself, sits down at the table, and eats)* That's right. The soup will put strength into you. That's what you need. Mustn't waste my time. I've got to finish a job. (Martin *goes back to his work. He hammers for a time, and then stops to watch the* Woman) I saw you in the street some days ago, I asked about you. Somebody told me you were staying with Maria Davidovna.

THE WOMAN. I went to Maria's. But that was a week ago. I've been looking for work, away over in the city. I was making my way back to Maria's, but all my strength went from me. I couldn't move another step. If you hadn't come to me, I believe I'd fallen into a faint. *(She begins to weep afresh.)*

MARTIN. Come, come. No more of that. It's all right now. Just eat some more of the soup. *(He works)* What was it brought you to these parts, friend?

THE WOMAN. My husband is a soldier. Seven months it is since they took him away. And never a word. I worked as a cook until baby was born, and then—well, no one cared to keep a woman with a child. It is three months now I've been struggling along. And food costs so much.

MARTIN. Ehk! Ehk! That's hard. Very hard.

THE WOMAN. I tried for a place as wet nurse, but no one would have me. I'm too thin, they say. I wandered about, hearing of this, hearing of that, and so I came to Maria Davidovna's.

MARTIN. Didn't she take you? She needs help, so they say.

THE WOMAN. Come again in a week, she told me; I'll have a job for you, then. What could I do? I wandered and starved. A week seemed like a year. But at last I am back again. It will be all right when we get to Maria Davidovna's, but we never would have reached there if it hadn't been for you. Now we are saved.

(She rises and goes over to the baby.)

MARTIN. *(Rising)* Have you no warmer clothes, friend?

THE WOMAN. *(With a shiver)* This is the time to wear warm clothes, but yesterday I had to pawn my last shawl for a twenty-kopeck piece.

MARTIN. To think of that now! *(He goes to the corner up Right and rummages. The Woman croons over the child. Martin comes over to the Woman with an old coat in his hand)* It's a moth-eaten, shabby old thing—I'm ashamed to offer it —but perhaps you might turn it to some use. *(The Woman looks at Martin, takes the coat and bursts into tears)* There, there. It's no use to me, that coat isn't. So much litter! I'm really glad to get rid of it.

(He turns away, and goes to the door.)

THE WOMAN. *(Putting on the coat)* May Christ bless you, little grandfather. *(She picks up her baby)* He must have sent you to your window. My little baby would have frozen to death. It was He surely who led you to look out, and take pity on me, an unfortunate.

MARTIN. *(Smiling)* Indeed he did that. I've been looking out of the window, friend, for a wise reason I can tell you. *(Suddenly he holds out a piece of money which he picks out of a bowl on his work bench)* Take this, for Christ's sake; redeem your shawl. *(The Woman, after looking at Martin, takes the money silently. She makes the sign of the cross and he does likewise. He opens the door and the Woman goes out. Martin closes the door. He sighs. Clears away the soup bowl and goes to resume his work. Suddenly he notices feet passing and hastens to the window. He shakes his head, muttering "Only the dvornik." He works. Again feet pass, and again Martin rises to observe them. Once more he is disappointed, but before sitting down he hesitates, goes back to the window. Finally he goes to the door, calling)* Stepanuitch! Stepanuitch! Stop shovelling that snow for a while. You must be cold. Come in, and I'll give you some tea. The samovar is all ready as it happens.

(Coughing is heard, and Stepanuitch, an old brokendown soldier with a shovel in his hand, appears in the doorway.)

STEPANUITCH. May Christ reward you for this, Martin! My bones ache!

(He tries to kick the snow from his boots, but staggers.)

MARTIN. Don't trouble to wipe your feet, I beg you. I'll clean it up. Customers come in and out and scatter the snow. It's nothing to me. *(He pours out tea)* Here now. Drink some tea.

STEPANUITCH. *(Coming forward to the table and drinking the glass of tea at a draught)* That's good! That warms you.

MARTIN. Yes, I'm a lucky one—here in my cellar I don't feel the cold. I ought to be grateful, but there it is—like as not I grumbled because of the cost of the fuel.

STEPANUITCH. I'd mind the cold less if it wasn't for the cough. If the Lord must send coughs, why doesn't He choose the summertime? We'd bear it better then, but they say He knows best.

(He places the glass, bottom up, on the saucer.)

MARTIN. *(Who has gone back to his work, taking a glass of tea with him)* Drink some more for your good health.

STEPANUITCH. No, no—no, I mustn't take more. *(But he refills his glass with trembling hand)* Ikh! In the old days—in the wars—we didn't get such tea. Many a time I've eaten snow to quench my thirst.

MARTIN. Think of that now.

STEPANUITCH. And nothing to eat but porridge, day after day, day after day, and you'd think yourself lucky to have half rations of that. Now I'm old and forgotten. Well, we do what we can.

(He finishes the tea and turns up his glass.)

MARTIN. Come, you mustn't stint yourself. Have some more.

STEPANUITCH. More? No, I mustn't think of it. No, no, no. *(He pours out another glass, nevertheless)* Yes, yes. Nothing to eat but porridge. Yes, and we'd eat snow to quench our thirst. *(*Martin *looks up at the window)* Are you expecting someone? Martin Avdyeitch?

MARTIN. Am I expecting someone? Well, I am and I am not.

STEPANUITCH. I'd better be going.

(He turns up his glass and crosses himself.)

MARTIN. No hurry, friend. It's only a fancy. Don't think you'd be in the way. *(A boy, eleven or twelve years of age, enters)* Is that you, Ilya? Come in.

STEPANUITCH. *(At the door)* Thanks to you, Martin Avdy-eitch. Thanks to you for treating me kindly.

MARTIN. You are welcome. Come in again. Always glad to see a friend. Come now, close that door, Ilya; we must not let in the cold. (Stepanuitch *goes out slowly, and coughing violently.* Ilya *comes forward.* Martin *has taken a pair of boy's boots from the shelf)* Ten kopecks it will be, and your mother owed me twenty for hers.

ILYA. That's what she told me—thirty kopecks. Here's half a ruble, and I'm to be very careful of the change.

MARTIN. That's right. Warm yourself at the stove before you go out again.

(Ilya *goes over to the stove.* Martin *hammers.)*

ILYA. I'd like to be a shoemaker.

MARTIN. Would you, Ilya? Well, well, plenty of time to decide.

(*An old* Applewoman *enters. She is robust and hearty. Her basket of apples is nearly empty, as she has almost sold out her stock. She also carries a bag of chips which she has collected. She puts down her burdens.)*

THE APPLEWOMAN. Ehk! Ehk! What a day! I can't think why the Lord sends such weather as this, unless it were for our sins.

MARTIN. Glad to see you, babushka. What can I do for you?

THE APPLEWOMAN. It's these boots. *(She takes them from basket)* They are little Liza's. They're in need of repair.

MARTIN. *(Examining them through his spectacles)* So they are—badly in need. Ekh! You should have brought them before.

THE APPLEWOMAN. Times are so bad. Where could I get the money?

MARTN. That's what they all say, and spend the more in the end. Well, well, I'll have them ready to-morrow.

(Ilya *has left the fire quietly and he is now near the door.)*

THE APPLEWOMAN. How much will they cost?

MARTIN. Thirty kopecks. And I will buy some of your apples.

THE APPLEWOMAN. That's fair, Martin Avdyeitch. So be it then. *(She turns and catches* Ilya *in the act of abstracting an apple from her basket. She seizes him by the collar.)* You

young thief! Good-for-nothing! *(She cuffs him)* I'll take you
to the policeman for this.

ILYA. *(Crying)* I didn't take it. What are you licking me
for? Let me go! Let me go! *(They struggle over to Right.)*

THE APPLEWOMAN. Yes, I'll let you go—when the policeman
has got you.

ILYA. Let me go! Let me go!

MARTIN. *(Coming forward)* There, there, babushka. Think
what you're saying. Don't be too hard on the boy. Forgive
him, for Christ's sake.

THE APPLEWOMAN. *(Swinging Ilya to her right)* I'll forgive
him so that he won't forget it till the trees grow roots in the
air. I'll take him to the police, the young villain.

MARTIN. Let him go, babushka. He'll never do it again.
Let him go, for Christ's sake. *(He takes Ilya from the old
woman. The latter tries to run, but Martin holds him)* Ask
the babushka's forgiveness, Ilya, and don't ever do it again.
I saw you try to take the apple.

ILYA. No I didn't—I—I—*(He wavers.)*

MARTIN. Think, Ilya.

ILYA. *(Suddenly bursting into tears)* Forgive me, babushka.
I didn't mean—I didn't think—forgive me.

MARTIN. There now. That's right. That's as it should be.
And here's an apple for you, Ilya. I will pay you for it,
babushka.

(He takes an apple from the basket, and hands it to Ilya.)

THE APPLEWOMAN. You ruin them that way, the young
rascals. He ought to be taught such a lesson as he'd never
forget.

MARTIN. Eh, babushka, that is right in our judgment, but
not according to God's. *(Putting his arm round Ilya's shoulder)* If Ilya is to be whipped for an apple, then what ought
to be done to us for our sins? *(The Applewoman is silent)*
God has commanded us to forgive, else we, too, may not be
forgiven. Everyone should be forgiven, and the thoughtless
especially.

(He crosses to Right Center.)

THE APPLEWOMAN. *(Shaking her head)* That's so, I suppose. But the trouble with the young ones these days is that
they are so much spoiled.

(Ilya *crosses up stage a little Center.*)

MARTIN. Then we who are older must teach them, surely.

THE APPLEWOMAN. That's just what I say. And I know something of children. Yes. *(She crosses Center to the bench, and sits)* I myself have had twelve of them, and only one daughter is left—she's the mother of Liza, whose boots I brought you—Liza's my grandchild—and just think, she's the only one I have. Yes, I've had twelve children, and but one grandchild. You'd think when you grew old you'd have children to care for you. But there it is. I look hearty, but I'm not so strong as I was. And yet I have to work. Well, God knows best. And what a good child is Liza! No one gives me such a welcome as she. When she sees me in the distance, "Babushka! Babushka!" she shouts, and comes running—I'm always afraid she'll fall and hurt herself. *(Her glance falls on* Ilya*)* Perhaps I was too hard. It was only a childish trick, I suppose. God be with him; the rascal.

(She stoops to pick up the bag of chips.)

ILYA. Let me carry it, babushka. We live near you. It's on the way.

THE APPLEWOMAN. *(Putting the bag on* Ilya's *back)* Ay, ay, you never know; you never know. *(She picks up the basket)* You're right, shoemaker; we ought to think what we're doing.

(Gerasim *returns.*)

MARTIN. Almost ready, gracious sir. Just a little polishing, that's all.

(He works at the completion of his job. The Applewoman *and* Ilya *go out.*)

GERASIM. It's getting dark in here.

MARTIN. That's nothing to me, gracious sir—this is my last job today. Soon I shall light my lamp and turn to my book.

GERASIM. Ah, yes, shoemaker; I remember you said you could read.

MARTIN. Praise be to God! My father was book-learned. He taught me my letters. But I neglected them shamefully, until after that pilgrim came and talked to me. "You can read, Martin," he said. "Buy a Gospel," he said, "and learn about our Lord." Well, I did as he said, and in the evening when my work is done I light my lamp and read.

(He starts up to observe a passer-by.)

GERASIM. Whom are you looking for, friend?

MARTIN. It's like this. Last night I was reading in the Gospel how our Lord was dining at the Pharisee's and how the repentant woman came and washed his feet with tears. And our Lord said to the Pharisee, "Thou gavest me no water for my feet. Thou gavest me no kiss. My head with oil thou didst not anoint." It made me think of myself. It seems, I said, that Pharisee must have been just such a man as I am. I, too, have thought only of myself—how I might have my tea, be warm and comfortable, and never to think about my guest. And who was that Pharisee's guest? The Lord Himself! If He had come to me, should I have done the same? I rested my head upon my arms—and I suppose I must have dozed, for suddenly I heard a voice call "Martin!" I started up. "Martin!" it called again. "Who's there?" I cried, and I looked all around the room. But there was no one. I sat down and began to doze again. But the voice came once more, quite plainly I heard it. "Martin! Martin!" it said. "Look to-morrow on the street. I am coming." *(Gerasim crosses himself)* I suppose it was a dream, but all today—I couldn't help it—I've been watching and watching. But He has not come. And now it is dark. It is too late. *(He sighs)* Ah well, well, old men have their fancies! Your boots are ready, gracious sir.

(He rises and offers the boots.)

GERASIM. *(Taking the boots and paying Martin)* God be with you, friend. The innkeeper did not lie to me. You are a good man, even if the Lord does not visit your dwelling. Goodnight, shoemaker!

> *(He crosses himself and goes out quietly. It is quite dark in the room. Martin takes the little lamp from the shelf, lights it, and places it on the table with the reflector toward the audience. He takes the Gospel from the shelf, sighs, and sits down. He slowly opens the book. A beautiful, rich, clear voice is heard as if from the left of the stage.)*

THE VOICE. Martin! Ah, Martin! *(Martin starts up, amazed)* Did you not recognize me?

MARTIN. Who?

THE VOICE. Me.

(Dimly the figure of the Soldier's Wife is seen in the dark corner above the stove.)

THE SOLDIER'S WIFE. It was I.

(By the Soldier's Wife *stands* Stepanuitch.)

STEPANUITCH. And it was I.

(Ilya *and the* Applewoman *joining the shadowy group.)*

ILYA. And it was I.

THE APPLEWOMAN. And it was I.

THE VOICE. Did you not recognize me, Martin? It was I.

(Martin *lifts the lamp and makes it shine towards the left. There is nothing. He turns the lamp toward the right where the figures were seen, but they have disappeared. He places the lamp back upon the table. Shakes his head. Sighs. Sits down. His eyes light on the book. He adjusts his spectacles to read.)*

MARTIN. *(Reading)* "I was an hungered and ye gave me meat; I was thirsty and ye gave me drink; I was a stranger and ye took me in."

(Martin *looks up for a moment, and then his eyes return to the book. The curtain begins slowly to fall.)*

"Inasmuch as ye have done it unto one of the least of these my brethren, ye have done it unto me."

(The curtain has fallen.)

NOTE. *The "ghost" effect can be very simply and satisfactorily obtained.* Martin *lighting his lamp attracts the eye to stage left and the spirits enter right unobserved. Similarly when he peers left for the voice (which comes from left) and shades the lamp away from stage right, the spirits quietly retire.*

The Captains and the Kings

A Play in One Act

by

CHANNING POLLOCK

Characters:

(In the order in which they speak)

THE GENERAL	THE RICH MAN
THE PRIME MINISTER	HIS WIFE
THE BISHOP	THE REVOLUTIONIST
THE SENATOR	THE CHILD
THE LEADER	THE FISHERMAN
HIS SECRETARY	GUARDS, ETC.

PRODUCER'S NOTE

Like the room in which they appear, they are as grand as circumstances permit; the men—except The Fisherman, of course—covered with gold insignia and medals. The period and costume of each is as follows:

THE GENERAL is of the time of Bismarck, and in the uniform of his rank and period.

THE PRIME MINISTER wears the court dress of the Empire of Napoleon.

THE BISHOP's robes are of the Middle Ages, but care must be exercised that they are of no particular church. He should be fat.

THE SENATOR is in the toga of ancient Rome.

THE LEADER wears a khaki uniform, with Sam Browne belt, puttees, and an invented emblem, conspicuously displayed.

HIS SECRETARY is in the garb of the notaries of Molière.

THE RICH MAN slightly exaggerates the typical rich man of our day.

HIS WIFE is in the dress and jewels of the Byzantine period.

THE REVOLUTIONIST wears the costume of her kind in the French Revolution, with red cap and red flag.

THE CHILD is in white, flowing, and very simple robes.

THE FISHERMAN is ragged—but his rags are purple. Also, he is barefoot, and a net, or seine, is over his shoulder.

TIME: *No particular time.*

SCENE: *A room in the palace of The Great Kingdom. This may be as simple, or as elaborate, as desired. The only essentials are a door at each side of the stage, one or two windows at back, and a table and chairs. Indeed, all of these, except the table and chairs, may be left to imagination, and the play presented without scenery. If the alternative is chosen, doors and windows should be as solid as possible, and of the sort usual in palaces—double doors downstage right, and upstage left; the windows long, and in either side of the flat. The walls may be hung with tapestries or paintings of Captains and Kings, and the carpet, draperies, and furniture may be ornate. There may even be a daise left, and carved and gilded eagles—or something of the sort—above doors, windows, and chairs. Nothing is really necessary, however, except the suggestion of a room.*

(*Before the curtain rises, or if there is no curtain, before dialogue begins, sounds of a huge assemblage offstage. There are cheers, and perhaps the distant music of a band—whatever can be accomplished with a phonograph and/or supernumeraries. On the stage are three men, dressed, as are all the characters, as described in the Producer's Note. The* PRIME MINISTER *stands at the table, inspecting a map. The* GENERAL *is looking out of a window, and the* BISHOP *is seated at stage left.*)

GENERAL. What a mob!

PRIME MINISTER. What a racket! How can a man think? Isn't there a quiet room in the palace?

BISHOP. None more secluded than this. What are they cheering now?

GENERAL. I don't know.

PRIME MINISTER. They don't know, either. They've been cheering for thousands of years—mobs like that; cheering or cursing, and none of them ever knew why.

BISHOP. They cheer what they're told to cheer, thank God!

PRIME MINISTER. They cheer whoever feeds them.

GENERAL. Or beats them.

BISHOP. Or gives them consolation.

PRIME MINISTER. You can "thank God" while they listen to what *we* tell 'em; when they listen to the other side, you can *pray* God; and God help 'em, *either* way.

(Outside door right, the sound of rifles lifted in salute, and then grounded.)

BISHOP. *(Wearily)* Whom are the guards saluting now? *(Enter* THE SENATOR*)* Ah, Senator!

SENATOR. Good morrow, Bishop . . . General . . . *and* Prime Minister. Where is our Leader?

BISHOP. He left here five minutes ago to speak to the multitude.

SENATOR. Over the radio?

BISHOP. No; from his balcony. You can't speak over the radio when nobody's home.

PRIME MINISTER. Why not?

SENATOR. What do you mean, nobody's home?

GENERAL. See for yourself.

BISHOP. They're all out to welcome The Great Ruler.

SENATOR. Which Great Ruler?

BISHOP. *The* Great Ruler, of course. The Ruler of The Great Kingdom.

SENATOR. But who says he's coming?

BISHOP. Everybody.

PRIME MINISTER. Everybody's said it ever since I can remember, but now they believe it. Even our Leader believes it a little, I think.

SENATOR. Why?

GENERAL. Where have *you* been?

SENATOR. Across the border on a secret mission. My plane only just landed.

BISHOP. And didn't you see the mob?

SENATOR. There are always mobs. What do they signify?

PRIME MINISTER. They give leaders someone to talk to.

How can you lead without a platform—or, lacking that, without a balcony or a radio? We were in conference when this bedlam broke loose.

SENATOR. Who started it?

GENERAL. A child.

BISHOP. "And a little child shall—"

PRIME MINISTER. *(Without paying any attention to THE BISHOP)* This is a strange child—sixteen or thereabouts. Two or three days ago, she had some . . . vision. She was arrested, of course—

GENERAL. And The Leader heard of it, and sent for her.

SENATOR. A bit mad, perhaps.

PRIME MINISTER. Quite mad, and, therefore, not to be dismissed lightly. For good or evil, it's only the mad who ever accomplish anything. The vision spoke to this girl, and told her she must prepare the people to receive their Ruler.

SENATOR. When?

PRIME MINISTER. Today. *(Cheers)* And so they rushed into the streets, and began cheering.

GENERAL. They're cheering The Leader now. He has appeared on the balcony.

BISHOP. Can you hear what he's saying?

GENERAL. Yes, but, at this distance, it's only words.

PRIME MINISTER. It's always words, and always the same words, but they serve. Isn't it curious, General, how people can rejoice in the power that enslaves them, and the glory in which their only part is cheering and dying?

SENATOR. In ancient Rome, we gave them bread and circuses.

PRIME MINISTER. That still does very well, but they must glimpse the power and the glory, too.

BISHOP. The glory that is within themselves?

PRIME MINISTER. No; oddly enough, I don't believe they ever thought of that. Their pride is in gold worn by someone else—in marble, and marching men.

GENERAL. They must have their toys.

PRIME MINISTER. They must have *importance*. They must believe themselves the best of their kind, and their kind the best in the universe. While that is true, they will leave their bodies to you, their souls to you *(indicating the* BISHOP) , and their minds to me—which is lucky for all of us.

BISHOP. Mankind is born to evil.

PRIME MINISTER. Mankind has never been better or worse than its leadership—which, being the case, explains everything.

(Cheers off.)

GENERAL. But if they threw off leadership—

PRIME MINISTER. Because they have bad eyes, would you pluck out their eyes?

(More cheers.)

GENERAL. The crowd is dispersing.

BISHOP. He must have persuaded them not to expect The Great Ruler.

PRIME MINISTER. Or reminded them how much more thrilling it would be to wait for a great movie star, or a great swimmer.

GENERAL. He is inspired—our Leader! *I* should have used machine guns.

PRIME MINISTER. So much easier than reasoning. Anyway, it will be quiet again, and we can get down to business.

SENATOR. Suppose The Ruler *does* come?

BISHOP. Don't talk nonsense! Why should he come now?

SENATOR. It would be a good time.

BISHOP. It would be the worst of all possible times. Why, we haven't *begun* to fulfill his commands. However, there's no danger. You expected him, Senator, in the last days of the Roman Empire. I expected him in the Middle Ages. The General looked for him a century ago, but none of us who serves him has ever seen him.

GENERAL. What matter, since we have served him well?

PRIME MINISTER. Do you think anyone really *wants* to see him?

SENATOR. We are paying our taxes.

GENERAL. And carrying his banners everywhere.

BISHOP. And giving him homage—and surely that's enough!

(The sound of the salute is repeated off left.)

GENERAL. *(Springing to attention)* Our Leader!

PRIME MINISTER. Gentlemen, our Leader!

(They all stand at the salute, as the Leader *enters at left.)*

Leader. *(After saluting)* Be seated, gentlemen. The people have gone back to their homes—and that's that!

General. How did you manage it, Excellency?

Leader. I told them to go. It's surprising how willingly they obey, if you have plenty of prisons.

Bishop. And if you promise them enough.

Prime Minister. Shall we look at the map, Excellency?

Leader. By all means. *(He goes to it, but his mind is elsewhere)* There was something unearthly about that Child. If it should happen that she was right—

Prime Minister. The palace has been hung with cloth of gold.

Leader. And his throne?

Prime Minister. Covered with purple and ermine, Excellency, and beside it are the scepter of diamonds and the jewelled crown.

Leader. *(To* Bishop*)* Have the candles been lighted in the cathedral?

Bishop. The candles are ready, but we cannot agree as to their order.

Leader. Is that important?

Bishop. Oh, of supreme importance. We have disputed the matter hundreds of years, and shed rivers of blood. Some of us insist the yellow candles should come first, and some say the green. There is a question of robes, too; should they be buttoned in front or behind? Shall we speak to him in our own tongue, or another? The words must be carefully chosen, and as for the music—

Leader. *(Wearied)* Is the guard posted, General?

General. A double guard, Excellency—and cannon. There will be a salute of twenty-one guns; then the trumpets. I believe in preparedness.

Senator. How shall we know if he comes?

Leader. The Child will know.

Prime Minister. Does it seem reasonable he should speak to a child rather than to Captains and Kings?

Bishop. We must all be as little children.

Prime Minister. *(Humorously)* We're certainly doing our best.

LEADER. A Great Ruler must be received with Great Honor. There is no harm done if we are ready, and he does not come, but if he comes, in all his magnificence, and we are *not* ready —that is unthinkable. I have given orders that, if The Child returns, she is to be admitted instantly. *(At map)* And now, gentlemen, where were we?

PRIME MINISTER. We were looking for lands that others had not seized.

LEADER. And we found—?

PRIME MINISTER. Nothing much. You see, Excellency, this has been going on for a long time.

SENATOR. Our Roman Legions—

BISHOP. Our pious Crusaders—

PRIME MINISTER. Our great Napoleon—

GENERAL. Ah, but we beat him!

LEADER. But ours is *the* superior race. It is our mission to carry culture and civilization to the ends of the earth.

GENERAL. Whether they like it or not!

LEADER. *(Pointing)* That's a nice bit of territory.

PRIME MINISTER. England's.

SENATOR. She carried civilization there a long time ago.

BISHOP. *And* Christianity.

PRIME MINISTER. So now the people are naked and starving.

LEADER. What are those greenish spots?

PRIME MINISTER. Dutch. *(Pointing)* America bought and paid for these people, and Japan and Italy are killing these —there and there.

LEADER. That is *our* divine right.

GENERAL. We shall have to destroy the rest of the world first.

PRIME MINISTER. But America may interfere.

LEADER. America has decided that it's none of her business. She didn't get her money back last time. The Great Ruler has made clear our mandate by giving us the best scientists and inventors. Yesterday one of them perfected a ray of light that will burn up whole armies!

PRIME MINISTER. Today, our secret service reports the same ray perfected by two other nations.

LEADER. Damnation!

PRIME MINISTER. Exactly.

Leader. *(Pointing)* Wait a moment! What have we here?

Senator. Only poor ignorant savages.

General. With no machine guns, or anything.

Prime Minister. And a rich, happy country.

Leader. We cannot leave that in the hands of a benighted, inferior race.

General. *(Pointing)* We will march across here.

Prime Minister. But we have a treaty with that nation.

General. So much the better; they will not be prepared.

Leader. Prime Minister, we must begin at once. Spread spies—lies—everywhere. Instruct the newspapers to publish accounts of outrages against our citizens, and our honor. I myself will speak over the radio. General, get out your military bands, and, Bishop, you tell them about the will of God.

Senator. There are inferior people in our own midst.

Leader. Of course; everyone is inferior to me, and, in some degree, to you.

Senator. I mean other races.

Bishop. And people who don't agree with us.

Leader. Are there still such? I thought we had exterminated them long ago. Well, you know what to do, Senator.

General. I can do it more quickly.

Bishop. Or I.

Leader. Do it together—as you always have—for the glory of God, and our Nation! *(Enter* Secretary, *right)* Well, Mr. Secretary?

Secretary. A Rich Man awaits without.

Senator. Without what?

Secretary. Without compunction. But he has brought His Wife.

Leader. Show them in. (Secretary *exits. The others rise)* Don't go, gentlemen. The Senator and I will need your moral support. We have just robbed this Man.

Bishop. Does that seem right?

Leader. Why not? We needed the money, and, anyway, he has robbed everyone else. Eventually, they will kill him, and us, and then new leaders will come, and everything will begin all over again. It is the law of life, gentlemen.

Bishop. In the name of The Great Ruler.

(THE SECRETARY *returns with* THE RICH MAN *and* HIS
  WIFE.)

SECRETARY. A Rich Man.

RICH MAN. A Very Rich Man.

HIS WIFE. And Wife.

LEADER. Welcome, my friends. (*To* WIFE) Try that easychair. I'll have my secretary bring you a cushion.

WIFE. No cushion.

LEADER. (*To* SECRETARY) No cushion. (SECRETARY *bows
low, and exits. To* WIFE) You look charming in that dress
of another time.

WIFE. All times are my time. I was born with civilization,
and shall outlive it.

BISHOP. They toil not; neither do they spin.

LEADER. (*To* RICH MAN) But *your* costume is modern.

RICH MAN. It has modern improvements; that's all. I
always begin in working clothes—lean, hard, eager, and frugal.
As I thrive, the nation thrives, and then both of us grow fat
and soft. However, no nation can get on without me. It has
been tried often, but never successfully.

WIFE. And wherever he goes, I go.

GENERAL. None of us seems to belong to any time in particular.

SENATOR. Because all of us have existed always.

BISHOP. (*To* WIFE) Have you heard that we are to expect
The Great Ruler?

WIFE. (*Polishing her scarlet fingernails*) Really? No, I
hadn't heard; I was playing bridge.

SENATOR. We are told he may come tonight.

WIFE. Sorry; I shall be dancing.

RICH MAN. And I shall be making money.

WIFE. (*Opening her vanity case*) That's all that interests
him, and I can't see why. (*She looks in the mirror.*)

PRIME MINISTER. Surely you can . . . *now.*

WIFE. What I mean is, the government taxes all our necessities—our yacht, our town house, our country house—

RICH MAN. It's hardly worth while trying to achieve anything. Why do you take what we earn, Excellency?

LEADER. To give to the poor.

RICH MAN. Why?

LEADER. Because they keep me in power.

RICH MAN. Is that all?

LEADER. Well, of course, I have to live, too. And palaces are very expensive. You have no idea.

WIFE. *(Using lipstick)* Haven't we? With eighteen servants!

LEADER. I have a million servants—every bureau is full of them, and every one of them votes for me.

RICH MAN. But the good of the people—

LEADER. My dear sir—among friends!

SENATOR. It's an old Roman custom. My Emperor soaked the rich to give to the poor.

RICH MAN. And what happened?

SENATOR. Oh, he was very popular.

RICH MAN. And then?

SENATOR. Well, in the end, of course, we went bankrupt.

RICH MAN. And *then?*

SENATOR. Don't you remember? Then *you* came back—lean and hard—and we started all over.

RICH MAN. *(To* LEADER*)* There ought to be a law—

SENATOR. *A* law! Thousands of 'em!

RICH MAN. —giving me whatever I can get. In return, I will keep the General, and his army, and they will keep you.

LEADER. But if the people starve—

GENERAL. We can send them out to conquer their enemies.

SENATOR. It's always been done that way.

BISHOP. In the name of The Great Ruler. *(Sotto voce to* RICH MAN*)* And, while I think of it, have we had your check toward building the new cathedral?

(An uproar offstage right, Voices of SOLDIERS: *"You can't go in there!" . . . "You can't see The Leader!" All on stage turn to the door.* THE GENERAL *draws his revolver.* THE SECRETARY *enters right.)*

SECRETARY. Excellency—

LEADER. What is this disturbance?

SECRETARY. A woman asks audience.

LEADER. Not The Child?

SECRETARY. No, Excellency; another mad woman. We sent her to prison, but it didn't do any good.

LEADER. Bring her in.

[SECRETARY *exits*

BISHOP. Is it safe?

LEADER. We will quiet her quickly. *(The* GUARD *admits the* REVOLUTIONIST) Who are you, woman, and what do you want?

REVOLUTIONIST. I am Revolution, and I want Justice!

LEADER. For whom?

REVOLUTIONIST. For the Workers of the World!

SENATOR. Haven't I seen you before somewhere?

PRIME MINISTER. Haven't I?

REVOLUTIONIST. Yes; both of you. I am thousands of years old.

LEADER. You don't look it.

REVOLUTIONIST. Every century I grow younger and stronger.

WIFE. Is it Steinach or Elizabeth Arden?

REVOLUTIONIST. In Greece, I was called Demos—the people. In France, I was The Terror. Now I am Communism.

RICH MAN. I demand—

LEADER. *(Ignoring him)* And how would you achieve Justice?

REVOLUTIONIST. *(Pointing to the* RICH MAN) By taking all he has.

PRIME MINISTER. He has just proposed taking all *you* have.

REVOLUTIONIST. Whoever is stronger robs who is not.

LEADER. I cannot permit that.

REVOLUTIONIST. Then down with everything! Down with the tyrants!

LEADER. And then?

PRIME MINISTER. Then she becomes the most cruel of tyrants.

REVOLUTIONIST. Someone must reign.

BISHOP. Of course; The Great Ruler.

REVOLUTIONIST. There is no such person. If there were, why doesn't he rule?

SENATOR. I never thought of that.

BISHOP. We rule for him.

LEADER. He may come today.

REVOLUTIONIST. Don't make me laugh! I, and I only, strive for Universal Brotherhood.

RICH MAN. Through robbery?

GENERAL. And murder?

SENATOR. And tyranny?

RICH MAN. All your life you have spread ruin.

REVOLUTIONIST. And *you?*

RICH MAN. I have created labor.

REVOLUTIONIST. And taken the fruits thereof.

RICH MAN. I have created wealth, comfort, progress.

REVOLUTONIST. For yourself only.

RICH MAN. I have made the world what it is today—a world of great machines, great production, great buildings, and art.

REVOLUTIONIST. And millions who have nothing to put in their mouths.

RICH MAN. At least they *have* mouths—and heads that do not fall from the guillotine.

REVOLUTIONIST. Liberty! Equality! Fraternity!

RICH MAN. The liberty of forced labor, the equality of chaos and impotence, the fraternity of Robespierre and Stalin! You have destroyed faith, and freedom, and all that is fair in the world. When you are done, I return to enthrone fitness, and order—

WIFE. *(Rouging her cheeks)* And Me.

REVOLUTIONIST. Great God, listen who speaks! Croesus, whose serfs died by droves in the mines of Lydia! Cheops, who built pyramids of human bones! Lucullus, who feasted while whole cities ate husks! You who, for countless ages, have driven men, starved women, taken childhood from children—drunk of their sweat, eaten of their flesh, and given them only misery and despair! Midas, whose food turns to gold, and whose ears to those of an ass!

GENERAL. Kill her!

REVOLUTIONIST. You, who have killed untold millions—marched them barefoot across frozen wastes, blown them from guns, left them writhing in agony on battlefields from Phoenicia to Madrid and Shanghai! *(To SENATOR)* You, who have enslaved the world with your laws! *(To PRIME MINISTER)* You, who have rotted it with your sneers! *(To BISHOP)* And you, who take bread from the poor to give them empty cathedrals and empty words!

LEADER. Silence, woman; you blaspheme!

REVOLUTIONIST. And, finally, you—partner of God—who, in every guise, in every century, have been the supreme thief and murderer—ten thousand kings and emperors and un-crowned monarchs who have ground the faces of ten thousand million of their creatures in the dust! Builders, all of you, and destroyers, all of you, and tell that to The Great Ruler when he comes!

VOICES. *(As in echo, afar off)* He comes! *(Nearer)* He comes!

OTHER VOICES. *(Off right)* The Great Ruler comes!

BISHOP. Oh, nonsense!

LEADER. I will believe it when I see The Child.

(THE CHILD enters through the open doors right.)

CHILD. He is here.

GENERAL. But where are his soldiers?

CHILD. He has none.

BISHOP. And his priests?

CHILD. He has none.

LEADER. And his heralds?

CHILD. Only I, who have seen his face.

PRIME MINISTER. What madness is this?

WIFE. Announced by a ragged beggar!

GENERAL. Without troops!

BISHOP. Or magnificence!

LEADER. This must not be. *(At window)* Cheer, you out there! The Great Ruler comes!

GENERAL. *(At door right)* Where is the guard? Present arms and blow your trumpets!

(The crowd cheers, and the trumpets blow.)

BISHOP. On your knees—all of you!

*(They kneel, except THE PRIME MINISTER, and THE REVO-
    LUTIONIST, who still doubt; THE LEADER, who cannot
    humble himself, and THE CHILD, who has seen his face.
    No one appears, and, after a moment the tumult dies.)*

LEADER. I see him not.

CHILD. Nevertheless, he is here.

*(Very simply and quietly, the FISHERMAN enters through
    the open doors right. The CHILD goes to him.)*

LEADER. But, Child, this is only a poor fisherman.

CHILD. Sir, what did you expect?

(The cheering is resumed, and, slowly and unwillingly, the doubters kneel.)

FISHERMAN. *(Simply and quietly—as throughout, except in his one angry speech)* Why do they cheer?

BISHOP. *(Rising)* They cheer in your praise.

FISHERMAN. Why should they praise one whom they heed not?

SENATOR. *(Rising; as do the others now)* But, Sire, a great ruler—

FISHERMAN. A great ruler is not praised, but followed. Only little men need mount upon thrones. They must have splendor without, who have none within.

LEADER. *You* cannot be The Great Ruler.

FISHERMAN. It is plain that I cannot be.

CHILD. Sir, I beg you to believe.

LEADER. But I don't understand.

BISHOP. *(Breaking through to* THE FISHERMAN*)* Will you give me your word?

FISHERMAN. *(Gently)* I gave you my word; what have you done with it?

BISHOP. We preach your—

FISHERMAN. What did I say that made you think I cared whether your candles are green or yellow?

SENATOR. We have promulgated your laws.

FISHERMAN. Which of them has advanced the Kingdom?

RICH MAN. *(Exulting)* Ah, but you should see what we have done with machinery!

FISHERMAN. What have you done with mankind?

RICH MAN. We have created new wonders of steel!

FISHERMAN. And left man as he was. You who wrangle here wrangle in words thousands of years old. Your deeds, and desires, and aspirations are unchanged. There is little difference between the youngest of you and the oldest. What shall it profit you to create marvels of steel rather than of mind and spirit?

REVOLUTIONIST. When you came in, I was talking of brotherhood.

FISHERMAN. But your banner is the color of blood.

REVOLUTIONIST. Blood brotherhood.

RICH MAN. *(To* REVOLUTIONIST*)* Am I your brother?

Revolutionist. Am I yours?

Fisherman. Why don't you try working together? It shouldn't be difficult, if you remember that each has what the other needs—and the world needs. Do any of you ever stop to think what the world needs? I never spoke of races, or creeds, or classes, but of that family which is the world.

Leader. But I have made your people great, and their nation powerful.

Fisherman. Is brute force great? Is power not of the mind?

Leader. *(Impatiently)* You don't understand; I have carried civilization to the ends of the earth.

Bishop. And Christianity.

Fisherman. No; I do not understand.

Prime Minister. We have taught—

Fisherman. What have you taught? Humility and faith and unselfishness and peace?

General. Without armies, there could be no justice and order.

Fisherman. Then why not use your armies *for* justice and order? If you must contend, why not in courts of justice, whose decision is enforced—if need be—by the combined forces of justice and order? When you have done that—when no man fights except for universal order and justice—then, and then only, shall I call you Civilized, and Christian, and Great. Now, your glory is tinsel, and your wisdom a vast and incredible stupidity. You had great gifts; what have you done with them? You had power, and you used it to enslave others. You had a fair world, and you have filled it with hate. Your thinkers destroy, and your artists produce ugliness and evil. Your wealth is a poverty of mind and character; your poverty is a wealth of impotence and envy; your law is the law of the jungle, and all your aspiration is for dust. You have so much and so little—every capacity except that to enjoy the fruits of capacity; every greatness but goodness, and every perception except that which takes in the stars. Help me, oh God, for this people's heart is waxed gross, and their ears are dull of hearing, and their eyes they have closed.

Bishop. This man blasphemes!

General. This man speaks treason!

Rich Man. He denies property rights!

SENATOR. And the law!

REVOLUTIONIST. And the rights of labor!

WIFE. And womanhood!

LEADER. And the Divine Right of Kings!

PRIME MINISTER. What fools you are to mistake a poor fisherman for The Great Ruler!

FISHERMAN. *(Sadly)* I am no Ruler. I am but a fisherman— a simple man, and you have forgotten that. *(To SENATOR)* You speak of my laws. I made no law, except love one another and be kind. *(To LEADER)* I claim no Divine Right of Kings, nor divinity, unless it be in my utterance, which is not mine, but the Infinite Wisdom. I am, as you say, a poor fisherman, who will come again.

CHILD. When will you come?

FISHERMAN. When they are like you, my child. For then I shall understand them, and they shall understand me.

PRIME MINISTER. *(Rushing to the open doors, right, in which —if possible—a crowd, in all kinds of costumes, has gathered)* Arrest this man!

REVOLUTIONIST. To the guillotine with him!

LEADER. To the concentration camp!

SENATOR. Crucify him!

(But the crowd parts, in silence, and, as simply as he came, THE FISHERMAN goes. As he does so, however, there is an even greater tumult of trumpets and cheering, which is silenced at last. The crowd and the others have turned to look after THE FISHERMAN.)

CHILD. He came, and you knew him not. Pray God you may know him when he comes again.

(The cheering and the trumpets resound; in the distance, slowly, the salute of twenty-one guns.)

CURTAIN

The Curtain

A Play in One Act

by

HALLIE FLANAGAN

Characters:

> PHILIP NORTON.
> RUTH, *his daughter.*
> SADE, *the girl across the hall.*
> LESTRANDE, *an officer of the New York police.*
> TWO POLICEMEN.

PLACE: New York City.

TIME: Present.

LENGTH: About fifteen minutes.

> *A small room in a New York apartment house is a com-
> bined living and sleeping room, furnished meagerly, but
> with some dignity and with a rather pathetic attempt at
> homelikeness. At the back, there is a shallow alcove, sepa-
> rated from the room by a curtain of dark material. To
> the right of the alcove is a window. To the left of the
> alcove is a screen placed in such a way that one catches
> only a glimpse of a cot with several cushions and a dress-
> ing table, simply equipped. In the center of the room
> there is a deal table, littered with papers, books, a type-
> writer, a desk lamp. A chair is back of the table. There
> is an easychair with a stool beside it. At the back a
> transom over the door discloses dim light from the outer
> hall. It is an autumn evening.*

(Through the window, one sees lights appear in the build-ing opposite. There is a sound of someone coming up-stairs. The door opens and a girl enters. She gropes along the wall and snaps an electric button. The table light flashes on, revealing RUTH. *She is slender, with a sensitive, beautiful face. She is simply dressed in a shabby, well-fitting black suit, and a black sailor hat. As if too tired to move, she remains leaning against the wall for a mo-ment. Then she sinks into the easychair. She sits there with closed eyes, raising her hands listlessly to remove her hat, which slips to the floor. There is a knock and a girl's voice is heard calling "Ruth!")*

RUTH. Come on in, Sade.

(The door opens and SADE, *flashily pretty, loquacious, comes in.)*

SADE. 'Lo, kid. Heard you come upstairs and knew you was all in. Been a fierce day?

RUTH. Like all the rest.

SADE. You take it too hard, kid—try to dub along with all work an' no play. Nothin' in it! Now you'd feel a lot better if you'd pep up, cold cream your face, an' come along to the dance with me an' Bert.

RUTH. You're awfully good, Sade, but—you know I can't. Besides I've a lot of typing to do tonight.

SADE. Your line sure is the bunk! No work for a week and you sit around and worry yourself sick, or else wear out shoe leather tryin' to find a regular job—and then some old party pops up with nine million letters to be typed before morning!

RUTH. It's all I can do.

SADE. Chuck it. I could get you a posish in at Crawley's tomorrow—you know that. 'Course, "clerk at Crawley's" doesn't sound as swell as—

RUTH. Oh, Sade—you know it's not that—but I keep hoping I'll get a really good job—and then too I know that Father—

SADE. See here, kid. I'm goin' to talk straight to you. *(She draws up the other chair and sits opposite* RUTH.) How long has it been since your father—since he—well—*(She hesitates.)*

RUTH. *(Bitterly)* Go on—say it. I mean it. You've no idea

what a relief it would be to hear one person say it right out
—"Since your father was sent to the penitentiary."

SADE. *(Uncomfortably)* I never did see any sense in callin'
a spade a spade if there's a politer name. But if you don't
mind my askin' you, dearie, didn't he leave you nothin' when
he went?

RUTH. He thought he left us quite a lot, but when everything was settled there was only a little. And then you see,
that was five years ago. Mother was sick for almost a year, and
after she died I took what money was left and learned this
(indicating the typewriter). You see I was sixteen when it
happened and I hadn't a regular education. Father and
Mother had taught me at home and I was ready for college—
but not ready to do anything practical.

SADE. Gosh! It must just about kill your dad to have you
dub along like this.

RUTH. *(Quickly)* Oh, he doesn't know.

SADE. Doesn't know?

RUTH. Of course not. Why, Sade, he thinks I'm the biggest
sort of a success. I believe I'll tell you a secret. Do you want
to know who I really am? Private Secretary to Jarvis of Jarvis
Steel! *(She laughs rather hysterically.)*

SADE. *(Awed)* Ruth! You never dared tell him *that*.

RUTH. Didn't I though? Why, Sade, I worked it out so
beautifully that I almost believe it myself at times.

SADE. I should think you'd be afraid to lie about a thing
like that. Why, he might write to Jarvis or somethin' and
find out.

RUTH. He is allowed no letters but mine. Think, Sade!
Those letters are all he has. And he's so proud of me—so
happy because I'm having a good time.

SADE. *(Blankly)* Good time?

RUTH. Yes. You see, Mrs. Jarvis has taken a fancy to me—
they take me out to the house and occasionally to the opera—
you should have read my description of *Carmen* last week!

SADE. *(Completely floored)* Well, I must say you're a queer
one. Now I'm not claimin' to be any plaster saint and I step
over the truth now and then when it's strictly necessary—but
to just make up stuff out of your head—

Ruth. It's not out of my head. It's out of my heart. And there's all the difference. *(Her voice changes entirely)* If they had taken *your* father, and shut him up alone, year after year, for something he never did—

Sade. Oh, I know. It's fierce. I'm not blamin' you for tellin' the yarns, kid—only I don't see how you think 'em up.

Ruth. It's easier than telling the truth.

Sade. Well, I gotta get dolled up for t'night. Wisht you'd go. Luce an' Marg is over to the room. Better drop in on 'em later.

Ruth. Perhaps I will. Thanks, Sade..

Sade. G'bye. *(She leaves, then sticks her head in at the door)* An' say—I wouldn't say nothin' about that Jarvis deal to no one else. Sounds too nutty.

Ruth. I won't. *(Left alone, ruth goes slowly to the alcove and draws back the curtain, revealing the portrait of a man with fine sensitive face, a spirited look, a gallant smile. ruth remains looking at the picture for some time. Then she slowly draws the curtain back in place, goes determinedly to the table, uncovers the typewriter, and starts work. She types for some time. Once she starts, as if hearing some sound. She listens intently, then resumes her work.)*

(The door opens and a man enters, closing the door quietly behind him. He removes a soft felt hat, revealing the face of the man in the picture, though without the smile. He stands unseen for some seconds, watching the girl.)

Norton. *(Quietly)* Ruth.

Ruth. Father! *(She seems stunned. She goes to him blindly. He takes her in his arms. Clinging to him desperately, she begins to sob.)*

Norton. There, there. Don't.

Ruth. I won't. But how—I don't understand?

Norton. It's come at last. I've been pardoned.

Ruth. Father! *(She kisses him. Then crosses to the table trying to control herself. Norton stands with bowed head, just as she left him)* Isn't it strange? I've thought for five years of what this would be like. I've thought of hundreds of things to say to you—but now there are no words.

Norton. No—there are no words. *(He comes to her)* Just

let me look at you. (*He takes her face in his hands and looks at her gravely, then turns abruptly away*) Margaret!

RUTH. Am I like her, Father?

NORTON. Yes. More like me—much more. I'm going to talk to you about that later—not now. (*He lifts one hand vaguely as if to ward off something*) Now I only want to look at you. Sit here. (*He sits in the chair, with* RUTH *on the stool at his feet*) Ruth, you've grown up.

RUTH. Haven't I?

NORTON. Yes—grown up—and become a young lady and private secretary at that. Child—I can't tell you how I feel about your work. For you to get such a position in spite of the handicap—I'm proud of you.

RUTH. I'm glad.

NORTON. It's the only thing that's kept my courage up. It's been something to hang onto. And it makes it a little easier for me to suggest something now.

RUTH. Tell me.

NORTON. Should you be much disappointed if we should have to be separated for a while longer?

RUTH. Separated?

NORTON. Just for a little time. You see when I had my interview with Governor Stewart a month ago, he offered to locate me in connection with some of his mines in Mexico.

RUTH. Mexico!

NORTON. He wants me to go at once.

RUTH. Now? Tonight?

NORTON. Yes. I can't take you until I'm located. I'll go down, get settled, and then send for you. Don't you think that would be wiser—especially since you have this position here?

RUTH. (*Slowly*) I don't know.

NORTON. Ruth, I'm trying to do the thing that's best for both of us. I can't let you risk anything. I've got to be sure that I can make good. It's been so long that I'm afraid of myself.

RUTH. I'm not afraid for you. I know you are going to succeed—only—I wanted to be there from the first. But if I can help better here—I'll stay.

NORTON. That's my girl. *(He sees that she is trying to control her disappointment, so leaves her and starts to walk about the room. He sees that the window shade is up and pulls it down nervously)* Windows! Hate windows. Eyes spying in on you out of the night. . . . I don't like this neighborhood for you, Ruthie.

RUTH. It's near my work.

NORTON. And I'm a little disappointed in your place here. Couldn't you be cosier?

RUTH. I'm—I'm in my room so seldom—I—

NORTON. Yes, yes. But I seem to remember that someone wrote me about a beautiful room—a fireplace—books—pictures—

RUTH. Father! Don't!

NORTON. Oh, I understand only too well. You wrote me those things to make me happy. And all the time you've been denying yourself to save your money for me. Isn't that it?

RUTH. *(Relieved that he has not guessed the whole secret)* Yes.

NORTON. You're not to do it any more. Understand? Take the money you've saved, get a better room, pretty clothes. And in a few months I'll send for you. It was a kind thing for you to do, dear, but it hurts me that you didn't tell me the truth.

RUTH. *(Slowly)* Do you think truth is so awfully important?

NORTON. *(Looking at her quickly)* What do you mean?

RUTH. Just that truth never seems very important to me. It so often hurts people.

NORTON. I don't understand you.

RUTH. It's very simple. If the truth is going to hurt people I love, I don't believe in telling it.

NORTON. Stop! I can't stand this!

RUTH. *(Amazed)* Why, Father—

NORTON. That's what I meant when I said you were more like me. Oh, I've feared this.

RUTH. I don't understand you.

NORTON. I must make you understand. Listen. Five years ago I was sent to the penitentiary for forgery.

RUTH. Oh, Father, why do you talk about it?

NORTON. Your mother died a year later, still believing me innocent.

RUTH. Of course we knew you were innocent.

NORTON. I was guilty.

RUTH. Guilty—no—no!

NORTON. Yes.

RUTH. I don't believe it.

NORTON. I was guilty. And the forgery they detected was only one of a long chain of lies.

RUTH. Oh—no!

NORTON. Be quiet. Don't speak to me. Sit down. *(He paces the floor)* I tell you I am going to do what I never have done before—tell the truth. God! When I sat there just now and heard you talk as you did of truth, it turned me cold to the very soul. It was my own voice speaking. It started with me at the university, I think. I was superficially brilliant. People expected me to succeed. When I couldn't quite make it on my own, it became increasingly easy to use fraud. Then—I met your mother and married her. *(He stands with bowed head.)*

RUTH. Father!

NORTON. *(Silencing her with a gesture)* Well—I got into a bonding company and things looked promising. People liked me—expected me to make good. But success didn't come. Then, somehow, opportunity came up, just as if arranged, in which by trickery, by double dealing, I could get ahead. There were all sorts of crooked deals—you wouldn't understand—and, Ruth, I used to justify it all just as you justified your lie to me—it was because I loved your mother —it was to give her everything—it was to justify her belief in me. As time went on, I used to try, every now and then, to stop—never because I felt any compunction, but because I was afraid of being caught.

RUTH. Oh.

NORTON. *(Again silencing her)* Most of all I was afraid of your mother's finding out. For she wasn't like we are, Ruthie. She hated a lie. She believed it must be truth always. She thought that truth would somehow bring things right.

RUTH. Does it?

NORTON. How should I know? I only know what lies bring. Well—so it went on. Years passed and still no one suspected. I never looked like a liar.

RUTH. Don't!

NORTON. There was always a curtain of lies between me and the world. But at last the curtain was torn aside—and everyone knew.

RUTH. Oh, Father, why did you tell me? It isn't that I can't forgive you. I do—oh, I do. It's just that—

NORTON. I know. But there is to be no curtain between you and me. You are to see now what I never saw until too late, that no good thing can come out of evil.

RUTH. What do you want me to do?

NORTON. I want you to promise me to put truth first—always.

RUTH. I promise. (NORTON *kisses her on the forehead. As he does so, far off, down the street, is heard a faint whistle.* RUTH *does not notice it, but* NORTON *stands motionless, listening. The whistle sounds again, still far away.* NORTON *goes to darkness*) Father?

NORTON. Hush! (*He goes to the door and locks it, goes to the table and snaps off the light, leaving the room in partial the window and listens. The whistle is heard again, a trifle nearer.* NORTON, *coming from the window*) They've found me.

RUTH. Found you?

NORTON. Yes. Don't stand there so. Don't you understand? They've tracked me here, I tell you.

RUTH. Father! Then you're not pardoned?

NORTON. Pardoned! God! Do they pardon us once they get us? I've escaped, I tell you, and I'll not be taken! Do you understand? Now listen. Everything else is as I told you. I can send for you later. There *is* a place ready for me in Mexico. I have my ticket—an hour is all I need.

RUTH. Father, Father, why didn't you tell me the truth?

NORTON. I wanted to spare you. That's too late. Now listen. You've got to get me out of this. Understand? (*He begins going noiselessly about the dark room, speaking very rapidly*) Any other door?

RUTH. (*Distractedly*) No.

NORTON. (*Pulling back the alcove curtain*) No good. (*He goes to the window*) This window—

RUTH. Leads into the street by the entrance.

NORTON. Other rooms opening off the hall?

RUTH. People in all of them.

NORTON. What's behind this screen?

RUTH. That's a closet—they'd look there at once.

NORTON. *(Suddenly going to pieces)* Ruth—for the love of God—

RUTH. *(Collecting herself as he collapses)* Wait. I know. Here. *(She opens the curtain of the alcove and motions him in)* Stay flat against the wall to your left. *(She leaves the curtain carelessly half open. Speaking half to herself)* You shouldn't have turned off the lights—they saw that—let me think—wait. *(She goes back of the screen. The sound of steps mounting the stairs is heard. There is a knocking at the door. Silence. The knocking is resumed. RUTH emerges from behind the screen. She has slipped into a loose dark robe and her hair is hanging. She turns on the table light. At the door, timidly)* Who is there?

LESTRANDE. Miss Norton?

RUTH. Yes. Who is it, please?

LESTRANDE. Officer Lestrande of the New York police.

RUTH. Police?

LESTRANDE. With a search warrant for an escaped convict. Philip Norton.

RUTH. He is not here.

LESTRANDE. Come now—we saw a shadow on the blind and the lights snapped off.

RUTH. I turned off the light, of course, before I went to bed.

LESTRANDE. Open the door, please. RUTH *opens the door, steps back to the table, and stands between it and the alcove. LESTRANDE enters, motions to two men who enter and remain near the door, and approaches* RUTH) Now, Miss, this is as hard on me as it is on you. But the law's the law. We tracked your father all afternoon, but he gave us the slip. But we know where he's headed for, so if he ain't here now—we'll wait.

RUTH. Officer, I'll be frank with you. If my father had come to me, I should have hidden him if possible. But look around you. What chance do you think a man would have hiding here?

LESTRANDE. A slim one. But we'll look all the same.

RUTH. Very well but— you're an hour too late.

(Her voice grows hysterical—she seems to be losing control of herself.)

LESTRANDE. Too late? Then he *has* been here?

RUTH. Too late—you're too late! You'll never take him —now—never—he's safe on the way to Canada—oh—what am I saying—wait—he hasn't been here at all—I—

LESTRANDE. Somepin' funny goin' on here.

FIRST POLICEMAN. Canada—get that?

RUTH. Or, no—no, I didn't say Canada. I don't know what I said. (LESTRANDE *drops back in some perplexity.* RUTH *goes to him*) Wait—wait—you said you were going to search—

LESTRANDE. We're going to search the northbound trains, that's what we're going to search. *(He turns toward the door. At this point the* SECOND POLICEMAN, *who has been studying* RUTH, *whispers to* LESTRANDE, *who speaks testily)* Oh, very well, very well. We'll look through the place, Miss.

> (RUTH *conceals her desperate disappointment; drops back to the curtain and sweeps it from right to left, concealing* NORTON *by the mass of the curtain held by her arm.*)

RUTH. Will you start here?

FIRST POLICEMAN. *(Aside)* She's just killin' time.

> *(They advance, but drop back in surprise at the sight of the portrait.)*

SECOND POLICEMAN. That's him, right enough.

RUTH. There is a closet behind the screen.

LESTRANDE. *(To the men)* Stay where you are. *(He goes behind the screen.* RUTH *slowly drops her arm. The curtain falls into place. She remains standing, looking straight ahead with a perfectly expressionless face.* LESTRANDE *emerges, rather shamefacedly, from behind the screen)* Beg pardon, Miss. Might have known you spoke the truth. *(He crosses to the door. At the word "truth" the girl goes limp. Just as* LESTRANDE *and the policemen reach the door she speaks.)*

RUTH. Wait. . . . My father is in the alcove. *(The men start forward.* PHILIP NORTON *emerges from behind the curtain. He stands for a moment as if dazed)* Forgive me!

NORTON. *(He turns slowly to her, takes her in his arms and kisses her. He puts her arms down from behind his neck. Then with a strange look of triumph, he turns to* LESTRANDE *and holds out his hands. The policemen get out handcuffs)* I am ready, gentlemen.

CURTAIN

The Coming of Light

by

MARCUS BACH

Characters:

> MILES COVERDALE, *a translator*
> JAMES NICHOLSON, *a printer*
> ANTONIA, *his stepmother*
> VESIAN, *a woman spy*
> CORYDON, *a soldier under King Henry VIII*

SCENE: London.

TIME: October 5, 1535.

LENGTH: About thirty minutes.

> *The curtain rises on a room dimly lighted by a single candle burning on a small table near a couch at back. What we see of the surroundings indicates little prosperity, and the simple furnishings serve to make the place barely comfortable. Over the couch, however, a somewhat luminous icon is affixed to the wall, and if the light permitted we might distinguish the portrait of a Madonna and Child.*
>
> *After a moment of silence the door at right back opens and admits two men. The first to enter is James Nicholson, thirty. The other is Miles Coverdale, in his early fifties. Both men wear suits of the period. White collars, almost shoulder-wide, extend over their mantles. On their heads are tight-fitting skullcaps.*

JAMES. *(In a whisper)* Antonia. Antonia. *(Turning to Coverdale)* Lay off your things.

ANTONIA. *(From the couch)* James?

JAMES. *(Crossing to the couch, speaking in a low voice)* Yes, Antonia. Are you all right?

ANTONIA. You must not worry about me. *(She sits up— an old woman and blind, with a kind, patient face.)*

JAMES. *(Giving her her cane)* I have brought him here.

ANTONIA. Who?

JAMES. Coverdale. Miles Coverdale, Antonia. You remember—

ANTONIA. Oh, yes. *(Then, to herself)* Miles Coverdale. . . . *(James motions to Coverdale, who lays a large manuscript on the table and comes over.)*

COVERDALE. Please don't get up. *(He gives her his hand)* James has told me about you, Antonia.

ANTONIA. *(Remaining seated, clasping his hand)* Miles Coverdale! *(With a smile)* If I could see—what would he be like?

JAMES Oh, he is tall and—

COVERDALE. *(Interrupting, genially)* A homely old fellow, Antonia, with a pinched face and a nose as flat as if he had slept on it half his life. His chin is covered with a growth of beard as thick as London's fog tonight. And if he'd take off his cap, which he never does, you would find a bald spot as big as your hand.

ANTONIA. But there's a heart—of which you said nothing. *(To herself)* And the heart is everything.

JAMES And that hand you hold, Antonia, that's the hand that finished the first English Bible. And it is here—in this room. *(He goes to the manuscript, looks at it and lays off his mantle.)*

ANTONIA. I know. *(Then, as she releases Coverdale's hand)* You were careful?

JAMES. Yes. And we'll be going into the bindery as soon as we have a bite of food. We have come a long way and with not a little difficulty.

ANTONIA. I'll get it for you. *(She starts to get up.)*

JAMES. No, Antonia. *(Coming to her with the manuscript)* Here—this is it—*(He puts it into her hands)*—Coverdale's Bible. It was printed in Antwerp, and we are going to bind it here tonight.

ANTONIA. *(Absorbed)* The Bible in English. . . .

COVERDALE. Yes, Antonia. The whole of the Scriptures—in English for the first time.

JAMES. Just as it says here, "Translated out of German and Latin into English." You know, Coverdale, I'd have changed that a bit.

COVERDALE. Yes?

JAMES. I'd simply have said, "Faithfully translated into English." I think it would go better here in London if we wouldn't give Germany any credit for it.

ANTONIA. *(Gently)* James—

JAMES. *(Laughing)* Forgive me, Antonia. *(He goes toward back and during the next speeches engages in setting the table with a few dishes and simple viands.)*

COVERDALE. I rather think England won't care much about the inscription.

ANTONIA. England will care only for light. But at what cost has this light come? *(To herself)* What cost. . . . *(Then)* What Wycliffe suffered we know. How John Huss died we know. And how Tyndale will die we have yet to see.

JAMES. Probably Tyndale will be released. When the book gets abroad—

ANTONIA. You say "when," and you do well, James. When tyrants rule, the just die in their faith. *(To Coverdale)* You worked with Tyndale, didn't you?

COVERDALE. Yes, I was near him when they tricked him to his arrest. Did you ever hear the account of that?

JAMES. Parts of it. *(He lights two more candles.)*

COVERDALE. An agent whom Tyndale had often befriended invited him to dinner. As they passed a certain side street the agent pointed his finger at Tyndale and indicated to some officers who were approaching that this was their man. And so they seized him. So they seized Jesus once, and so they seized Huss, of whom you spoke. So they may seize us, Nicholson. . . .

ANTONIA. God will shield you.

COVERDALE. So we pray, Antonia. But whatever befalls it will be enough if only his Word is preserved.

JAMES. *(With inward fear)* There is danger, of course. But it was Cromwell himself who came to you with the commission to continue the translation.

COVERDALE. Sometimes the bishops are stronger than royalty.

ANTONIA. Beware of the Emperor. *(Then, to herself)* Beware of the Emperor.

COVERDALE. What if it is God's will that his book go forward with the blood of martyrs? Have you not heard it said,

"Blessed are they which are persecuted for righteousness' sake, for theirs is the kingdom of heaven"?

ANTONIA. Words of Jesus?

COVERDALE. *(Gently)* You will hear them soon, Antonia, in your own language. Hear of the day the Master was followed by a great multitude—and to speak to them he went into a mount. Let me find it for you. . . . *(He pages through the manuscript.)*

JAMES. And what was that you told me about him restoring sight to the blind—and I said Antonia should hear that?

ANTONIA. Yes, that. . . .

COVERDALE. Ah, there is so much. . . . It is like being dazzled by a sudden light—like finding oneself in a treasury after having looked for coins in the street. . . . Here, Antonia—

ANTONIA. *(Leaning forward upon her cane)* Yes?

COVERDALE. *(Reading)* "And he cometh nigh unto Bethsaida; and they bring unto him one who is blind and beseech him to touch him. Jesus takes him by the hand and leads him away. Once out of the city Jesus spat upon the eyes and putting his hands upon the man asks if he can see anything. And the man says, I see men like trees walking and light has come unto me. And Jesus says, See that thou tell no man what has happened unto thee."

ANTONIA. Blessed Master! And now unto us is that light come!

COVERDALE. Yes, Antonia. And it will be worth everything that has been endured before—and everything that must be endured hereafter.

ANTONIA. *(To herself)* Men like trees walking. . . .

COVERDALE. *(Absorbed)* Today—October fifth, 1535, Five years ago all copies of the Pentateuch were burned. And two years earlier some fifteen thousand copies of the first English New Testament translation were destroyed. I stood with Tyndale that night and he turned to me and said, "I, too, am on the pyre."

JAMES. *(Disturbed)* But there is no danger, Coverdale. King Henry has his divorce now and upon petition for an English Bible he gave his consent. Doesn't that show he is in sympathy with the Church?

ANTONIA. Have you never learned, James, that men fear light more than the dark?

COVERDALE. *(To James)* Are you afraid?

JAMES. *(After a moment of silence)* I brought you here unafraid, didn't I? Tonight we bind God's Word and tomorrow—why tomorrow I wouldn't be afraid to show it to the King! I could attach an inscription saying, "To the Emperor and Prince King Henry the Eighth."

COVERDALE. No.

JAMES. Why not?

COVERDALE. Because I have seen men suffer and die for this book. I have heard their prayers and they asked only that it should go to England undefiled.

ANTONIA. *(To herself)* Men like trees walking. . . .

COVERDALE. And also because God does not need the favor of kings and men.

ANTONIA. Now, one word more from the holy book and then a bite to eat. Have you light enough, James?

JAMES. Yes, Antonia.

COVERDALE. *(Opening the manuscript again)* Where shall one turn? One might as well do as it was said of Luther, "He let God open the book for him." And so he'd lay his German Bible before him and let it open where it would. So—here— you, Antonia, open it and wherever your fingers fall let that be the word for us tonight.

ANTONIA. God direct me then. For this may be his way of speaking to his children. *(She opens the manuscript and puts her fingers on a page.)*

COVERDALE. *(Reading)* "Blessed is the man that walketh not in the counsel of the ungodly, nor standeth in the way of sinners, nor sitteth in the seat of the scornful. But his delight is in the law of the Lord; and in his law doth he meditate day and night. And he shall be like a tree planted by the rivers of water, that bringeth forth his fruit in—" *(He is interrupted by a knock at the door.)*

JAMES. *(Whispering)* Who is that?

ANTONIA. Go into the bindery—quickly—

COVERDALE. *(Closing the book and guarding it)* This will not be destroyed now.

ANTONIA. *(Getting up)* Please—into the shop. *(The rap is repeated.)*

JAMES. Yes, come.

COVERDALE. *(He hides the manuscript on the couch)* This is a better way.

ANTONIA. What have you done?

COVERDALE. I have hidden it.

ANTONIA. Sit down then—here at the table. *(She starts toward the door, feeling her way with her cane. The men sit down at their places.)*

COVERDALE. *(Bowing his head)* Our Father which art in heaven, hallowed be thy name. Let thy kingdom come. Thy will be fulfilled, as well in earth, as it is in heaven. Give us this day our daily bread. And forgive us our debts as we forgive our debtors. But deliver us from evil. For thine is the kingdom and the power, and the glory forever. Amen. *(Meanwhile Antonia has opened the door to Vesian, a woman in her early thirties, commonly attired.)*

ANTONIA. Good evening.

VESIAN. *(Just before the prayer is ended)* Do men still pray that prayer in London?

JAMES. *(When prayer is ended)* Were you looking for someone?

VESIAN. I beg your pardon. I lost my way in the fog and—

ANTONIA. Who is it, James?

VESIAN. *(Drawing away)* Is she—blind?

JAMES. Yes. But who are you and—

VESIAN. Won't you believe me when I say I'm lost? It is usually so, is it not? Men pray, but when their spirits are tested they become as other men. I have been walking—half the night it seems—and I come here hungry.

COVERDALE. Here, Nicholson, let her take my place.

ANTONIA. There will be plenty for all. *(She locks the door.)*

JAMES. Of course. You have come into the home of James Nicholson, a printer. This is my stepmother, Antonia. And this is a friend.

COVERDALE. Miles Coverdale.

VESIAN. *(James has offered her his chair)* Thank you. But where is your place now?

JAMES. Be welcome to what we have.

VESIAN. *(Indicating Antonia)* And she?

JAMES. Antonia has eaten earlier tonight.

ANTONIA. *(To herself as she goes to back)* "Men like trees." . . .

VESIAN. What is that she says? *(For a few moments no one speaks. Antonia sets out another plate.)*

ANTONIA. You must eat, too, James. *(He seats himself and partakes of the food with the others.)*

COVERDALE. The fog is bad tonight, isn't it?

VESIAN. Have you been out in it?

COVERDALE. Oh, yes, earlier. *(Again there is silence.)*

VESIAN. Are you—Protestants?

COVERDALE. We are.

VESIAN. I thought you might be when I heard you pray. . . .

ANTONIA. Where are you going?

VESIAN. I—*(For a moment she is confused as the staring eyes of Antonia turn in her direction.)*

JAMES. It doesn't matter.

VESIAN. If I could trust you. But I can trust you after hearing you pray. . . . I was going to a friend's—to secure some leaves of a German Testament. Why—why do you look at me so? Are you not in sympathy with the Bible?

COVERDALE. Do you read German?

VESIAN. A little. But since there is no other way to get the Scriptures—Of course you have heard of William Tyndale. How easily he might have given England an English Bible. But he was too credulous—and he failed.

COVERDALE. Why do you think he failed?

VESIAN. Didn't he? One night at Paul's Cross they burned thousands of his Testaments. Some say that there are only two left in all England. The Cardinal sat on his throne and watched them lead heretics to their death. They, too, were burned on the autumn night—and many of them were compelled to light the pyres with their own hands. Has Tyndale failed?

COVERDALE. *(Studying her)* This German Bible you mentioned—how was that brought to England?

VESIAN. It was smuggled from Cologne. Of course you know that they have been smuggled into the country with flax since the embargo was lifted.

ANTONIA. *(Still staring in her direction)* And you love the Word of God so much that you will try and read it in a foreign tongue?

VESIAN. Some day, we hope, someone will again take up Tyndale's work.

COVERDALE. Tyndale is working now—in the Tower.

VESIAN. No translation will ever come from the Tower. Nothing comes from the Tower but suffering.

JAMES. But Tyndale's friends, what of them? Sir Monmouth—

VESIAN. Sir Monmouth will be taken, too. That is, I fear he will be taken. *(There is a moment of silence.)*

ANTONIA. *(Quietly, but in a sinister voice)* I wish I could see you—I wish I could see a woman who loves the Word of God so much she'll brave the London fog for it. *(Vesian stirs uneasily.)*

COVERDALE. *(Strangely)* Antonia. . . .

VESIAN. Of course, I don't want it only for myself. You see—*(She turns from Antonia, distracted)* Why does she stare at me like that?

COVERDALE. *(Intensely)* How can she stare when she is blind?

JAMES. Antonia. . . . *(Antonia turns away.)*

VESIAN. *(Her self-possession returning)* No, I do not want it only for myself. Someone I know—dying—wanting a word of comfort. You are a printer. You should know where there might be a German Bible or a fragment of it.

JAMES. No, I do not.

COVERDALE. Perhaps I could help you, my friend. *(His eyes meet Vesian's. There is a moment of silence.)*

VESIAN. *(Uneasy under his gaze)* I know. We are all in this. We are all in danger, are we not? We know what they have done to those who have had traffic with the book—how they have cut off their hands and gouged out their eyes. And you—*(She looks squarely at Coverdale.)*

COVERDALE. *(Quietly)* Yes—I?

VESIAN. I do not know your business, but you and I, even she—*(She indicates Antonia)*—we are all under suspicion if we profess to be interested in the Scriptures.

COVERDALE. Shouldn't that make us feel a kinship one with

the other? Didn't the Master say, "When ye have lifted up the
Son of Man, then shall ye know that I am he . . . and then
are ye my disciples indeed"?

VESIAN. You know the Scriptures well. . . .

ANTONIA. *(Half to herself)* "And he shall be like a tree,
planted by the rivers of water. . . ."

VESIAN. *(Getting up)* Well, I thank you for your kindness.

JAMES. But where are you going?

VESIAN. *(Becoming more crafty)* To continue my search
and hoping that heaven will help me to success.

COVERDALE. *(Quietly)* How would you like God to speak
to you in your own tongue—in English?

VESIAN. Oh, sir, will we ever see that day?

ANTONIA. *(As before)* "Blessed are they that are persecuted
for righteousness' sake. . . ."

VESIAN. Why does she keep saying those things?

JAMES. Antonia. . . .

COVERDALE. *(Quietly, to Vesian)* You are afraid.

VESIAN. Do you know where there is a Bible?

COVERDALE. *(After a moment)* Yes. *(Antonia gasps audibly.
There is a moment of suspense.)*

VESIAN. You are very kind.

JAMES. *(Betraying a certain fear)* Coverdale, if we—

COVERDALE. *(Going to the couch)* Yes, I know where there
is a Bible.

ANTONIA. *(In a whisper)* Blessed Master—

VESIAN. Well—

COVERDALE. *(Returning with the manuscript)* You see before you, my friend, the Bible in your own tongue. English
—for which the King has scattered blood. It is here, the words
of the prophets, the apostles, and the Master.

VESIAN. The English Bible—

JAMES. The English Bible.

COVERDALE. *(To Vesian)* Now, read.

VESIAN. *(Nervously)* Why should I read?

ANTONIA. *(Almost sharply)* You have eyes to read.

COVERDALE. For this reason it has come to you, my friend!

VESIAN. *(Nervously, attempting to hide her eagerness)* Let
me see the front of it.

ANTONIA. Beware!

JAMES. Antonia. . . .

COVERDALE. *(Showing Vesian the title page)* There—

VESIAN. *(Reading)* "Translated out of German and Latin into English by Miles Coverdale." *(She looks at him)* I see *(Then)* You men are very brave!

ANTONIA. *(Excitedly)* Judas has come!

VESIAN. Yes! *(Her whole attitude changes and she attempts to get possession of the manuscript. Coverdale is too quick for her and keeps it firmly in hand.)*

JAMES. Spy!

ANTONIA. Spy! Spy!

COVERDALE. *(To Vesian)* What you would do, do quickly!

VESIAN. *(Bitterly, jeering)* Save yourselves! *(She rushes to the door, throws aside the bolt and is gone.)*

JAMES. Spy!

ANTONIA. You must go—both of you!

JAMES. *(To Coverdale)* Did you suspect?

COVERDALE. Yes.

ANTONIA. Quick—go quickly! God will protect you.

COVERDALE. God will protect us here as well.

JAMES. *(Who has gone for his mantle)* You are staying!

COVERDALE. We came here to bind the Word of God. Let us go on with it.

JAMES. Not I!

COVERDALE. We cannot turn back.

ANTONIA. For the sake of the Word—take it, and fly. In a moment they will be here.

COVERDALE. And why should we leave you, since we have all been spied upon? Isn't there danger for you as well?

JAMES. We must all go!

ANTONIA. No danger will come to me. . . . For me this little room has always been the world. Into it tonight has come a great light. I ask no more. *(She swoons slightly.)*

JAMES. Antonia!

ANTONIA. A great light!

COVERDALE. *(He and James proceed to take her to her couch)* And you think we would leave you?

ANTONIA. *(Her voice weaker)* You must not think of me.

JAMES. Quietly now, Antonia, and lie still.

ANTONIA. If I could have seen her. . . .

COVERDALE. You did see her, Antonia, better than any of us. But the Master came not to send peace but a sword, and tonight that sword will strike our hearts.

ANTONIA. Let nothing stand between England and the Word of God.

COVERDALE. No.

JAMES. Here, drink this, Antonia. Then let me get a doctor for you.

ANTONIA. No. It will pass again. But if I were going—to Him—

JAMES. Oh, Antonia—

ANTONIA. *(In a weaker voice)* If this were the hour appointed for me—

COVERDALE. Don't try to speak now.

ANTONIA. Bring me the light.

JAMES. What?

ANTONIA. His Word.

JAMES. *(Softly to Coverdale)* I'll go for someone. Wait here. And if anyone comes—

COVERDALE. Have no fear.

JAMES. *(At the door)* And bolt this door. *(He goes.)*

ANTONIA. His Word. . . . For this, too, was his Word given —that when men came to die—when darkness came—they might have light. . . . James?

COVERDALE. James will be back, Antonia.

ANTONIA. James must not be afraid.

COVERDALE. No.

ANTONIA. But I was afraid. And I was afraid of this hour —before his Word came to me. . . . Read. *(Very softly)* "He shall be like a tree planted by the rivers of water—"

COVERDALE. *(Reading)* "And he shall be like a tree planted by the rivers of water, that bringeth forth his fruit in his season; his leaf also shall not wither; and whatsoever he doeth shall prosper. The ungodly are not so; but are like the chaff which the wind driveth away." *(There is a knock at the door)* "Therefore the ungodly shall not stand in the judgment—"

CORYDON. *(Outside, simultaneously with Coverdale's next reading)* Is anyone there? Open, please. Open in the name of the King! I say, are you going to open—

(A heavy hand is laid on the door and Corydon, finding it

unlocked, enters. He is straight, severe, attired as a soldier of the King. He stops instinctively as he sees the dim figures of Coverdale and Antonia and hears the voice of Coverdale complete the Bible reading.)

COVERDALE. "—nor sinners in the congregation of the righteous. For the Lord knoweth the way of the righteous; but the way of the ungodly shall perish."

ANTONIA. Blessed Master, keep and preserve thy Word and thy servant from harm! *(She repeats these words as a whispered prayer during the next few speeches.)*

CORYDON. *(Standing motionless)* Miles Coverdale! I arrest you in the name of his Majesty King Henry the Eighth!

COVERDALE. *(Quietly)* On what charges, my friend?

CORYDON. Heresy!

COVERDALE. How do they accuse me of heresy?

CORYDON. *(Not moving from his place)* Will you come?

COVERDALE. One word. I am under commission of his Excellency Sir Thomas Cromwell.

CORYDON. *(Interrupting sharply)* The King has obligations to others besides Thomas Cromwell. It is forbidden that any man should have or draw any text of Holy Scripture into English without license of the Bishop. Will you bring your book and come or shall I—*(Antonia gets up slowly. Corydon looks at her.)*

ANTONIA. And what will be done to him?

CORYDON. We have a Tower in London. And we have fire.

COVERDALE. *(Close to Antonia)* Ask, rather, what will be done to the book.

ANTONIA. Nothing! I will keep it! I will keep it and no one shall take it from me. *(She has taken the book from Coverdale and shields it with her remaining strength)* Let them gouge out my dead eyes—let them take my life, for my life is already spent. But take this book from me and all England will rise against the King!

JAMES. *(Having entered)* Antonia! *(He comes to her side.)*

ANTONIA. All England will rise against the—King. *(Then, softly)* No—another must shield the book. You—James—and— *(Coverdale takes the book from her failing hands and they lay her on the couch.)*

CORYDON. *(Sharply, but not moving)* Enough of this!

ANTONIA. *(Scarcely audible)* "Our Father who art in heaven." . . . *(She continues the prayer through the next speeches. James is at her side.)*

COVERDALE. *(To Corydon)* What will you do?

CORYDON. *(Advancing)* Remember Huss and Tyndale! *(A moment of silent suspense)* You are not afraid?

COVERDALE. No, my friend. God has watched over me until this hour and I have no doubt he will guard me now.

CORYDON. A daring fellow, eh?

COVERDALE. No, a servant.

CORYDON. But not of the King.

COVERDALE. Of a King, yes.

CORYDON. And you, printer, if you value your tongue—come along!

COVERDALE. We value nothing henceforth save to do the will of God!

CORYDON. Once more—give me that book!

COVERDALE. Come, take it. *(Corydon advances a few steps threateningly.)*

JAMES. Give it to him!

COVERDALE. *(Sharply)* Never!

CORYDON. With one thrust of this sword I can send both you and your blasphemous book into perdition.

COVERDALE. My Master vanquished perdition. Think you his Word can then perish therein?

JAMES. Let me speak! *(To Coverdale)* Don't you know that what he says is true? So strong is Henry's arm that even the Church has learned to bow to it. Now, why should we—we who are in possession of the most hated and most loved of treasures—why should we sacrifice ourselves and it upon these strange altars? Are we not men? Then let us reason together. Is there no alternative? *(To Corydon)* What do you wish but to please your King?

CORYDON. What talk is this?

JAMES *(To Coverdale)* And what do you wish but to please your heavenly King by making his Word known to our countrymen?

COVERDALE. I wish nothing save that. Neither life nor renown.

CORYDON. *(To James)* You are very shrewd.

JAMES. *(To Corydon)* If, then, to please your King you could bring him this book—not for him to destroy, but for him to disseminate among his subjects—

COVERDALE. What are you saying?

JAMES. Once I overheard that the King was willing to answer the request of the convocation. He is to have said, "If the Bible, as Tyndale predicted, is to be born in exile, I will nourish it on English soil." Do you not see? Here it is—complete—to receive his commendation!

CORYDON. I will be blunt. Let that honor be mine and I will shield you both and see that the book reaches King Henry's hands.

COVERDALE. The Word of God needs no commendation from an earthly king!

CORYDON. Stubborn fellow! You forget there are guards and soldiers even now within call. Guards and soldiers who would rather have the request of the Bishop fulfilled than the whims of the Emperor.

JAMES. Coverdale, don't you see? Perhaps this, too, is the hand of God!

ANTONIA. Anything—that light may come!

JAMES. Yes, Antonia!

COVERDALE. *(Quietly)* Anything—that light may come?

CORYDON. *(Impatiently)* Well?

COVERDALE. And why do you think this book would so quickly find favor in the eyes of the King?

JAMES. Print on the book these words, "To the Most Noble and Gracious King Henry the Eighth this Book is dedicated by his humble subject, Miles Coverdale." *(To Corydon)* Isn't that the way?

CORYDON. *(Significantly)* I know the Emperor. . . .

JAMES. I will print it at once and bind it together.

ANTONIA. That light may come. . . .

COVERDALE. Yes, Antonia. *(He turns the manuscript over in his hands)* Here is the light of the world—made brighter by the blood of those who loved it. Born in exile—yes, that is what Tyndale said. And I ask only that it bring the exiled back to God.

JAMES. Surely there is need for diplomacy here if we would gain our ends.

COVERDALE. I will make a confession unto you. I was loath to meddle with this work of translating because I realized my own insufficiency therein and recognized that I was lacking in tongues. Notwithstanding, when I considered how great pity it was that we should want it so, and the desire of many others to translate it—others even less able than I—I made bold to undertake the work from necessity. But to say the truth before God, it was neither my labor nor desire to have this work put into my hands.

JAMES. God bless you, Coverdale!

CORYDON. We care not what power drove you to the writing of it. Come, then, inscribe it to the Emperor. Where is your printery?

JAMES. This way. *(He indicates a door at left)* But *(Indicating Antonia)*—

COVERDALE. GO. I will stay with her.

CORYDON. *(To Coverdale)* Will you give it to me?

COVERDALE. *(Handing him the manuscript)* I do not give it to you. It is placed into your hands by the spirit of Wycliffe, and Huss, and Luther. Take it, and God grant you hold your word.

JAMES. This way, sir. *(He and Corydon exit into the bindery.)*

COVERDALE. *(Quietly after they have gone)* Even here—diplomacy?

ANTONIA. What is it you say?

COVERDALE. *(Coming to her)* Antonia—that book—if it is not in the hearts of men it will avail nothing.

ANTONIA. But being there it will rob even death of its terror.

COVERDALE. *(Absorbed)* To the Most Noble and Gracious Prince King Henry the Eighth. . . . Antonia, sometimes I fear. . . . And some day England may ask how much of Tyndale's courage was mine.

ANTONIA. No, my friend, some day England will say that only in this manner could it have gotten its Bible freely into the hands of its subjects.

COVERDALE. Then you don't think his Word will suffer for what I have done tonight—dedicating this book to a tyrant king?

ANTONIA. God has strange ways and strange men to work his will. This night an English Bible finds its place in English hearts.

COVERDALE. I pray you may be right, Antonia. *(He kneels beside the couch.)*

ANTONIA. *(Placing a hand upon his head)* And may He bless his humble subject, Miles Coverdale.

Roger Williams

A Play of Democracy

by

MARCUS BACH

Characters:

ROGER WILLIAMS	THOMAS ANGELL
MARY, *his wife*	A MAGISTRATE
DAVID ALDEN	FIRST DEPUTY
MARCY, *wife of David*	SECOND DEPUTY
MRS. EVERETT NEAL	

LENGTH: *About thirty minutes.*

SCENE: *A room in the home of Roger Williams, Salem, Massachusetts. The time is Monday, January 6, 1635. The room serves as kitchen, living room, and study, and is sparsely furnished.*

(The curtain rises on Mary Williams, wife of Roger, who, "possessed by sickness and a deep concern for her husband, has grown beyond her years of three and thirty." At the moment she is engaged in setting a table. There is a knock at the door. Mary casts anxious, fearful eyes toward the door as the voice of Mrs. David Alden is heard outside.)

MRS. ALDEN. *(Offstage)* Mrs. Williams!

(Mary hurries to the door, throws back the bolt.)

MARY. Come in, Mrs. Alden. Tell me what's happened!

(Mrs. Alden enters. She is in her late fifties, a "good, albeit gossipy, neighbor.")

MRS. ALDEN. They are letting him go!

MARY. Are they truly!

MRS. ALDEN. *(Laying off her things)* I saw the judge himself bring your husband to the courthouse door and everyone cheered.

MARY. But is he to be free?

MRS. ALDEN. I heard the Judge say to all the crowd standing

---

out there in the cold, "The Commonwealth of Massachusetts
has spared the life of this man."

MARY. Thank God!

MRS. ALDEN. There was a great cheer went up. I turned and
ran fast as my legs would go here to your home. I did want
to be the first to tell you.

MARY. *(To herself)* It's true then. . . .

MRS. ALDEN. We've been neighbors here in Salem too long
for anyone else to bring you this good news.

MARY. I should have been there. I should have been at
Roger's side.

MRS. ALDEN. You're not well enough to leave the house. You
should be in bed.

MARY. But it's over now, isn't it?

MRS. ALDEN. Sit down. Sit down and I'll set the table for
Brother Williams and you.

MARY. *(Fearfully)* It doesn't seem real somehow—that they
let him go.

MRS. ALDEN. Do you think they'd put a man to death just
for saying what he believed? And with you just bringing
another baby into the Commonwealth? With the Roger Williams' being among our first citizens!

MARY. There was such feeling against him!

MRS. ALDEN. Now, now, it's all over.

MARY. Please let me help. We'll set out the syrup and the
cakes. There is fresh milk in the kitchen.

MRS. ALDEN. David said he would bring some partridge.

MARY. Your husband shouldn't do that.

MRS. ALDEN. Why not? All he has to do is shoot them out
of the back window.

MARY. *(Amused and happy)* I know, but he is always shooting things out of the back window for us. *(There is a sound
at the door)* Listen! That's Roger! *(Roger Williams enters)*
Roger, you are home! You are free! *(Mary goes into his arms.)*

*(Roger is thirty-seven. He is of "Welsh temperament, ex-
citable, ardent in feeling, generous, courageous, and firm,
a nature which, perhaps, has a touch of obstinacy.")*

ROGER. *(Holding her in his arms)* Yes, Mary, I am home.

MRS. ALDEN. *(Proudly)* I've already told her the good news.

MARY. *(Taking Roger's coat)* Sit down, my dear. Sit down and rest. I was so worried.

ROGER. How are the children?

MRS. ALDEN. I'll see to them. *(Mrs. Alden goes.)*

MARY. Roger—what is it? You're free, aren't you?

ROGER. They have spared me execution.

MARY. I know.

ROGER. But they have accorded us a great disgrace.

MARY. How?

ROGER. Don't you know?

MARY. I know nothing. Mrs. Alden said—

ROGER. Banishment.

MARY. *(In quiet terror)* Banishment!

ROGER. From the Commonwealth.

MARY. Oh, no.

ROGER. We are to be driven out like lepers. We are to take our children and never set foot in Massachusetts again. And why we should want to. . . . But our lives are deeply implanted in this soil. We built this house—our last child was born here. Ah, they have touched us at a tender spot, indeed. Mary, it is a great price that you must pay for my ideals.

MARY. A greater price for you. All you asked was that each man be allowed to worship God.

ROGER. You see how alone we are. I walked from the court without a single voice raised in my behalf. The crowd made way for me. No one spoke. No one so much as touched my hand—

MARY. Mrs. Alden said they cheered. . . .

ROGER. At first, yes. Before this awful brand was stamped on me. I walked alone, then.

MARY. *(Quietly)* Well, then, Roger, banishment will not be worse.

ROGER. *(With emotion)* Mary, do you know what it means? Wilderness, the cold, with no friends but Indians, and no home. If we had money we might make our way to the colony in Virginia. But can we go there? I am labeled a religious bigot, a heretic, an outlaw. Tell me, Mary, can you still believe in me?

MARY. With all my heart.

ROGER. I can't ask it of you. You are scarcely strong enough to be up, to say nothing of travel.

MARY. Are we to go so soon?

ROGER. Within the week. We are, of course, to sell all our goods. We are to take nothing except such as is prescribed by the court.

MARY. What must be, must be, Roger.

(Mrs. Alden comes in.)

MRS. ALDEN. *(Picking up her coat)* Where that husband of mine is keeping himself—I told him to bring the partridges the minute I heard the judge pronounce you free. What's the matter? I thought you would both be singing.

MARY. How are the children, Mrs. Alden?

MRS. ALDEN. Sleeping sound as could be. They're two beautiful girls, Brother Williams. Especially the last. The one I helped name. Freedom Williams. There's not a prettier name than that in Salem. If there's ever another—will you name her Marcy—after me?

ROGER. We'll see, Mrs. Alden.

MRS. ALDEN. Thank you. *(She goes out.)*

ROGER. We did call our child Freedom. . . . We were very optimistic.

MARY. We must always be optimistic, Roger. If we are to be driven out, we will go with our heads up.

ROGER. There is an alternative.

MARY. What?

ROGER. I have the privilege to recant.

MARY. And that—?

ROGER. Not a public recantation. I need simply affirm to authorities of the Commonwealth that I renounce what I have proclaimed as the "liberty of conscience"—the "right of each man to worship in his own faith and to choose his own congregation and House of Prayer." If I recant we need not be exiles.

MARY. You often said that those principles were a part of you, Roger. You said they were things you believed in enough to suffer for.

ROGER. I, yes. But not you, Mary. Why should you suffer? Why the children?

MARY. I have cast my life with you. We came here as strangers, we can go elsewhere as strangers.

ROGER. On the contrary. We came here and were welcomed with open arms. This is our home. This must be our home. I cannot ask you to do this. Look out at the snow—the frozen river—the wilderness! We are to go there!

MARY. Together, Roger!

ROGER. *(Turning from her impulsively)* Friendless, homeless, poor!

MARY. *(After a moment)* You think you could recant?

ROGER. I would do much for you, Mary.

MARY. Roger—when you walked out of that door this morning I did not know whether you would ever return to me. Men have been killed before because of their religious beliefs. And yet, had you turned back to me—had you said you would recant—had you asked me to choose—I doubt whether I would have held you back. . . .

ROGER. *(Quietly)* Whether a man ought to give his life for a principle—for an idea in which he believes—that is something that has never been proved.

MARY. There is only one answer—a man must be true to himself.

ROGER. But I have no right to take you into exile! Into what might be death for all of us! You know we are alone, Mary!

(Enter David Alden and Marcy. They are talking, i.e., Marcy is talking. David is a man of sixty or sixty-five, typical of the conventional American pioneer.)

DAVID. This is no time to be talking about partridges!

MRS. ALDEN. A body has got to eat!

DAVID. The gun is behind the kitchen door. Go back and shoot one yourself.

MRS. ALDEN. I've a mind to!

DAVID. *(Sincerely and hesitantly)* Mr. Williams—is there anything I can do?

MRS. ALDEN. Is it as bad as David says, Brother Williams?

ROGER. You have been good neighbors to us. *(He turns away.)*

MRS. ALDEN. You won't have to leave before spring, will you, Mrs. Williams?

DAVID. *(Impatiently)* Within the week!

MRS. ALDEN. You didn't tell me that! But the children—and winter! Where will you go?

MARY. This new world is a large world, Mrs. Alden. *(Mary goes out.)*

MRS. ALDEN. But there is no place like Massachusetts *(She catches herself)* Begging your pardon, Brother Williams.

DAVID. Marcy! *(He indicates that she should go out to Mary. Mrs. Alden goes.)*

ROGER. *(Quietly)* She may be right, David. There may be no place like this.

DAVID. *(Hesitantly)* Mr. Williams—I'm not a learned man, but I have always admired you for standing up for what you believed. You have many friends here.

ROGER. Thank you, David. But at times like this you need not be afraid of wounding me with the truth. I have no friends.

DAVID. I stood in the crowd after you walked away. I have never seen anything like that, sir.

ROGER. *(Grimly)* Nor I. . . .

DAVID. No one spoke. I saw strong men with tears in their eyes. I saw women with their hands clenching their shawls. You will say that not even I came out to meet you, Mr. Williams, but there was a reason for that. Something seemed to pass over the whole crowd of us. Something I cannot explain.

ROGER. What do you mean?

DAVID. It seems we all understood something that we never understood before. Don't ask me to explain.

ROGER. *(Gently and tenderly)* You have done very well. You stood with me at court three months ago when this happened. You are here today, which is more than I can say of any other man.

DAVID. I want you to know that my team of horses is yours whenever—if ever you will want to use them. . . .

ROGER. I may not need to. . . . I may stay.

DAVID. But—they have hanged men who disobeyed the order of exile.

ROGER. And they have forgiven those who recanted, even to making them officials in the Commonwealth. *(Mary returns)* I tell you I can't do this! I can't take you from your home, Mary!

(There is a knock at the door. David, who is near the door, opens it after a glance at Roger. Enter an old lady, Mrs.

Everett Neal. She is modestly dressed and is a gentle, lovable character.)

MRS. NEAL. Mr. Williams, I know you will forgive me for coming. I am Mrs. Everett Neal. I am a Puritan, sir, and though there are many things on which we would never agree, I believe with you that every person ought to be allowed to worship God in his own way. That is the hope of this new land.

ROGER. *(Obstinately)* Sometimes what we believe in the dark must be proclaimed in the day.

MRS. NEAL. *(With sincerity)* Yes, and that takes great courage. *(She takes a small book from beneath her shawl)* I with the crowd this morning. I heard your sentence of banishment. It seemed that something went out of our Common-have brought something, sir. A book of the Scriptures. I wish you would be good enough to write your name in it for me. It is a foolish, sentimental thing. But would you? I stood wealth when the Judge spoke those words. It seemed that the same thing from which we fled the Old World was taking root here in the free soil of Massachusetts. I am not one to rise against the law, sir, but I have not forgotten why we crossed the sea.

MARY. Come, Mrs. Neal. Sit down.

DAVID. Wasn't that what took hold of all of us this morning? Didn't I tell you, Mr. Williams!

MRS. NEAL. The people all felt that. They stood for a long time after the Judge went back into the hall. They turned and watched you walk to your home—there were women with children in their arms. They had been standing since early morning. They went home quietly.

ROGER. Give me the book.

(Roger takes the book with emotion and goes out.)

MARY. *(To David)* Is that true about the people, Mr. Alden?

DAVID. Yes, Mrs. Williams. He thinks because they let him walk alone that it was for a different reason. I'll show him! Half the town will be at your door before nightfall!

MARY. And yet the sentence must be carried out?

DAVID. That is the law. But it will be easier when you know you have friends who will say good-bye. *(David goes out.)*

MARY. *(Almost to herself)* The people are his friends. . . .

MRS. NEAL. I have been here many years, Mrs. Williams. I have seen the State and the Church accuse heretics and take lives. Though they banish Roger Williams his message will not be banished. But it is terrible for you! Surely there is nothing worse than to be driven from one's home.

(Roger returns.)

MARY. Roger! Do you hear what she says? There are those who will bless you!

ROGER. *(With a quiet chuckle to hide his emotions)* You are a very sentimental person, Mary. And you, Mrs. Everett Neal, if you are ever caught with this book you will surely have to follow me into exile. *(Roger hands her the book.)*

MRS. NEAL. Thank you, sir. *(She opens the book and reads)* "God only is King over the conscience of men."

ROGER. *(Grimly)* What I have written, that have I written!

(Enter a Magistrate with two Deputies.)

MAGISTRATE. Roger Williams! The court is not unmindful that its sentence carries with it certain grave implications. We are aware that recently a daughter was born to Mary Williams. We know, too, that you have no fortune wherewith to transport your family across the sea. In view of these and other matters I have been ordered to deal leniently with you.

ROGER. Leniently?

MAGISTRATE. I am authorized to accept your oath of recantation. If you will renounce but one of the charges against you, we will show extreme leniency. Renounce them all and your citizenship in the Commonwealth will be restored.

(The Magistrate unrolls a parchment.)

FIRST DEPUTY. *(To Roger)* Step forward.

ROGER. What persuaded you to come here?

FIRST DEPUTY. The law has been satisfied. We hope now to satisfy the people.

MAGISTRATE. *(Reading with authority)* Do you still affirm that His Majesty, King James, lied when he vowed he was the first Christian prince to have discovered this land?

(Roger turns to Mary.)

MARY. Say only what you believe!

ROGER. *(To the Magistrate)* I so affirm.

MAGISTRATE. Do you still affirm that our present King, Charles of England, has no right to seize this new territory without consent of the Indians?

ROGER. I made that very clear throughout my trial.

SECOND DEPUTY. *(Heatedly)* And the court made it clear that Christian kings are invested with a right, by virtue of their Christianity, to take and give away the lands and countries of other men!

ROGER. I will never submit to that though they take my life!

MAGISTRATE. Roger Williams, do you now contend that "an oath ought not to be tendered to an unregenerate"?

ROGER. I do, since thereby he is taking the name of God in vain.

MAGISTRATE. Do you affirm that it is not necessary to give thanks before meals?

ROGER. I said that such an act is a personal matter and should not be compelled by the laws of the Commonwealth.

SECOND DEPUTY. If it is unwise to pray a blessing on a meal, it is unwise to eat!

MAGISTRATE. Do you still deny that an alliance between Church and State is a valid, spiritual union?

ROGER. That I do with all my heart!

MAGISTRATE. Finally, Roger Williams, will you utterly renounce your ecclesiastical tyranny or do you still affirm that freedom of conscience is the natural right of man? *(The Magistrate lowers the parchment and looks at Roger steadily)* For I warn you, sir, your arrogance is grave and distasteful to the authorities and clergy of the Commonwealth. Unless you retract this pernicious doctrine it may go harder with you than you deem.

ROGER. Is anything harder than banishment within the week?

MAGISTRATE. There may be banishment before sundown!

ROGER. What!

MARY. How can that be!

MAGISTRATE. The order of the Inquisitorial Council.

ROGER. Why this sudden threat?

FIRST DEPUTY. The people are restless.

ROGER. Ah, that is it! *(He turns to Mrs. Neal)* The people!

They ask it, do they? Is this the friendship you spoke about?
Is this what David Alden meant?

Mrs. Neal. *(To the Magistrate)* No, the people, sir, are
with Mr. Williams. They were so affected they could not
speak.

Magistrate. Silence!

Roger. *(Going to his wife impulsively)* Mary!

Magistrate. Recant and be free!

Mary. Roger, don't you see! They fear an uprising of the
people for you—not against you—

Magistrate. For the last time, will you recant?

Roger. *(After a moment, quietly and profoundly)* Gentlemen—there goes many a ship to sea, with many hundred souls
on board whose weal and woe is common. This is a true
picture of our Commonwealth. It has happened that sometimes both Catholics and Protestants, Jews and Turks, may be
embarked together . . . and yet none of these is forced to come
to the ship's worship, nor is compelled to another's way of
faith. This, gentlemen, is the liberty of conscience for which
I plead. This is what I believe in my heart. I can say no more.

First Deputy. Thou hast accused thyself for the last time!

Magistrate. Whereas, then, thou has broached and di-
vulged these dangerous tenets without retraction . . . it is
ordered that thou shalt be driven from this jurisdiction before
nightfall never more to return hereto! The Deputies will see
that this command is fulfilled! *(The Magistrate turns and
goes out followed by the Deputies.)*

Mrs. Neal. God bless you, Mr. Williams. *(Mrs. Neal goes
out.)*

Roger. Why did I do this? Why, Mary?

Mary. You could not do otherwise.

Roger. Now, what do you think? Can I go? Can you stay
here until I have prepared a place for us somewhere. Is it
possible I can leave you with two small children—?

Mary. I will come to you. You remember once we went to
Narragansett Bay. We crossed the river. There were friendly
Indians there. I remember the sachem of Pokanoket. And
you said, "Sometimes these Indians almost seem like my
people."

Roger. You are a brave woman. Braver than I, I think.

And what you have said about the Indians is true. They know
I am their friend.

MARY. There is just one thing I wish I knew—

ROGER. And that—?

MARY. —the people here in Salem—

ROGER. *(Agitated)* See, you doubt! And I doubt! I tell
you no one so much as raised an eye to me. I walked through
a city of the dead. The voice of banishment drummed in my
ears. That is why I must wander about suffering for this truth.
Is it what men want? Or am I a heretic to them as well as to
the court?

MARY. But Mrs. Neal and David Alden—

ROGER. *(As before)* I thought you doubted! I felt you
doubted, Mary! Look at me! There is still time. They will
still be glad to have me recant.

MARY. Listen!

*(Outside, far distant, is the sound of voices. Mrs. Alden
comes in, scarcely stops, crosses and goes out.)*

MRS. ALDEN. There's a great crowd coming with David at
the head. If he's up to some mischief I'll attend to him. *(She
hurries out.)*

ROGER. Mary, no matter whether it is mischief or a blessing, I am glad for what I did. I do not know why, but I am.

MARY. And I am glad, Roger. And very proud.

*(David comes in with Thomas Angell. Thomas is about
forty-five, rugged, likeable, obviously slightly embarrassed
by the presence of Roger, whom he has always admired
and held in awe.)*

ROGER. Well, gentlemen?

DAVID. Mr. Williams, there are many people anxious to
see you.

ROGER. *(Tersely)* They will have to come quickly. I am to
leave today.

DAVID. We know. That is why Thomas Angell is here with
me.

ROGER. Well, Thomas, you have always been my friend.

THOMAS. *(Simply)* Mr. Williams, there are some among us
who wish to follow you.

ROGER. Follow me? What do you mean, Thomas?

THOMAS. There is Joshua Verin, John Smith, Francis

Wickes, Thomas Oleny, and others. They are at their homes now preparing for the journey.

ROGER. Into banishment—with me!

THOMAS. Yes, Mr. Williams.

ROGER. *(Falteringly)* No, Thomas, you do not know what you're saying!

THOMAS. We are agreed, sir, if you will give us permission. There is a new land—there can be a new freedom!

ROGER. You hear what he says, Mary!

MARY. It is a great thing, Thomas Angell.

ROGER. *(To David)* And the people—? What do they say?

DAVID. They are under the law. There is nothing they can do. But they want to show you that they are your friends.

MARY. Let them come in—as many as can!

(David starts to go.)

ROGER. Wait, David, I want to thank you. You were right, then, in what you said. And as for you, Mr. Angell, and the others who have this great confidence, I assure you it will not be misplaced. We will go to the mouth of the Moshassuck River and there, by the grace of God, undertake a settlement which will permit freedom of worship and liberty of faith.

THOMAS. As you have often said, Mr. Williams, that should be the right of every man.

ROGER. We will bargain honestly with the Pokanokets. If need be we will learn their language. They will be our people. *(There is a shot outside, some distance from the house) What's that?*

MARY. The deputies—?

DAVID. *(Suddenly)* It sounded like my gun! Marcy! *(He goes quickly.)*

MARY. *(Laughing)* The partridges!

ROGER. *(Seriously)* Thomas, if we should ever found a settlement as we plan, we will call it Providence. Surely God's great hand is guiding us this day.

THOMAS. The river is open. We have many canoes. We can go far tonight if you are willing.

ROGER. *(With emotion)* To the cove at Tockwotten. Then to Fox Point and—finally to the spring at the mouth of the Moshassuck—

(Enter David and Mrs. Alden, agitated.)

DAVID. Such a thing! As though we didn't have enough trouble for one day!

MARY. What happened, Mrs. Alden?

MRS. ALDEN. I missed it! *(To Roger)* And I did so want to see you have a good meal today, Brother Williams.

ROGER. Your intentions were good even though your aim wasn't.

(The Magistrate enters in authority.)

MAGISTRATE. Marcy Alden!

MRS. ALDEN. Oh, my!

DAVID. Now what is it?

MAGISTRATE. You are accused of discharging a weapon between the hours of nine and one o'clock, which is a misdemeanor under the law. You are ordered to spend one day and one night in the town jail.

MRS. ALDEN. *(Trembling)* Oh, no!

DAVID. Such a thing!

MAGISTRATE. Come along.

MRS. ALDEN. *(Going into Mary's arms)* Oh, Mrs. Williams!

DAVID. *(To the Magistrate)* Is there nothing we can do?

MAGISTRATE. It is the law. Even Mr. Williams knows that. The hour from twelve to one is to be an hour of meditation and silence.

ROGER. What time is it now?

MAGISTRATE. Twenty to one by the sun-clock in your own yard.

MRS. ALDEN. They make these laws without even telling us. It's not fair.

MARY. It will not be so bad. I will be waiting for you tomorrow.

MAGISTRATE. Be thankful it wasn't the Sabbath. You might have been hanged!

MRS. ALDEN. It's a bad country when they have so many laws.

ROGER. It's a good country, Mrs. Alden.

MRS. ALDEN. I know what you mean. Good-by, Brother Williams. Good-by, Mrs. Williams.

ROGER. Good-by, Mrs. Alden. And be of good courage. We will yet eat partridges in peace.

MRS. ALDEN. I hope so. I hope so, Brother Williams.

MAGISTRATE. Come! I am in no humor for bantering!

DAVID. *(Gently)* Come, Marcy.

MRS. ALDEN. It is dreadful days we are living in—dreadful days.

MAGISTRATE. As for you, Roger Williams, see that you read the time of day aright.

ROGER. That I will. *(The Magistrate goes out with David and Mrs. Alden)* As soon as you men are ready, Thomas, join me here. Bring such goods as you can. But more than that, bring great courage for the new city of Providence!

THOMAS. Yes, Mr. Williams. *(Thomas goes.)*

ROGER. *(Tenderly)* It is never so dark but that there is some light, Mary.

MARY. It is a great thing for the people to do.

ROGER. For them I must do much. And, yet, but for you I might have failed.

CURTAIN

To Speak of Freedom

A Literacy Play

by

GEORGE NEW

Characters:

NARRATOR
A MISSIONARY
GONZALEZ
THREE VOICES
A PERSON OF IMPORTANCE

TOMASA
THE VILLAGE CHIEF
TWO MEN OF THE VILLAGE
OTHER VILLAGERS

TIME: Present.

PLACE: Mexico.

LENGTH: About twenty minutes.

SETTING: *This play may be staged very simply. To the right of the stage there is a desk with a box of cigars on it, a chair behind it, and another chair in front of it. This suggests the office of the Person of Importance. To the left of the stage are several rough benches and an easel. These suggest the open-air school. In the center of the stage, away from the audience there is a bench. At the opening of the play this has a briefcase on it. It first suggests a room in the church, later a hill above the village. A curtain may or may not be used.*

The Narrator *appears before the curtain, if there is one. If not, he stands at the left of the stage.*

NARRATOR. In the Spanish-speaking countries to the south, in the English-speaking to the north, in every country of the vast two continents of the western hemisphere millions of men, white, brown, and black, wait with questions in their eyes and with no voice to speak. These are illiterates who can neither read nor write. They are not stupid men. They are men like you and me. There is only one difference. No gov-

241

ernment, no church has cared enough to give them a voice, to find them and teach them. But there are governments which care. There are churches which care. There are men who care—men who labor ceaselessly to give these silent millions a voice—a voice to speak of freedom.

This is the story of one of those who cared. It might be the story of anyone of a thousand missionaries and teachers. It is not the story of a wealthy man nor of a famous man. It is the story of a Mexican boy who reached out his hand to his neighbors—of Gonzalez who teaches school in the little Indian village of Taxhay in the State of Hidalgo, Mexico.

The story begins seven years ago in a Baptist Church in Los Angeles. Young Gonzalez goes down to the church almost every Sunday evening. This evening he and his friends have listened to a missionary just returned from the Philippines. They have heard how the Moros of Mindanao were taught to read and write and how they learned to teach others. Gonzalez has been very silent while the story is told. Now the others have gone down to the church basement for games, but Gonzalez has waited to speak with the missionary.

Gonzalez *and the* Missionary *come in together from the Right. They cross to the center bench. The* Missionary *carries some papers, which he puts in the briefcase.*

MISSIONARY. Aren't you going to miss the party downstairs?

GONZALEZ. Sir—I wanted to ask a question.

MISSIONARY. Of course.

GONZALEZ. The Moros you told us about—the Spanish thought they were stupid and could not learn?

MISSIONARY. Yes, the Spanish and many Americans, too. They were considered incorrigible troublemakers.

GONZALEZ. And all they needed was an opportunity?

MISSIONARY. All they needed was an opportunity—and kindness. They were troubled and lonely. They were eager to be our friends when we showed them that we cared. I think they will yet prove to us, those Filipinos, what good friends they are. But here, you are missing the games—

GONZALEZ. The people who need help—they are not all in the Philippines.

MISSIONARY. Oh, no. The least of them are in the Philippines. Listen *(He takes a marked book from the briefcase and reads)*:

"In Asia and Africa alone nine persons out of ten are illiterate—half the human race. There are millions in every country in Latin America."

You are from Mexico?

GONZALEZ. Yes. I am a Mexican. My parents brought me to Los Angeles when I was a little boy, but I remember things you help me understand—an old Indian forced to put his thumbprints on an agreement he did not understand because he could not read nor sign his name.

MISSIONARY. Yes, it is sad. People who could help do not hear those who can only suffer silently because they have no voice. You are in school?

GONZALEZ. I will graduate from high school in the spring.

MISSIONARY. Congratulations to you. Will you go on to college?

GONZALEZ. I don't know. I would like to go. My family is poor.

MISSIONARY. If you want to go you will find a way.

GONZALEZ. Perhaps I will find a job in Los Angeles. There is much to learn in the city.

MISSIONARY. You have thought of going back to Mexico?

GONZALEZ. Oh, my friends are American. I feel North American.

MISSIONARY. The government of Mexico is making a great effort to teach the Indians. But it is difficult. There is little money. There are few schools and few teachers. You understand, you could be a teacher.

GONZALEZ. Oh, I hadn't thought about going back to Mexico. I am happy in the United States. I wouldn't want to leave my friends. What could I do? I am only seventeen. *(Slowly)* Yes—I might be a teacher.

MISSIONARY. Each of us must find his own way and his own work. Well, come. We'll both miss the party.

(He takes Gonzalez' arm, picks up briefcase. They go out right.)

NARRATOR. Gonzalez did not forget his talk with the missionary, and one day after school he went to the library to read about Mexico. He read about the tiny village schools which were painfully, one by one, emerging in the hidden forests of the tropics in the south and the lofty valleys of the mountains. Slowly, with suffering and confusion, a whole nation was finding its voice. Gonzalez thought about it as he walked home that day.

(Gonzalez *enters right with some books under his arm. He crosses to the center of the stage.*)

He could see that the way was not easy. Other voices were raised which would never let the great office of a free people be heard.

(*The Voices are loud and insistent.*)

FIRST VOICE. (*Off left*) The Indians are savages, incapable of civilization. They are dirty and stupid. They do not even speak Spanish. Now they are to be educated at government expense. It is a great folly. It is a great waste of money.

GONZALEZ. (*Looking off left*) But I have learned that no people is stupid. There is wisdom to be found in the ways of every people. It is the duty of those who have light to take it to others.

SECOND VOICE. (*Off right*) These new ways are madness. The ways of the fathers are the ways to be trusted. Let these meddling outsiders stay away. Indians have no need of the city man's books and written signs. They will only bring wickedness and disaster. Let the women continue to grind the corn. Let the men not look up from their labor in the fields.

GONZALEZ. (*Looking right*) Yes, there is wisdom in the old ways. If the Indian learns to read and write he will better understand it, and he will bring it to men in the cities who do not understand. But there is disaster in the old ways, too. The soil grows thin and washes into the sea. The eyes of the children grow dull, and they are not children but old people. The women are the slaves of the corn they must grind for six hours each day. The evil in the old ways makes the people and the country poor.

THIRD VOICE. (*Off left*) It is impossible to educate the

Indians. There is no money. There are no schools. In Mexico there are some forty races and as many languages. There is no way to make these people understand one another.

GONZALEZ. *(Left)* But there is a way. I've read that Dr. Laubach has discovered a way. People in India and Africa, all over the world, are learning to read and write their own languages. Each one who learns can help another.

VOICES. It is stupid meddling. It will not succeed.

It is dangerous folly. It will not succeed.

The people do not want it. It will not succeed.

Forget it, Gonzalez. Forget it. Forget it.

GONZALEZ. *(Coming toward the audience)* Now I begin to see. I cannot forget it. I could not be happy if I did not try to share all that I have learned. I would be a coward if I stayed here, and my life would be worth nothing. There is something that I can do. I can go where I am needed. I can teach people to read. (Gonzalez *goes off left.)*

NARRATOR. So it happened that the next year Gonzalez did not go to work in Los Angeles. Instead he took a second-class bus down the winding length of the Pan-American highway, and with every mile that brought him closer to Mexico City his heart sang louder. He was going back to his people and his work. He would be a rural schoolteacher. He would show the people of his village that there were people who wanted to be their friends. He was happy. In Mexico City he was accepted for enrollment in the training school for rural teachers. He worked very hard, and many people noticed what a fine student he was.

One day Gonzalez received a letter asking him to come to the office of a certain person of importance. Gonzalez did not know what to expect.

(The Person of Importance *enters right and stands by the desk.* Gonzalez *enters left.)*

THE PERSON. Gonzalez?

GONZALEZ. Yes, Señor. *(They shake hands.)*

THE PERSON. Here, have a seat. (Gonzalez *sits in the chair before the desk.* The Person *sits on the desk)* I am happy to meet you, young man. You are a fine student, I hear. I'm interested in promising young men. There's a place for them in my business. It pays me to be interested. Here, have a cigar. *(He offers* Gonzalez *a cigar from the box.)*

Gonzalez. No, thank you, Señor. (The Person *takes a cigar and lights it.)*

The Person. I hear you want to go out into the hills. Want to teach the Indians to read or something.

Gonzalez. Yes, Señor. That is the dream which brought me back to Mexico.

The Person. Well, I may as well be frank. *(He seats himself behind the desk)* That's all nonsense. It can't possibly come to any good. It's just stirring up trouble. The Indians are an inferior people. It's in their blood. They're shiftless and lazy. They need bosses, not education.

Gonzalez. There are some people who believe that the hope of Mexico is the education of the Indians.

The Person. Revolutionary double talk! Don't take it seriously. Look here, son, you're a well-trained, bright young man. That's why you're in my office. You know English and you know Spanish. I can offer you a real job, a job with a salary and a future. You can stay here in Mexico City—enjoy life.

Gonzalez. I'm sorry Señor. You are kind. Someone told me once that each of us must find his way and his work. (Gonzalez *stands)* I've found my job.

The Person. *(Rising)* Hmmm. I can't understand you young people. Wasting the best part of your life up in those lonely mountains. How do you expect us to carry on down here without you? *(He crosses to* Gonzalez) But you'll be back soon enough. Sooner or later you'll be back. Come in and see me, son. Come in and see me. *(He pats* Gonzalez *paternally on the back as they go out left.)*

Narrator. So instead of staying in Mexico City Gonzalez started out one day to the little Otamy Indian village of Taxhay, a community of three hundred and thirty people. First he took a bus up the highway, and then, for the last four hours, he hiked along a foot trail, over hills and down ravines, and finally he reached the high ridge of the last mountain. There below were the leaf-covered shacks of the village, the fields of corn, the chickens and the goats, and the children playing in the dooryards. Gonzalez had never been so happy.

The next weeks were very busy. Gonzalez went from hut to hut to meet the people, who were always very quiet. But the children came every day for their lessons, which were held in the shade of a Pinone tree. One day Gonzalez persuaded a group of men and women to come and see how easy it was to learn to read. Then he felt that a wonderful new light would soon shine in the village.

But it was very dry. The corn did not prosper. Without corn the winter would bring hunger and illness. There began to be whisperings in the huts, but Gonzalez did not hear them. He was too busy copying the charts for the reading lessons.

(Gonzalez *enters left with the chart. He puts it on the easel, which is turned so that the audience does not at first see the face of the chart. While* The Voices *speak,* Gonzalez *is very busy finishing the chart.*)

First Voice. God is displeased. It is the stranger, the school teacher who is to blame. This is what comes of the new ways.

Second Voice. God is jealous. We save our pesos to build a school. Instead we should give them to God to make rain. Now God is displeased and will make the children ill.

Third Voice. We did not ask the teacher to come here. He belongs to the city, not the country. He does not come to make us wise, but to make us appear foolish. Let him go back to the city.

Voices. We must get rid of him.

We must get rid of him.

We must get rid of him.

Narrator. That day a very silent group of villagers came for the reading lesson. (Gonzalez *turns the literacy chart so that the audience may see it. A group of villagers file in from the left. Some of them sit on the rough benches. Others stand behind the benches.*)

Gonzalez. Good afternoon, my friends. I am very pleased. In a short time many of you have made great progress. Soon

you will be able to help others in the rancheria who have not
come to the lessons. You will be teachers, too. Soon you will
be able to tell them what a wonderful thing it is to be able
to take up a book and be able to understand wise men in far
places or to put on paper messages to be carried across the
mountain. With the new knowledge we will make Taxhay a
beautiful, prosperous village.

Who will read first what they see on the chart? *(There is no
reply. Indicating one of the men)* Come, Señor, will you read?

THE MAN. Not today, Señor teacher. My eyes water.

GONZALEZ. *(Indicating one of the women)* Señora, you are
a fine pupil. Will you not shame the men with your skill?

THE WOMAN. Not today, Señor. I have no heart for reading.

GONZALEZ. Come, come. We must all take each step as it
approaches us. Remember, it is our privilege to show the way
to the others. Who will help us this morning and read first?
*(Tomasa, a young girl who has been standing behind the
women at the back, raises her hand and comes forward.)* You,
Tomasa! You will show us the way when we hesitate.

TOMASA. I will try.

GONZALEZ. Come forward. You will succeed. *(Tomasa comes
and stands by the chart)* We will show everyone what a simple
thing reading is, will we not? *(They exchange smiles.)*

GONZALEZ. You have only to tell us what you see. *Gonzalez
points to the words on each line of the chart. Tomasa answers
hesitantly, with great concentration.*

TOMASA. Pato. Raton. Balanza. Vaca. Casa.

GONZALEZ. Perfect! You are a fine pupil. Now, we will
cover the pictures and you will tell us what the signs represent. (Gonzalez *covers the pictures on the chart with a large
white handkerchief, which he takes from his pocket. He again
points to the words.)*

TOMASA. *Pato. Raton. Balanza. Vaca. Casa.*

GONZALEZ. Exactly! You set a fine example. Now will you
choose someone to follow you, and you may help them if they
need it. Who shall it be? (Tomasa *starts to choose. The Head
Man rises from his seat.)*

HEAD MAN. Tomasa! Come! There must be no more reading. (Tomasa *looks at* Gonzalez, *then runs to the back of the room.*)

GONZALEZ. I do not understand. You want to learn to read. You have come to learn.

HEAD MAN. No. We do not want to learn new ways. These are our hills. These are our father's hills. We will cover them with corn as our fathers did. We will live as our fathers did. That is our wisdom.

GONZALEZ. Yes, these are your hills, and this is your village. I have come to give the hills back to you. You must trust me. If you learn to read you will discover how to hold the precious earth of your hills. You will learn that you must not plant corn alone, for it makes your earth poor. You will learn not to cut the pinones which hold the lifegiving moisture in the earth. You will learn to till your fields so that they do not wash into the valleys. *(A Second Man rises.)*

SECOND MAN. We do not trust what you tell us. You are a foreigner. You should not be here. Your knowledge belongs to the city. We do not trust the city.

GONZALEZ. I have not come to take anything from you. I am a friend with a gift. I do not belong to the city. If you will let me stay with you, your village will be my village. You will teach me your ways and your wisdom. What I bring you does not belong to the city. It belongs to your village. It belongs to all men everywhere. (Gonzalez *points to the chart*) These are signs with which men may share their love and wisdom. Without them; the silence creeps up. *(A Third Man rises.)*

THIRD MAN. We must not listen to you. What you teach is not pleasing to God. He stops the rain, and the corn does not grow. God will make us hungry if you do not go. We must do as we have always done.

GONZALEZ. Listen, my friends. God is not angry with you. The rain will come as it has always come. If it comes late this season, and if the crop is poor, that is a test of the patience of God's children. God does not demand that you run in fear from house to house gathering pesos with which to bribe him. Instead, remember this: God has brought us together in this village. God has given you your land and your children. We must learn to use our land well that it may be an unspoiled gift to our children. With love we must build a school for our children. God did not intend them to live in silent loneliness. He intended that the earth should be ours and that we should be brothers one of another. That is why we learn to read. *(There is muttering among the villagers.)*

CROWD OF VOICES. What the teacher says is right.

No, he is a stranger.

God wants a sacrifice.

He has come to help us.

He must go. We must send him away.

GONZALEZ. I will speak my last words to you. I came to you from a great distance because I had a dream for you. I saw your village, and it was a shining village. It was beautiful with flowers and the laughing faces of many children. The women were singing all day, and the men greeted one another with great love. Your village was one of many villages, and each village was friendly to those around it. The wisdom of the people was carried from village to village. And all the villages, all the people's wisdom—all this was Mexico. And Mexico spoke to all the nations. *(He picks up the chart)* This chart—your learning—is a promise of those things. That is why I teach you. *(He replaces the chart)* Now you must decide whether I am to stay or go. You must choose. If I stay, we will build a shining village. But you will have to make a sacrifice—and not for rain. We are all poor, but we must tax ourselves to build a school. It will belong alike to the youngest and the oldest. We must all agree to work to build it together. If you will not do that, then with sadness I must leave you. You must think of what I have said and decide. There is nothing more for me to say to you. *(After a moment the* Head Man *silently leaves left. The others follow.* Tomasa *goes last with a backward look.)*

NARRATOR. Gonzalez climbed silently and slowly to the top of the hill and looked down on the village. He was troubled. *(Gonzalez goes to the bench, center, and sits)* First there had been his own desire to stay in Los Angeles and he an American. He loved his friends there, and the city held much promise. Then there had been those who told him the Indians were stupid and unwilling to learn. He had not believed them. He knew their interests well enough. Now he faced prejudice and fear. He had come as a friend. If the people would not trust him, what could he do? He could only wait with patience.

VOICE. *(Off left)* Gonzalez! Gonzalez! *(Gonzalez jumps to his feet. Looks off left)* Gonzalez!

NARRATOR. It was the head man of the village, hurrying up the mountainside. *(The* Head Man *enters left and goes to* Gonzalez *with hands outstretched.)*

HEAD MAN. Gonzalez, we have decided. You must stay with us. We will build the school. Our village will not be silent. We will make Taxhay a shining village. We will teach one another.

GONZALEZ. *(Embracing him)* We are friends. It is good to be friends. *(Gonzalez indicates the space above the bench)* Here on this high hill where all the village can see, let us build a white cross. It will be a sign for Taxhay. We will look at it, and each of us in his heart will know what it means. We will look at it, and we will know that Taxhay is not alone. *(They clasp hands. A cross of light appears between them. If there are curtains, they close.)*

NARRATOR. If you traveled down the Pan-American highway, you might stop short of Mexico City at the tiny village of Los Troncas. There you would start the four-hour hike across the hills to Taxhay. You would know that you were approaching the village when you saw the gleam of the white cross on the hill. You would look down from it to the fine school below. Gonzalez might hike out to greet you, and he would surely take you down to a fine meal, which his wife, Tomasa, would be preparing for the guest. After you had eaten you might go out with Gonzalez to look at the sky and the cross, dark against its vastness. There in the silence you might almost hear the unstilled voices of brown and black and white men—voices to join the voice of Taxhay—to speak of freedom.

Empty Hands

A One-act Play of India

by

HELEN M. CLARK

Characters:

BENTLEY, an American missionary of about thirty-five years of age. His face is young, but his hair, in strange contrast, is streaked with white.

MARK, an American in his late twenties.

MAXWELL, a small, dried-up little Scotsman of indefinite age.

LUKKA, a Hindu manservant.

JOGIE, a small Hindu boy, about twelve years of age.

THE BRAHMIN, a young Hindu, about twenty-five.

ANNAMURI, a Hindu woman. She is young, small, dark.

TIME: Present.

LENGTH: About thirty minutes.

SETTING: *The scene is a room in Bentley's house, built beside the Road of the Pilgrims, which leads to one of India's many shrines; a plain, high-ceilinged, white-walled room, with a window center back, covered by bamboo blinds. The door at the right, which stands open during the play, leads to the veranda. The door at the left leads to the rest of the house. There is a plain table at the left, a comfortable chair to the left and a plain chair to the right of the table, another plain chair at the right of the stage, and a bench upstage by the window. The room is lighted rather dimly, the one kerosene lamp on the table leaving most of it in shadow. There are a few books on the table, among them a primer and a well worn English Bible. On the walls are pictures or hangings, and above the table a reproduction of Hoffmann's "Christ and the Rich Young Ruler," or a picture of Thorwaldsen's statue of Christ, "Come Unto Me," or some other painting in which the hands of Christ are shown as empty. From out-*

*side comes the muffled sound of the monsoon rain, falling
steadily, heavily. This sound continues during the play
until its cessation is indicated.*

TIME: Early evening.

(At curtain rise the stage is empty. Then Jogie darts in the
door left and scurries across the stage to the door right.
But the rain discourages him, and he runs back and ducks
in under the table, where he sits, very small and quiet,
with his knees drawn up to his chin. Then Bentley enters
left, stands looking about the room.)

BENTLEY. (Crossing right and calling out the door) Jogie!
Jogie!
*Jogie does not move. Bentley turns and goes over to the
table.*
BENTLEY. (Casually) Do you like it under the table, Jogie?
*Getting no answer, he bends over and looks under at Jogie.
Jogie stares up at him. Bentley beckons to the boy to
come out. Jogie does and, on his feet, ducks his chin and
stands looking up at Bentley furtively.*
BENTLEY. Why did you run away from me and hide under
the table? (No answer) What's wrong, Jogie?
JOGIE. Nothing, Sahib.
BENTLEY. Then why did you skitter out of sight like a
scared rabbit when you heard me coming? That's been an
admission of guilt since Eden, Jogie. (He puts his hand under
Jogie's chin, lifts his head and touches the corners of his
mouth) Um-h'm! Sugar again.
JOGIE. Yes, Sahib.
BENTLEY. You could have asked, Jogie.
JOGIE. Yes, Sahib.
BENTLEY. Why didn't you, then?
JOGIE. I do not know, Sahib. The sugar was there—and the
Sahib was not. That is, I thought the Sahib was not—
BENTLEY. But, unfortunately, the Sahib was. And yesterday
you promised me you wouldn't steal any more, Jogie.
JOGIE. Yes, Sahib. But when I saw the sugar, I forgot. I
thought only of how sweet it was.

BENTLEY. *(Walking right)* O very small Adam, what am I going to do with you to make you remember your promise?

JOGIE. The Sahib may beat me if he wishes.

BENTLEY. Would you be sorry if I did?

JOGIE. No, Sahib. But I would cry very loudly and weep very much—and then perhaps the Sahib would be pleased—and forget.

BENTLEY. Oh! I see. You will make a very loud noise and then I will forget that my sugar has been stolen.

JOGIE. Yes, Sahib. But—will the Sahib make it a very small beating? Because it was only a very little sugar, Sahib. In the palm of the hand. *(He turns around, hunches his shoulders, screws up his face.)*

BENTLEY. *(Crossing back to table)* No. No beating. You had enough of those before you came to me to last a lifetime. *(Jogie turns to face him again)* But I've got to make you remember your promise some way. Have you also forgotten what I taught you, Jogie?

JOGIE. *(Uneasily)* The Sahib has taught me many things. And it is difficult to remember all of them.

BENTLEY. About stealing.

JOGIE. Does the Sahib mean the word of his God?

BENTLEY. Yes. Have you forgotten?

JOGIE. *(After a slight hesitation)* No, Sahib.

BENTLEY. Say it, then.

JOGIE. Thou shalt not steal.

BENTLEY. That's something, anyway. If you know the rule, then it's just a matter of application. And now—to improve your memory on promises, suppose you go stand by the wall there and say that over out loud until I tell you to stop.

JOGIE. Yes, Sahib. *(He goes over to the wall right, stands facing it)* Here, Sahib?

BENTLEY. Yes.

JOGIE. *(Shifting downstage a little)* Or—perhaps here, Sahib?

BENTLEY. *(Firmly)* Right there.

JOGIE. Yes, Sahib.

(Bentley takes a book and sits at left of table. Jogie watches him.)

BENTLEY. Go on, Jogie. And face to the wall.

JOGIE. Yes, Sahib. I but wanted to see if the Sahib was listening.

BENTLEY. The Sahib is.

JOGIE. Yes, Sahib. Now I will say it. Thou shalt not steal. Thou shalt not steal. Thou shalt not steal. *(He gets very much interested in something above him on the wall)* Thou shalt not steal. Thou shalt not—*(He stops to watch whatever it is.)*

BENTLEY. *(Looking up)* Go on, Jogie.

JOGIE. Sahib, there is something crawling—

BENTLEY. Never mind. Go on.

JOGIE. Yes, Sahib. Thou shalt not steal. Thou shalt not steal. I am a creature of the dust. I am a worm that crawls in the dust. I am a very little worm that crawls under the dust. *(A furtive glance at Bentley)* Thou shalt not steal. There is dust upon my head—and a great sorrow in my belly. It is like the pain for which the Sahib gives the evil-tasting medicine. *(Looking around quickly)* Only for this I do not need the medicine, Sahib. Truly. *(Face to wall again)* Thou shalt not steal. I am a small and miserable worm—truly the smallest and most miserable of worms—and the Sahib is my father and my mother—and I think it is a spider, Sahib. Thou shalt not steal. The Sahib has said that his God sees everything. Then must his God know that it was a very little sugar that I took —no more than would stick to the palm of my hand after I had wetted it with my tongue—so. *(He illustrates by licking his palm, then looks upward)* And truly the Sahib's God knows it was very sweet and pleasant upon my tongue. It *is* a spider, Sahib. (NOTE: *Do not let Jogie clown through next part of speech)* Thou shalt not steal. And truly the Sahib is a great man. He has builded this house for his God upon the Road of the Pilgrims, and sits within to talk of his God to those who come to his door. Thou shalt not steal. And the pilgrims who walk upon the road to the shrine turn aside to listen to the wisdom of the Sahib, for he is a very wise man. The Sahib is a very good man, also. The Sahib is a very holy man, also. I will ask the Sahib's God to make me as wise as the Sahib. *(He glances about to see if this makes any impression. Bentley takes no notice. Jogie sighs)* Thou shalt not steal. It is a good saying—it is a very wise saying—but difficult to obey. Very difficult—when there is sugar—and it is strange that the Sahib's God should notice such a very little sugar. Thou shalt not steal. *(He glances about again. Finding he is still being ignored, he lifts his voice in a wail)* Aie! Aie! My belly is full of pain because the Sahib is very angry.

BENTLEY. The Sahib is not angry, but he is grieved because you do not think of him as a friend.

JOGIE. *(Turning to face him)* I do not understand, Sahib.

BENTLEY. When one wishes something from a friend, one asks, Jogie.

JOGIE. Yes, Sahib.

BENTLEY. And when one takes from a friend what is not asked and given for the asking—one hurts a friend very much.

JOGIE. Has the Sahib also a pain in his belly?

BENTLEY. Yes—I'm afraid I have, Jogie.

JOGIE. Perhaps if the Sahib took the medicine—

BENTLEY. Medicine won't help my pain, Jogie—any more than it will yours.

Jogie considers this. Then he goes over to the table.

JOGIE. Is it just because of the sugar that it hurts, Sahib? It was only a very little sugar I took.

BENTLEY. And nothing more, Jogie?

(Jogie shuffles his feet uneasily, looks down, then at Bentley, then takes something out of his waistband and holds it out. Bentley takes it. It is a watch fob.)

JOGIE. It—it was so very bright, Sahib—and I meant but to look at it—so I took it in my hand. You knew, Sahib?

BENTLEY. Yes, Jogie, I knew. But I wanted you to give it back to me yourself.

JOGIE. The Sahib's God sees everything—and so does the Sahib.

BENTLEY. This hurt me more than the sugar, because the fob was my father's—and so it is precious to me.

JOGIE. I am sorry, Sahib.

BENTLEY. You see, Jogie, two people cannot live happily in the same house if they cannot trust each other.

JOGIE. You will not send me away? Please do not. I will remember next time, Sahib. Truly I will. Do not send me away!

BENTLEY. No, of course not, Jogie. We'll just—try again.

Jogie. Yes, Sahib. And I will promise again.

Bentley. Is the pain better now, Jogie?

Jogie. *(Brightening suddenly)* Yes, Sahib. It is better. It is gone!

Bentley. And mine, also.

Jogie. And are we—are we friends again, Sahib?

Bentley. Of course, Jogie.

Jogie. Ah! Now I have a very good feeling inside. Need I stand by the wall again, Sahib?

Bentley. No. No more. Sit here beside me and we'll have a reading lesson. You missed it this afternoon, you know.

Jogie. *(Sighs)* Yes, Sahib. But it is very difficult to learn—this reading! *(Sits on floor beside Bentley's chair.)*

Bentley. *(Opening the primer)* But if you wish to be as wise as the Sahib, you'll have to learn it. Here. This page.

Jogie. Yes, Sahib. But I wish I had not wished. *(He sighs, then studies the page laboriously, marking each word with his finger and muttering to himself.)*

(Lukka, a manservant, enters left.)

Lukka. Sahib?

Bentley. Yes, Lukka?

Lukka. Shall I light the lantern, Sahib?

Bentley. Of course.

Lukka. There will not be any pilgrims upon the road to-night, Sahib.

Bentley. Probably not. Yet light it, Lukka.

Lukka. As the Sahib wishes. *(He goes out on the veranda and presently a faint light shows through the doorway.)*

Jogie. *(Struggling with a word)* What is this, Sahib?

Bentley. "Many." You ought to know that.

Jogie. Sahib, these words are as many leaves in a heap—all alike. How shall I tell one from the other?

Lukka. *(Re-enters)* It is done, Sahib.

Bentley. Thank you, Lukka.

Lukka. Yes, Sahib. *(He exits left.)*

Jogie. And this, Sahib?

Bentley. "Grow."

Jogie. "Grow." Truly this is hard to do, Sahib.

Bentley. The road to wisdom is always hard, Jogie.

JOGIE. I do not think I will be a wise man. I will be a holy man. A Sadhu does not have to read.

BENTLEY. The road to true holiness is also hard. And a holy man must remember promises.

JOGIE. Yes, Sahib. *(Sighs a long sigh.)*

Annamuri enters left.

ANNAMURI. Sahib!

BENTLEY. What is it, Annamuri? Is the child awake?

ANNAMURI. No, Sahib. He sleeps. But he breathes with difficulty and his sleep is restless. He cries out now and again. Sahib—I am afraid.

BENTLEY. You mustn't be afraid. I'm sure he'll be all right.

ANNAMURI. He is so little—and our only son—

BENTLEY. I know. But don't worry. Go back and watch him, and call me when he wakes. But remember, sleep is his best medicine.

ANNAMURI. Yes, Sahib. *(She starts to go, hesitates, then comes back to face Bentley across the table)* Sahib?

BENTLEY. Yes?

ANNAMURI. *(Holding out her hand, in which is a small brass charm on a cord)* It is the charm that used to hang about my son's neck. Will the Sahib take it—and keep it?

BENTLEY. Why?

ANNAMURI. Sahib, my husband says that perhaps we should hang it about the child's neck again—that we may have the help of the old gods as well as our new God. He says it was blessed by the priest—and so might cure the sickness.

BENTLEY. Do you want to put it back, Annamuri?

ANNAMURI. No, Sahib. You said it was not right, now that we are Christian. Yet my husband holds it in his hand and looks at the child—and there is something within me that urges, "Put it back!" So will you please take it, Sahib—and put it where we cannot see it?

BENTLEY. *(Taking the charm)* It wouldn't help the child —neither would it do him any harm. It has no power in itself. But if you put your trust in it—

ANNAMURI. I know, Sahib. That is wrong. It is only that we are so afraid.

BENTLEY. I understand, Annamuri. But try not to be. Because I'm quite certain the child will be better when he wakes. *(Puts charm on table.)*

ANNAMURI. Yes, Sahib. *(Looks at charm, takes it up, then drops it)* No! The ways of your God are better, Sahib. That I know—in my heart. He—he will not be angry because—because sometimes the old ways. . . .

BENTLEY. No, Annamuri. God understands. He has a Son, too.

ANNAMURI. Yes, Sahib. And I will trust him—no matter —no matter what may come. For you and your God have dealt kindly with us, Sahib.

BENTLEY. Thank you, Annamuri. And if you need more help in this and I can give it . . .

ANNAMURI. Yes, Sahib. I will come. *(Goes to door, turns)* Thank you, Sahib. *(She goes out left.)*

JOGIE. The gardener does not read. I think I will be a gardener.

> *(There is a faint clatter on the veranda, and Maxwell comes to the door right. He takes off his helmet and raincoat and shakes them outside as he talks.)*

MAXWELL. How are you, Bent?

BENTLEY. *(Rising and going around the table)* Hello, Henry! Come in!

MAXWELL. As soon as I wring myself out. Whew! It's a fine night for ducks, I'm thinking.

BENTLEY. *(Sitting on table)* And Scotsmen? *(Calls left)* Lukka!

MAXWELL. Aye, and Scotsmen. It's weather after me own heart. A bit of rain and I blossom like a rose. Only I'm wishing it wasn't quite so like a warm showerbath.

Lukka enters and Maxwell hands him the raincoat.

Better hang it out on the veranda, Lukka, where it can drip and bother nobody.

LUKKA. Yes, Sahib. *(He goes out on the veranda with the coat, returns in a few seconds and exits left.)*

MAXWELL. *(Putting his helmet on the bench and rolling down his trouser legs, which are turned up nearly to his knees)* I just thought I'd swim over and see if you could play a bit of chess. It's not likely you'll be bothered with any pilgrims tonight. Beyond the village the road's as empty as a Scotsman's purse—except for a hundred bottomless puddles into which I fell with exasperating regularity.

BENTLEY. *(Laughing)* "Dr. Foster went to Gloucester
            In a shower of rain.
            He stepped in a puddle
            Up to his middle,
            And never went there again."

MAXWELL. And a sensible man he was! *(Takes out a handkerchief and wipes his face and hands)* Hetty told me I was a bit gone in the head to be coming here in the rain—but I said even a missionary is entitled to go daft once in a while. *(Seeing the charm which Bentley is holding)* What's yon thing you're dangling?

BENTLEY. A charm. It used to hang about the neck of the gardener's little son. The boy's ill—

MAXWELL *(Quickly)* Cholera?

BENTLEY. No. Old-fashioned croup. His mother brought this to me so she wouldn't be tempted to put it back on the boy. You see, Henry, they're trying.

MAXWELL. Aye. It's not easy to break with the old beliefs and superstitions. Well, how about it? Have you time for a game or no?

BENTLEY. As things look right now, yes. Jogie—get the chessboard and the chessmen, please.

JOGIE. Yes, Sahib. *(He scrambles up and exits left.)*

MAXWELL. How are you making out with yon wee laddie?

BENTLEY. I have hopes.

MAXWELL. Well, that's something. Are his ideas of morality any the stronger?

BENTLEY. I think so. Of course, we have our ups and downs in the matter. His most persistent failing is a nonchalant disregard for private ownership.

MAXWELL. And but naturally. You can't undo in a minute all he got into his head in eleven or twelve years of begging and thieving and what not. But he's not much like the bundle of bones and sores we picked up beside the road, so far gone with sickness and hunger it's a wonder to me he lived at all.

BENTLEY. *(As he goes back to left of table)* I know. But I

don't think I'll ever get him filled up, Henry. He's all stomach.

MAXWELL. Aye, probably. And no different from most small boys in that. *(He sits right of table.)*

JOGIE. *(Entering with a chessboard and box of chessmen and placing them on table)* Here, Sahib.

BENTLEY. Thank you, Jogie.

JOGIE. Yes, Sahib. *(He tries to dodge out the door again, but Bentley catches him.)*

BENTLEY. Wait, Jogie. Not until you've finished your lesson.

JOGIE. *(With a sigh)* Yes, Sahib. *(He takes his book and sits over by the door right.)*

Bentley sits down left of table.

MAXWELL. *(Getting out the chessmen)* I'm feeling in top form tonight, so I hope you're not averse to losing.

BENTLEY. I usually do, anyway.

MAXWELL. Because you won't keep your mind on the game. You'd give me a better run for it if you did. But since I can't find anyone else in this benighted country willing to play with me, I'll have to put up with you. A poor chess player's better than none at all.

Something outside attracts Jogie's attention at this point.

BENTLEY. I'm sorry. I suppose it's because I've so little time for the game.

MAXWELL. Aye. That's it. Every year I have to wait for the rains to wash the pilgrims off the road before there's even a chance of finding you with a free evening—or part of one. Because if we get through one game tonight it'll be a miracle.

JOGIE. *(Excitedly)* Sahib! Sahib! Someone comes!

MAXWELL. Aye. What did I tell you? I had a feeling this would happen.

BENTLEY. A pilgrim, Jogie?

JOGIE. No. It is a sahib who comes. He walks strangely. *(He gets up and backs away from the door)* Something is wrong, Sahib. *(He scoots across to door left and stands there watching, big-eyed.)*

> *(Mark appears in the doorway right, and stands there, holding to the side of the door, his head down. He is hatless, rain-soaked, mud-splashed, exhausted. Bentley rises quickly.)*

MAXWELL. *(Also rising)* What—

As Bentley goes toward him, Mark lifts his head.

BENTLEY. *(Stopping center, surprised)* Mark!

MAXWELL. Mark Douglas! Mark!

Mark lets go of door, walks uncertainly toward Bentley, staggers. Bentley catches him, steadies him.

MARK. Thanks! I—I'm all right now.

BENTLEY. Here. Better sit down. *(Puts him in chair right.)*

MAXWELL. Lad, where have you been? What's wrong? Are you ill, lad?

MARK. No. No. I—I'm just—awfully tired—

MAXWELL. *(Peering out the door)* Is there no one with you?

MARK. No one. I came alone.

MAXWELL. Alone! Do you mean to say—

MARK. I was on the train. It stopped. I saw the name of the village—I remembered you were here, Bent—so I got off the train—and came to find you. I—I want to talk to you. I've got to talk to someone. If I don't, I'll go mad! I've got to talk to you!

BENTLEY. Not until you've put on some dry clothes, old man. You can't sit and chat in those wet things. Lukka! Lukka! *(He puts his fingers on Mark's pulse)* And—how long since you've eaten anything?

MARK. I—I don't know—I don't remember—I can't think —my head feels funny—*(He sags forward suddenly.)*

MAXWELL. *(Catching him)* Laddie!

BENTLEY. Wait! Hold him!

(He goes out left quickly. Mark recovers a little, but sits slumped forward, holding his head. Outside the rain slackens, ceases. In a few seconds Bentley returns with a small glass of medicine.)

BENTLEY. Here, Mark! Drink this.

Mark does, slowly. Lukka enters left.

BENTLEY. There! That'll help. You'll feel better in a minute.

LUKKA. You called, Sahib?

BENTLEY. The Sahib has need of dry clothes, Lukka. And Jogie—get warm water for washing—and towels. Hurry!

JOGIE. Yes, Sahib. *(Exits left.)*

BENTLEY. Think you can stand now? *(Mark rises cau-*

tiously) All right. Come with me. *(He takes Mark out left, Lukka following.)*

> *Maxwell goes to the door left, looks after them, shakes his head, returns to the table and sits on the end of it, shifting the chessmen around absently. After a minute Bentley re-enters, alone.*

BENTLEY. *(Speaking over his shoulder)* And then bring tea, Lukka. *(To Maxwell, as he crosses right)* Strange! The boy's half starved.

MAXWELL. Not so strange. You've heard, of course?

BENTLEY. *(Turning)* No. What's wrong?

MAXWELL. His brother died—last week.

BENTLEY. Terry?

MAXWELL. Aye. Just finished his medical training—had his appointment to the field here and his passage booked—and was killed by a drunken driver the night before he was to have sailed.

BENTLEY. I see.

MAXWELL. Wilson sent me word. He was the one who had to break the news to Mark. Said Mark took it with hardly a sign of emotion. Just listened—walked out—and disappeared.

BENTLEY. Disappeared!

MAXWELL. Right out of sight. That was eight days ago —and they've been hunting for him ever since. Quietly, of course. Wilson told me to watch for him in case he headed this way. I didn't think it likely he would—but here he is. Odd that he came to you, though. You haven't seen him for quite a few years, have you?

BENTLEY. *(Crossing up to window)* Not since I came here.

MAXWELL. He needs help, that's evident. It's only a great trouble would send him stumbling up here alone through the rain. And it's something more than the shock of Terry's death, I'm thinking. *(Bentley nods)* You've given help to a lot of men, Bent. Do you think you can— to him?

BENTLEY. I can try. If he'll tell me what's wrong.

MAXWELL. If what I think's wrong—you can do more for him than I can, likely.

BENTLEY. Yet—perhaps it would be better if we talked alone. Would you mind, Henry?

MAXWELL. Not at all. I came for a chess game—but it

wasn't the night for a miracle, it seems. *(He goes to chair right and rolls up his trouser legs, then puts on his helmet)* I'll trot down to the village and send a wire to Wilson and tell him we've got Mark here—and not to worry about the lad. He's in good hands. *(He goes to the door, turns)* And I'm thinking the Lord brought him to the right place, Bent. Good night.

BENTLEY. Good night, Henry. And thank you.

MAXWELL. Not necessary to mention it. Good night again.

(He goes. Bentley crosses to door right and stands looking out. Lukka enters left with a tray of tea things, sets it on the table.)

LUKKA. The tea, Sahib.

BENTLEY. Thank you, Lukka.

LUKKA. Shall I pour it, Sahib?

BENTLEY. No, thanks. I'll do that when Douglas Sahib comes. Will you put those chess things away? We won't be needing them.

LUKKA. Yes, Sahib. *(He gathers up the chessmen and the board)* Is there anything else, Sahib?

BENTLEY. Tell the cook to get hot soup ready. That's all.

LUKKA. Yes, Sahib. *(He exits left.)*

(Bentley crosses to the table, pours the tea. As he sets the second cup down, Mark enters left. He has on a clean shirt and trousers, slippers on his bare feet, and his hair has been combed. He stops by the door hesitantly.)

MARK. Where's Maxwell?

BENTLEY. Gone home. Have a chair? *(Mark comes around and sits down right of table)* Care for sugar in your tea?

MARK. Yes, thanks.

BENTLEY. *(Putting sugar in Mark's cup and handing it to him)* Here.

MARK. Thanks. *(He takes the cup, sips absently.)*

(Bentley takes his cup, goes right, and stands leaning against the wall by the door, watching Mark.)

BENTLEY. Quite a long time since we last saw each other, isn't it?

MARK. What? Oh, yes. Yes, it is.

BENTLEY. Before I was sent home.

MARK. I heard that you'd come back—on your own.

Bentley. *(Laughing)* Rather a joke, that. They told me I'd never be able to come back—and yet, here I am. And I was to live quietly if I wanted to live at all. But I didn't quite see why I couldn't live just as quietly in India as in the States —only money was the problem until an uncle of mine solved it by leaving me a lot of money, because, he said, I was the only one in the family who had sense enough to be a complete fool. Don't forget you're drinking tea.

Mark. Oh! Oh, yes.

Bentley. So I came back, and, like the fellow in the poem, I built this house by the side of the road and tried to be a friend to India going by my door. And it hasn't hurt me. I'm still very much alive. Try some of those biscuits there.

Mark. What?

Bentley. I said—try a biscuit.

Mark. Oh! Thanks! *(He takes one but does not eat it; just sits and crumbles it in his fingers.)*

Bentley. *(Turning, and looking out the door)* The Road of the Pilgrims! I like that name for a road, don't you? That's why I came here. And I watch the pilgrims go by every year —thousands of them—on their way to the shrine. India— seeking eternally and hopelessly for her soul's salvation!

Mark. Do any of the pilgrims come in here—to talk to you?

Bentley. *(Facing him again)* Yes. Quite a few. I give them a place to rest—and, if I can, the true answer to their seeking —God. Some of them call this the House of Rest. Others, the House of the Light—because I keep a lantern burning on the veranda every night.

Mark. That's how they told me to find you—to follow the road—until I saw the light.

Bentley. And they call me the Keeper of the Light. That gives me a lot to live up to. But this isn't a regular mission, of course. The only extra thing I have is a small dispensary. Maxwell, down in the village, tends to the rest. He has the church and the school and—

Mark. *(Interrupting)* Bent! Bent, I've got to talk to you!

Bentley. *(Crosses back to the table, sets down his cup)* All right, Mark. Go ahead now. *(Sits on table close to Mark)* I've just been chatting until you drank your tea. What's the matter?

MARK. You—you've heard—about Terry?

BENTLEY. Maxwell just told me. I'm sorry, Mark.

MARK. You—you remember him? How full he was of life —of laughter?

BENTLEY. Yes, I remember. The last time I saw him he was sitting on the veranda making bookmarks to distribute at Christmas. He painted me one while I waited—and told me at the same time all about how he was going to be a doctor when he grew up. I still have that bookmark. Keep it in my Bible there.

MARK. That was his dream—his plan—to be a doctor—and come here to India and work. And then he had to die—like that—before he could do anything at all. He had to die—so uselessly, so needlessly—

(Bentley puts his hand on Mark's shoulder, but he says nothing.)

MARK. He loved India. He promised all he had to this work here—his life—everything. All he asked was to serve— to help others—and he never had a chance to begin. Millions of useless people can go on living for years—but Terry, who could have done so much—has to die—

BENTLEY. *(Quietly)* And what about you, Mark?

MARK. What?

BENTLEY. What has this done to you?

MARK. To me? *(He gives a short, queer laugh)* After Wilson told me, I tried to think—I tried to understand—I tried to accept. I even tried to pray—but I couldn't. I couldn't—because I found there was nothing to pray to. No God— nothing—

BENTLEY. Mark—

MARK. Nothing but blackness. I tried to reach through it —find something beyond—but there was just emptiness. It's gone—everything I believed—God—everything!

BENTLEY. Why do you say that?

MARK. If there were a God, this wouldn't have happened, Bent. It couldn't have happened. Terry had such a clear, bright faith. He believed in God. He put his whole life, his work, everything he had, into the hands of God—and this is what he got. It's a ghastly sort of joke. And ever since I heard, there's been crazy laughter screaming in my head. It's all I can hear! *(He rises, goes right, turns to face Bentley)* If there were a God—why did he let Terry die that way? Why? You can't answer that, can you? Can you?

BENTLEY. *(Rises, goes slowly around to left of table)* No. I can't answer.

MARK. You're honest, at least. You don't hand out the hackneyed cant—trust, accept, "Thy will be done!" God's will—that Terry should be crushed to death! *(He comes back to the table)* The Lord giveth—the Lord taketh away—blessed be the name of the Lord! Rot! It's all lies, I tell you! Lies! *(He drops down in his chair, his face in his hands.)*

BENTLEY. *(Crosses slowly to door right, stands looking out, his back to Mark)*: All of us encounter death, Mark—if we live any years at all. And all of us—when youth dies—rebel at the seeming waste of it. And I suppose all of us, at one time or another, run up to the gate of Heaven and beat our hands against it and cry, "Why, why, why?" into the strange silence of God.

MARK. Did you—ever?

BENTLEY. Once. When the girl I loved died.

MARK. You got no answer?

BENTLEY. None—yet. I'm waiting.

MARK. And you—still believe?

BENTLEY. Yes.

MARK. You're a fool! A fool! We're all fools! There's nothing, I tell you! Nothing!

BENTLEY. *(Turns to face him and there is a touch of anger in his voice)* Why did you come here, Mark?

MARK. What?

BENTLEY. Why did you come here? For an audience—or for help?

MARK. I—I don't know. I had to talk to someone. I had to.

BENTLEY. And now that you've told me?

MARK. I—I thought perhaps you could help—

BENTLEY. There are things I might say—but I'm afraid they'd be hackneyed cant you rebelled at a minute ago. *(After a slight pause)* Where are you going from here, Mark? Back?

MARK. No. No, I can't go back. I'm done with that. I can't go on teaching what's meaningless—untrue. Let India go on with her own gods—they're as good as any. *(Then, almost in a whisper)* But I'm afraid, Bent. This blackness, I'm lost in it—I'm afraid—because there's nothing in the blackness to hang on to—I'm lost—*(Covers his face with his hands)* Help me, Bent!

(Bentley goes to him quickly, takes his pulse again. Annamuri comes in left.)

ANNAMURI. Sahib?

BENTLEY. Yes?

ANNAMURI. The child is awake, Sahib. And he is better.

BENTLEY. Very well. I'll come. *(To Mark)* She's the wife of my gardener and her small son's ill. I'll have to go with her for a few minutes. I'm not going to talk to you tonight, Mark. You're not in a condition to listen sanely to God's side of this argument. But you were sent here for a reason. You must have been or you wouldn't have gotten off the train. That means the answer you want is here—but we'll have to wait until we know what it is. And right now you need food and rest more than anything I can say.

MARK. I can't sleep—I don't want to eat—

BENTLEY. Try, anyway. Eat what you can of what Lukka brings. Then lie down and rest, and when I get back I'll give you something to make you sleep.

(He goes out left, followed by Annamuri. Mark walks over to the door right, stands looking out into the night. Lukka comes in left.)

LUKKA. Sahib?

MARK. Yes?

LUKKA. If the Sahib will come, I will show him where he sleeps.

MARK. Not now. Later.

LUKKA. But Bentley Sahib said—

MARK. *(Sharply)* Later!

LUKKA. Very well, Sahib. *(He takes the tea things and exits left.)*

Mark comes back to the left of the table, picks up the Bible and hunts through it until he finds a bookmark. As he takes it, his eye catches a verse on the page.

MARK. *(Half to himself)* "And Barnabas determined to take with them John, whose surname was Mark. But Paul thought

not good to take him with them, who departed from them
from Pamphylia, and went not with them to the work. . . ."
*(He shrugs impatiently, shuts the Bible and shoves it to one
side, looks at the bookmark)* "To Bentley—from Terry. Merry
Christmas!" Terry! *(He crushes the bookmark in his hand
and sinks down in the chair left of the table, resting his forehead on his folded arms.)*

*(A Hindu enters the door right. He is, by the cord about his
neck, a Brahmin, but because he is on a pilgrimage, his
turban and clothes are of the poorest quality. He pauses
in the doorway, looking in at Mark uncertainly. Then
he speaks.)*

BRAHMIN. Sahib?

MARK. *(Starting up)* What? Oh!

BRAHMIN. I may enter, Sahib?

MARK. Yes. Of course.

*The Brahmin comes forward a step or two; then, seeing
Mark's face better, pauses.*

BRAHMIN. I am sorry, Sahib. I have come at a time when
you would be alone. I will go.

MARK. No. It's all right. Stay if you wish. *(He rises, goes
to window, stands there with his back to the room.)*

BRAHMIN. Thank you, Sahib. *(He folds the shawl over his
left shoulder and sits on the floor at right.)*

MARK. You were—looking for someone?

BRAHMIN. I am a pilgrim, Sahib. I go to the holy place
at the end of the road.

MARK. In the rains?

BRAHMIN. What matter the rains, Sahib, if I may find that
which I seek?

MARK. Your name?

BRAHMIN. I have no name, Sahib. Nor shall I have—until
I find the end of my searching—peace.

MARK. *(Turning about quickly)* You're searching for peace?

BRAHMIN. Yes, Sahib. For peace. That my soul may rest.

MARK. Peace! *(He laughs suddenly.)*

BRAHMIN. *(Startled and offended)* Sahib!

MARK. I'm sorry. I wasn't laughing at you. Have you
searched long?

BRAHMIN. For many moons, Sahib, upon many roads, and at many shrines.

MARK. Why?

BRAHMIN. Because there is something within me that drives me on like dust before the wind. It is a sickness of the heart, Sahib, that will not let me rest. I kneel in the holy places and cry to the gods—but they answer not—and I rise and go, unsatisfied. I seek healing, but I have not found it. I seek light and yet I stumble in darkness—

MARK. Darkness! *(Walks to table.)*

BRAHMIN. The Sahib walks in sorrow, also?

MARK. *(His back to the Brahmin)* Why—why do you say that?

BRAHMIN. It is in the eyes of the Sahib. It is upon the face of the Sahib. Does this sorrow follow upon the heels of death, Sahib?

MARK. I—I have lost a brother.

BRAHMIN. And I a son, Sahib. He was very small. He had just learned to laugh. Does the Sahib also seek peace?

MARK. Yes.

BRAHMIN. Then are we brothers, Sahib. Pilgrims upon the holy way. May your search be soon ended, Sahib.

MARK. *(Turning to face him)* Why did you come here?

BRAHMIN. Because I go to pray in the holy place at the end of the road, Sahib.

MARK. I mean—to this house?

BRAHMIN. Because, Sahib, in my wanderings I saw a strange thing that made me wonder—a strange thing I cannot forget —that I do not understand—and I would know, Sahib, what it means.

MARK. Oh!

BRAHMIN. I may speak of it to my brother upon the way?

MARK. If you wish. *(He crosses back to the window, stands watching the Brahmin.)*

BRAHMIN. As I went upon my pilgrimage, Sahib, from holy place to holy place, I passed a shrine I knew not, and within it was the picture of a God I knew not. And I asked one who stood near what might be the name of the God within the shrine—and he said it was a picture of the Christians' God.

MARK. Oh!

(Here Bentley appears in the door left. Neither man notices him, and after a glance into the room, he withdraws quietly.)

BRAHMIN. Then I looked again and beheld this strange thing of which I would speak. Sahib, I have bowed before the gods of India—and always these gods hold something in their hands. But this God—the Christians' God—held nothing. He stood so, Sahib, with hands outstretched—and those hands were empty.

MARK. Empty!

BRAHMIN. And that was what made me wonder—that the hands should be empty—that they held nothing. That was eight moons ago, Sahib, and I have gone far upon the way, and yet I cannot forget those empty hands.

MARK. Empty hands. Holding nothing.

BRAHMIN. I have asked here and there, and one told me if I would seek the House of the Light upon the Road of the Pilgrims, I would find one who could answer me. One who served this God whose hands are empty. A holy man—the Keeper of the Light. And so, Sahib, I have come to you.

MARK. But I—you're mistaken. I'm not the Keeper of the Light—

(But the Brahmin has not heard. He has seen the picture back of the table. He rises, goes toward it.)

BRAHMIN. There he is, Sahib. The picture is not the same —but again the hands are empty. *(Turning to Mark)* Why is it so, Sahib? Why does your God stand with empty hands? Has he nothing to offer to those who serve him? Or is he begging something from those who worship him—something to fill his hands? Is he a poor God, Sahib? Is he a God who takes—yet gives nothing?

MARK. Empty hands—empty promises—

BRAHMIN. Sahib?

MARK. *(Bitterly)* I was thinking of the words he spoke when he held out his hands: "Come unto me all ye that labor and are heavy laden—and I will give you rest."

BRAHMIN. *(Missing the sneering bitterness, catching only the words)* Rest? Sahib, will you say those words again?

MARK. *(A little startled)* "Come unto me all ye that labor and are heavy laden—and I will give you rest."

BRAHMIN. Rest. Peace. These are things that cannot be held in the hands. Peace of soul—that which I have been seeking. Sahib, tell me, for what price does your God offer this rest?

MARK. *(Mockingly)* For no price. All one has to do is ask.

BRAHMIN. One asks? Nothing more?

MARK. Nothing. Except believe. Simple, isn't it?

BRAHMIN. It cannot be. So much for so little. Peace of soul but for the asking. *(Turns to look at picture again)* Yet if it be true—if this be the end of my searching—if I have found the healing for this weary sickness in my soul that I have carried like a weight of great stones for so many dusty miles—Sahib, tell me again—*(He turns and looks at Mark, a long, searching look)* Nay, the Sahib jests.

MARK. What?

BRAHMIN. The Sahib speaks in mockery. I am sorry, for I asked truly. I thought I had come from the darkness into the light—but now I see I was mistaken. The Sahib has no light to give. I will go, Sahib. *(Starts for door.)*

MARK. *(Stepping in front of him quickly)* Wait! Why did you say I mocked you?

BRAHMIN. If the Sahib spoke the truth about his God—that his God gives peace of soul for the asking—then would the Sahib himself ask for and receive this peace—and suffer no more pain and sorrow of heart. Not even because of death. The God I seek is one greater than death. Your God is not. The picture of your God is a true picture, Sahib. His hands are empty. He holds nothing—he gives nothing. It is strange that you should serve such a God—but the ways of Sahibs are strange. *(He crosses to the door.)*

MARK. Wait! I told you I'm not the Keeper of the Light. I'm not the one you want to talk to about this. It's Bentley Sahib and he'll be here presently and he can tell you—

BRAHMIN. No, Sahib. I have failed. There is nothing for me here. I must go on. It may be that I shall find what I seek at the holy place at the end of this road, where I shall pray and wait for the dawn to come.

MARK. But—

BRAHMIN. *(Going to Mark)* And you who also walk in the darkness of sorrow—whose empty-handed God can give you nothing—will you come with me? It may be that we shall find peace together.

MARK. No, I—

BRAHMIN. You will not, Sahib? Then—may you find peace in your own way upon a road of your own choosing. *(He touches his forehead and turns to go.)*

BENTLEY. *(Stepping quickly through door left)* Are you going to let him go, Mark?

(Mark and the Brahmin both turn. The Brahmin waits just inside the door.)

MARK. Bent! Bent, you—you heard?

BENTLEY. *(Coming to end of table)* I heard. All of it. Are you going to let him go?

MARK. *(Going to him)* You talk to him, Bent. Tell him what he wants to know. Answer his questions—help him.

BENTLEY. Why?

MARK. You must, Bent. Because he came to you for help. Talk to him. Answer him.

BENTLEY. No.

MARK. What?

BENTLEY. Because he came to you. You'll have to answer him yourself, Mark.

MARK. But I—I can't. You know I can't—

BENTLEY. Answer him, Mark. Or he goes unanswered.

MARK. You mean you won't—

BENTLEY. No. I have nothing to say to him.

MARK. *(Grabbing him)* Bent, you're crazy! You've got to talk to him!

BRAHMIN. Sahibs, I have caused strife between you. I am sorry. I will go.

MARK. No! Wait! You've got to talk to him, Bent. You've got to. Because if he goes out that door, he'll walk in darkness forever.

BENTLEY. *(Sitting left of table)* And what difference does that make to you?

MARK. *(Across the table)* You can't let him do that, Bent. You don't know how horrible the darkness is—and the empti-

ness—and the sickness in your heart. They call you the
Keeper of the Light. That's what he's hunting for—light.
Give it to him!

BENTLEY. Can I offer a man warmth from a fire built with
stones?

MARK. What do you mean?

BENTLEY. What shall I give him, Mark? Hackneyed cant?
Lies? Let him go out into the darkness—be lost in the night
over India. What do you care? Let him spend his life trudging
from shrine to shrine seeking peace for his soul. He won't find
it—but what is it to you? Let him hunt for God. If you're
right and there is none, he won't find him—but his own gods
are good enough for him. Let him go. He's just one of millions—someone you once passed on the road. You can forget
him.

MARK. Bent! Are you mad?

BENTLEY. If he's nothing to you, he's nothing to me. Let
him go, Mark.

MARK. No! No, I won't let him go! Not this way! (*He
turns to the Brahmin in the slight hysteria of fatigue and emotion*) I'll try to tell you—it's here, the peace you want—the
light in the darkness—if he won't give it to you, I've got to!
I've got to help you—tell you—make you see—find a way
through this blackness somehow—and help you—

BRAHMIN. (*Coming to him*) Sahib!

MARK. It's all mixed up—crazy—I'm lost—but I've got to
show you the light—and I've got to find it myself first. I've
got to show you the words He spoke are true—that He does
give peace for the asking—and healing—that His hands hold
more than any man can take—I've got to reach through this
blackness and find Him again—I've got to pray—but I can't
think—I can't find words—(*Clasping the Brahmin's hand*) Will
you help me—brother?

BRAHMIN. In what way, my brother?

MARK. You want peace of heart. So do I. Pray with me—

BRAHMIN. As you will. But speak the words—for I know
not the name of your God.

MARK. (*Looking up*) I've got to find You again—for him
—for myself—Christ—Christ of the empty hands—help us—
the two of us—

(There is a silence, a strange stillness. Neither man moves. Nor does Bentley. Then, slowly, Mark and the Brahmin unclasp hands. The Brahmin looks at his hand. Mark looks at his hand. Then they stare at each other in a sort of wonder. The Brahmin speaks first.)

BRAHMIN. Did you feel it also, Sahib? The touch—so light —as if your hand were clasped by another?

(Mark nods, unable to speak.)

BRAHMIN. Brother, is your heart as mine is now—at peace?

MARK. Yes. *(Turns upstage)* Yes.

BRAHMIN. The pain—the sickness of heart—it was healed by the touch upon my hand. It is the end of my seeking. I have found peace. Here will I stay and serve the God whose touch is healing. No more I know of him—but he is now my God.

BENTLEY. *(Quietly)* And you will forsake all other gods—if he asks it?

BRAHMIN. Even so, Sahib. *(He draws back, hands clasped together, head bowed.)*

BENTLEY. *(Rises, goes to Mark)* Mark?

MARK. *(Starts, turns to him)* Oh!

BENTLEY. I had to do that, Mark. Because I knew if I could make you light the light for another—you'd light it again for yourself. I didn't think you'd send him away into the darkness. Is it all right now, Mark?

MARK. I felt it—the touch of His hand—on mine. Yes. It's all right. Everything.

BENTLEY. Even if there is no answer—about Terry?

MARK. Yes. I can wait for that—now.

BRAHMIN. Sahibs, now I know why his hands are empty. It is so he may clasp the hands of those who come seeking— and so give their souls peace. *(To Mark)* That is the reason, Sahib.

MARK. Yes. Yes—that's why.

CURTAIN

The Builders

A Dramatic Service of Worship

by

FRANCES DYER ECKARDT

Characters:

THE BOY	THE SON
THE MAN	JOHN
MR. HIGGINS	SYLVIA
THE HUSBAND	MISS PATTERSON
THE WIFE	FRED
MAMA	

SCENE: The sanctuary of a little rural church.

TIME: Present.

LENGTH: Thirty minutes.

> *The pulpit may be center and back, with two rows of pews to either side and at right angles to the altar. Or the pulpit may be to one side, facing directly across the stage, with two rows of pews across from it, placed straight up and down stage. With this setting, there may be a small table between the pulpit and the pews. The pulpit should be on a slightly raised level. Directly beneath it is placed a basket of flowers. And somewhere, there should be a window, with the sun shining through, to throw a soft beam of light across the scene.*
>
> *The Boy quietly takes his place on the front pew. Through an outer door of the church auditorium, to the rear, there enters a man in his middle years. He is a man of poise and authority—one who evidently fills a responsible position in some community—but there is about him at this moment an air of hesitancy, of unsureness, which makes him appear quite humble. He is like a man who comes home to a familiar place, glad at being there, yet fearing*

Printed in *motive*, October, 1942. Copyright, 1942, by Board of Education of the Methodist Church. Used by permission of the author. All rights of reproduction performance and permission to produce reserved by the author, Mrs. Rockwell C. Smith, Garrett Institute, Evanston, Illinois. Royalty for first performance $2.50, for next five performances $1.00 each. For additional performances, arrange with author. Single copies available from Walter H. Baker, 178 Tremont St., Boston, Mass.

*the impact of the past. Slowly he walks to the front of
the church, to the stage, and the altar. There he pauses
and gazes about him, finally lifting his face to the light
of the window. He speaks softly.*

Man. I'd forgotten about that window, with the sun shining through. . . . (*He looks about him, slowly*) Nothing's
changed. . . . By George, I've never been away! I'm just a
little kid named Rusty, and I've slipped in here to take a nap
where it's cool! . . . (*He shakes his head with a smile*) That's
one thing the old church was good for—

(*The* Boy *has been asleep, curled up in a corner of the front
pew, left. Now he stretches, yawns, and sits up, looking
at the* Man. *He speaks naturally, as if he were simply
continuing a conversation.*)

Boy. Gee, it's funny how tired a fella can get sometimes,
just fooling around!

Man. (*He turns quickly, to face the* Boy.) Good heavens,
Boy, you startled me! I didn't see you there.

Boy. (*Sitting up straight*) I'm sorry I scared you, Mister.
I thought you was talking to me.

Man. That's all right.—What makes you so sleepy this
afternoon?

Boy. Well, I got up at four, 'cause the perch are biting
pretty good right now, and that's the time to catch 'em. But
it sure gets a fella yawnin', time he's through dinner.

Man. Yes, I remember. . . . (*After a moment, he looks more
closely at the* Boy, *as if puzzled by some faint recognition*)
Whose youngster are you, anyhow? I'd swear I've seen you
before.

Boy. (*He rises, and goes toward the* Man, *his voice wistful*)
Gee, don't you know me, Mister? I thought you'd always remember me.

Man. Remember you? . . . (*He gazes at the* Boy, *who nods
hopefully back at him*) But I've been away for years!

Boy. (*Very simply*) I know, I've been waiting for you to
come back.

Man. Waiting? (*The* Boy *nods. For a moment the* Man
looks at him in silence. When he speaks again, there is a note

of beginning realization in his voice.) You look the way . . .
I used to look.

BOY. *(Softly)* You do remember, don't you?

MAN. *(Slowly, looking into the* Boy's *eyes)* Yes. . . . I remember—Rusty.

BOY. That's me, Mister. I thought for a minute you'd
forgotten all about me.

MAN. *(He turns away, speaking a little sadly)* One forgets
so many things.

BOY. *(Following him)* But I think about you an awful lot.

MAN. *(Facing him, with a smile)* Do you, Rusty?

BOY. Sure. That's why I'm glad you're here.—Did you come
back all alone?

MAN. *(He crosses in front of the* Boy, *to the left. There is
a hint of constraint in his manner.)* No, my son is with me.
I'm waiting for him now. We're driving through on a long
trip, and he wanted to stop. He'd never seen my old home.

BOY. Gee, Mister, what's he like?

MAN. He's a handsome young man, Rusty. Just graduated
from college.

BOY. What's he going to be?

MAN. *(His constraint grows)* He wants to be a preacher.

BOY. Does he?—I always thought that's what you'd be. It's
a sort of an honor, having a preacher in the family!

MAN. *(And now the constraint changes to bitterness)* My
son has strange ideas about that. He wants to shut himself
away in the country—in a little church like this—where no one
will ever see or hear of him again.

BOY. I like it out here.

MAN. My son's a brilliant fellow. It's no work for him. A
useless sacrifice!

BOY. Maybe he'll change his mind.

MAN. *(Tonelessly)* Maybe he will. *(He sits in the front
pew, left, his head bowed.)*

BOY. All the preachers that come here, seems like they
want to go somewhere else. 'Cept Mr. Higgins. I think he'd
like to stay, only he's afraid people don't like him.

MAN. Mr. Higgins. . . . *(He has forgotten the* Boy, *and
speaks as if he were alone)* How clearly the past comes back!

As if life had changed as little as the sun still shining through the windows of this old church. As if Mr. Higgins himself were standing in the pulpit there, reading the Scripture I loved to listen to. . . .

(Mr. Higgins *comes to the altar from the left. He is an elderly man, with bowed, defeated shoulders, ill at ease, withdrawn, stiff in manner. Only when he reads the prophetic passages from the Scripture does he seem to attain full power and confidence.—As he crosses the stage toward the pulpit, the* Boy *faces him.*)

BOY. *(With a touch of awe)* G-good afternoon, Mr. Higgins.

HIGGINS. *(Pausing)* Good afternoon, my boy. I am glad to see you enjoying the quiet of this beautiful sanctuary. Are you meditating, perhaps, on the Sunday school lesson for tomorrow?

BOY. We-ll, not exactly. . . .

HIGGINS. I see. Just being quiet. . . . *(He continues, as he talks, toward the pulpit)* Well, it is a good place to come . . . in the proper spirit. But this is a holy place, not to be desecrated by frivolous dissipation.

BOY. N-no, sir. *(Eagerly, as* Higgins *opens the big Bible on the pulpit)* Please, sir, are you going to read something?

HIGGINS. I am marking the Scripture for tomorrow's service.

BOY. Why don't you practice it? Don't you think you might do better if you practiced it?

HIGGINS. Do you find my reading very unsatisfactory?

BOY. Gee, no, Mr. Higgins! I—I think it's bully! I—I just thought maybe you'd let me listen—

HIGGINS. *(With mild reproof)* You must watch your language, my boy. It is sometimes a little careless.

BOY. *(Sitting right if pulpit is back center, or, if pulpit is right, sitting at the table center, in one of the chairs)* Y-yes, sir.

HIGGINS. *(He reads, after a pause, from Ecclesiastes, gradually losing himself in the poetry and beauty of the words, his voice full and resonant.)*

Remember now thy Creator in the days of thy youth, while the evil days come not, nor the years draw nigh, when thou shalt say, I have no pleasure in them;

While the sun, or the light, or the moon, or the stars, be not darkened, nor the clouds return after the rain:

In the day when the keepers of the house shall tremble, and the strong men shall bow themselves, and the grinders cease because they are few, and those that look out of the windows be darkened,

And the doors shall be shut in the streets, when the sound of the grinding is low, and he shall rise up at the voice of the bird, and all the daughters of music shall be brought low; . . .

Or ever the silver cord be loosed, or the golden bowl be broken, or the pitcher be broken at the fountain, or the wheel broken at the cistern.

Then shall the dust return to the earth as it was: and the spirit shall return unto God who gave it. . . .

(For a moment Mr. Higgins *stands in silence, his face lifted to the sunlight. Then the* Boy *speaks breathlessly, as if breaking a spell.)*

BOY. Gee, Mr. Higgins—I mean—I never thought about that before, Mr. Higgins—that a bird has a *voice*—that it talks with, I mean—not just a song. . . .

HIGGINS. I am glad to find you listening to the language of the Scriptures. It will reveal much to you that is new and beautiful.

BOY. *(Impulsively)* I wish I could read it like you do—I wish I could be a preacher like you, Mr. Higgins!

HIGGINS. *(Touched and sad)* Like me? *(He shakes his head)* . . . I am a very poor preacher, my boy. My days have been long, and I have failed. *(He speaks from the depths of his longing)* There is work to be done, if only I knew how; but I am weak, and it was not given me to reach men's hearts. . . . *(He lays his hand in silence a moment on the Bible, then closes it, and slowly leaves the pulpit, crossing left. He speaks to himself, the* Boy *forgotten)* Some day, I pray, a better man may come. *(He goes, with bowed head. The* Boy, *behind him, puts out his hand, and calls softly.)*

BOY. Mr. Higgins. . . . Mr. Higgins—*(But* Mr. Higgins *does not hear. The* Boy *runs sobbing to the* Man, *who rises, and touches him gently)* He's gone, and I didn't tell him! I didn't tell him I love him!

Man. Words aren't always needed, Rusty. I think perhaps he understood without your telling him. *(He leaves the* Boy *seated left and walks center, thoughtfully, as he continues speaking)* Love, with him, was a matter of deeds, not something to be spoken of. . . . *(He sits quietly right or back center, his head resting on his hand. After a moment, a young* Husband *and* Wife *enter together left, and come hand in hand to the altar, facing it in silence.)*

Wife. Here's just where we stood. . . . *(She smiles)* I feel as if I were being married all over again!

Husband. Would it be worth doing?

Wife. I think so—on the whole. *(Then suddenly clinging to him and crying out)* Oh John—I don't want to go away! We belong here. This church is part of us!

Husband. We're not really leaving it, Sylvia. Wherever we go, we'll take it with us.

Wife. *(Softly)* A church not built with hands. . . .

Husband. That's it, my dear. A *fellowship* . . . of which we'll always be a part. That we can help to build, no matter where we are! *(He takes her in his arms, and the* Boy *left clears his throat warningly. They turn toward him, startled.)*

Wife. Oh!

Boy. It's only me.

Husband. Well, Rusty!

Wife. Hello there, little boy.

Boy. Are you going away somewhere?

Husband. Yes, we're going to the city, Rusty.

Wife. Shall we take you with us?

Boy. I don't think I'd like it.

Husband. You have to go where your work takes you.

Boy. I'm going to get a job right here, where I can go fishing, and have a horse, 'n lots of fresh air.

Husband. I hope you can!

Wife. And think of us, Rusty, Sunday mornings—

Boy. I'll think about you while Mr. Higgins says the prayer.

Husband. *(Laughing)* That will give you plenty of time!

Wife. Dearest, it's almost time.

Husband. Yes. . . . Goodbye, Rusty.

Wife. Be a good boy, Rusty—

BOY. Oh, sure. G'bye. *(They go off left, and the* BOY *watches them leave, then lies on his back on pew left, picking up some Sunday school leaflets lying there loose, from which he makes darts)* I wish they wouldn't go away.

MAN. *(Meditatively, still seated)* What did John and Sylvia find in this little church? A sense of human fellowship, I suppose—of friendliness. . . .

BOY. *(Throwing darts)* I bet I can hit the ceiling with this, I bet I can, I can. *(He throws.* Miss Patterson, *a busy, wiry, shabby little woman, bustles in left.)* Aw, gee, there must be a draught!

PATTERSON. My goodness, Russell Burley, what are you doing? You just let Mr. Higgins catch you, throwing paper darts! *(She sees the material with which he is making another dart)* With *my lesson leaflets!* You *naughty* boy! *(She puts down on table, or corner of pew, a pile of printed material which she carries.)*

BOY. *(Sitting up)* It's all right, Miss Patterson. They're for last Sunday.

PATTERSON. Well, be sure you pick them up.

BOY. Yes, Miss Patterson. *(He does so.)*

PATTERSON. *(Busily, at work on her papers)* These new quarterlies are such a job. I like to get everything sorted out before Sunday morning. Here—help me get them into piles. That's a good child.

BOY. *(Examining one of the books, with interest)* Does our class get this one, with the picture of the picnic?

PATTERSON. The *picnic?* Oh. That's the loaves and fishes story. . . . Yes, that's yours.

BOY. I'll keep one out to look at. *(He is kneeling on the floor, with a pile of the books.)*

PATTERSON. *(Sitting)* Seems like I'm always finding you in here, child. Such a funny little boy. Why do you come?

BOY. I don't know. I just like it here. It feels cool, and quiet—like putting your face down into the grass. And you can think about things. . . .

PATTERSON. Well, fancy a youngster talking like that! But that's all right. I like it here, too.

BOY. Why do you like it here?

PATTERSON. Why do I like it here? *(She shakes her head)*

I doubt I can tell you, child. . . . *(She lays aside her papers and folds her hands in her lap, sitting still a moment before she quietly speaks)* This is the place where I can be myself. Where it don't matter how old I am, or what I look like, or where I live. . . . Where I can come and have a job to do, along with other people, and they take me for what I am, and no questions asked . . . where I can hold my head up, and know I'm of some use in the world. . . . *(She is quiet again for a little while, and then she briskly piles up her papers, with a little laugh)* There, child, you see it wasn't much use asking! But you'll understand, some day.

Boy. *(Slowly)* I guess I just need to think about it a little.

Patterson. Boys your age shouldn't think too much. You get out and play, and forget such things for a while; and come around to my house sometime when you're hungry, and we'll see what's in the cookie jar! *(She rises as she speaks, and crosses right.)*

Boy. Gee, I will, Miss Patterson!

Man. *(Rising to face* Miss Patterson, *as she comes right and speaking softly)* I do understand, old friend! . . .

(She walks past him, unseeing. The Boy *calls to the* Man, *as he looks after her.)*

Boy. Look, Mister. *(He is trying to stand on his hands)* Look Mister, can you do this? Look! Like this.

Man. *(Laughing)* You always liked to show off, didn't you? *(He crosses, to left and sits.)*

Boy. *(Continuing his efforts)* It's not hard, once you get in practice.

(The Janitor *enters from right with mop and cleaning rag.)*

Janitor. Hey there, youngster—watch out for them flowers. You want to behave that way, you git outside!

Boy. I won't hurt anything. I'm an expert. See?

Janitor. *(Gruffly)* Come on, now. Clear. I need the room.

Boy. No. . . . Let me help you, Fred—please!

Janitor. You! Never held a broom in your life, I'll wager.

Boy. I have so! I help Mama every Saturday. Here, I'll mop. *(He seizes the mop.)*

Janitor. Well, go to it. I've no objection. Plenty of chores to home, fur's that goes. *(He busies himself with dusting.)*

BOY. *(Mopping vigorously)* Have you got your new little calf yet?

JANITOR. Oh, sure. Come two days ago.

BOY. Gee, did it? Is it a he or a she?

JANITOR. It's a she, thank the good Lord.

BOY. What's the good Lord got to do with it?

JANITOR. *(Sternly)* Boy, don't you git flip! All blessings is the Lord's. The increase of the fields is His; He owns the cattle on a thousand hills!

BOY. Do you s'pose maybe God is a kind of farmer? *(He leans on the mop to consider this idea.)*

JANITOR. *(Pausing in his work to answer)* Well, now, not meanin' anything disrespectful, I sometimes think He is. Certain it is, a person finds Him easier out among the trees and meadows, and where there's animals that's kind to one another. . . . Set a little church like this down in the open places, and God walks in the door, no matter whether the paint is on and the choir can sing and the preacher preach, or not. . . . Seems like where you got Nature, you jes' natur'lly got the best start toward heaven!

BOY. *(Thinking it over)* Do you s'pose, Fred, if God likes it so well out in the country—outdoors, 'n everything—He'd really care if I went fishing on Sunday sometimes—real early in the morning, you know? Or swimming?

JANITOR. That's as may be. You ask Mr. Higgins that.

BOY. I know what *he'd* say.

JANITOR. Well, you do as he says, and you won't come to no harm. *(He puts out his hand for the mop)* Here, I'll take the mop now, and thank ye kindly, lad. Don't stay inside too long, here—gittin' queer ideas.

BOY. I won't. Can I help you again, sometimes?

JANITOR. You can that, and welcome! *(He goes off, left.)*

MAN. *(Coming to the Boy, and smiling down on him)* You're a strange little fellow, Rusty. It rather brings me up short, meeting you here. Tell me, now that you've seen me, are you terribly disappointed?

BOY. Well, you're different, Mister—from what I expected, you know. Only I don't worry about that so much, 'cause we're friends.

MAN. Yes, Rusty. We're friends. And friends don't let each other down, do they? *(He turns away, walking slowly left.)*

BOY. Are you thinking, Mister?

MAN. Yes, Rusty, I'm thinking.

BOY. 'Bout something awful important?

MAN. About you . . . and about my son.

BOY. That wants to be a preacher?

MAN. Yes. . . . *(Again a tinge of bitterness in his voice)* A country preacher. *(He sits, lost in silence.)*

BOY. *(Sitting beside him)* I'll think, too. I'll think about fishing on Sunday.

(After a pause, Mama enters from the right, carrying flowers. She is a woman of spiritual poise and power, graceful and calm. She goes to the basket of flowers beneath the pulpit.)

BOY. *(Softly, to the* Man*)* Look! There's my Mama! *(He runs over to her)* Hello, Mama!

MAMA. *(Startled)* Why, Rusty! I thought you were playing baseball!

BOY. I was, but we finished.

MAMA. And did you win?

BOY. Well, almost. Only they got ahead the last inning.

MAMA. *(Comfortingly)* It must have been a close game. *(She turns again to the flowers, speaking rather absently)* Here, darling, hold these a minute, will you? *(She hands him some of the blossoms, and kneels to arrange the basket)* I want Mr. Higgins to find an especially nice bouquet at the altar tomorrow. He's so very fond of flowers. . . .

BOY. *(Standing behind her, troubled)* Mama. . . .

MAMA. *(Without turning)* Yes, dear?

BOY. Mama—why is Mr. Higgins a failure?

MAMA. *(Stopping her work, and looking at him in surprise)* A failure, dear? Why do you call him that?

BOY. That's what he said. When he came to look up the Scripture. He said, "My days have been long, and I have failed." . . . Do you s'pose it's 'cause people go to sleep sometimes, when he's preaching?

MAMA. *(Smiling)* No, dear, I don't believe so. *(She pauses, considering)* It's just that some people call him a failure, and so he's come to think he is one.

BOY. *(Impatiently)* But why do they, if he isn't?

MAMA. They have a queer way of measuring success, Rusty. . . . They think it grows out of what a church has to give a minister: money . . . position . . . a talented congregation. . . . *(She speaks very simply, with sadness)* We can't give Mr. Higgins very much. We just need him.

BOY. *(Shaking his head thoughtfully)* I don't think Mr. Higgins cares about money.

MAMA. *(Choosing her words carefully)* No, I think he wants only to serve, and sometimes feels unhappy because he doesn't quite know how. You see . . . he didn't plan, perhaps, to be a country preacher, and he isn't a farmer, so it's hard for him to understand the things that are problems to people like us. . . . But that doesn't make him a failure; it just means that we must work harder than ever to help him, doesn't it?

BOY. Yes, Mama.

MAMA. *(Her face is lifted to the sunlight, her eyes on the distance)* Perhaps if we do that, if we all work together, we can build something new out of what we have. Perhaps we can take the friendliness, and beauty, and strength of the country, and make them into a church a minister will be proud to serve! . . . *(She blinks a mist of tears from her eyes, and reaches out with a little smile to take the Boy's hand in hers)* Well! . . . That's quite a lecture for my little boy, isn't it? *(And then, gaily)* I tell you what we'll do. We'll have Mr. Higgins over for dinner tomorrow, and we'll just let him see how much we like him, shall we?

BOY. Yes, Mama! Will we have fried chicken?

MAMA. I think we might. And speaking of meals—it's almost supper time right now. You come home with me, and wash off that mud behind your ears!

BOY. Aw, gee, it doesn't show!

MAMA. Come along, dear. . . . *(She pushes him ahead of her, and they go off right.)*

MAN. *(Standing, and putting out his hand to them)* Don't go! . . . *(He looks after them a moment, then turns toward the altar, with bowed head. For a moment he stands there in silence, and then a young man comes briskly and happily down the aisle from the rear of the church. He is whistling, but breaks off to call.)*

SON. Hello, Dad! I've been looking for you. *(He comes to stage from left.)*

(The Man *turns slowly, to face his* Son.)

MAN. *(Almost as if he were waking from a dream)* Hello, Son. I'm afraid I lost all track of time.

SON. Doesn't matter. I've been wandering around outside here, looking things over.

MAN. How do you like the church?

SON. *(Laughing)* Well, not having your sophisticated tastes, I think it's about perfect! *(He walks right, looking about him)* Give me a little room like this, with the sun shining in and you can have your old cathedrals!

MAN. *(Smiling)* Just a country boy at heart, eh?

SON. You know it, Dad. Call me silly if you like, but I'm sold on the idea.

MAN. You'd really be satisfied to settle down—in a little place like this.

SON. *(With all the vigor and enthusiasm of youth in his voice)* Satisfied? I can't imagine a more exciting life! This is where things are happening, Dad. It's just as if all the little churches in America had been building . . . *building* . . . slowly, patiently, and now, suddenly, a new church was rising out of the earth, shining and glorious. . . . I don't know how to make you see what I mean, but if I could—it's all I'd need to go ahead!

MAN. *(Quietly)* It's strange you should speak that way of building. . . . I once heard your grandmother use the same words. . . .

SON. She was one of the builders.

MAN. I've been remembering others who were. . . . *(He speaks slowly, with a new light in his voice)* I think I understand for the first time something of what they were building.

SON. *(A little wistfully)* And of what I'd like to build, too, Dad?

MAN. Yes, Son. . . . Your old Dad's ready to admit you've got something. You go on to school, and study to be a country preacher if you want to. I think he'll back you.

SON. *(His voice joyful)* Dad, with you talking like that, I can do anything!

MAN. We'll build together, Son.

SON. Together! *(They clasp hands. Very softly, the organ has begun the tune of the congregational hymn, "Finlandia." Now, as the play ends, and the* Man *and* Son *walk together down the aisle of the church, the music increases in volume.)*

MAN. Now, suppose we walk down for a look at the Common. I want to show you where that baseball diamond used to be. . . .

Sentence

by

LILLIAN CARMICHAEL

Characters:

DAN KELLY   AMOS APPLETHWAITE, his lawyer
MRS. KELLY, his mother   MARY HARMON

TIME: Present.

LENGTH: About twenty minutes.

SCENE: *An antechamber, a dreary little room that opens into
a courtroom. Three oak chairs are in a row at the back;
a desk at left front with a cuspidor beside it and another
chair, almost center stage; a filing case near the door at
right back. Dan Kelly's trial for manslaughter has just
ended and he is here with his lawyer awaiting the return
of the jury. Dan sits on the desk, crumpled dejectedly.
He is young, in his early twenties; his head is bandaged,
and his clothes, though well-cut, are somehow wilted to
match their wearer. Dan's lawyer, a hearty man by name
of Amos Applethwaite, is walking up and down the room,
smoking a cigar. He speaks with bluff, false cheeriness.*

APPLETHWAITE. Well, buck up, Dan. *(Looking at his watch)*
Four o'clock—the jury ought to be in any time now. Five
hours of it—they won't want much more.

DAN. How do you know?

APPLETHWAITE. It stands to reason.

DAN. That Scotch bird looked to me the sort who'd hold
out all week.

APPLETHWAITE. Well, a hung jury wouldn't be bad.

DAN. Better than a hung neck.

APPLETHWAITE. My dear boy! I've told you often the worst
we can fear is a short prison term. Death in a collision at
night that way, and the victim a young doctor—not as if it
had been a child or an old person or a woman. And you with
your head still bandaged—most fortunate, that bandage. Even
if they regard your intoxication as proved.

From *Why Should I?* copyright, 1937, used by permission of the pub-
lishers, Abingdon-Cokesbury Press, 150 Fifth Avenue, New York, N. Y.

DAN. Oh, shut up.

APPLETHWAITE. *(Hurt)* Well, I'm just trying to buck you up. Even if they think you were drunk—

DAN. *(Interrupting)* I was.

APPLETHWAITE. *(Looking at the door)* S-s-sh! As I was saying, even with that, and even with this Mary Harmon about in her widow's weeds—

DAN. *(Interrupting again)* Weeds?

APPLETHWAITE. Poetic license. I grant young Mrs. Harmon's appearance is far from weedy—worse luck. It's been our biggest handicap to have your victim's widow about in the jury's eye all the time.

DAN. My victim's?

APPLETHWAITE. Well, the deceased's, if you prefer—the deceased's. What I was saying, even if they think you were drunk, as Mary Harmon testified, the worst we could fear is a short prison term. Not more than five years.

DAN. Five years!

APPLETHWAITE. Oh, there'll be an appeal, of course. Your mother insists on that, and I've plenty of exceptions. *(Turning as a knock is heard at the door)* Here's your mother now, probably. *(Applethwaite opens the door.)*

(Enter Mrs. Kelly, Dan's mother, closing the door behind her. A quiet aristocrat of a woman, she smiles at the lawyer.)

MRS. KELLY. They said I might come in here with Dan, Mr. Applethwaite.

APPLETHWAITE. *(Relieved to have her)* Yes, assuredly, Mrs. Kelly. *(Pulling out the chair by the desk)* Sit down here. Well, now your mother's with you, my boy, I'll go out and see what I can hear. Be right back. *(Exit, closing the door.)*

(Dan remains slumped on the desk. Mrs. Kelly watches him intently. She does not take the chair, only stands beside the desk.)

DAN. Earning his five hundred bucks right up to the last, old Applethwaite seems to be.

MRS. KELLY. He's been very kind.

DAN. *(Spreading out his five fingers and looking at them)* Five—always a rum number for me, mother, five is. Five hundred gone on Applethwaite, five drinks that night. Four, I'd been steady, and six, I'd been laid out. But five—

MRS. KELLY. Does your head hurt? *(She adjusts the bandage)* It'll be all right, Dan.

DAN. *(Getting off the desk and pacing the floor)* Five women on the jury, and five moles on that Scotchman's chin. Five years.

MRS. KELLY. Oh, no, darling! The appeal—Mr. Applethwaite said—

DAN. *(Interrupting and looking about the room rather desperately)* What if I beat it now?

MRS. KELLY. What if you—escaped?

DAN. The bond forfeited. And I'd have to have money.

MRS. KELLY. *(Suddenly eager)* I could sell the house.

DAN. *(Subsiding, coming to sit hopelessly on the desk again)* And live in the park.

MRS. KELLY. *(Almost whispering)* Oh, do go, Dan! South America. You can send me word and I'll come. We could get out of the building together. It's four now—I'll tell them we're just slipping out for some tea. . . .

DAN. It's no use; they'd have me in the first block. Besides. . . . *(A pause.)*

MRS. KELLY. *(Calm again)* Yes, I know.

DAN. Five years. Well, you can cash in on that insurance policy, mother. That and the house. Better rent the house.

MRS. KELLY. I'd rent it and come to live in—

DAN. The prison town?

MRS. KELLY. Let's not, dear. It's—it's really ridiculous. Appeal, and Mr. Applethwaite as clever as he is.

DAN. And that widow as pretty.

MRS. KELLY. *(Betraying her intensity again)* Pretty? I shouldn't call her pretty—horribly bitter girl. Why does Mary Harmon hate you so!

DAN. I happened to have killed her husband.

MRS. KELLY. Not *killed!* A dark night and a collision—

DAN. And me drunk.

MRS. KELLY. *(Glancing at the door)* Don't! They haven't —they haven't proved that.

DAN. The jury thinks they have. Better, if we'd admitted it—at least gone down in honesty.

MRS. KELLY. If I went to Mary Harmon again—

DAN. Again?

MRS. KELLY. Oh! Well, yes, I did go to her, Dan, last

week. She has a son, a little child. I said, "Mrs. Harmon, suppose your son grew up and—

DAN. Well?

MRS. KELLY. She said she'd rather then her son would go to—prison.

DAN. Bet she would too. Rum thing, as pretty a girl as that looking like a woman who lunches on scrapiron.

(A knock at the door.)

MRS. KELLY. *(Calling)* Yes, Mr. Applethwaite? Come in.

MARY HARMON. *(Offstage)* It's not Mr. Applethwaite.

MRS. KELLY. *(Low, to Dan)* She's here! Mary Harmon!

DAN. *(Shrinking back)* Tell her to go away.

MRS. KELLY. No, she must have changed her mind, Dan. She'll help us.

DAN. Not a chance. She just wants to accuse me again— and that sort of thing. I've had all I can stick! Send her away!

MARY. May I come in?

(Enter Mary Harmon. She is a personable young woman dressed simply in black. She speaks with formal courtesy.)

May I talk with you a little, Mrs. Kelly?

MRS. KELLY. Oh, yes, Mrs. Harmon. Of course. Shall we go into the other room?

MARY. No, I want your son to hear.

MRS. KELLY. Well, I really don't know if it's allowed, Mrs. Harmon.

MARY. I asked them. I said, "May the complaining witness speak to the defendant while the jury is out?" They said it was unusual, but legal.

MRS. KELLY. *(She has stepped between Dan and Mary)* What is it you wish to say to me?

MARY. May I sit down?

MRS. KELLY. Yes, certainly. Dan, bring Mrs. Harmon a chair.

(Dan gets off the desk and brings Mary a chair from the back. He places it at right front. Mary sits upon it, thanking him calmly. Their eyes meet as she glances up. Dan turns awkwardly away and goes back to the desk. Mrs. Kelly has seated herself in the chair by the desk, pushing it about to face Mary's. A pause.)

MRS. KELLY. Well?

MARY. I have a proposition to make to you.

MRS. KELLY. *(Concealing her eager hope)* Oh, certainly.

MARY. *(Bringing her chair closer and leaning forward)* You came to me last week, Mrs. Kelly. Suppose my own son were grown, you said, and had killed another person because he was too intoxicated to drive safely.

MRS. KELLY. I didn't say—

MARY. *(Interrupting)* Not in those words, but you meant that. And I answered that I would choose then to have my son take his punishment in prison.

MRS. KELLY. Yes, but I never admitted that Dan was intoxicated, Mrs. Harmon. He wasn't intoxicated.

MARY. No? Were you there, as I was, to see his car come crazily at us out of the night? Then the jar, and the crash, and the darkness. Then lights approaching, and I saw my husband—

MRS. KELLY. Oh, naturally, it seems thus to you now, Mrs. Harmon, but—

MARY. *(Interrupting)* And your son crawling out from under his car, stupefied—drunk.

MRS. KELLY. He'd been injured!

MARY. *(To Dan)* Weren't you drunk?

DAN. Yes, I was drunk.

MRS. KELLY. Dan!

DAN. It's no matter now, mother.

MARY. Yes, it is. That's why I'm here.

MRS. KELLY. *(With cool formality again)* Indeed?

MARY. Yes. I have an offer.

MRS. KELLY. If this is a ruse, Mrs. Harmon—

MARY. It's not a ruse. I'm risking prison myself, probably, for obstructing justice, or something like that. *(To Dan)* In a few minutes now, Mr. Kelly, the jury will probably bring in a verdict of guilty, and, if it does, you'll be sentenced to at least five years in the penitentiary.

MRS. KELLY. Oh, no!

MARY. Five years. You'll appeal and probably lose; and maybe appeal again, and lose again, till your mother's money is all gone. Five years then, and your mother pinching along outside on some little near-genteel job in a tearoom, perhaps.

MRS. KELLY. Mrs. Harmon, you have no warrant to—

MARY. *(Interrupting)* Yes, I have a warrant.

DAN. Let her talk, mother.

MARY. Thank you, Mr. Kelly. Well, as I said, I'm here to dicker.

MRS. KELLY. Dicker?

DAN. What have we left to dicker with?

MARY. Not money—I'm no blackmailer. Did you ever make a speech, Mr. Kelly?

DAN. Huh?

MARY. It's quite to the point; an idea that just came to me. You're an electrical engineer, I understand. Don't they make speeches at board meetings, and the like?

DAN. Not me.

MARY. You could learn. All the better if you're not a professional orator.

MRS. KELLY. This is scarcely a time for jests, Mrs. Harmon.

MARY. Jests? I'm achingly serious.

MRS. KELLY. Pray tell us what you mean then.

MARY. This *(To Dan)*: I'm thinking of your being in prison for five years. What use is that to me or—my husband? Would you agree, if I withdraw before your next trial—oh, leave the country, even; I've relatives in Canada. Would you agree— *(She hesitates.)*

DAN. Agree to what?

MARY. Agree to give five years of your life to the work of teaching others not to drive while drunk?

(Enter Applethwaite.)

APPLETHWAITE. The jury's coming in! *(Starts as he sees Mary.)* Oh, Mrs. Harmon—good afternoon. Come on, Dan.

MRS. KELLY. *(Who has risen)* Must he—hear the verdict out there, Mr. Applethwaite?

APPLETHWAITE. Afraid so, Mrs. Kelly. I've saved you a seat.

MRS. KELLY. I can't . . . I can't go. I'll stay here.

APPLETHWAITE. Good idea. Come on, Dan.

DAN. *(Stopping to put an arm around his mother)* It'll be all right.

MRS. KELLY. *(On abrupt resolve)* Mr. Applethwaite, Mrs. Harmon has said she would withdraw before the next trial, if my son agrees—

APPLETHWAITE. *(Interrupting)* But that's no use, you know.

Appeals take the testimony given here as to facts. Unless
Mrs. Harmon wishes to deny her testimony now, and have me
move for a mistrial.

MRS. KELLY. Oh, won't you, Mrs. Harmon?

MARY. What would it mean? *(She rises to face Applethwaite.)*

APPLETHWAITE. Well, perjury for you, I'm afraid, unless a
doctor certified that you were hysterical at the time. If you
wish to deny—

DAN. She doesn't. Come on. *(To Mary)* Stay here with
my mother, won't you?

MARY. Yes, I will.

*(The two men go out. The women look at each other.
Mary sits down again in her chair at right front. Mrs.
Kelly stands by her chair.)*

MRS. KELLY. *(Challengingly)* He has never been a drunk-
ard, for all you think. Just that night, with the other young
men. Just that once, was he so.

MARY. Once can be as many as a thousand.

MRS. KELLY. I suppose so. Dan's father died when he was
small, almost the age of your son. Strange, it was nearly the
same—fishing, and a boat overturned because another man. . . .

MARY. This earth is much too tricky a planet not to keep
one's senses clear.

MRS. KELLY. You don't want Dan to go to prison?

MARY. Not now. I did, I wanted it terribly. But then when
the jury went out—*(She leans forward with her arms on her
knees and stares off dreamily)* Do you believe the dead talk
to us, Mrs. Kelly?

MRS. KELLY. *(Steadying herself with a hand on her chair)*
Why?

MARY. It was as if my husband's voice spoke to me then,
back in my brain. As if it said, "What have you done, Mary,
shackling this man?" He was like that, a doctor, you know;
he never blamed anyone. Revenge was just silly, he thought,
just a hangover from barbarism. Better to pick up the pieces
of things and glue them together, he said. And when the
jury went out, it was as if I heard his voice.

MRS. KELLY. So you came in here.

MARY. I didn't want to—five hours of deciding. But I came.

MRS. KELLY. *(Listening)* Do you hear anything out there?

MARY. No—this door must be soundproof. It takes quite a while, I've heard, with all the ceremonies.

MRS. KELLY. What is it you wanted Dan to do?

MARY. As the price of my withdrawal? I wanted him to give those years he might have spent in prison—give them to teaching boys not to imitate him. He's young and muscular; boys listen to a man like that more than to the feeble old ladies they send about. Oh, I hadn't worked it out much—talk places that boys gather, I thought, talk even on street corners, sort of Salvation-Army style. But it's too late, I see, now.

MRS. KELLY. No! In the trial, yes—but a pardon—if you'd help me get a pardon. Wouldn't your wish have weight with the Governor?

MARY. I doubt it. Justice isn't a faucet you can turn off, Mrs. Kelly.

MRS. KELLY. But they may not regard his intoxication as proved. Then those statutes wouldn't apply, it would be just an accident such as anyone might have. Mr. Applethwaite says they won't regard Dan's intoxication as proved.

MARY. But your son admitted he was drunk.

MRS. KELLY. Not out there.

MARY. Does that make a difference?

MRS. KELLY. *(Sitting down and leaning on the desk)* Oh, I can't—I can't bear it. Prison!

(Mary crosses to bend over her. The door opens heartily. Applethwaite comes in.)

APPLETHWAITE. Well, well, well!

MARY. *(Straightening and turning)* Why—what—?

APPLETHWAITE. *(Embarrassed)* Oh, you here still, Mrs. Harmon—well, you'll understand.

MRS. KELLY. What is it?

APPLETHWAITE. Acquitted, my dear lady!

MARY. Acquitted?

APPLETHWAITE. Why yes, Mrs. Harmon. You see, they thought that head injury made the evidence of intoxication too slight—thought it produced the symptoms that you interpreted as intoxication. So this verdict is no denial of your testimony. Acquittal, just as I told you to expect, Mrs. Kelly. The newsmen want to take your picture.

(Mrs. Kelly has risen, steadying herself by holding to Mary, who has turned her face away. Applethwaite is jubilant. He comes over and takes Mrs. Kelly's arm.)

APPLETHWAITE. If you'll just step out here where the light is better, Mrs. Kelly. All the big journals want your picture, naturally—alone and then with your son and then with me and then the three of us. Come on.

MRS. KELLY. *(Who is not at all aware of what Applethwaite is talking about)* Dan—where is he?

APPLETHWAITE. Out here being photographed. Come on.

(Mrs. Kelly glances at Mary and then lets herself be led out. Mary stands motionless, looking down at the desk. Presently Dan enters. He closes the door. Mary does not glance about until he speaks.)

DAN. Mary—Mrs. Harmon—

MARY. *(Turning, speaking in cold formality)* I congratulate you, Mr. Kelly.

(Dan crosses to the desk. They look at each other for a long pause.)

DAN. Why should you congratulate me?

MARY. Because you're acquitted.

DAN. I'm not acquitted.

MARY. He said—

DAN. *(Interrupting)* Who, Applethwaite? Yes, acquitted out there. But not in here.

MARY. What do you mean?

DAN. I've come for my sentence.

MARY. You'll do it anyway?

DAN. Yes. Five years' sentence, if my judge chooses. Does she?

MARY. I think she does, Dan.

(Dan accepts her proffered hand. They stand looking at each other.)

CURTAIN

Speaking of Pictures

by

MARION WEFER

Characters:

PHILIP HENDERSON, college student, about twenty years old.

BETSY, his sister, eighteen.

TOMMY, his brother, sixteen.

SANDRA, a newcomer, nineteen.

JIM, a friend of the Henderson's, eighteen.

PAT, Jim's sister, fourteen.

TIME: Present.

LENGTH: About twenty-five minutes.

SETTING: *The back lawn of the Henderson home. Entrances are at left and right. The right leads into the street. The left leads into the kitchen door. There are two shallow steps, left front, before the door. At the center back is an outdoor fireplace with fuel ready for a picnic. To the left of this is a long garden settee, or several chairs of garden furniture. To the right is a fairly long trestle table with a backless bench beside it. The lawn is enclosed by a hedge.*

As the scene opens Philip is seated on the steps, left front. Betsy is practicing First Aid on him and has put his arm in a sling. She uses a large triangular bandage and has her manual open on the step. She steps back to admire the completed sling.

BETSY. There now, Handsome! Your stylish sling, I mean! *(Whips it off while Philip sits patiently)* That's that! Relax! Your arm isn't broken any more!

PHILIP. *(Stretches it)* That's my good luck, my muscular ministering angel! Can I go, now? *(Starts to rise.)*

BETSY. *(Pushes him back)* You cannot! Sit still! Be a sport, Phil, I want to try those pressure points again! *(Thrusts manual into his lap)* Look here! You went through the windshield and cut your throat! *(Gets him beneath the chin with the*

Used by permission of the author. Printed in Classmate, October 25, 1942, Nashville, Tennessee.

301

flat of one hand and fumbles vigorously along the edge of his jaw with the other) Where's your artery at? This one always gets me—

Philip. *(Puts up protesting hand; chokes)* Hey! Take it easy, Sis!

Betsy. Quiet, Brother! I'm saving your young life—

Philip. *(As well as he can)* Have to—choke me—to death to—do it?

Betsy. *(With dignity)* I'm simply applying "digital press-ure"! There! Got it! Everything's under control! *(Removes hands)* You're saved!

Philip. *(Feels neck tenderly)* Sez you! May I never come nearer to a necktie party! *(Hands book to her)* Enough's enough, Bets!

Betsy. *(Ignores book; coaxes)* I don't suppose you'd mind letting me give you artificial respiration?

Philip. *(Bounces up hastily)* Don't you suppose it! Take your book and run along. You've got to get supper anyway with the folks away!

Betsy. *(Wistfully)* All you have to do is to lie flat on your face!

Philip. *(With exasperation)* Look here, my zealous Night-ingale, I've broken my arms and legs for you! I've cracked my collar bone and sprained my ankle! I've had a variety of fancy hemorrhages and all the pleasures of being hanged! I won't be drowned!

Betsy. *(Ever so sweetly)* You could be struck by lightning if you'd rather! They—artificially respirate—for that!

Philip. *(Pulls a face)* I still don't like the idea!

Betsy. Picklepuss! I do think you might!

Philip. Just a little angel of mercy, aren't you?

Betsy. Well, I take my test tomorrow. Timing's terribly important in artificial respiration. *(Illustrates with both hands)* You get your fingers on the ribs and you press in—and out—and in—and out—! Not too fast, you understand? Something like playing the accordion in waltz time! *(She advances on Philip with intention.)*

Philip. *(Fends her off)* O.K.! I get the idea! But accordion playing on my ribs is out! Sit down and I'll quiz you. *(Sits down with resignation. From the house comes the sound of a cornet, clarinet, or what-have-you, inexpertly played. Philip jumps)* Great suffering cats and little kittens! Did you hear what I heard?

BETSY. Stick around home, college boy, and you'll get used to it. It's only Tommy—definitely not Dorsey! *(Another blast from the player.)*

PHILIP. I believe you. The kid tells me he wants to make the band so he can go places next winter.

BETSY. Those snaps you sent home gave him ideas. Some trick photographer you're getting to be! Look at you now with your pockets full of pictures! *(Music again with a very sour note)* Personally, I'd be embarrassed! You made a mistake and you tell the world! The folks are kind of against the band proposition. They would be!

PHILIP. I can think of a few reasons.

BETSY. But theirs are such icky ones! We're not mere children! Tommy can take care of himself! So can I!

PHILIP. Kind of sure of yourself, aren't you? What's all this I hear about you and the crowd going clear across the county to Sachetti's?

BETSY. If you're quizzing me, Professor, that's not in the book!

PHILIP. So you won't talk? *(Shrugs, takes book, leafs through it)* O.K., then, we'll stick to the book. Here's one you may be needing if the crowd makes a habit of Sachetti's. What do you do for a case of poisoning—alcoholic variety?

BETSY. *(Pouts)* The folks have been talking to you.

PHILIP. They have. You've got them bothered. They want me to make a noise like a Dutch uncle. So I'm a bit bothered myself.

BETSY. Oh, the folks make such a fuss over nothing! We didn't even like the place. We just went there on account of Sandra.

PHILIP. That new girl? I've never met the lady.

BETSY. You will. *(The music blares as badly as ever)* Tommy's that way about her. Maybe it's love. *(Calls into house)* Hey, Tommy, pipe down! Button it!

TOMMY. *(Offstage)* Say, when do we eat?

PHILIP. It isn't love.

BETSY. *(Calling as before)* When the potatoes are baked.

Come out and listen to Phil being a Cutch uncle. *(A derisive toot.)*

PHILIP. A little "digital pressure" might help! Tell me about this Sandra. How come the crowd's going her way?

BETSY. Oh, she's something special. She's got style—and poise, and things like that! She just came here to live a few months ago; she and her mother. I guess her father's dead. She never speaks about him. But she's been more places! New York and Hollywood—

PHILIP. Gets around, doesn't she?

BETSY. One winter they lived right in the city where the university is. She said she knew a lot of the boys but she didn't remember you.

PHILIP. I don't suppose I circulate in Sandra's circle. And who am I to be remembered?

BETSY. I gave you a nice build-up. Told her you were on the paper and won prizes with your candid-camera shots.

PHILIP. Local yokel makes good? I bet she was struck all of a heap.

BETSY. Well, I do think she's found out we're not such a corny crowd. That's why we went to Sachetti's. Just to show her! As a matter of fact, we have better times at Charley's Milk Bar. Only that sounds so blah!

PHILIP. Sandra prefers Sachetti's?

BETSY. She didn't say much. Honestly, Phil, that party was a flop! The place isn't such a much, and the way they charge you for practically nothing at all—! It's wicked!

PHILIP. Well, then, show your independence! Go where you please! If you like Charley's Milk Bar take Sandra in tow, sail right in like the Spirit of '76 and call for a double malted! I'll bet she'll say, "Make mine chocolate!"

BETSY. *(With complete unbelief)* Yes, she would!

PHILIP. She'll lap it up and like it!

BETSY. You're definitely dizzy! Feature Sandra in a milk bar!

PHILIP. Unless she's dieting or something, why not? You'll find the best people in 'em. The kind that do things and have to keep their heads. Listen, if you're going to let this Sandra—and the lady's beginning to get in my teeth—if you're going to let her lead you around you'd better come through with a 100 per cent answer to this poisoning proposition.

(Shoots out an inquisitorial finger at her) You're in Sachetti's with the crowd! Somebody goes out like a light! How's about it, First Aider?

BETSY. *(Quickly)* I know the answer! Don't tell me! You try to make them throw—you give the patient an "emetic"!

PHILIP. Sounds more professional that way, but it isn't any prettier! Thinking of some of the, let's call 'em "poisoning cases" I've seen, I'd say, "Try and do it!"

BETSY. Well, if they won't take it, the book says quote, usually the patient will sleep off the condition in a few hours. Unquote. Next question, Professor!

PHILIP. Switch the subject on me, would you? Just walk out and leave 'em lay? *(Leafs through book)* Let's chat about stimulants. Say, this one's news to me! *(Reads)* "Whiskey and brandy are not proper first-aid stimulants and should not be used." Is that right? All I know about first aid is what I see in the movies. Why, there, the first thing they do is rush a drink to whoever gets knocked out, and up pops the patient very happy about the whole affair!

BETSY. We had words about that in class. Mary Gibbs said it wasn't true. But the instructor says the book knows best. It has to! It's official! They'd have all the doctors in the nation on their neck if they pulled a boner!

PHILIP. *(Rereading, still surprised)* What do you know! "Not proper stimulants and should not be used." And more than that—*(Reads)* "Their use may cause considerable harm." *(Holds up book)* American Red Cross First Aid Textbook, Revised, With 114 Illustrations! Does Sandra study First Aid? She'd better!

(Tommy bursts through the door)

TOMMY. Hey, Betsy, are the potatoes done when they bust all over the oven? I took one out, and by golly, it hit the ceiling!

BETSY. The potatoes? Oh, my stars! I forgot to prick 'em! *(Goes out left on the run.)*

TOMMY. *(Looking after her)* What a swell cook she turned out to be! *(Sits down)* Say, Phil, show me the rest of your pictures. Some of those you sent home were neat.

PHILIP. *(Takes a few from pocket of coat)* Sure. I was just going through them, sorting out negatives and such.

TOMMY. Going in for any more contests?

PHILIP. Could be. I've got some action stuff that—*(Sound of an auto horn right. Tommy jumps up and waves.)*

TOMMY. Hi!

PAT AND SANDRA. *(Offstage)* Hi, Tommy! Where's Betsy?

TOMMY. She's around. Come on in. How was the water? *(Philip, who has been looking sharply at the group, shuffles through his pictures, studies one, looks out toward group incredulously as the unseen voices carol back.*

PAT AND SANDRA. Marvelous! Simply marvelous! We're coming in!

PHILIP. *(Slips pictures into coat pocket)* Is that—Sandra?

TOMMY. *(Goes down steps and crosses to meet friends, speaking as he does so)* Sure that's Sandra. No one like her in this town. Come ahead and see if I care! *(He meets the three, Sandra, Pat, and Jim, as they come on carrying large paper bags and cardboard boxes. Pat is dressed in obvious imitation of Sandra. She imitates her mannerisms, and her hair is strained into Sandra's exaggerated coiffure. Sandra herself is a pretty girl with make-up a bit too vivid, dress more extreme than Betsy's simple sports frock, and an effusive manner that has become habitual to her. Her abundant good will and bouncing vitality make her attractive. She chatters as she crosses.)*

SANDRA. So I said to Jim—*(Tommy takes a bag from her)* Oh, thanks, Tommy, you lamb—I said, "I think it's wonderful of Betsy to give up going out to the pool with us and stay home and study first aid and cook supper for her brothers and all!" I mean, I think it really is! I told Jim, "Betsy Henderson has more character than any girl I ever knew!"—*(Tommy offers to take box)* No, I'll carry this one. It's a cake. I made it. After I fed the first one to the neighbor's chickens! Boy! I had me a time fussing around the kitchen—messing up more dishes—so I said we'd just barge in and throw a party! Can we do the dogs here like we did at the very first party I went to in this town? We had more fun!

TOMMY. Sure you can! Say, this is wonderful! It was tops of you to think of it! *(Bawls in door)* Hey, Betsy! Look who's here with a flock of food! Surprise! Surprise! *(Turns back to friends, remembers Phil, who has been standing looking grave and rather formidable)* Sandra, this is Phil, the college man, you know. Phil, this is Sandra.

SANDRA. *(Beaming)* Hiyah! I've heard a lot about you.

PHILIP. *(Cordially but quietly)* How are you?

(Sandra looks at him quickly. The others are absorbed in their bundles. Pat edges up to Tommy. Betsy appears in the door with an apron on. She pushes back her hair.)

BETSY. Hi, folks! You're the answer to the maiden's prayer! I was just scraping the family supper off the ceiling. You boys bring the things in and we'll fix up trays—

SANDRA. I brought paper plates and things. Can we have a bonfire afterwards and sing?

TOMMY. Swell! I'll bring my cornet!

PAT. *(Meltingly)* Oh, Tommy, will you?

BETSY. Not at this party, he won't! Sandra, you and Phil get the fire started. You're too fancy for a kitchen maid. Come on, Pat and you fellows—

PAT. I'll take the cake, Sandra.

SANDRA. *(Giving it to her)* See that Tommy keeps his finger out of the icing! He gets juvenile moments!

TOMMY. I resent that. *(Notices Pat for the first time as she comes up the step with a bag on each arm and the cake box held by the string under which she has slipped a finger)* Yipe! What have you done to your hair, kid?

PAT. *(Loftily going out)* I like it this way. It's not so— juvenile! *(The others follow her with the exception of Sandra and Phil, who are at the bottom of the steps, left, front.)*

SANDRA. *(Happily)* Well, Fireman, let's do something constructive with matches. Got any? Or do we rub two sticks together?

PHILIP. *(Hunts in pockets, drawing out packet of pictures as he fishes)* Nothing like that, even in these wilds.

SANDRA. *(With curiosity)* Are those some of your pictures? Do let me see. Betsy says you're a whiz; take prizes and all that; and you're on the paper at the university. Do you know Bob Treadwell, or Buzz Hardy, or Red Wallis?

PHILIP. *(Shakes head, balances pictures on hand)* Not so well. I used to trail that crowd with my camera for action shots, but their actions were a little too swift for me to catch up with. However—*(Selects a picture, hesitates, hands it to her)* Since he's a friend of yours, and you know he doesn't always look that way—

SANDRA. *(Looks at picture, laughs)* That's Buzz! Some picture!

PHILIP. *(Watching her curiously)* Definitely not his best.

SANDRA. *(Still laughing)* You got plenty of action! Buzz always fancied himself as a rug-cutter when he'd had a couple. That might have been at the inter-fraternity party. Any others? *(Returns picture.)*

PHILIP. It was. *(Flips through pictures, selects another, looks at her)* I've another.

SANDRA. *(Puts out hand)* Let's see. Might be somebody I know.

PHILIP. *(Keeps picture)* Could be.

SANDRA. Well, what are you holding out on me?

PHILIP. *(Keeps picture)* I was only shooting around trying indoor work. The light was better than I thought.

SANDRA. *(Impatiently)* Come across. It must be something special.

PHILIP. *(Still holds it)* I've never shown this one.

SANDRA. Why not? Come on, college man!

PHILIP. *(Gives it to her)* Didn't think it would be fair to —the subject. And I didn't know her.

SANDRA. *(Looking at picture)* Oooh! Oh, it isn't—

PHILIP. Think you could help me out?

SANDRA. *(Still looking at picture in a dazed way)* But I didn't—I couldn't have—did I really—? *(Lets picture drop.)*

PHILIP. *(Picks up picture)* Candid camera.

SANDRA. *(Turns on him)* Honestly, have you never shown it? Honestly? Not to Betsy—or Tommy—or anyone?

PHILIP. Not to anyone. Honestly.

SANDRA. *(With hand out)* Give it to me then!

PHILIP. No.

SANDRA. *(Slowly)* I know you don't like me. I saw that right away. You're—the perfect sort, I expect. *(Appealingly, humbly)* The crowd here, they treat me as if I belonged! Are you going to show them that picture?

PHILIP. I wouldn't want to.

SANDRA. Then give it to me. Please!

PHILIP. You know what you are to the crowd here? The new girl; the city girl; the girl that's been places and knows her way around! They're all prepared to follow your lead, from Betsy to that funny kid, Pat.

SANDRA. Well, if they are—so what?

PHILIP. You're leading them the wrong way. I heard about Sachetti's. So I keep the picture.

SANDRA. Oh, but you must—(*Enter Betsy carrying a broiler and a tray with hot dogs. The others follow with food, paper plates, napkins, mustard, the cake. Philip slips the picture into his coat pocket.*)

BETSY. Haven't you started the fire yet, Useless? (*Crosses to table, left, followed by others*) I don't mean you, Sandra. You wouldn't know. (*The others put their food down, talking as they do so.*)

TOMMY. I'll show you how to build a fire any time you want, Sandra. Boy, am I hungry!

PAT. (*At his heels*) Want a bitsy bite of cake?

TOMMY. I do not. I want one hot dog, well done!

BETSY. (*Laying hands on brother*) Phil, take off that coat and build us our fire! (*She takes the coat which he slips out of, perforce, and lays it over the bench by the table. Philip starts making the fire*) Did he get started on camera stuff, Sandra? He's good enough, but wacky!

(*Tommy, followed by Pat, with Jim next, settle on the settee, right, Betsy and Sandra are by the table, left.*)

SANDRA. I'll butter these rolls, Betsy.

BETSY. Thanks. I'll do the dogs. Did we bring everything?

JIM. Everything but; the kitchen sink. Need any help, Sandra?

SANDRA. (*With a speculative eye on Philip and on his coat*) No, thanks! Sit still and we'll give you service.

JIMI. Well, if you don't need any help—(*Unfolds napkin. Philip straightens up after building fire and starts to come toward bench where his coat is. Betsy takes a broiler of dogs to the fire and watches them. Jim, Tommy, and Pat watch her.*)

TOMMY. Well done for me, Bets!

JIM. Me, too! (*Sandra, aware of Philip's movement, comes around the table before he can reach his coat, extracts the picture from the pocket, slips back behind the table, and offers him a buttered roll with winning politeness.)*

PHILIP. *(Puts on coat)* Very, very funny. Only I have the negative. *(Takes it out of other pocket)* In the other pocket. Pity!

SANDRA. *(Comes around the table. Speaks bitterly)* You think of everything, don't you, college man? You've—all the makings of a good enemy. *(Her tone changes to sincere appeal)* Give me a chance, won't you? You don't understand. *(She turns away from him, takes a plate of rolls from the table, and crosses right and serves the others, returns left to stand near Betsy, who is busy at the fireplace. Philip sits on the bench in front of the table. The light is dimmer and the fireglow illuminates the scene more and more.)*

TOMMY. How about some harmony? Anybody want me to get my cornet?

BETSY. Nobody does, believe me, brother! These are getting done!

JIM. Nobody loves the music maker. How about showing your pictures, Phil?

BETSY. If it wasn't for his picture show these dogs would be done! Somebody tell a story.

TOMMY. What do you say we go to Sachetti's afterwards?

PAT. Oh, yes. Let's! I've never been!

JIM. *(Pats her head patronizingly)* Not you, Pat. Not for the juvenile!

PAT. *(Furious)* Why, you big lug! Sandra told me when she was my age—

SANDRA. Hush, children, hush! I'll tell you a story.

BETSY. Pinch him for me, Pat! That's a brother! Always belittlin'! Go ahead, Sandra! Make it good.

SANDRA. Maybe I'll show you pictures, too.

JIM. Good for you!

SANDRA. Once upon a time—

TOMMY. Want some sound effects? I'll get—

SANDRA. It's not that kind of a story. It's not very dramatic.

PAT. Is it funny?

SANDRA. No, Pat. It isn't funny. But I think I'll tell it anyway. *(Hesitates a minute, then plunges ahead, speaking quickly, but distinctly)* Once upon a time there was a little girl. And she had a father and a mother and—

BETSY. *(Gabbles rapidly)* And they all lived together in a little house in the middle of a wood!

PHILIP. *(Quietly)* Button it, Betsy. *(Betsy catches his gravity as the others of the group do also. The lights are quite dim and the group is lighted by the fire glow.)*

SANDRA. No they didn't. They lived in hotels and boarding-houses, and sometimes furnished rooms. Ever since she could remember. They moved around a lot, on account of the little girl's father. He—he changed his job so often. The little girl's mother went to business, so there wasn't anyone around to tell the girl things and she had to learn a lot by herself. So she got some things all wrong. She thought she had to do what everyone else did. She thought she had to do the things the crowd did, and she couldn't be very choosy about the crowd because she hadn't any chance to be particular. She had to take what she could pick up—or else be lonely. And she didn't like being lonely. Well, one day her father—went away. We won't talk about that. Her mother said they'd stop moving; she was so tired of moving; and they'd have a real home. They did, and they loved it, and the girl had real friends, the kind she's never known before. She liked them. She wanted to do things their way. But—I guess this is the funny part, Pat—her new friends wanted to do things the way they thought was her way. You see, she'd—strutted a bit—put on an act—before she really knew them. She wanted them to like her and it was the only way she knew. They didn't know she'd given up her old crowd way. She gave it up the day she visited her father—at the sanitarium. *(There is a pause.)*

BETSY. Thanks, Sandra. I guess we all get the idea. From now on, Sachetti's is—out! Phil! Hand me a plate. These are done! *(She piles up the dogs and starts serving them, first to Sandra, then to the others. The tension breaks as they help themselves.)*

PAT. But I'm all mixed up! Didn't—

TOMMY. *(Hastily hoping to distract her)* Pass the mustard!

PAT. *(Passes it, but persists)* Didn't you say you had pictures or something?

SANDRA. *(Takes picture from pocket)* Why yes, Pat. I've a picture of a girl being—terribly juvenile. Catch! *(As she extends the picture Philip steps forward quickly and intercepts it.)*

PHILIP. Mind, Pat? I'm keen on pictures.

PAT. *(Offended)* You might have let me see it!

TOMMY. *(Hastily)* Have another dog! Have some mustard!
You know I'm beginning to like that funny-looking hairdo.

PAT. *(Meltingly)* Oh, Tommy!

PHILIP. *(Who is pretending to examine the picture by fire-
light)* Whoever took that was crazy. *(He lets it fall into the
fire as he meets Sandra's eyes.)*

BETSY. Why, you big butter-fingers! It's ruined! Sandra,
do you have the negative?

SANDRA. No. But I don't care at all.

JIM. Get your friend to print you another.

SANDRA. He isn't any friend of mine. *(Betsy crosses to table
and looks over articles.)*

BETSY. There! I knew there was something! I need the big
cake knife and some more plates.

TOMMY. *(Very lazily)* What do we need plates for anyway?

BETSY. *(Mentally dividing cake with a poised forefinger)*
Maybe you like coconut cake with mustard. I don't. And the
rest aren't crazy, either.

SANDRA. I'll get the plates! Save your strength for K.P.
later, gentlemen! *(Crosses towards steps, left.)*

PHILIP. *(Follows her quickly)* I'll bring the knife, Bets.

BETSY. Suppose we clear up a bit. *(She collects plates, napkins, and so forth, and the others help, moving back and forward quietly. Sandra and Phil are to the front, left. Sandra
is about to go up the steps.)*

PHILIP. Sandra. *(Sandra turns and looks at him.)*

PHILIP. *(Takes packet out of pocket, peels off a negative,
hands it to her)* Yours. I'm sorry.

SANDRA. *(Taking it)* That's all right. Thanks.

PHILIP. I was mistaken about you. But you're mistaken
about me, too.

SANDRA. Perhaps. What do you mean?

PHILIP. You said I'd the makings of a good enemy. Wrong!
I've the makings of a good friend. How's about it?

SANDRA. *(Studies him a minute, suddenly puts out her hand
with a smile)* O.K., friend!

CURTAIN

Among Thieves

A Religious Drama in One Act

by

HELEN M. CLARK

Characters:

THE CAPTAIN	THE LIEUTENANT
THE SOLDIER	THE PRISONER
THE BOY	THE PREACHER

NOTE: *The Captain, the Soldier, the Boy, and the Lieutenant wear the nondescript, tattered, rag-tag uniforms common to all revolutionaries or guerrilla soldiers the world over. They carry knives and swords, but no guns are in evidence. The Prisoner wears a uniform, but it is so torn and blood-stained that it cannot be identified as that of any particular nation. The Preacher wears the clothes of a laborer.*

TIME: Indeterminate.

SETTING: *A place of rocks and trees close against a steep hill-side. The only light is the dull glow from the embers of a dying fire deep in a circle of stones, down center; a light so dim that from all about it the blackness comes crowding in. There is a wind blowing high overhead, as if across the top of sheltering hills. The wind rises in a shrill gust, wails away down an unseen glen, rustling the leaves of unseen trees, dies to a whisper.*

(Then the SOLDIER *is heard, coming down a hill at right. Metal clicks softly against metal with every step. Water splashes lightly as he wades through a small stream at the foot of the hill. Then, coming closer to the fire, he stops and speaks. His is a hearty, mature voice, softened a little by caution.)*

SOLDIER. Where are you, lad? Will you speak up?
(The voice that answers is that of a boy, fourteen or fifteen; a voice young, eager, alive. The BOY *is sitting on the ground to the left of the fire.)*

BOY. I'm over here. Why?

SOLDIER. I just wanted to know which bump around the fire was you, so I wouldn't be treading on you unexpected, that's all. You'd likely squawk loud enough to raise the dead —to say nothing of all honest men sound asleep in their beds hereabouts. (*He comes up to the right of the fire.*)

BOY. (*Resenting the teasing*) Aw! No, I wouldn't! (*Then, eagerly*) Is there any sign of them yet?

SOLDIER. No. But there's hardly been time. Where's the Captain?

BOY. He went off down the glen a few minutes ago. He's awfully restless. Keeps walking around the fire and listening—

SOLDIER. Aye. It's uneasy business, this waiting. It gets a man the way nothing else does. Too bad that wounded arm the Captain's got kept him from going with the rest of them tonight. He's not happy, hanging around here.

BOY. Well, he might've gone anyway, seems to me.

SOLDIER. No, no, lad. In this raiding business you got to have two good hands for fighting and two good legs for running. Otherwise, you get retired—quick and permanent. (*He chuckles as he sits on a rock right of the fire.*)

BOY. I wish they'd let me go on a raid some night.

SOLDIER. When you've had a bit more training for it, laddie. You've got to be clever as a fox to get away and keep away from the government men.

BOY. Aw, they're no good!

SOLDIER. That's where you're wrong, lad. Don't underrate them. There're some pretty smart men in the government's army. That's why you've got to learn to be just a bit smarter before we'll let you tangle with them. There's a whole lot more to this game, you know, than just being mad at these foreigners and wanting to kill them.

BOY. It'd be fun, though. Hiding in the rocks, waiting, jumping out when they come by—fighting them—killing them—

SOLDIER. (*Chuckling*) Killing! That's pretty brave talk from a lad who shut his eyes and put his hands over his ears and cried a bit when we killed the little goat for eating day before yesterday.

BOY. Aw! That—well, that was different. It was just a baby thing—and it had such a soft, silky head—and it followed me around the camp like a puppy—But these foreigners—I could kill them, all right. Because I hate them plenty!

SOLDIER. Aye. But hate or no hate, you got to learn to lad. And, at the start, killing's not easy. For your kind, keep your eyes open when you stick your sword into a man, anyway.

BOY. What do you mean—for my kind?

SOLDIER. That you got too much heart in you, lad.

BOY. Aw!

SOLDIER. Oh, it's nothing to be ashamed of. Maybe I was a bit like you—once. I can still remember the first man I put a sword through. He wasn't much older than you, either. I can remember the sort of puzzled look on his face—and the queer, frightened whimper he gave before he choked on his own blood and died. And I just stood there like a ninny, looking down at him. Sort of surprised me that it was so easy to kill. He bothered me a bit, that first one. But I got over it. I've finished off hundreds since—and I sleep like a baby. You get used to killing—like everything else.

(The wind rises shrilly.)

BOY. The wind's a lot stronger, isn't it?

SOLDIER. Aye. The night's thickening. Be rain before morning, likely. If so, it's a bit of luck for us—with a late moon rising.

BOY. I could see stars overhead a little while ago. They're gone now.

SOLDIER. Aye. Means we'll have to get home by dead reckoning when we go. Which reminds me, that's another thing you've got to learn, lad, before you can be sent with the others.

BOY. What?

SOLDIER. To smell your way across the country in the dark when there's not a star to guide you; when there's storm about you—or mist so thick you can't see your hand held in front of your nose. And you got to learn to move so quiet in the dark that not even a grass blade whispers. And more, you got to know these hills and moors so well that when you step on a pebble in the dark, you know just where it lies—or when you touch a leaf, you know which side of the bush it hangs on. And you got to learn to tell the time by how the night smells and feels—so daylight won't sneak up on you and catch you out of hiding. Take a good sniff now, lad. What's your nose say to you about this place we're sitting?

BOY. Well, I can smell charred wood—hot stones—ashes—dust—

SOLDIER. And no more?

BOY. No-o. Grass, maybe.

SOLDIER. You should be able to smell the rain coming on the wind. And the wetness of the brook there, so you'd not go splashing across it careless-like. You ought to smell that tangle of willows and bushes up the glen. That'd tell you it's maybe a good spot for hiding but not for running. And the thorn bushes on the far bank, so you'd not blunder into them unexpected like. And the stretch of grass and flowers up the hill that'd tell you there's open ground and safe travelling. And even the leather in my boots—and the bit of cheese I got here in my pocket.

BOY. You're just joking.

SOLDIER. No, lad. I'm serious. Because if you get lost in the night—go wandering about noisy and blind—you're liable to collide with the government patrols—and you know what'll happen then. And it's not a pretty way to die, lad.

BOY. I know. I saw when—when they did it—to my father. He died that way.

SOLDIER. Aye. I know. You've got reason enough for hating them, lad. So have the rest of us. But to them we're outlaws—and if they catch us, that's what's at the end of the road for us.

BOY. It—it's an awful way to die—hung up like that—

SOLDIER. Aye. But don't be worrying about it, laddie. We're not caught yet—and most of us die fighting, anyway. Is there any wood near you? We might stir up this fire—be a bit warmer while we wait.

BOY. There was a stick by this rock—Yes. Here.

SOLDIER. Thanks, lad. Now let's see—

(But as his hand reaches into the dim light above the fire, another voice speaks from the left; the voice of a young man—an educated voice, yet hard, a voice used to giving commands and having them obeyed.)

CAPTAIN. Let that fire alone!

SOLDIER. *(Starting, withdraws his hand)* That you, Captain?

CAPTAIN. Yes. Don't put any more wood on that fire.

SOLDIER. Aye, sir, if you say not. But it wouldn't show, deep down here between the hills.

CAPTAIN. The clouds have come too low. There might be a reflection. We won't risk it. We're too close in.

SOLDIER. Aye. We'll let it be as it is, then. But there, laddie, is what I meant. You see how the Captain could come up the glen in the dark with not a sound?

CAPTAIN. You might have heard me if your ears hadn't been full of your own chatter. *(He moves closer to the fire.)*

SOLDIER. I was only giving the lad a few bits of advice, Captain. Youngsters like him need a lot of talking to, first and last, before they amount to anything.

CAPTAIN. No doubt—though how much he'll amount to on what you tell him's a question. Did the sentry on the hill have anything to report?

SOLDIER. Not a blooming thing. It's as quiet as a graveyard in all directions.

CAPTAIN. Too quiet. They ought to be coming back.

SOLDIER. The time's not been as long as it seems, Captain. It passes slow, just waiting like this. Besides, the soldiers mightn't have come along right on schedule. Gold's tiring stuff to carry, you know, even when it's tied to pack hores.

BOY. Then the soldiers ought to be glad when we take it away from them.

SOLDER. Aye, lad, but they won't be. Nor grateful for the nice long rest we'll be giving them after we've got their gold.

CAPTAIN. Their gold! Squeezed and gouged out of the poor wretches they call subjects—and every piece of it stained with blood! *(Laughs shortly)* And they say we're robbers!

SOLDIER. Aye. And cutthroats. Only difference between us and them is they can cut throats legally—and with the government's blessing. *(Sings raucously.)*

> "Oh, it's great to be a soldier,
>   A soldier of the king!
>   You get such pretty medals
>   For your bloody murdering—"

CAPTAIN. Shut up, you fool! You'll wake the whole countryside with that blatting.

Soldier. Aye, Captain. Sorry. But remind me, laddie, some-time when we're in a safer spot, and I'll teach you that song. It's a good one. Be as much as your life's worth to whistle it in the hearing of any government man, it makes them that mad. But some time when you're safely hid in a crowd—

Captain. Don't put ideas like that into his head! Lad?

Boy. Yes, sir?

Captain. You'd better go up and get another report from the sentry on the hill.

Boy. Yes, sir. *(He rises and stumbles out right, splashing noisily through the brook.)*

Soldier. *(After him)* Easy, lad, easy! You'll be scaring the wee minnows! *(Laughs; to* Captain*)* He's clumsy-footed as a puppy, that one.

(There is a gust of wind. The Captain *comes up close to the fire, left.)*

Captain. They couldn't have taken the gold by another road to the coast.

Soldier. No, no, Captain. The boys in town had the word straight. We've got our men waiting at the right place.

Captain. If it wasn't for this arm—I should have gone, anyway.

Soldier. The Lieutenant can handle it all right, Captain. He's not so long on brains, but he remembers orders pretty well. It's just that you're not used to waiting like this.

Captain. I suppose that's it. *(He sits on a rock left of the fire.)* Waiting gives me too much time to think—and wonder —and grow afraid—

Soldier. Um! The lad's aching to take part in a raid, Captain.

Captain. He's not ready yet.

Soldier. I know that. Not for the kind of thing we're doing tonight. But I was thinking—next time we get an easy job —something like wiping out a patrol—let me take him along. I'll be responsible for him. And lads like a bit of excitement now and then. How about it, Captain?

Captain. No. It'd be too dangerous.

Soldier. He's not so bad on the fighting end. I've been training him myself.

Captain. That's not what I'd worry about. But suppose

something happened and they took him alive—tried to make him talk? How long do you think he'd hold his tongue under torture?

SOLDIER. Aye. I get it. Guess you're right there. Still, he's got to start in some time.

CAPTAIN. There's no hurry about it. We've men enough yet without him. And life's good at his age. Let him live—a little longer.

(There is a silence between them. The wind shrills down the glen.)

SOLDIER. Nice little job we did a few days ago, wasn't it? Twenty-five of them left to rot in the sun. And more of them tonight—and the gold, to boot.

CAPTAIN. We're just taking back our own.

SOLDIER. Aye. But that's not the way they'll see it. They'll have patrols swarming around here tomorrow like flies on a carcass.

CAPTAIN. They'll not find anything.

SOLDIER. No. Be as if we'd melted and run down a crack. By the way, Captain, some of the boys have been wondering if it isn't time for us to start organizing a real army.

CAPTAIN. I don't want an army.

SOLDIER. But, Captain—

CAPTAIN. I've told you before we can do more damage to them this way—with a small, well-trained body of men that can gather or scatter on a moment's notice—and without attracting attention. An army's too difficult to equip—to hide —and moves too slowly.

SOLDIER. There's lots of men willing to join up with you, Captain, if you'll take them.

CAPTAIN. They're willing, I know. But you can't make an army out of an untrained rabble in a few weeks—or even months. And it takes more than courage and a hope to stand against a fighting machine like the government's.

SOLDIER. Aye. They got a fine army—much as I hate to admit it. They're good fighters, these foreigners.

CAPTAIN. That's what a lot of men have found out—too late. That any fight in the open with these foreigners isn't a battle. It's a massacre.

SOLDIERS. Aye. I know. So do some thousands of dead ones.

CAPTAIN. And there's less danger of betrayal among a few. One word—one hint, even—that any number of men are gathering together anywhere, and the government soldiers'll come like vultures. No, this way's best, with a few men, so we can move quickly—strike quickly—and hide quickly.

SOLDIER. Like rats in holes.

CAPTAIN. Why not? Rats can weaken a foundation and destroy it—gnawing it. And some day, when the leader comes who can rouse this nation—make it follow him—fight for him—

SOLDIER. And he'll have a plenty tough time doing that, I'm thinking, because there're a lot of folks don't seem to care, one way or the other, who rules them. And a lot of them even like these foreigners and their way of running things.

CAPTAIN. Traitors! Boot-lickers! Slaves simpering and scraping before their masters—smiling when they get kicked out of the way—and crawling back for more—faugh! We lead a hard life—and we're hunted men—but at least we're free men.

SOLDIER. Aye. We're free men—until we're caught and hung up in the sun to dry.

CAPTAIN. We've kept out of their hands so far.

SOLDIER. Aye. And maybe we can keep on dodging them until we die of old age—but I'd hate to bet on it, Captain. These foreigners got a long arm—and they don't give up easy.

CAPTAIN. Well, what if they do catch us—and we die? They can't kill the thing we're fighting for. There'll be other men who love liberty to take our places and carry on. And some day—we'll win.

SOLDIER. Aye. We can hope that, anyway. Meantime, we'll keep on cutting the throats of as many foreigners as we can lay hands on—and generally making life miserable for them one way and another. Here comes the laddie again. *(Chuckles)* Wonder if he'll ever learn to move across the landscape any gentler than a lumbering ox?

(The wind rises. The BOY *comes splashing across the stream and in right.)*

CAPTAIN. Any news, lad?

BOY. No, sir. Nothing yet.

CAPTAIN. They should be getting back.

SOLDIER. Take it easy, Captain. The night's still young. They'll come.

BOY. I wish we could see the stars. Then we could tell how long it's been since—

SOLDIER. Wait, lad!

BOY. What's wrong?

SOLDIER. Quiet! Listen, Captain! Someone's coming down the hill there.

CAPTAIN. It might be—

SOLDIER. No. None of ours'd be heading in from that direction. And it's just one man. Still now.

(The three of them draw back into the shadows left, waiting tensely. The wind whispers. Off right, in the darkness, a stone rattles under a passing foot. Water splashes softly as someone steps into the brook.)

CAPTAIN. Who's there? Who's there, I say?

(Out of the darkness, right, a voice answers, the voice of a young man, quiet, courteous.)

PREACHER. I beg your pardon? Did I startle you? *(He enters at right.)*

CAPTAIN. Who are you? What are you doing here?

PREACHER. I was taking a short cut home across the hills, and I saw your fire here in the glen and came down.

SOLDIER. Huh! *(Relief in his voice)* It's all right, Captain. I know him. He's a young fellow who goes around through the towns here, talking to people. Most of what he says don't make much sense, but he's all right. Folks call him the Preacher.

CAPTAIN. *(With contempt)* Preacher!

SOLDIER. Aye. Glad you stopped, Preacher. We're herders —and the night's kind of long and lonesome for us, sitting here. Come on up to the fire and chat a bit—if you got time. *(He slips his sword back into its sheath audibly.)*

PREACHER. You say you're herders?

SOLDIER. That's right, Preacher.

PREACHER. There are no sheep or cattle feeding on these hills. And that was a sword being sheathed. You're not herders.

Soldier. H'm! Well—guess you got us there, Preacher. You've pretty good ears on you.

Preacher. And those who wear swords are—soldiers.

Captain. We might be soldiers. And again—we might be thieves. But whatever we are, we're no company for honest men. So on your way, Preacher—and forget you saw us.

Soldier. Wait, Captain! Hadn't we better keep him here now until we go? So's he can't say anything down in the town about seeing us? Because if the boys are delayed, or anything —well, no use taking chances.

Captain. No, I suppose not. But why did he have to—? Hold him, then.

Soldier. Aye, Captain. Sorry, Preacher. You don't know what this is all about—and I know you didn't mean to get into it—but since you did, we'll sort of have to detain you— temporary. But don't be afraid. We won't hurt you. Come on and sit down. Here's a nice rock by the fire. How about it?

Preacher. As you wish. (*He comes quietly and sits on the rock indicated at right of fire.*)

Soldier. That's it. All nice and cozy. Sorry the fire's so near gone, but since we're aiming to move on in a few min- utes—You don't mind waiting, I hope? Won't be long.

Preacher. No. I don't mind.

Captain. Quiet, all of you! I thought—

(*The wind rises above them. There is a moment while they all listen.*)

Boy. Nothing—yet.

Captain. I don't like this. Something must have gone wrong. Perhaps we'd better—

Soldier. Now, now, Captain. Don't worry. Nothing could go wrong. It was all too well planned. Here—sit down and have a chat with the Preacher. That'll get your mind off— other things. And you'll find him kind of—interesting. Maybe.

Captain. I doubt it. I've no use for preachers and their cant.

Preacher. There's a shipment of gold being sent to the coast tonight.

Boy. (*Soft gasp*) Oh!

Soldier. (*Hastily*) Now, wherever did you get that notion,

Preacher? We—well, we heard some was being shipped down next week, maybe.

PREACHER. It's being sent tonight—secretly.

CAPTAIN. Where did you hear that?

SOLDIER. Funny, isn't it, how things like that sort of get blown around the country like thistle seeds? 'Specially if it's supposed to be a government secret. Then everybody and his pet goat knows about it.

CAPTAIN. By what road is it going down, Preacher? Do you know that, too?

PREACHER. By the road where robbers lie in wait.

BOY. Robbers! Don't you call us that! They stole it from us first! Now we're taking it back! Tonight!

SOLDIER. Lad, keep still!

BOY. It's our gold! Ours! We've got a right to take it—

SOLDIER. Keep still, I said! Don't go shooting off your face to every passer-by. I ought to bop you for that!

CAPTAIN. Never mind. The damage is done—and I don't know that it matters. Now do you know what we are, Preacher?

PREACHER. You named yourselves thieves.

BOY. For taking back what's been stolen from us?

CAPTAIN. Quiet, lad! We call ourselves patriots, Preacher. We're men outside the law, yes. Hunted men—because we love our country—want her free of foreign aggression, foreign rulers.

PREACHER. I see. And patriotism, you think, excuses robbery and murder?

SOLDIER. We sure do, Preacher, when it's these foreigners as get robbed and killed. You can't be soft in this game.

CAPTAIN. Let's get this straight. Which side are you on in this, Preacher? Ours—or the government's?

PREACHER. I'm on no side. Because I'm interested only in men.

CAPTAIN. What do you mean by that?

PREACHER. You divide men by race—boundaries—social barriers—ideas—and a thousand other ways. I don't. All men are alike to me.

BOY. You mean even these foreigners that've taken our

country away from us—and our freedom—and made us slaves?

PREACHER. They're men, too.

BOY. They're not! They're beasts! Ugly, cruel beasts! They hunt us down and put us in prison and torture us and kill us—just because we want to be free!

SOLDIER. Easy, laddie! Easy, now!

BOY. This is our country! Ours! And they've no right to be here! No right at all, I tell you!

PREACHER. No. They're not here by any right. Nevertheless, they are here and hold authority—and must be endured —for a time—

CAPTAIN. Endured? And so you'd have us give in to them and let them clamp chains on us without protest? You'd have us do nothing about the situation—make no effort to be free?

PREACHER. I believe all men ought to be free, yes. But freedom's not just a matter of overthrowing one form of government and setting up another. Freedom's born of truth and tolerance and understanding—and love for one's fellow men—

CAPTAIN. Rot!

PREACHER. And you can't get it by force. Force destroys freedom. It destroys everything worth while.

CAPTAIN. Oh! So you're one of those, are you?

SOLDIER. I told you he was a bit on the crazy side, Captain. He'll go on like that for hours—all about loving people no matter who they are—and about all men being brothers, or something. But if you don't take him too serious, he's sort of amusing.

CAPTAIN. Amusing! He's sickening! Look at him! Young, strong, healthy—and yet he's content to go about drooling pacifist rot. And I know why. That stuff's a good cloak for cowards—gives a man a chance to hide behind words when he's yellow—afraid to fight!

PREACHER. Afraid? Yours is a simple code, isn't it, Captain? If a man strikes you—strike back. If he hurts you—hurt back. If he kills you—someone else must kill him.

SOLDIER. Of course, Preacher. It's always been that way, hasn't it?

PREACER. Yes, I'm afraid it has. It's a code as old as men. Yet it's built on fear and fear alone. When you say, "I hate," you mean, "I'm afraid."

Boy. No! That's not true!

Preacher. And that's why a man shows greater bravery, higher courage, when he doesn't strike back, hurt back, do murder for murder. When he doesn't hate, he's not afraid—

Captain. More rot! I've never seen one of that kind yet that wasn't yellow clear through.

Preacher. You call yourself a soldier, I believe, Captain?

Captain. I am a soldier. And a patriot. And I believe in the right of this nation to be free. In the right of all little nations to be free. In the right of men to live under a government of their own choosing—not one forced on them against their will by aggression, by a stronger, bigger nation. And I'm willing to die for what I believe. Which is more than you'll ever do for that slop you're talking, Preacher. You haven't guts enough to die for anything!

Preacher. (Not answering that) And how would you make this nation free?

Captain. By fighting for it. By killing every foreigner I can.

Preacher. By murdering men.

Boy. They're not men! They're beasts! Beasts, I tell you! They killed my father! They took him—and hung him up! I saw him die They killed him—because he wanted to be free!

Soldier. Easy, laddie!

Boy. They've no right here. They came and conquered us —took away our country—because their army's bigger and stronger. They say we're not as good as they are. That we're slaves—animals—not human. They make us crawl in the dust in front of them—and if we dare to whisper against them, they kill us—

Soldier. Easy, now, lad! What good's it do to yell all that at the Preacher? He knows, anyway.

Captain. But the boy's stated our case very clearly, Preacher. Our right to be free men—our right to be men at all—has been taken from us. Why shouldn't we fight to get it back? What's your answer to that?

Preacher. You've been wronged, yes. But one wrong's never corrected by another. All you'll ever accomplish this way is your own destruction.

Captain. Bosh! There's only one way to get anything in this world, and that's to fight for it!

BOY. We've got to fight for our freedom and our country! We've got to!

PREACHER. The only way to get anything is to fight for it? Strange that men go on believing that against all the record of the years. Because everything that's been set up by force in this world's been knocked down the same way. Every kingdom, every empire, every government built by the sword has been destroyed by the sword—men who live by the sword die by it—and yet men never learn.

CAPTAIN. You talk too much, Preacher.

PREACHER. Does the truth in my words disturb you?

CAPTAIN. No. Their stupidity!

PREACHER. Are they so foolish? How many men out of your own band have died, Captain, since you began this? And what have their deaths gained? Is the freedom you seek one step nearer?

SOLDIER. We know it'll take time, Preacher. Years, maybe. And every death on our side's been paid for by ten on theirs. You can believe what you like about it—but it's no use preaching a sermon to us. Because we think different. That our way's right.

PREACHER. Well, suppose you win what you want in your way? Suppose you drive out these foreigners, set up new rulers, call yourselves free again? You'll still be faced with differences of opinion—divisions—factions. What of them?

CAPTAIN. They're easily dealt with.

PREACHER. More killing, I suppose?

BOY. If they won't be on our side, we'll have to kill them.

CAPTAIN. We've got to make this a strong nation so this won't happen again. We've got to be one people. We can't be torn apart, weakened by factions, minority groups. That's what destroyed us before. It can't be again.

SOLDIER. We got to get rid of opposition some way, Preacher. Can't have too much of it around. It's dangerous.

PREACHER. Then all you propose to do is substitute one tyranny for another? Grant to men the privilege of dying on their brothers' swords instead of their enemies'? Give them more of hate and fear and intolerance? If so, then you haven't the right to be free men. You don't know what real freedom is.

CAPTAIN. I know I've had all I want of this nonsense!

SOLDIER. Take it easy, Captain. He don't mean any harm. He just ain't straight in the head.

CAPTAIN. That's evident. Only a fool or a crazy man would talk that rubbish. We'll do this our own way, Preacher, without any advice from you. Go on spouting all the pretty ideas you like. Your words'll never change anything. They're just sop for weaklings. Love! Brotherhood! Non-resistance! Pah! Force is the only thing men respect—and it's the only way to get what you want—and keep it.

BOY. We'll drive these foreigners out of here! See if we don't!

PREACHER. You'll drive them back beyond something you call a boundary. But you'd still be afraid. You'd build big armies and spend the national income for weapons to guard that boundary. And then those who live on the other side would grow afraid—think you threatened their security—out of that mutual fear would spring war—you see how it has no end?

SOLDIER. Just no stopping him, is there?

PREACHER. They're strange things, boundaries. Imaginary lines men draw around a piece of the earth—lines they guard with forts and soldiers—lines behind which they herd together, shaking with fear and hating those who live on the other side of a line that isn't really there. That's why my kingdom will be a kingdom without boundaries. A kingdom for all men—no matter who they are.

CAPTAIN. Your kingdom!

SOLDIER. That's another thing he likes to talk about, Captain. Some screwy sort of kingdom. I don't quite get it—but you know how these batties are, sometimes. Get to thinking they're kings, or something?

CAPTAIN. King! Oh! Sorry I didn't recognize your Majesty —but you should have worn your crown. Perhaps we'd better cut some twigs off the thorn bushes up there and weave you one—so there'll be no mistake in the future.

BOY. A king with a crown of thorns! (Laughs) That'd be good, wouldn't it?

SOLDIER. Oh, he ain't that mad, Captain! That is, I mean—

CAPTAIN. Then he's a fool!

(A low, sharp whistle off left, repeated once.)

BOY. There's the signal!

SOLDIER. There it is, Captain. They've come. *(He answers the signal with two short whistles.)*

(A voice speaks off left, the harsh, hard voice of a brutal man.)

LIEUTENANT. Captain! Are you there, Captain?

CAPTAIN. Yes. *(Then, as the* LIEUTENANT *enters left)* You got it?

LIEUTENANT. We got it, Captain. No trouble at all. Jumped on them in the pass and had the whole business done in a few minutes. And didn't lose us but two men.

CAPTAIN. And the gold?

LIEUTENANT. Right with us.

CAPTAIN. Good! Tell the men to scatter out and head back across the river to the main camp with it. I'll wait here. If there's any pursuit before you're out of danger, we'll draw it off toward the southwest.

LIEUTENANT. There won't be anybody chasing us, Captain. Least, not from that bunch of soldiers. We did a thorough job. That is—except for the one we got with us.

CAPTAIN. The one you—I said no prisoners!

LIEUTENANT. Sure. I know. But this one was still fighting when we wanted to run—so we just wrapped him up and brought him along. He's one of their officers.

CAPTAIN. Where is he?

LIEUTENANT. Down the glen where he caved in and dropped. Seemed to be as far as he could get right then. I thought the boys'd like a little fun tomorrow—sort of a celebration. And when they get through with him, we can drop what's left of him somewhere so's these rats can see what'll happen to them when we get them alive.

CAPTAIN. I said no prisoners and I meant it, but since you've dragged him this far— Go order the men to get on, and then bring him here.

LIEUTENANT. Sure, Captain.

[*He exits left into the darkness.*

SOLDIER. Well, that's that, Captain. I told you the Lieutenant could handle the job all right. But we'd better not stick here too long. Won't be healthy in a bit.

CAPTAIN. Just until we're sure no patrol's following close enough to catch any of the raiding party. *(Then, lower)* Two —killed.

SOLDIER. Could've been a lot worse, Captain.

LIEUTENANT. *(Returning left with the* PRISONER *stumbling wearily behind him.)* Here he is, Captain. We handled him pretty rough, so he's not feeling so good this minute.

BOY. Is he tied?

LIEUTENANT. Nice and tight, young un. Gagged, too. So you needn't be afraid.

BOY. I'm not afraid of him—or any of them!

LIEUTENANT. Big talk, big talk, little Weeper over Goats!

BOY. Aw! Forget it!

CAPTAIN. Take the gag out of his mouth.

LIEUTENANT. He might holler, Captain.

CAPTAIN. Not more than once. Take it out. I want to talk to him.

LIEUTENANT. All right, Captain, if you say. Get over here, you! *(Pushes the* PRISONER *around back of the fire.)* Ugh! This gag's all bloody. He must've got cut on the head. Not that I care.

SOLDIER. No. Getting blood on your hands oughtn't to bother you any.

(The LIEUTENANT *thinks this a good joke and laughs. The* PRISONER *gives a gasp as the gag is removed from his mouth.)*

LIEUTENANT. There! Now come here! Let's have a look at what we got. *(For just a few seconds a white face appears in the dim light above the fire. Then it is jerked back into the shadows)* Kind of a young un, ain't you? But that's all right. You'll last longer after we get going on you. The old uns always die too quick—spoil the fun.

(The PRISONER *speaks, at first in a thick, rather muffled voice; then, as the effect of the gagging wears off, in a clear, aristocratic young voice, a voice edged with pain and weariness, yet defiant.)*

PRISONER. Water!

LIEUTENANT. Will you listen to him now? Asking us for a drink!

PRISONER. Water!

Preacher. Aren't you going to give it to him?

Lieutenant. Huh? *(Goes over to the* Preacher.) Say who's this fellow? He ain't anybody I know.

Soldier. Oh, he's all right. Harmless. Just a sort of country preacher.

Lieutenant. Preacher, eh! I don't like the breed—anything about 'em. How'd he get in on our party?

Soldier. Oh, just sort of walked in—accidental like. Now he's stopping by request.

Lieutenant. Oh! You're not taking him into camp, I hope?

Soldier. No. Don't worry. We're leaving him here.

Prisoner. Water—please—

Preacher. Aren't you going to give this boy a drink?

Lieutenant. Me? I should say not. And you want to know why, Preacher Man? Because I saw a gang of his kind dragging some of our men off to prison—and, when one of them asked for water, he got his teeth knocked down his throat. Come to think of it, that might not be such a bad answer to this guy—

Captain. None of that, Lieutenant!

Lieutenant. Him and his breed! Slimy rats!

Preacher. He's a man—and your brother.

Lieutenant. Brother! Brother! He's my—*(This is almost too much for him)* Say, what is this, anyway?

Prisoner. Water!

Lieutenant. Brother! Pah! And this is all his kind'll ever get from me! *(He strikes the* Prisoner, *who goes down on his knees.)*

Captain. I said none of that! Let him alone!

Prisoner. *(Thickly)* If I were free—had a sword—

Lieutenant. Pah! *(Gives the* Prisoner *a push with his foot that tumbles him forward on his face)* Get down where you belong, brother! In the dirt!

Captain. That's enough of that. I mean it. Leave him here and get on after the men.

Lieutenant. But, Captain—

Captain. Go on, I say!

Lieutenant. What about this fellow?

Captain. I'll attend to him in my own way. Get on.

Lieutenant. Yes, sir. But remember, Captain, we got use for him tomorrow—me and the boys.　　　　　　[*He exits left.*

CAPTAIN. Be careful at the ford.

LIEUTENANT. *(Off)* Sure, Captain.

CAPTAIN. Lad?

BOY. Yes, sir?

CAPTAIN. Go tell the sentries to stay in place and watch for pursuit—until I signal.

BOY. Yes, sir. *(He runs off into the darkness right.)*

(There is a silence about the fire. The wind shrills overhead. The PREACHER goes quietly to the PRISONER and helps him to his feet. He gets up wearily, slowly, painfully, and stands unsteadily, breathing in short, hard gasps.)

CAPTAIN. Sit down—if you want to.

PRISONER. I prefer—to stand.

CAPTAIN. Suit yourself.

SOLDIER. Better rest while you can, soldier. Won't be any chance after we get going.

PRISONER. I still—prefer to stand.

SOLDIER. Stubborn cuss, eh? All right, then. Stand. What do I care?

PREACHER. This boy's wounded. Aren't you going to help him?

SOLDIER. Me? And why should I, Preacher? He's nothing to me.

PREACHER. How about you, Captain?

CAPTAIN. He's nothing to me, either.

PREACHER. Do you mind if I help him?

CAPTAIN. Not if you want to.

PREACHER. *(To PRISONER)* If you'll sit down here—

PRISONER. Take your hands off me! I said—I'd stand!

PREACHER. But—

PRISONER. I don't want help from you! Let me alone!

PREACHER. Please.

PRISONER. I said— *(He gives up and sits down on a rock back of the fire)* All right. I suppose—it doesn't matter.

PREACHER. I've a cup here. I'll get you some water from the brook.   [*He goes out right.*

SOLDIER. H'm! Not such a sprightly specimen the lieutenant picked up. Seems to me he might've done better.

CAPTAIN. I told that fool no prisoners.

SOLDIER. Aye. He'll be a drag on us if we have to get on in a hurry. So maybe we'd better finish him here before we go. Still, it'll be kind of too bad not to let the boys have their fun with him—We'll wait and see.

BOY. *(Coming in right)* I told the sentries, Captain.

CAPTAIN. All right. Now sit down and keep quiet. We've got to listen. *(He moves left, away from the fire.)*

BOY. Yes, sir. *(Sits right of fire)* What's the Preacher doing by the brook?

SOLDIER. Oh—he's busy being brotherly.

PREACHER. *(Re-enters right)* Here's water.

PRISONER. My hands are tied—

PREACHER. I'll hold the cup for you.

PRISONER. *(After a long drink)* Thank you.

SOLDIER. Polite, ain't you?

PRISONER. When I've reason to be!

PREACHER. Now I'll bandage your wounds. Let's see—there's this cut on your head—

PRISONER. And one on my right arm—

SOLDIER. *(Sarcastically)* Nice little hospital we're running! Shall I kick up the fire and make a light for you to work by, Preacher?

PREACHER. It's not necessary. My eyes have grown used to the night. I can see well enough. But this boy's cruelly tied. Won't you take these bonds off?

SOLDIER. And give him a chance to skip out? Oh, no, Preacher!

PREACHER. He hasn't the strength to run far. Besides, I can't bandage the wound on his arm when he's tied this way.

SOLDIER. Well—how about it, Captain? Shall I untie him for the Preacher?

CAPTAIN. I don't care. Yes. Do it.

SOLDIER. I hate to trust this fellow, Preacher. His kind's tricky. I'll untie him—but I'm going to stand right here and watch him while he's loose. And just remember that, Soldier! There!

PREACHER. Thank you. Now let's see— Your head, first. It's only a shallow cut. *(He takes two handkerchiefs from his pocket, tears them, and binds the wounds on the PRISONER'S head and arm.)*

SOLDIER. But you're wasting your time on a dead man, Preacher.

PREACHER. This man's not going to die.

SOLDIER. *(Laughs)* Will you listen to that, Captain? You know, Preacher, I'm almost of a mind to take you along with us so you can watch him die tomorrow. It'll be something to see. The boys know a lot of cute tricks— What're you shaking for, soldier?

PREACHER. Are you cold? Here—I'll put my coat over your shoulders.

SOLDIER. Cold! Huh! That's not why he's shaking, Preacher. He's afraid.

PRISONER. Not of you—nor of death!

SOLDIER. You're lying, soldier. You're scared stiff.

PRISONER. Give me a sword and I'll show you! Give me a sword! I'll fight you! All of you at once!

SOLDIER. Humph! You talk big like the lad here. Come down to it, you're not much older than he is, are you?

PRISONER. Will you give me a sword?

BOY. Go on. Give him one—and let me fight him!

SOLDIER. And if he did, I'd lay ten to one he'd beat you, lad, and him fighting with his left hand like he'd have to. Can't you see, you thick-head, he's trying to talk us into letting him die easy—because he knows what's ahead of him?

PREACHER. And why must you do that to him?

CAPTAIN. Because he stands for all we hate. He's one of these conquerors—and we're dust beneath his feet—slaves— dogs—

PRISONER. That's what you are, all right! A rabble of mangy curs!

SOLDIER. You'd do better to keep your mouth shut, soldier! We don't forget easy.

CAPTAIN. No. Let him talk. I want your friend here to listen to him. You hear, Preacher? He calls us curs—mangy curs—because we love our country—and want to rid it of his kind. Because we want to be free.

PRISONER. You were free once—and all you did was fight among yourselves. You didn't know the meaning of law and order until we came and gave it to you. You weren't fit to be free men. You had slave minds. All we did was make you what you really are.

CAPTAIN. Go on. And listen well, Preacher.

PRISONER. I know your kind. Patriots you call yourselves! Patriots! Outlaws—thieves—murderers! That's what you are!

CAPTAIN. Listen well, Preacher.

PRISONER. And do you think by killing a few of us here and there—five—ten—twenty—you're going to make us give up what we've conquered? You fools! What we've taken, we keep, and neither you nor ten thousand like you can frighten us or destroy us or drive us away! And we've caught plenty of rats like you. You'll be hunted to death in a few more months—hung up for a lesson to the rest of this rabble—and that'll be the end of you—and we'll still be here!

CAPTAIN. You hear, Preacher? Now you know why we kill every one of his breed that we can.

PREACHER. I heard. But those are just words wrung out of the pain in a boy's body—and the fear is in his heart.

CAPTAIN. It's the creed of all his kind—that they're super-men—empire builders—destined to rule the earth. But they die just as easily as we lesser men.

SOLDIER. Just as easy, Preacher—and stay dead just as long.

BOY. Listen! I thought I heard something!

SOLDIER. Quiet, lad! Let's see. *(They are all silent for a moment, tense, listening. But there is no sound except the whisper of the wind)* Nothing yet. But we'd best get out of here now, Captain, while the going's good. Only—this fellow's in no condition to take along. Lost so much blood he can hardly sit up. Just be a bother. So—

CAPTAIN. Go ahead. Get it done.

SOLDIER. Aye, Captain. Come here, lad.

BOY. What do you want?

SOLDIER. You been aching to kill one of them, haven't you?

BOY. You mean—

SOLDIER. Here's my sword—and your chance to get your first one. Go to it.

BOY. Oh! Sure!

PREACHER. *(Moving in front of the* PRISONER*)* You can't do that, lad. You can't kill him.

BOY. Yes, I can. I hate him! I hate all of them! They killed my father!

PREACHER. Think, lad! It's doing murder. There's no

blood on your hands now—but once you kill, they're stained forever.

BOY. I don't care! I hate him, I tell you—and I'm going to kill him!

PREACHER. He's wounded—helpless—unarmed—

BOY. Get out of my way!

PREACHER. No, lad. I can't let you do this.

CAPTAIN. Stop interfering, Preacher. It's not your affair. At least this'll be a quick death for him—without torture.

PREACHER. Why must it be death for him at all?

SOLDIER. That's all his kind ever gives us, Preacher.

PREACHER. That's the way of beasts. Kill and be killed. But you're men.

SOLDIER. Not to his way of thinking we aren't.

PREACHER. If you behave like beasts, what else can he think? Act as men should. Do what you'd want other men to do to you—

SOLDIER. Preacher, I swear if you don't shut up, I'll— Go on, boy, and get it over. We got to be going. Out of the way, Preacher! Out of the way! Prick him with the sword, lad, and he'll move fast enough.

BOY. Get out of my way! You can't stop me from killing him! Get out of my way, or I'll—I'll kill you, too! Get out of my way, or—(*His voice drops suddenly into silence. He stands staring at the* PREACHER.)

SOLDIER. What's the matter, lad?

BOY. I—I don't know.

PREACHER. Put out your hand, lad. Not the one with the sword in it, but the other. Put out your hand and touch this boy. That's it.

BOY. (*Obeying*) I—I touched his throat—and it's soft—like the head of the little goat—I felt the beating of the pulse there —quick—afraid—

PREACHER. Can you still it forever?

BOY. I—I can't—the sword's heavy as lead—I can't lift it! I can't do it—I'm afraid—I can't kill him!

SOLDIER. Huh! Fine soldier you are, lad! Here—give me the sword and I'll attend to it. One side, Preacher!

PREACHER. (*Grasping the* SOLDIER's *arm*) Wait!

SOLDIER. Say! You sure got a grip on you, Preacher. If the rest of you's as strong as your hand, I'd hate to tangle with you. But no use us making a fight out of this. It's got to be done.

PREACHER. No. It doesn't have to be done. You can't let this boy be killed, Captain.

CAPTAIN. Why not? He'd show us no mercy in a like circumstance.

PREACHER. But you'll be merciful.

CAPTAIN. And why should I?

PREACHER. Because he's your brother.

CAPTAIN. Brother! Will you stop prating that word?

SOLDIER. He's no kin of ours, Preacher.

PREACHER. What difference is there between you? Aren't you men? Aren't your bodies built alike? Haven't you all minds and hearts and souls?

CAPTAIN. He's our enemy.

PREACHER. Why?

CAPTAIN. I had a country once. His kind took it from me. I had brothers once—and a father. They fought for freedom —and were dragged away into slavery and death. Their ghosts stand between us, Preacher.

SOLDIER. And I had a wife once—a baby son. They were trampled to death when his kind charged on a helpless crowd in the streets. Their ghosts stand between us.

BOY. And I had a father once. They killed him. He's between us.

CAPTAIN. And between us lie all the wrongs he and his kind have done to us—the death and sorrow and injustices inflicted upon us—the yoke of slavery they make us wear— and the blood of our dead crying out from the ground under our feet.

PREACHER. And which of these can his death make right? Is there one wrong that this boy's blood can blot from the book of history?

CAPTAIN. I'm not concerned with that. Only in balancing the account.

PREACHER. He and all he stands for will pass away in time. But the death of this one boy won't hasten the passing by so much as a minute. Believe me.

CAPTAIN. If he dies, there'll be one less swine in the world.

PREACHER. One less man. Let him live.

CAPTAIN. He dies. Now.

PREACHER. As one more useless sacrifice upon the reeking altar of hate? Let him live. He's your brother.

CAPTAIN. Does he call me brother? No. He calls me slave.

PREACHER. And rightly.

CAPTAIN. What do you mean—rightly?

PREACHER. No man is free who's slave to hate and fear—as you are.

CAPTAIN. Be careful, Preacher!

PREACHER. I told you that freedom's born of tolerance and understanding and love for one's fellow men. Those in the heart of a man make him free—keep him free. That's the truth—and you know it.

CAPTAIN. I said—

PREACHER. You call yourself a free man—but you're not that unless you prove your right to the name—that you really understand what freedom is. Right here in this glen is the whole senseless struggle of man against man in a nutshell. Here you are—two men—and between you a wall of your own making—of hate and fear and lack of understanding.

CAPTAIN. I tell you—

PREACHER. You look at this boy—but you don't see him. You see only a great wrong that's been in the world since the beginning—the wrong of all empire won by force—of all imperialism built on murder—the wrong of all war and greed and selfishness—the wrong of the only answer men have ever made to force—blow for blow—hate for hate—wrong for wrong —death for death. Just that—over and over again—solving nothing—getting nowhere.

CAPTAIN. Stop preaching and get out of my way!

PREACHER. And is all this any more his fault than yours? Will his death correct it? Look, Captain. Really look. What do you see? A monster? A nation of monsters? Or just one hurt, frightened boy?

CAPTAIN. Out of my way, I said!

PREACHER. You're the older—and in this hour the stronger. Which do you choose to be, Captain? The slave he called you—or the man you know yourself to be? Are you big enough, fine enough, great enough, free enough to do what all men ought to do—return good for evil, love for hate—and let this boy go?

SOLDIER. Go on, Captain, and get it over. We're wasting time.

CAPTAIN. Stand aside! *(He pushes by the* PREACHER, *grabs the* PRISONER *by the shoulder, yanks him to his feet. The* PRISONER *gives an involuntary moan of pain and goes limps. The* CAPTAIN *catches him to keep him from falling—and the* PRISONER *clings to him)* Here! Don't hold to me like this! What's the matter with you?

PRISONER. I—I'm sorry. It was a dizziness—in my head—Will you wait—just a minute—until I'm able—to stand alone? I'd rather die—that way—

CAPTAIN. *(In an odd tone)* You are just a boy. How old are you?

PRISONER. Nineteen.

CAPTAIN. Nineteen. *(He lowers the* PRISONER *to his rock again)* Nineteen! Why can't they send men against us instead of children!

SOLDIER. He's big enough and old enough to do us plenty of damage, Captain. You going to finish him—or shall I?

PREACHER. *(Softly)* Slave—or free man?

PRISONER. *(Slowly)* I'm sorry I called you that. Because he's right about this, you know.

CAPTAIN. Right?

PRISONER. Yes. You see, all my life I've been taught that we were the greatest nation in the world—sort of superior beings—that it's our destiny to conquer and rule the earth. And I've been proud of this empire we built out of the dead bodies of little nations. I thought it was our right to do it that way. I've been proud to be what I am—a soldier of the empire. But it wasn't until I came out here that I realized there was another side to all this. I noticed it first when I rode through the streets of your cities and saw eyes staring at me—sullen, hating eyes. That's our only reward. Hate.

CAPTAIN. Do you wonder?

PRISONER. No. Not now. I'm beginning to understand. It's a natural consequence of what we've done—the way we've built our empire—with force. We bred it in you. We oughtn't to wonder when it's returned with interest. It—it's justice, I suppose. You see, I never saw you as men before. I never thought of you as men. I never talked to you as men. It never occurred to me that you had bodies and minds and hearts that could be hurt—feel pain. That is, any more, perhaps, than dumb brutes feel pain. Because I was taught to think of you that way. But he's right. We are men. There's no difference between us. Neither of us is better than the other.

SOLDIER. So you know that at last, do you?

PRISONER. Yes. I know—now—when it's too late.

CAPTAIN. And why this change of opinion?

PRISONER. I don't exactly know. Perhaps it's because of what he did. This man here. The one you call the Preacher.

CAPTAIN. What?

PRISONER. Yes. He's one of you—my enemy—but he gave me water—his coat—tied up my hurts—and tried to save my life. You can't hate a man who does that for you. And you —you could have let me fall just now—but instead you caught me—held me up—as if I were a comrade. I hated you a few minutes ago. I don't, now. I'm not even afraid any more. I know there's a wall between us that oughtn't to be there—but I'm afraid we've built it too high—too strong—with too many wrongs—and now tonight we can't reach across it, you and I. So perhaps we'll have to wait until we meet in some other world beyond this to clasp hands and say what we ought to say because you saved this boy's life—in a like circumstance

SOLDIER. *(In wonder)* Well, I'll be—

PRISONER. I know. I sound crazy. These things this Preacher said — they sound crazy, too — like a madman's words — but maybe, after all, we're the ones who are mad. All we've done with armies and wars and conquests and hating is mess things up. But good for evil—love for hate—do what you'd like all men to do to you— Yes, it's mad. But it might make a saner, better world—if we'd courage enough to try it. I don't know. I never will know—now. *(To PREACHER)* Will you help me to stand? *(The PREACHER helps him to his feet)* You'd better take your coat now. And thank you for trying to save my life.

(He turns to the CAPTAIN*)* I'll be honest in the face of death. They're greater wrongs on our side than on yours. And so if my death'll even the balances in any way—I'm ready.

(The wind whispers softly across the hills.)

PREACHER. *(Quietly)* Can you be as great as he, Captain?

CAPTAIN. All right, Preacher. You win. You can have him.

SOLDIER. But see here, Captain—

BOY. You mean—you're going to let him go?

CAPTAIN. Just that.

SOLDIER. You're crazy, Captain!

CAPTAIN. Perhaps. But he goes free.

BOY. I—I'm glad!

(A whistle off right.)

SOLDIER. The signal, Captain! We got to be going. But there's still time to kill him—

CAPTAIN. No. Go on! *(He whistles twice into the darkness.)*

SOLDIER. Well—I suppose one more or less won't matter. But my hat's off to you, Preacher! I didn't think you could do it—just talking. Come on, lad—   [*They go off right.*

(The CAPTAIN *remains, poised, listening.)*

PREACHER. Blessed are the merciful—for they shall obtain mercy.

CAPTAIN. That's likely. If they catch me, I'll be hung just as high as if I'd never done this.

PREACHER. No. Because you've been merciful—because you saved this boy's life—in a like circumstance I'll save yours —one day.

CAPTAIN. *(Laughs)* You'll save my life! Ha! I'll believe that when it happens. Frankly, Preacher, for both our sakes, I hope we never meet again.

PREACHER. Yet we will meet again—upon another day and upon another hill. And when we meet, then perhaps you'll remember this promise I make to you—Bar Abbas.

CAPTAIN. How do you know my name?

SOLDIER. *(Off right)* Captain, hurry! There's some disturbance over toward the town. Come on. We got to go.

CAPTAIN. Coming! Good-bye, Preacher. And as for you, Roman—don't cross my path again. Only a fool tempts fate twice.

PREACHER. Good-bye, Bar Abbas. Until we meet.

CAPTAIN. I haven't seen enough of your face to know you if I do.

PREACHER. You will know me, Bar Abbas—for I shall be wearing a crown of thorns.

CAPTAIN. Humph!   [*He goes into the darkness at right. (There is a silence. The wind whispers down the glen.)*

PRISONER. They—they've gone!

PREACHER. Yes. They've gone.

PRISONER. They've gone. And—I'm alive. The rain's beginning to fall—I can feel the drops on my face—on my hands! I'm alive! Free! I'm alive!

PREACHER. I am come that men may have life— Shall we go, Roman?

PRISONER. Why did you do this for me? Who are you? Where did you come from?

PREACHER. From Nazareth. I'm a carpenter there. Come—

CURTAIN

Subject and Classification Index

Characters

2 Characters
IT'S EASTER, DR. JORDAN

3 Characters
THE SHEPHERD'S STORY

4 Characters
SENTENCE
THE CURTAIN (2 extras)

5 Characters
COMING OF LIGHT

6 Characters
AMONG THIEVES
SPEAKING OF PICTURES
WHERE LOVE IS
TO SPEAK OF FREEDOM
(extras)

7 Characters
THE BIRTH OF THE SONG,
 "SILENT NIGHT"
EMPTY HANDS
THE SYMBOL OF A CROSS

8 Characters
THE CLOTH OF SENDONY
(extras)
A CHILD IS BORN (extras)

9 Characters
WHITE CHRISTMAS
ROGER WILLIAMS
THE BUILDERS

10 Characters
NO ROOM IN THE HOTEL

11 Characters
THE CAPTAINS AND THE
 KINGS

18 Characters
THE CHRISTMAS CAROL
(less with doubles)

*Performance Time**

10 or 15 minutes
THE SHEPHERD'S STORY
THE CURTAIN

20 or 25 minutes
THE SYMBOL OF A CROSS
TO SPEAK OF FREEDOM
SENTENCE
SPEAKING OF PICTURES

30 or 40 minutes
NO ROOM IN THE HOTEL
WHERE LOVE IS
THE CHRISTMAS CAROL
THE BIRTH OF THE SONG,
 "SILENT NIGT"
WHITE CHRISTMAS
A CHILD IS BORN
ROGER WILLIAMS
THE COMING OF LIGHT
IT'S EASTER, DR. JORDAN
AMONG THIEVES
THE BUILDERS
EMPTY HANDS
THE CAPTAINS AND THE
 KINGS

1 hour or 1½ hours
THE CLOTH OF SENDONY

---

* Most of these plays may be performed in the shorter time indicated. The amount of music used will affect the length. Some may cut where condensation is necessary.